The Forensic
Comicologist

TO SCOTT,

The Forensic Comicologist

Insights from a Life in Comics

JAMIE NEWBOLD

Foreword by MICHELLE NOLAN

McFarland & Company, Inc., Publishers
Jefferson, North Carolina

LIBRARY OF CONGRESS CATALOGUING-IN-PUBLICATION DATA

Names: Newbold, Jamie, 1955– author. |
Nolan, Michelle, 1948– writer of foreword.
Title: The forensic comicologist : insights from a life in comics /
Jamie Newbold ; foreword by Michelle Nolan.
Description: Jefferson, North Carolina : McFarland & Company, Inc.,
Publishers, 2018 | Includes bibliographical references and index.
Identifiers: LCCN 2018017612 | ISBN 9781476672670
(softcover : acid free paper) ∞
Subjects: LCSH: Comic books, strips, etc.—Collectors and collecting. |
Comic books, strips, etc.—History and criticism. | Comic-book stores.
Classification: LCC PN6714 .N49 2018 | DDC 741.5075—dc23
LC record available at https://lccn.loc.gov/2018017612

BRITISH LIBRARY CATALOGUING DATA ARE AVAILABLE

ISBN (print) 978-1-4766-7267-0
ISBN (ebook) 978-1-4766-3122-6

The front cover image is of Jamie Newbold

Printed in the United States of America

*McFarland & Company, Inc., Publishers
Box 611, Jefferson, North Carolina 28640
www.mcfarlandpub.com*

Table of Contents

Foreword

by Michelle Nolan

You're about to read a unique book by a unique author.

Jamie Newbold is the only known person with two decades of experience as a full-fledged police officer followed by two decades as the owner of a full-service comic book store. Thus, this fascinating fellow justifiably can call himself "The Forensic Comicologist." You are about to read the first extensive biography of a leading comic book retailer—one who is also a first-time author.

Jamie, from whom I have purchased hundreds of vintage comic books, is more than a trusted friend. He's also a fount of information about all aspects of collecting comics, which has emerged since the curiosity the hobby was in the 1960s to a much-respected pastime known by millions nationwide.

Those of you in your fifties or older will remember when you were called a whole lot worse than "nerd." It was more or less OK to read—and even save—comics when you were 10 or 12 years old, maybe even 14 on the cusp of high school.

After that? Well, you'll recall suffering catcalls and worse when a group of friends would spot you looking through a comic book rack. After all, the racks weren't labeled, "Hey, Kids! Comics!" for nothing.

Many people do not realize the tortures we collectors—yes, we were often self-proclaimed collectors, not savers!—of comics suffered in the 1950s and 1960s, and even into the 1970s in many parts of the United States.

Miss an issue? Horrors! You might not see it for years. Finding a store that sold every title you cared about? No such place, anywhere in America. I seriously doubt, in the post–World War II Baby Boomer years of 1946–1964, and even well beyond, if any retailer in America sold every issue of every comic book title.

More than 200 to 300 issues appeared on the racks every month during the height of comics readership in the early 1950s. They weren't all monthly titles, but rather issues of everything from your monthly *Action Comics* to your yearly *Archie Annual*. Even in the late 1950s and early 1960s, the early Silver Age era, when far fewer titles were published by far fewer companies than just 10 to 20 years earlier, well over 100 issues per month were constantly published.

As a budding comic book historian, I knew even then, because my first "real" job was racking comics for a local drugstore every Tuesday and Thursday, in exchange for free comics and something much more important—first crack at the rack!

Nobody, but nobody, could carry them all. Nobody would have wanted to, considering the 10-cent and 12-cent comics of the day didn't make nearly as much money as magazines and paperbacks. Comic books, in fact, were loss leaders in many locations.

But I was lucky. My dad was a great friend of the owner of the largest newsstand in San Jose (now known better as the heart of Silicon Valley). He came the closest to having all the current comics. On Saturdays in the late 1950s and early 1960s, after scouring three nearby used-book stores for back issues—that's where we found old comics—I would broom and clean the place in exchange for—you guessed it! Comics!

People younger than 50, however, often don't know how stressful it was to collect comics.

This is where Jamie Newbold comes in. As he details in this book, he began reading comics circa 1960, when he was 5 years old, thanks to his father, and loved comics so much that about 15 years later, he was among the first to work at the second comic book store established in San Diego.

I lived about 500 miles north in San Jose during the school years, and about 1,400 miles north in Northwest Washington state during summers, so I never really knew Jamie until later. But, as you will see, he was busy, busy, endlessly busy in the 1960s and 1970s, learning how to read comics and eventually how to buy, trade and sell them.

His story is endlessly fascinating. I am several years older than Jamie, so how well I know, since I was a partner in what is generally considered the nation's first free-standing comic book store, established March 3, 1968, in downtown San Jose by Bud Plant, myself (I signed the business license) and five other friends. There was no way the local magazine distribution monopoly would allow our hole-in-the-wall comic book business to carry new comics, but we did sell old comics. Thousands and thousands of them. We opened the store—it really was the brainchild of Bud and two buddies, Jim Buser and the late John Barrett—hoping to make money, but primarily hoping people would bring in their collections—and their parents' collections!—of old comics.

It worked! *Captain America* #1 came into the shop! The Golden Age *Green Lantern* #1 (not to mention the Silver Age *Green Lantern* #1) came into the shop! *Superman* #2 came into the shop! And untold thousands of others.

That's why I know how excited Jamie must have been, when he discovered how to uncover old comics! In the 1960s and 1970s, this was information hoarded and not readily shared with others.

Fast-forward several decades—you can read all about it inside—and Jamie ultimately was to establish his own store, Southern California Comics, circa 1997, toward the end of his dangerous days as a San Diego police officer.

There's no doubt in my mind that I have gone through many more thousands of comics than the vast majority of collectors and even many retailers. But surely not more than Jamie! This guy tells you in this book all about the thousands of collections he has gone through in search of Gold, Silver, and Bronze! That's comic books from the 1930s through the 1970s and early 1980s. (He also tells you, in his own inimitable style, why searching for comics from the last three decades or so can be immensely frustrating.) Even if you are an established collector, you likely will learn a lot from Jamie's story.

Jamie has mixed commercial success with a wacky sense of humor, such as displays at his store of the most beat-up comics he has ever been offered and the grungiest money he has taken in as legal tender! Jamie, a great family man, also tells you how he has mixed business success with family love.

Just as I was lucky to grow up in the heart of a great comic book scene in the Bay Area of Northern California, Jamie was fortunate to grow up in San Diego, a beautiful city that just happened to develop the greatest of all conventions, now called Comic-Con International, after its humble beginnings as the Golden State Comic Convention in March and August 1970.

If you have ever dreamed of opening a comic book store, Jamie's book will be an eye-opener! You will either be more determined than ever, or you will go back to collecting and reading—and appreciating people with the aptitude of Jamie Newbold!

Michelle Nolan has been a comics historian and a newspaper and magazine feature writer for more than 50 years. She received an Inkpot Award from Comic-Con International in San Diego for her work as a comics and pop cultural historian and entrepreneur. She has published more than 10,000 stories and columns, including more than 500 on comic book history.

Preface

Four years ago a group of my employees, friends, and a couple of others took a shot at doing a reality television show centered at my store, Southern California Comics. We'd been posting our weekly comic book review videos on YouTube to the acclaim of no one. The TV show was the next step. We had a director, equipment, and scripts, and we shot some footage. Our director utilized help from a local documentary producer and got us three meetings with the AMC Network. The first two meetings were encouraging and they sent us back before the camera to shoot additional footage. Ultimately, however, we weren't good enough for TV.

I was featured in one of the segments of our proposed TV show, titled *The Forensic Comicologist*. I was the "scientist guy" teaching subjects such as comic book grading, what restoration meant, and how to shop for great comics. My wife even had a lab coat embroidered with Forensic Comicologist and my name. I thought the segments were pretty good, but I might have been alone in that thought. The non-comic book people involved with the project were bored with the concept and offered little encouragement.

I had beers with a friend, Ian Strelsky, soon after the TV show attempts ended. We commiserated over what might have been. He saw I wasn't completely separated from the idea, so he suggested I write a book. After all, I wrote articles for *Comic Book Marketplace* and *Overstreet Price Guide*. I knew my business, having plied the trade for decades. Why not write a book?

I thought about it for a week. I knew that it would be a daunting project. Until now, the longest articles I'd ever written were no more than seven pages, though I did have the history of thousands of hand-scripted police reports to add to my writing skill-sets. They tended to force a modicum of grammar and proper syntax on cops since our reports were read by attorneys and judges. So yeah, I thought I could gut it out with some help and produce a book about the pitfalls of collecting comics. My police officer legacy might help people take the book seriously. Plus, I'm a stickler for fair play and justice. I don't think there's enough of either in the comic book collecting world. I know there's plenty of people blogging, streaming and threading on various web sites and chat sites. Many witnesses and concerned parties post or share horror stories—stories that center on a particular crook or troublesome event. Some people proffer solutions while others cry out for justice. Too many of these souls lack real-world answers or have no practical experience fighting the battles. There must be someone out there who can collate stories and facts to teach collectors how to protect themselves. So...

In the fall of 2013 I started writing and writing and stopping and writing; three years later, I finished the book. Sometimes it was hard to stay on target. Work and health issues caused me to stall. Doubt in my abilities and direction halted my advance, but each time I grew determined to try again until I couldn't stop. Stopping became an insult to all my effort. I needed to do what others had not: write a book that really gets to the heart of comic book collecting.

Years of store ownership taught me that a lot of people frequently get in trouble spending money on comics. I became the informal "Answer Man" at my store and got more than a few people out of the deep end with comic book collecting. I realized a written tutorial would be the only way to encompass everything I had to say about comic book collecting.

I figured I had something to say and if no one listened, at least I would have done no harm. Some aspects of this book may seem out of date by the time this reaches the public. eBay's policies change, PayPal's policies change, and grading companies wrestle with changes. Keeping everything accurate and evergreen turned out to be a great challenge. Concepts in a chapter written in 2013 could be obsolete in 2016. I may have a sheaf of addendums to write for an on-line edition or a second printing.

I have a wealth of stories within and without the world of comics. I'm lucky that beer, fatigue and age still allow me to hold onto a vast number of the best ones. I'm very fortunate that I have friends and customers who, when called upon, contributed their own memories. I credit them in each posting of their memoirs. These stories don't necessarily line up with the themes of each chapter. I decided that they were fine wherever I put them, acting as a sort of distraction if any particular chapter began to bog the reader down. I asked for written contributions, but I wouldn't recommend that for any future book writers out there. People just didn't want to put in that much effort, so I started taking dictation and found the results satisfying.

I have lots of people to thank for this project: Ian Strelsky in the beginning and Michelle Nolan, my editor, at the end. The middle of this daisy chain includes: my employees past and present (Matt Rios and Rob Mediavilla); my customers (the ones who followed along); my friends, who indulged my far-fetched and dull concept; and Will Given, a University of California San Diego professor who got my head on straight when It seemed I lacked direction.

I want to thank my son, Michael Newbold, and his family. Most of all I want to thank my wife Kim. She never once doubted me and texted me a month before I finished the book telling me how proud she was of my desire and almost-ceaseless effort.

Introduction
A Collecting Culture

It all begins with my father. His youthful years in Cedar Rapids, Iowa, were harsh in the 1920s and 1930s. His father died in 1919, the year my dad, Jim Newbold, was born. My grandmother remarried, but her new husband was abusive to the family. My father related few details, but made it clear that his childhood in the 1920s and Depression-era 1930s was hard on his family.

His escape from the Depression was the fantasy characters in the newspaper comics and the movies. Jim Newbold grew up with Big Little Books and pulps (more on these subjects later).

He loved Buck Rogers and Alley Oop. He loved so much of that fiction that he eventually progressed into the budding world of sci-fi of the 1930s. He read pulp magazines and short stories to fill his days and nights with unknown worlds of the fantastic and ultra-scientific. He engulfed himself in adventures that lightened his life and addicted him to reading. He went to the movies and lost time in the glow of a black-and-white collage of sci-fi serials.

In 1941, he was drafted into the U.S. Army months prior to the bombing at Pearl Harbor. My father served with the 34th Infantry of the Fifth Army, service that included our country's earliest conflicts with the Nazis in North Africa. By 1945, my father had survived over two years of combat in Africa, Sicily, and Italy. He even survived a brief imprisonment in a German POW camp in North Africa before being rescued by the British. Freedom, followed by more combat and a final reprieve from his command, sent him to the south of France to fight the remainder of his war from a desk behind the lines.

My dad was drafted before America entered World War II. The United States involvement in World War II brought my dad from a stateside post into French North Africa as part of the U.S. invasion known as "Operation Torch." Eventually his unit ended up in the outskirts of Tunis, Tunisia, captured by the Germans after a vicious battle across sand dunes. My father, along with other soldiers, was marched to a prisoner of war camp run by Italians. My father was never a veteran to talk about his war. For me it's all just bits and pieces I coaxed out of him. What I do know is that he spent a weekend in that POW camp before a British tank and some soldiers rolled up to the main gate. The Italians surrendered immediately without firing a shot against the big cannon pointed at their blockhouse. The Americans were rescued and my dad was eventually thrown back into the war for two more weary years.

Comic books were never a big part of my father's life. The characters he relished rarely wore colorful costumes unless they were on the big screen (Flash Gordon, Buck Rogers, etc.) and they were only in black and white. His tastes ran to the next generation of sci-fi: the paperback novels. He loved books of the imagination mixed with science.

By the middle of the 1950s, my dad had many things going for him. Married with a newborn, he had fatherhood to add to his accomplishments. His form of escapism, though, remained sci-fi stories and movies. His small family lived in and around Los Angeles and Pasadena, California. My dad finished college and took his first administrative job at Los Angeles City College. His off-time entertainment remained reading his favorite fiction. The books and magazines he read were found at newsstands and used book stores all over the county. It was only a matter of time until his voracious appetite for pop culture steered him towards comic books.

EC Comics was a premier comic book publisher in its postwar infancy. Soldiers returning from war were not just spending money on superhero comics, so other genres were finding popularity. The comic book theme that attracted my father was satire in the form of everyone's favorite, *Mad*.

My dad never really spoke to me about comics from that period. Rather, his collection of the earliest issues of *Mad* comics and the ensuing magazine version illustrated where his tastes in paneled art existed. (*Mad* was first published as a comic book before EC transformed it into *Mad Magazine* for its own survival.) So many vets steered towards non-superhero comics that costumed characters could easily have become extinct. Horror, sci-fi, romance, crime, and mystery comic books dominated magazine racks everywhere. Younger kids found Disney and funny-animal comics plentiful. Girls and young adults saw a myriad of teen, romance and humor comics.

EC Comics, producers of *Mad*, also made the best quality non-superhero comics. EC classed up the newsstands with well-written and often better-drawn westerns, crime, and goofy kid comics of the late 1940s. M.C. Gaines was at the helm of EC Comics and stayed safe publishing the kinds of comics he thought his readers wanted, including Bible stories and funny animals. His accidental death in 1947 transferred the dynamic company to his son's control. William became the editor by default and was poised to make a change in comics that time has labeled revolutionary. I will address that in a later chapter.

William Gaines reinvented the style of his comic book company and created comic books to match this 1950s generation of avid, war-matured readers. He tested the market with a sampler of crime, horror, sci-fi, and war titles, each with writing that matched the sophistication of its readers. These were no-holds-barred tales with the shock of the stories and awe of the art. Gaines and his editors knew within the first year that they were onto something. They added more titles or changed the direction of others. One new title was a 32-page comic simply called *Mad* (1952), EC's first humor comic. With biting topical wit, *Mad* poked fun at contemporary mores as well as entertainment culture and politics. *Mad* ran for 23 issues as a comic book with some of the best collaborative talent in the industry—an industry watched very closely by parents, teachers and politicians at a time when some perceived comic books as corruptive influences. The satiric look upon society was just the punny humor former soldiers like my father were maladjusted enough to enjoy, as 1950s America changed around them.

By the middle of the decade, comics in general and EC in particular were fighting public scrutiny and potential government censorship. Comics as they were being presented in the 1950s mortified thousands of American adults. Their sensibilities of the period were shocked by comic book content and negative press articles. A roaring maelstrom of pressure was directed at comic books. Unsubstantiated accusations that comics led to juvenile delinquency influenced politicians, churches, parents, and educators. A clarion call to stop comic books rang out nationwide. It was time for comics to change or go! Bill Gaines, always with a keen eye towards the future, opted to change. He allowed his comics to mutate into more palpable stories. They did not last. Conversely, he took *Mad* in a different direction: he converted it to a magazine with #24 to avoid the oppression and censorship of the 1950s, particularly towards comics (fleshed out in a later chapter).

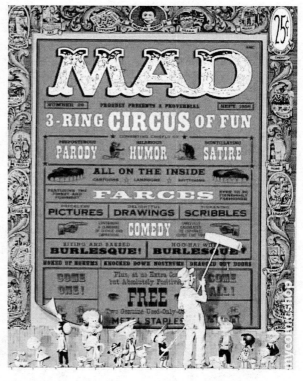

The publishing dynasty known as *MAD* began in comic book form in 1952. EC Comics' talented pool put together this topical and hilarious satire comic, allowing it to survive in magazine format when comic books came under fire by critics, censors and our own government. *MAD* #1 (1952) © EC Publications. Used with permission.

Lurid magazines had long been around, tailored for mostly male readers. Crime and sex-ridden tales were told in vivid details designed to shock and titillate. Those salacious stories were featured in men's magazines, crime magazines, and scandalous Hollywood periodicals. They occupied newsstands nationwide and operated with a certain amount of impunity. After all, they were geared towards adults. Comics would still exist, but in an environment safe for children. Non-comic book powers-that-be did not consider adult readership as a factor. Powerful individuals looking for soapbox success wanted control over something that would unify opposition and consolidate power. Comics remained that target.

Gaines shifted comic books to that format and forever released *Mad* from those restraints. The tempo of satiric wit and "humor in a jugular vein" observations made my father laugh harder. My father found the first magazine issues of *Mad* so enthralling in 1955 that he began collecting them. He handed them over to me when he felt I could appreciate them.

Now, like most kids, my earliest memories are vague, memories only retained perhaps by explosive events. Seriously. My earliest memory is of my dad blowing up then-legal fireworks outside our house on lower Azusa in Temple City (outside L.A.). I must have been around two or three years of age. I have a clear recollection of that 4th of July night. This tangible detail of my life extends to my father's childlike reverence of fireworks, even up to his death. Holiday fireworks were big events for Midwest kids back in my dad's day. Like fireworks, sci-fi and comic strips were memories my dad carried from childhood that could not be ripped away even by the horrors of his years of combat.

By the time I was able to read, I remember looking at the paperback books my father collected. He read books sometimes two or three at a time. I loved anything with dinosaurs on the cover. My dad recognized my attraction to monsters, dinosaurs, and the like. Monster movies were in vogue about this time. Dinosaurs and monster movies occupied my Saturday afternoons in San Diego. *Science Fiction Theater* hosted by "Moona Lisa" kept my friends and me glued to the TV on hot August afternoons. The *Superman* TV series was in syndication on local networks, so I got to watch George Reeves in action. (My father graduated from USC in 1953. Jack Larson, Jimmy Olsen from the original *Superman* TV show, was my dad's classmate.)

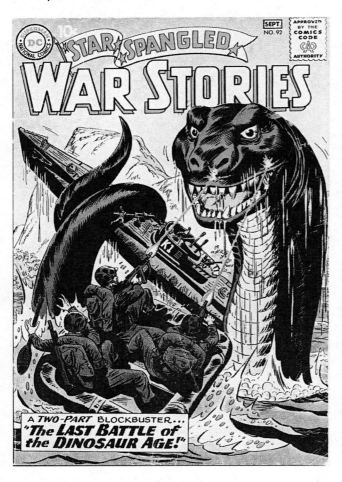

My war veteran father shared my love of comics and dinosaurs with his wartime past. Some of these old *Star Spangled War Stories* comics are the earliest memories I have of comic books in my hands. *Star Spangled War Stories* #92 (1960) (© DC Comics. Used with permission).

By the end of the 1950s, my dad took an administrative position at San Diego City College. He was a college administrator and head librarian (naturally), and doubled as college chairman for a time. Because of his college duties, he worked long hours one day a week on Mondays.

My devotion to dinosaurs and monsters was fanatical. My father bought me science books on dinosaurs. Of course, there was a limit to that material, so he looked elsewhere. I was about six, maybe seven years of age. One Monday night, my father came home late after a typical long work day. I was in bed when he brought me my earliest comic book memory. He sat on my bed beside me and laid a comic book across my blanket. The cover was the coolest thing I'd ever seen: a dinosaur fighting a World War II U.S. Army tank and its crew. Cool!! My father and I read the comic together with my dad using different voices for each character. He even mouthed reading sounds the dinos made. Comic books and dinosaurs! I wanted more of this! A hobby was born. That issue was from the dinosaur run of *Star*

Spangled War Stories from DC. Pterodactyls and T-rexes fought G.I.s on every cover of that comic book in the early 1960s.

A Fan's Recollection
By Ken Marr

I was born in San Diego in 1955. When I was growing up in the suburbs, comics were always around in kids' homes. I think more kids read comics than collected them. My first comics were hand-me-downs from my brother and his friends. I still have them, all torn and written on. When I started collecting I didn't think of it like that. I bought, found or somehow ended up with Archie titles, Disneys, Dells, DCs, ACGs, Harveys and later Marvels.

I remember going down to a grocery store called DeFalcos at a shopping center near my neighborhood. They had two spinner racks for comic books. My friend John and I would walk there every Saturday morning, get our comics and go home. My grandparents lived in Pacific Beach, not far from me. On the way to their house was the Pacific Beach Bookstore next to a lawnmower shop. The bookstore had a lot of comic book back issues for five and ten cents. I bought lots of great stuff there, like *Adventure Comics* #247, *Showcase* #22, and *Brave and the Bold* #57. The hunt was on for origin issues and first appearances. My other grandparents lived in Coronado opposite downtown San Diego. My grandfather would give me money to get "funny books" from the Day And Night Store on Orange Avenue. The barbershop next door also had comics that one of the barbers brought in and would trade for old and new issues. Got a *Tales of Suspense* #40 there.

On some Saturdays my dad would take me downtown, where he gave clarinet lessons. From there I'd walk to Lanning's Bookstore. Peggy Lanning, the owner's wife, ran the store from behind a counter next to the front window (she always had her small dog with her). Peggy always had a shopping cart in front of her store filled with coverless comics for a penny apiece. Kids could have one if they traded in two other copies first. She kept the really expensive stuff in the back of her store, but I never got to see them. She was very fussy about letting too many teenagers into the store at one time, so I don't remember ever getting an escort to go back and look at the better stuff. I do remember a huge bird cage by the front door occupied by a very talkative mynah bird. That bird was responsible for destroying more comic books than any other bird I've ever known. That's because the cage was lined with comic books for the bird droppings. You want a real shock, just read the titles of the comics that's weren't yet covered in you-know-what. Ohhh, the perfidity!

By the way, Lanning's was just one of about seven stores close together in the downtown area that carried old, used comic books in the latter part of the 1960s. I arrived on the scene around 1972 when I got my driver's license, so I might have missed some of the heady days of used bookstores chock full of old comics. I explored those stores but didn't see the wealth of comic books others have boasted to me about from their pasts.

In the summer the local newspaper ran free ads for kids for a week or two. Lots of kids put free ads in the paper selling comics. I'd call around and find sellers who lived close to me. I'd ride my bike to their homes and make purchases. I remember those purchases added up quick and stacks of back issues began reaching the ceiling in my bedroom.

Around 1967 I started buying Marvels. I owned a few and saw them on the racks, but the stories were always continued. That was a hassle if I couldn't get subsequent issues. Still, I started buying every title every week. I started with DCs but Marvel was king.

My friend John saw an ad offering to buy comics from a guy named Richard Alf (future San Diego Comic Con co-founder). John had Richard come to his house and sold all his DCs and Marvels.

I stopped collecting in high school. After high school I saw a *Sandman* comic book on the racks: *Sandman* by Jack Kirby. Kirby was at DC! That started me up again!

I moved out of my house sometime after that. Lucky for me, my mom did not throw out my comics. She knew how much I loved them and appreciated that comics helped me learn how to read. I still have most of the comics I've ever owned.

Fast forward a couple of years and my friends and I are stretched out in the living room reading *Superman* comics. Comics were hard to come by in my neighborhood. The only places to get them were miles away. Most of the parents on my street would not cater to the comic whims of their kids. My dad brought comics home, usually DCs, for any kid to read. My mother was like most mothers. She did not care about comics one way or another. She knew I liked to read and saw the wisdom in letting me read comics. Once, she sat next to me while I was reading a *Superman* comic. She told me the most extraordinary thing. She told me she knew Superman; grew up with him, in fact.

After my dad graduated from college, he and my mom briefly split up. She moved back into her folks' house on Rio Grande in Pasadena. I was a baby. I've since revisited that beautiful house, built in the 1920s. I don't remember that earliest year of my childhood. To my mom, her memories were of friendships, sports, and family in those golden years of Los Angeles. By high school, she was a star athlete at John Muir High School (track) and knew Jackie Robinson. She was two years older than Jackie, but my mom claimed that they shared at least one class together. She said she sat next to Jackie because seating was assigned alphabetically (her maiden name is Rousseau). She recollected having sunflower seed spitting contests with him at lunchtime!

There was another boy she occasionally walked to school with. He was a tall, good-looking boy, a quiet guy who she rarely saw outside of school and lived just across the street. His name was George Reeves (ne: George Bessolo). I could not believe that my mom knew Superman! She told me this in the 1960s, a few years after the *Superman* TV show's demise (and that of its star). The show was in syndication on local TV so I got to watch episodes that I was too young to comprehend during its original run.

I peppered her with questions. She did not remember anything earth-shattering that came from their casual talks on the way to school. They tended to walk together in the mornings but rarely after school. They were about three years apart in age, so they spent no class time together. She did not see him much after school and never saw him outside of school days. She

My mom grew up across the street from George Reeves and his mother. George was a strait-laced guy and an actor destined to be the second person to don the Superman costume for the screen.

did have opportunities to meet his mother, whom my mom felt dominated and controlled George. My mom did not particularly like her.

After my father died in 2002, my wife and I took my mom to visit her old neighborhood. Her memories were still sharp as to various landmarks from her past, including George Reeves's childhood house. The beautiful house still stands across the street from where I once lived with my mother and grandparents. George Reeves is long gone.

I registered a sentimental connection to the comic book culture. Both my folks had erstwhile links to comic book characters (Jimmy Olsen and Superman). How could I not explore the connection in my own way?

I bought comics where and when I could. There were no comic book stores per se in town. Lanning's Books in downtown San Diego and a few newsstands represented about all there was for comic book back issues. There was little regard or respect for comics. Lanning's had a birdcage near the front door and used comic books to line the cage.

By my first year of high school my dad and I drove to comic book specialty stores that had been operational in Hollywood for a while. Our first trip up there was around

In 1965 I managed to whine enough to coax my dad into driving across the city to a magazine stand so I could buy comics (rather, he could buy me comics). I landed on a copy of *Justice League of America* #37. It was an exciting two-part story featuring the Justice Society of America. The end of the story left me cliffhanging for another month. Unfortunately, I never got my return trip to pick up issue #38, so I was left hanging for years before I finally finished the tale. It was that mentality that helped lead me into collecting full runs of comic books. *Justice League of America* #37 (1965) and #38 (1965) (© DC Comics. Used with permission).

1969 or 1970. My dad found two stores in that area within walking distance of each other, so Cherokee Books and Collector's Book Store institutionalized comics for me. Both places were legendary for their back-issue selections. They fulfilled anyone's desire for old comics.

Collector's Book Store was a large business on Hollywood Blvd. near Vine. I distinctly remember a long counter top in front of a large wall, all filled with comics and other collectibles. The owners built a wall of pullout drawers faced with whatever title was contained within. If I wanted to fill in the run of a particular title, perhaps *Batman*, I looked for the drawer covered with a sample issue of *Batman* and dug around inside.

Cherokee Books was an actual bookstore with comics upstairs in the back. The Blum family owned the store, and Burt, a son, ran the comics end. To get to the comics, I walked up a narrow, winding staircase to the second floor. The comics were housed within wooden shelving that lined one side of the stairway. The comics were organized by titles and issues, but nothing was bagged up. If I wanted something, I pulled at the issue until I pried it free of the overly packed bookshelves. The imminent exposure to damage for the comic books was always present.

My dad and I once made a weekend of it in Hollywood. We went shopping along the strip for comics and books, stopping by a military surplus store called the Supply Sergeant to look at cool equipment. On one of these trips my father rented a motel room, and we killed that evening at the movies watching *Werewolves on Wheels* (1971). Bikers, chicks and gore, and I was only a teenager watching that stuff with my dad! My father was not one to shy away from an R rating with his kid.

Cherokee Book Shop was a unique bookstore on Hollywood Blvd. back when comic book collecting was just leaving its infancy. Burt, the owner's son (center), ran the comic book end of the business in the small upstairs office at the back of the store.

My Hollywood purchases were the beginnings of my serious efforts at comic collecting. I made subsequent trips to both stores throughout high school.

I found Mecca, though, when Comic-Con in San Diego was born in 1970.

Mike Copeland is a store customer at Southern California Comics and a senior volunteer for SD Comic-Con. Recently, he jotted down some memories of comic book collecting and shared them with me:

The summer heat and humidity always remind me of comics and comic book stores. I didn't discover comic book stores until I was 11 years old. Until then, I bought most of my comics at convenience stores, newsstands and a magazine shop that I later found out was a front for organized gambling. Obtaining and reading comics (mostly *Star Wars*) was all great fun, but I missed quite a few issues. I was completely unaware of how easy it was to find the missed issues, provided one could find a comic book store nearby.

Heroes World, a collector's store that was fairly close to my parents' house, seemed to be closed most of the time. The few times I managed to get Mom or Dad to drive me over there when they were open were bittersweet. I was able to find some of the issues I was missing, but they were not always in the best of shape. Very few of the comics were stored in plastic bags and those that were did not have backing boards with them. This was around 1980, and the idea of storing comics to keep them in good shape was somewhat foreign to me and to this particular store as well. I did manage to convince Dad to drive me to Comic Kingdom on University Avenue. This store had the back issues I needed, and they were stored in plastic bags. Their comics needed it. There was so much smoking going on in the place it looked to be permanently on fire. I would obtain my books and enjoy reading them as I developed the beginning stages of emphysema.

Two years passed. I had managed to quit reading comics cold turkey. I was in middle school now, and admitting you read comics to anyone lowered you on the coolness scale below a person who collected spores as a hobby. Besides, I was into other important things, such as sports, video games, and girls. Then a friend brought into class one day a copy of Simon and Kirby's *Fantastic Four* collection. One look at the painted cover brought back to me the almost forgotten stirrings of curiosity and desire. I instantly became hooked and started, despite the health risks, to obtain *Fantastic Four* and *Star Wars* comics.

Now, being older and wiser, I made lists before I went to the stores. Friends also were a big help. One friend from church gave me a bunch of old comics he didn't want any more. I took on odd jobs such as yard work and housecleaning to support my habit. New, cleaner stores opened closer to my parents' house. I discovered Comic-Con. I obtained my driver's license. My collection grew.

I found that there was enough interest when I was a senior in high school to form a comic book club. There were, however, still some problems. One girl I had a crush on told me I must be immature for reading "that crap." Another group informed me that because I didn't regularly read the comics they liked, I shouldn't consider myself a "real" collector. Another group was actually offended when I told them they should check out *Watchmen* or *Dark Knight Returns*. *Watchmen*, I was told, was too violent, and no one wanted to read about a bunch of characters that no one had heard of. Also, *Dark Knight Returns* was terrible, I was told: Batman was passé, the artwork wasn't very good, and no Batman adventure could be that interesting without Robin.

College found me branching out a bit. I could relate to Spider-Man. I enjoyed the new Image and Valiant comics. Dark Horse published *Star Wars* again! And I had a good, supportive group of friends who liked the fact that I read comics. Any kind of comics! Those who also read comics would engage me in conversations about the merit of reading some books over others, or what issues did we think would increase in value. The fact that none of our predictions about the value of comics increasing were correct didn't matter. It was the discussions and the debates that were the most fun.

   Those times got even better. I graduated from college. I got a job teaching high school science. I had pictures and posters of my favorite characters on my classroom walls. Students would ask me which characters would win in a fight. Friends and colleagues would ask me which comic book movies they should go see. My girlfriend asked me to marry her at Comic-Con and gave me a Green Lantern power ring to celebrate our engagement. When someone asked me if I'm a nerd, I replied, "Yes, and I'm proud of it!"

   Dad once said that I would eventually stop reading comics. Well, Dad, it's now 37 years and there is no end in sight. I still enjoy obtaining and reading comics. Now, if I could only get rid of this old, annoying cough....

The Watchmen first appeared in a DC promotional. They didn't even warrant a cover blurb. *DC Spotlight* (1985) (© DC Comics. Used with permission).

My friends and I used to drive up to the Rose Bowl in the early 1970s to shop at "The World's Largest Swap Meet." Eventually, we set up to sell at the Rose Bowl and tried it a couple of times.

The first time we went as dealers, my buddy Ski had a short conversation with a woman that I didn't overhear. He did tell her he'd see her at the swap meet the next month. Sales were okay for back issues, but nothing to celebrate.

We returned a month later and set up in about the same spot we had before. We conducted business into the early afternoon while a friend of mine shopped. Ski had asked to make a stop out in Malibu after we closed down at the swap meet. He said he had brought some comic books for the lady he met the month before. They had it all worked out in advance. We were to drive out to her place along the cliffs off Pacific Coast Highway to sell her some old comics Ski had foraged. Her name was Janet.

The drive was about half an hour with a few delays using an old folding map to find her home. Along the way Ski mentioned that Janet was married to an actor named Martin. He said that Martin had recently starred in an acclaimed "made for TV" drama called *The Execution of Private Slovik*. I'd seen the movie and blurted out, "You mean Martin Sheen! You're taking us to Martin Sheen's house to sell comic books to his wife?!" Too cool!

Ski, not wanting to be demonstrative, said, "Yeah, I thought I told you."

I replied, "No!!" while Matt wondered who Martin Sheen was.

We met her at the front door of their single-level ranch-style house along the cliffs overlooking the ocean. She brought us into the kitchen and fed us milk and cookies while Ski showed her the comics she was waiting so patiently for.

I don't remember what comics they were. These were comics she remembered as a kid and was so glad that a comic book guy she met at the swap meet had them to sell, albeit after a thirty-day wait.

We spent about forty-five minutes there, all in the kitchen. During that time I watched a couple of pre-teens, a boy and a girl, bouncing on a trampoline right outside the kitchen slider in the Sheens' backyard. To this day I swear it was a twelve-year-old Emilio Estevez and his sister (Janet said they were her kids). But the biggest surprise was when she yelled out for Martin!

Their house had a large living/playroom area opposite the kitchen. The whole time we were there, the TV was on in the furthest part of that living room area. When she shouted out his name, the great actor Martin Sheen popped up from a couch opposite the TV. We didn't even know he was there. Janet asked him to come into the kitchen and for 15 minutes we ate homemade cookies and taught Martin Sheen a thing or two about the comic book collecting culture.

Martin was really cool about our being there and seemed genuinely curious about what made comic collecting a growing concern. He didn't talk to us about his life; it was about our comics! And this was right before he traveled to the Philippines to begin filming *Apocalypse Now*. Not one word about what would become his tour de force performance to date in pictures.

Anyway, Ski made a little money off Janet, the Sheens made us feel at home, and we left with a wonderful encounter and story.

I wonder if Emilio remembers us....

San Diego's Comic Convention began in 1970 at the U.S. Grant Hotel for a one-day show in March and UCSD college campus in August. By 1972 the "Golden State Comic Con" had changed its name to "San Diego Comic Con." It held its first annual show as the SDCC at the El Cortez Hotel in downtown San Diego. This was my first Con. There were

The El Cortez Hotel in San Diego. This venerable 1920s icon was ground zero for the earlier San Diego Comic Conventions. It's fondly remembered as the party palace for comic book fans of the 1970s.

900 male attendees and three girls! I've been attending ever since. I matured from collector to seller at those shows. I even worked at the comic book store opened by one of the Comic-Con founders. From these beginnings I began to sell comics and my "everything comics" gluttony flourished at comic book conventions.

Comic-cons by the late 1970s had become a consistent source of income for me. Shows sprang up all over California and I hit many of them, from San Diego to San Francisco. The shows gave me an education while I was making money. I learned how to buy, sell, and trade in the trenches. Defending my grading and arguing prices with an opposite taught me valuable skill-sets.

A career as a police officer superseded my comic book life by the early 1980s. It would take a decade of occasional comic book dabbling before I would return to my four-color roots.

I was a construction worker and a comic book collector in the 1970s. Odd jobs were my specialty, but I worked for two contractors and one construction company at separate intervals. I was forewarned by one of my bosses that being a carpenter was a rough career later in life with little guarantee of big income. A friend of mine just out of the Marine Corps suggested I cut my hair and get a job with the police department in our hometown. San Diego PD was always hiring back then, so I applied and was hired in time for the spring 1980 academy.

I served for 19 years, working normal, everyday patrol, and then a succession of specialized assignments focused mainly on drug and gang enforcement. I was finding out along the way that like construction, police work was also hard on the body the older I got. By the mid–1990s I sustained a series of injuries that were increasingly difficult to recover from. Mounting pain and physical limitations forced me to seek early retirement.

I wasn't certain I would ever work again, but comic books and Southern California Comics saved the day.

By the early 1990s I found myself single again. My son, Mike, lived with his mother not far from me. Comics were more a part of his life than mine. Sure, I purchased some new comics along with his on our weekly trips to Sun Comics. For the most part, I found little desire to spend much money on entertainment until I was settled financially. Since this is a book about comics, we can fast forward through this section of my life and address the year 1994.

It was the summer and just weeks before Comic Con (soon to change its name to Comic-Con International). I dug out a couple of old, dusty suitcases from storage. I needed some cash so I figured that luggage held the answers. I had used the battered suitcases as storage for some of my hobby stuff, including comic books and memorabilia. I had only a

The San Diego Convention Center hosts the annual Comic-Con International comic book convention. As beautiful as this gigantic facility is, it's been outgrown by the massive crowds that want to attend the show, but can't get passes.

vague memory of what I'd stored in there roughly two decades before. I opened the two suitcases and found my old EC Comics collection, along with pounds of odds and ends. I spread all that stuff on the floor around me and took stock. There were all kinds of old comics, some pulps, artwork, lithographs, undergrounds, fanzines, and more. Even my ex-girlfriend's copy of *The Anarchist Cookbook*!

I contacted my friend Ed Farrell to ask a favor. Ed still maintained a booth at Comic-Con after two decades. Ed graciously let me borrow some table and wall space at the upcoming Comic-Con.

Within days the show was upon me. I finished prepping my inventory. I had not done a show in years, since before the 1980s, but here I was again. San Diego's Comic-Con was much smaller in 1994 than 2014 even though it occupied a much more cavernous building than in the 1980s. The early 1990s had produced San Diego's new convention center at the harbor on the once swampy shoreline bordered by manufacturing warehouses. The building was a jewel in San Diego's downtown redevelopment. Unfortunately, it proved to be too small for larger attractions. An expansion in the mid–2000s added square footage, but even that was not enough to contain the mad growth of Comic-Con.

Ed and I set up on the first day of the 1994 Con and constructed a booth that would fit all the products we could force into it. It was a wise call bringing too much stuff because I sold plenty of it.

After four days of sales, I was satisfied. I made money, played a little, and even bought art at the auction. At that time the Con occupied just a few of the existing halls. Much of the show-and-tell displays were contained in the Exhibitors Hall. Art auctions were held in Exhibit Hall A opposite the dealers' booths. Comic book dealers were more numerous at the show then. The price to set up attracted dealers big and small. Back then, spaces were allotted for tables (without booth consideration) and could be had for $500. The booths were over $1,000. I was on a strict budget, so I spent a couple of seasons occupying single tables, or conjoining tables with friends.

There was more floor space than was needed, so nobody fought for exhibitors' spots. You could actually be set up next to a booth that remained unoccupied through the show and just ooze over to take advantage of the extra space (if you could get away with it!).

The success of that show reawakened a long-dormant desire within me to rejoin the hobby. I made a small amount of disposable income from that weekend of sales. Since I had managed to hold onto my EC collection all those years, I tentatively checked out copies for sale at that show. Subsequent smaller shows in the region were well-attended by comic book back issue guys. I prowled the back issue boxes and wall displays for more EC comics to fill runs. I spent hundreds of dollars. I was having fun! The bug had bit, and I was once again a comic collector.

I met my future business partner, Gino Siragusa, at one of the small local shows in Mission Valley. We recognized each other from comic-cons of the past, but did not know each other. Gino was perusing the contents of a dealer's box of Golden Age books while I examined a table top covered with the seller's better EC Comics. There's that EC connection again!

Inevitably, Gino and I began to talk, and a permanent friendship resulted. Gino already had a business partner, Bob Capoocia, at the convention level. I met Bob a short time later. The three of us figured we could work in tandem at regional conventions, selling comics side-by-side.

Trips to L.A., San Francisco, and Phoenix strengthened our business ties and enabled aggressive purchasing tactics. We were becoming more experienced at the art of selling comics and acquiring comic collections. Our growing inventories filled three homes. Our wives were not pleased. They pushed for alternative storage. The combined boxes of comics and other ephemera took up an estimated 1,000 square feet squeezed into our garages and spare bedrooms. Our wives saw the increasing growth of filled comic book boxes at each residence as clutter and an affront to their freedom of movement at home.

Gino, Bob and I discussed off-site storage but ruled out storage units as impractical for our goals. We figured we could easily afford a thousand square feet of something we could move into. Our requirements outclassed the bareness of an unlit storage facility. Bathrooms, power, and stricter security were necessary. Plus, we wanted to open our massive inventory to the public when suitable. We needed something with greater public access. Enter the warehouse business model, unique among the world of comic book stores.

I'll be frank about this store idea. Neither of us knew who would run it or how it would work. I was recovering from surgery to repair injuries I'd suffered as a cop. (I was still on the job technically but I was one of the long-term walking wounded.) I had some free time while I was on long-term medical leave, so I took an idea and made it a reality. The thought was that we would store all of our inventories in one commercial rental and open it on weekends to the public.

The idea of a store is much simpler than the act of creating one. With little or no money, most people can get started with cheap rent in a shabby shopping center in a lower-income neighborhood. With money (something we did without), a comic fan can start up in any neighborhood. Or a strip mall. Or a shopping center. Or you can open up in a shabby building in a nice neighborhood!

With limited funds, I took on the task of hunting down a venue for our future store. The three of us were dedicated to this. Our capital investment amounted to $3,000, so pickings were probably going to be slim.

I chose a warehouse complex off a main freeway. I'd checked out similar industrial buildings in a part of San Diego known for manufacturing, wholesale distribution and retail. The monthly rates in most of these locations were affordable. They generally consisted of numerous ground-level suites, many buried in the midst of large industrial complexes, making it challenging for customers to find us, therefore guaranteeing us virtually no walk-in traffic off the boulevard. The key was finding a place central to the freeway system and close to my home. I chose a glamour-challenged suite in a block of warehouses in an old industrial center of San Diego, Kearny Mesa, which was twelve minutes from my house by surface streets. The rent was well under $1,000 for an equal amount of square footage, power (poor lighting), one bathroom (no hot water, and dirty), and an office. It was being vacated by a small body jewelry concern, so we were able to sign the lease and move in by October of 1997.

Bob, Gino, and I moved hundreds of boxes to the new location late that year. Furnishings were purchased or built by hand. Our office housed the cash register and our countertop was a venerable wooden used office desk, purchased at auction from the County of San Diego. Boxes had to be sorted with weeks of partner participation to organize the massive inventory. I was more or less fulltime at sorting and store operation, but pain from my injury limited my mobility. Sorting comic books was therapy to keep my mind distracted from the healing process that eventually left me with only a partial recovery.

The store seemed to take forever to get off the ground. By the spring of 1998 we'd already advertised the store in the phone book. Tables and wall-mounted shelves held rows of sorted comics. Our new Diamond Comic Distribution account was still months away. Comic book dealing morphed into learning the ropes of a retail storefront operation.

Unfortunately, taxes, permit fees and operation costs consumed our meager funds. Predictably, business did not take off. It just sort of fluttered on with some good days and lots of bad. Since we had back issues and only back issues, we missed out on the kinds of sales from new books other stores paid their bills with. The account with Diamond and subsequent new product shipments brought some business. Rent was produced any way we could generate it, usually tapping into personal cash.

Our strong suit was and still is the San Diego Comic Convention/Comic-Con International. Continual sales at comic cons often produced enough money to pay our bills. We would not have to sacrifice personal money often. Consequently, the rent got paid before we did or before collections were purchased. We depended on back issue purchases at various cons to carry our inventory forward. Each fresh collection drove business to us. The cons produced more buying opportunities than the store. One unfortunate missed opportunity exemplifies this period:

An ex-pat American from Mexico called with an interest in selling his comics. He was in his 60s and still owned the comics from his youth. I was alone the day he arrived at our store. He carried a large cardboard box through our open roll-up door and set it on top of one of our portable folding tables. The box was two feet cubed and heavy. He opened the folded flaps and grabbed a fistful of the contents: they were ECs! Hundreds of EC comics! All loose and piled on top of each other. The haphazard fashion the old gentleman used was guaranteed to damage the boxed copies. I carefully removed a small portion of the pile starting with a fat run of *Shock SuspenStories*. Issue #1 was on top and was accompanied by some copies of *Weird Science* and *Weird Fantasy*. The issues were piled up in some semblance of order. I stopped digging. There had to be hundreds of issues, all original, owned by this same man since the time he purchased them new, all unique one-offs. I wanted them badly. As an EC collector, my fan side started to broil. As a business owner, I saw major dollar signs, but our business couldn't afford it.

We had enough for rent, but not for rent and the ECs. The best I could offer at that time was maybe $2,500. He was a gruff, surly sort and not very patient. I divulged my cash dilemma, which did not charm him or reduce his price. In years to come, I would find money for just about any collection turned my way, but at this moment, I was fiscally unarmed. No way could I pony up the cash at the old man's speed. He was also losing his cool and telling me that if I couldn't buy them, he'd find someone who would. I had nowhere to turn to. I was stuck. He was frustrated that he made the trip from Ensenada (about two hours) for nothing. I asked him to give me a price break. He not only refused, but packed up the loose books and said he'd rather destroy them than give them away cheap. Then he walked, actually muttering under his breath. I swore that would never happen again. My partners commiserated later that day. "*C'est la vie.*"

That's enough about that.

Our store took forever to gain customers and cover our bills. Small collections and new weekly comics expanded our stock and diversity. Within a few years of daily struggle, more and more customers successfully discovered our hidden location. Regulars formed and monthly pull-list subscribers grew in number. We expanded into two more vacant suites, increasing to 2,500 square feet. By 2006, we'd acquired the contents and customers from several recently closed comic book stores. I always said that we would let business force us to expand in order to stay within our means. We've seen other stores do just the opposite, by expanding their size in hopes of bringing in more business. Many of those guys closed in failure sometime after.

Our inventory became massive, with over 400 boxes of comics on display at any given time. Conversely, the partnership reduced by one as Bob separated for personal reasons. A string of employees filtered through the shop. As they changed, so did the store's setup. Furnishings were upgraded and attempts to beautify our store's basement-like appearance had marginal success. A lot of money was spent, but we would never be "*très chic*." So the money would better suit us if we continued spending it on comic book collections instead of decor.

Our store had taken years of sales toil to produce enough income to pay its employees, debts, and finally us. Those years force-fed us a form of comic book labor I typify as trench warfare. It has been an almost daily cycle of buying and selling comic books with interested parties arriving at the store to sell all kinds of pop-culture merchandise, yet merchandise acquisitions that required a lot of haggling.

Years of negotiations in this arena were ramped up by the consistent flow of cash-hungry clients. We became adept at finessing collections from one party and then onto the next party. My particular purchasing skills were initially built upon repetitive comic cons, but those were few. Annually, small shows were habitually attended by the same buyers and sellers. New collection opportunities at these shows were uncommon. Our store, Southern California Comics, drew people from all over with more every month. Purchasing skills were honed with increased encounters from a variety of buyers and sellers.

There's a lot of collectible comic book stuff out there. We theorized that one fallen deal would quickly be replaced by one or two completed deals. There was no need to get panicky or adopt a hoarder's mentality. The money was there; the purchases were there. We just needed to be patient and calm, and better collections would be ours. That theory was sound thinking.

I represented the store for almost all of the buys. Circumstances had moved Gino out of San Diego. Our partnership remained, but I was the sole operative. The decisions to buy and sell were all mine. With confidence drawn from over three decades of my hobby-to-business experience, the store was wide open for some of the wildest collections I could imagine. All manner of people reached out to us to sell their comics: inheritors, storage hunters, old hobbyists, burnt-out collectors and amateur opportunists—all kinds of comic book possessors. We found ourselves satiated with collections the likes of which we once dreamed about. Well, maybe less than satiated, since one collection in hand is never as good as the next one somewhere out there!

I'm talking about comic collections with the likes of *Batman* #1–#250, boxes of Timelys, Golden Age runs of *Superman*, and more. Significant, original-owner collections from the 1950s and 1960s happened twice a year like clockwork. Collections of Silver Age from first-hand and secondhand collectors were more frequent. Large collections of contemporary comics rolled in throughout any given year. Some contacts required trucks to haul the stuff back to our store. Purchase yields ranged from more than 20,000 common modern comics to single issues that later sold for tens of thousands of dollars.

This is a good point to explain a more subtle challenge to retain positioning in our business. You can't get all this stuff from an often savvy public without gaining their trust. The best way to achieve that is offering fair buy-in prices. Pricing them with numbers acceptable to both parties, and with those prices explained, helps to seal deals. I prefer an open line of communication during conversations with the sellers. It sets them at ease and smoothes out misconceptions. The stone-faced look I've gotten from closeted dealers in the past just encouraged me to go elsewhere. To reach these ends, one needs to ensure that nobody gets burned. The best prevention against making a bad bargain is a good understanding of the product. Knowing the condition or grade of the comic allows us to know the value with certainty. Remarkably, too many people don't respect the need to fully understand the comics they sell to us.

Repeatedly attaching accurate value to collections is a science. It's a skill not taught in college. I learned it through hundreds of hours while playing comic books with others. Our business became adept at looking over collections containing thousands of comics and generating quick, on-the-money appraisals. "Quick" is relative, but generally it is a time frame that pleases the owner. Methodically, my team could handle larger collections several times a week. With an open dialogue discussing our thought processes, a prospective seller often felt the trust necessary to sign off on the big sale. That repetitive style of successful accumulation built us a solid reputation.

By 2014, our store's reputation for accuracy, honesty, and diversity earned us our best accolades to date. Our store was nominated for an Eisner "Spirit" Award. We made the first cut and dropped into a list of thirty-seven nominees from out of thousands of potential store applicants. Next, the CGC Collectors Society named our store as one of the top ten dealers in the world. We were number ten on the list and the only small store. Our reputation matched the selection criteria set forth by the bullet points to make the list. Our membership within the pantheon of some of the world's greatest comic book fans was established when the *Overstreet Price Guide* reinforced our contributions within the marketplace.

Our business has maintained a high positive feedback rating on eBay going back to our start in 1998. Our Yelp.com feedback rating remained the highest in town as of 2016. Yelp comments drive our sales as much as any public feedback. Our store has garnered accolades for our inventory and our prominence. We have been featured on local and national news on many occasions. We received an award from the San Diego Police Department for our charitable donations to an inner city youth program. We've donated thousands of comic books to youth organizations, schools, hospitals, county children's centers, and the military. Through ARC, an organization that sponsors afterschool programs, we've mentored a comic book club at the local high school. I subsequently hired two of my students for the store.

Over the years, I remained frustrated by collectors who missed all the easy lessons I learned about comic book collecting. I still encounter many comic book fans who have no idea what they are doing. The more knowledge I gained, the less, it seemed, a lot of my buyers understood. Watching my own customers' purchasing mistakes illustrates the rampancy of misinformation. There is a majority of collectors stuck in neutral with no plan to educate themselves as buyers and collectors and to develop skills designed to protect their wallets. Frazzled buyers are still getting ripped off online and in person. Hence, our store draws in plenty of people looking for a little advice. They want some mentoring after having been burned too often.

My background as a former police officer guaranteed I'd be connected to investigations regarding stolen comics. Cops are challenged daily with crimes involving property theft. Those crimes yield suspects in possession. That possession can only be prosecuted if the police can prove either that the thief stole the items, or knew he or she was in possession of stolen items. If the string of events connects a thief to a theft with witnesses or evidence, then the arrest is made and prosecution will be forthcoming (probably). Thieves are often stopped for other reasons and happen to be in possession of stolen property. The police are obligated to determine the origins and status of that property. The goal is to detain the thief while they conduct that investigation.

I once took a police report about stolen comic books. This report was taken in the 1990s in the local community of Ocean Beach. As the beat officer, I was dispatched to a residence to take the report of a burglary. A thief had forced entry into the back of a beach bungalow. The rear of the bungalow faced an alley, and alleys are frequent access points for thieves (fewer witnesses, even in daytime). The victim's name was Ray, and he made the report. His loss included tools, fishing gear … and comic books. And not just any comic books: 1940s *Captain America*s. *Cap* is still a highly desirable and uncommon title!

I collected as much information and potential fingerprint evidence as could be found and gave Ray a crime case number.

Now as fortune would have it, Comic-Con was just a month or two away. Since this was in the days before Craig's List and eBay, I reasoned that those comics stood a reasonably good chance of showing up at Con. Back then anybody could still get a ticket into the show, and exhibitors' booths were readily available.

That year my vendor's booth at that Con was set up nearer the back of the building. Ray, my crime victim from earlier, saw me and hurried over. He knew I'd be at the show, so he had searched me out. Ray told me that he took my advice and got an attendee badge to the show to look for his stolen comics. Lo and behold, he said, he found them at a nearby dealer's booth. He was in a hurry to get me over to that booth, but I slowed him down to discuss tactics. My thoughts were to allow me to scope out the booth, validate his claim, and then hotwire security to lock the booth down and prevent any mischief.

Ray's *Cap*s should have been identical to anybody else's *Cap*s, but they were not. He happened to own a collection of 3-ring binder hole-punched issues. They were easily distinguishable from any other issues because of those holes.

Ray took me to the proof, and I could see plain as day that Ray's comics were on the table in front of me. We said nothing to the dealer, but I had Ray stand by to watch the action at the booth while I got help. I used my police ID to get security's attention and had them accompany me back to Ray. Ray stood with me and security as I spoke to the dealer. By the way, I recognized the guy from sometime in the past. He lived in an airplane hangar in an East County airport and sold comics from the place—his idea of supplementing his retirement. I've forgotten his name, so for story purposes I'll call him "Tom." Tom denied that the comics were stolen. Then he denied knowing they were stolen. Then he gave up the identity of the guy who sold the comics to him.

I had security stand by while I stepped aside and placed a phone call to the detective who was assigned to the original burglary case. The detective was on-duty and instructed me to have security collect the stolen comics while I wrote down Tom's information from his driver's license. It's great being a cop at Comic-Con. You get instant respect and no nonsense. I explained to Tom that he was in possession of stolen property and that it would be up to the detective to decide if he was in any trouble. Remember, just owning stolen property is not enough. The owner has to know it's stolen and the law has to be able to prove that without any doubt. Tom was out the books, as well as another dealer. Tom had sold some copies to the other dealer at Con, and he, in turn, tried to flip them at his booth.

Ray and his comics went with me to the office of convention security. I borrowed a Polaroid camera from security that they used to take photos of their detainees. Per the detective's instructions I took instant pictures of the recovered comic books so that the comics could be released to Ray. The photos replaced the comics as evidence for potential court purposes. Ray got his stolen comic books back.

By the way, the original burglar was identified as an alley neighbor of Ray's. Ray did not know him, but within a few days the police sure did!

Comic books are stolen all the time. Determining if comics are stolen, though, can be a chore. Crime cases involving stolen comics can only go so far. One stolen copy of *Avengers* #265 (1986) looks like another, and can't really be distinguished in the field from a copy legitimately purchased. Also, the value of the comics can determine the severity of prosecution. Cops detain suspects all the time with a smidgen of suspicion or probable cause. The police need elements of the crime to line up to make the detention turn into an arrest.

In retirement I received occasional calls from investigators regarding stolen comic books. The contact usually involves a suspicious person in possession of identifiable stolen property including comic books. The officers ask me to help them figure out if they can gig (arrest) the suspect for stolen comics along with the other stuff. Yes, if the comics can be connected to a victim. No, if they cannot. If victims don't make crime cases, then the chances of seeing their property returned are almost nonexistent. If the crime occurred but the victim is unaware of it, then the detention may provide clues to the victim's identity. Then a crime case can be established and the arrest is made.

Our store is occasionally contacted by victims of comic book theft. They notify us of the loss in the hope that the collection might surface at our store. Suspects have tried to sell us stolen stuff in the past. The victim's warning call does stand a good chance of producing a recovery. I've found over the years that most people report their comic book losses from their homes or from storage. What doesn't get reported often enough are thefts from comic book conventions. Those victims are out of luck if no one in authority knows about the loss.

I've received calls from insurers about comic books as well. One such call was to assist an insurer with validating a claim. A then-recent firestorm had destroyed several hundred homes throughout the county of San Diego. One fire victim in particular lost his house and his expensive comic book collection. He filed an insurance claim with Allstate Homeowners Insurance and included the comics in the loss. One of the comics had an estimated value of around $25,000, according to the claimant. The insurer desired proof of possession, but the claimant had none. The insurer asked the claimant to provide provenance for the book, assuming that an owner of such an expensive comic book would have the name of the person he got it from. The claimant seemed vague to the insurance investigator. He did not have a name, but said he got it at a comic book store here in town. He provided the name of the store, but said they went out of business years ago.

The investigator was pretty sharp in coming to me. I established my years as a San

Diego comic book collector. I told him there's not a comic book store in San Diego I haven't been to or known about. I told him the store name the claimant provided was bogus. The investigator's gut feeling was that the claimant was lying, but proof was tough to come by. He thanked me and told me he'd keep in touch.

Weeks passed before I got a call-back from that insurance investigator. He had re-contacted the claimant to conduct a short interview for follow-up reasons. By using interrogation techniques, he managed to get the claimant to drop his guard and change his story about the expensive comic's origin. The investigator pulled out some paperwork and showed him that his current statements did not match what he'd said previously. He also questioned the man regarding the supposed comic book store. The claimant repeated the name he'd given previously and swore that's where he got it. When the investigator used my information to invalidate the claimant's story, he refused to speak further. He even went so far as to threaten the investigator with a lawsuit if his company didn't cough up the money. The investigator terminated that interview. In his subsequent phone call to me, he said that it was now up to his company to accept or reject the claim on that comic book and others. Thanks to my information, he said, his recommendation to his company on the claimant's behalf would be brutal.

There have been other questions about stolen or damaged comic books posed to me by police investigators and private companies. It's quite clear that crimes involving comics are unknown to many people outside our hobby. Collectors, too, can be mystified about the logistics and realities of owning exotic or expensive comic collections.

It grew clear to me that some sort of voluntary mentoring could help educate a lot of people. Someone with authority who could dispense knowledge like a doctor dispenses medical aid, someone who could teach others how to collect smartly and protect their investments, someone who could guide and assist collectors to understand how their collecting fits into the scheme of things, someone who could educate collectors about advantages and pitfalls in the world of comic collecting.

That someone would be the Forensic Comicologist.

1

Forensic Comicology

Forensic (defined): relating to the use of scientific knowledge or methods in solving crimes or legal problems; scientific analysis of physical evidence (as from a crime scene).

Merriam-Webster Dictionary officially recognized and printed the word "forensic": 1659.

Comicology (defined): the science of collecting comic books.

First known use: 2011.

What is a forensic comicologist?

A forensic comicologist is an expert in the field of law enforcement and its relationship to the pathology of comic books. I am a forensic comicologist. My goal is to invite other collectors, buyers and sellers to learn the science and business sides of dealing in comic books. We are a small but heavily acknowledged force within the world of comic books in general.

In 1975, my friend Ski hooked me up with Richard Alf, who hired me on the spot to work at his store, Richard Alf's Comic Kingdom. This arrangement allowed me to sell my own comics at comic book conventions without conflict. I sold at Comic-Con from my own inventory while working for Comic Kingdom selling their inventory. Comics were easy to come by, and new comics became sought-after back issues relatively quickly (retail locations in the mid–1970s were not yet saturated throughout San Diego, and comic books could be hard to find even new). New comics were cover priced twenty-five cents, then thirty cents, and then on and on. Back issues could be acquired cheap from collections coming into the store.

Working at a comic book store in the 1970s was hip; at least it felt that way. All my friends and cohorts felt that something was happening that was bigger than us. Comic book talk was everywhere. Stores carrying comic books were slowly popping up, and some comic book stores were actually growing into chain stores.

My work at Comic Kingdom was rudimentary. I either filed back issues away in a curtained-off portion in the back of the store, or I stood at a counter at the front of the store and sold comics. Early comic book retailing pioneer Greg Pharis was hired after me to run the store for Richard Alf, who always seemed to be somewhere else. Richard hired a third guy, a Navy sailor named Hans, to help out on weekends. Hans was older than the rest of us, but he used the atmosphere of the store to mentally escape his job. Hans was not unique. San Diego was a military town filled with marines and sailors from all over the country. They all needed various forms of escapism, especially since this was right after the tail end of the Vietnam War.

Hans was special in another way, too. He brought his birth certificate into the shop one day to show off the stamp on one corner of the document. The inked stamp was a genuine, honest-to-God swastika. It seems Hans was born in 1944 in Nazi Germany, and all German birth certificates at the time bore that stamp. Of course, Hans was not a Nazi baby, and his parents wanted out of that war-torn country. They managed to leave after the war and moved to the United States. Hans joined the Navy and was happy to be stationed in San Diego.

I have to say that the real peach about working at a comic book store in San Diego wasn't the store; it was the incredible opportunity the store offered to guys like me who focused on the annual comic book convention. All the Con bigwigs and lesser-known fans hung out at Richard's store. After all, Richard was a co-founder of the San Diego show and knew everybody. I was just twenty years old with few connections into that world, but after the end of my two-year tenure working for Richard, I knew enough people to become somewhat connected at shows.

I could get in free thanks to one acquaintance or another. I could crash at various hotel rooms if I was stranded downtown late at night. I went to the best parties and hung out with guys who could or did become famous. Well, as famous as a local comic book fan or artist could become.

The office of the Department of Forensic Comicology.

I was lucky enough to catch both Jerry Siegel and Joe Schuster at San Diego Comic-Con sometime in the mid–1970s while they were signing autographs. The postcards were there for both men to sign. I think they were both surprised at the amount of attention and celebration they received in front of an audience of comic book fans. (© DC Comics. Used with permission.)

Richard bought comic book collections off the street, through want ads and at conventions. He knew a lot of people, and that gained him referrals for collections to buy. Richard never shared the knowledge of the amounts he paid for other people's comics. He also didn't seem too picky. I knew local guys with cooler but smaller inventories. He just seemed to be getting bulk, and probably for pennies on the dollar considering that the average back issue in 1975 was probably less than $2 retail.

I feel that in some way my original partners and I modeled our store after the

1970s ambiance of not just a comic book store from back then, but a Comic Kingdom store from back then!

Richard Alf had been purchasing new weekly comics through the local periodical distributor ARA when I first hired on. Back in New York, the direct comic distribution system had just been born in the mid 1970s. Alf took tentative steps, ordering a few new titles from Phil Seuling's company, formed just two years earlier. Alf was tired of getting tiny discounts from ARA even though unsold copies were fully returnable. He was in touch with the East Coast and saw the direction our market was headed. The discounts were better and the unsolds would sell later at the store, through the mail or at the convention. One of the first new titles he ordered through Seuling was 1976's *Howard the Duck* #1. Alf was lenient with store manager Greg Pharis and me. When Greg ordered the comics from Seuling, Richard increased the order to accommodate Greg and me so we could buy some copies wholesale for ourselves. Greg and I took those copies cover priced at 25 cents each, and sold them at San Diego Comic-Con. I remember having more than 20 copies I took to the show that summer: I made a killing at $40 a copy! Imagine if the fates had fashioned comic book speculators five years earlier than planned. We'd all have invested in Neal Adams *Batman* art!

San Diego's first comic book speculators were freshly minted!

Some store owners speculated on new comics for resale early on. Speculation is no mystery term. Like investments in any profit-making enterprise, we comic book people speculated on new comics as they hit the stands. Just like today, forty years ago we thought new titles with first appearances or some other key component would sell for more later.

I have a longtime friend who helped a San Francisco store icon sell off some of his inventory. In this case the inventory consisted of a case of *Incredible Hulk* #181s (the book of the Millennials!). (There will be more on this concept in a later chapter.) My buddy will remain anonymous in this telling. He disclosed that the store owner (long since retired) had the foresight to retain a case of that comic book for reasons we can only speculate. There was nothing from what my friend told me that indicated the owner had once reflected on this issue and decided it would be worth a fortune someday. He just happened to keep a case for himself, to sell two decades later. Anyway, I ended up buying ten copies from my buddy back around 1999 at a show in Oakland. Even as recently as the end of the '90s, the book was still not that expensive. I bought all ten for about $75 apiece, in grades ranging from Fine to Near Mint. I ended up selling off a few to a couple of friends for a little more than I paid. The others went full retail with the best copy, a raw 9.4, selling for $450. Big money back then!

Close your mouth, reader. I get to tell this story because I'm old and know some people, nothing more.

Comic Kingdom was the second comic book store to open in San Diego. Pacific Comics was the first by at least a few months. Both stores were of minimal square footage with neither yet overwhelmed with boxes of back issues, at least as far as the public could tell. Our store eventually fell prey to over-indulgence and the owner was forced to rent a warehouse to hold the growing wealth of back issues. That plan was justified with the growth of the mail-order arm of the business. Pacific Comics has its own history of expansion, metamorphosis and an ultimate ending, perhaps prematurely.

CHARLES M. SCHULZ
2162 COFFEE LANE
SEBASTOPOL, CALIFORNIA

July 5, 1966

Jamie Newbold
5509 Mt. Acara
San Diego, California

Dear Jamie,

I was glad to hear that you enjoyed the latest TV special. All of us who worked together on it were very pleased with it, too.

The next special will be shown sometime around Halloween and will be primarily about Linus and the Great Pumpkin.

Kindest regards.

Sincerely,
Charles M. Schulz

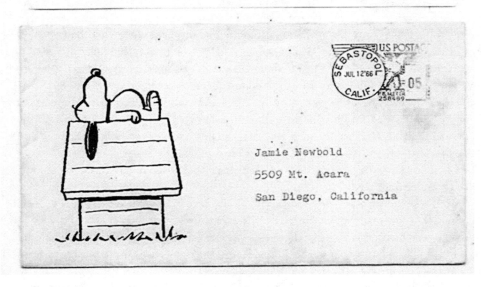

Jamie Newbold
5509 Mt. Acara
San Diego, California

I was a big fan of Peanuts as a kid. I was such a super-fan that I wrote Charles Schulz a letter at the age of eleven. Getting a response was the highlight of my year!

I did field work as an amateur paleontologist working at digs in San Diego and throughout Southern California's deserts (sponsored by museum classes and private organizations). That work included lab time at the La Brea Tar Pits in Hancock Park in Los Angeles. This was a growth experience for me, the first where I left town to work. I borrowed one of my parents' cars, a 1969 Ford station wagon, and made the two-hour drive to Beverly Hills to work at the park bordered by a museum complex. The La Brea Tar Pits are a tremendous part of Los Angeles' natural history and its dominance as an oil-producing city.

Back in the early 1970s the park was roughly sixty years old, having been mined for the past sixty years for its rich depository of mammal fossils going back tens of thousands of years.

My work at the museum was based upon my desire to be a paleontologist. I took museum classes in San Diego in junior high and high school in the late 1960s and 1970s. The tar pits seemed like a necessary and fun step toward my field experience in that science. So I found contacts at the San Diego Natural History Museum who set me up with a personnel coordinator at the La Brea site. That contact set me up as a volunteer for the summer of 1973. In June of that summer my adventure began.

Working at the pits is not as foul as it sounds. New volunteers don't even go near the pits. Just one or two were being actively excavated. The others were bubbling ponds fenced off to protect the public; unfortunately, the park sits on active unseen tar pockets that still are alive with bacteria. The bacteria form pockets of methane that occasionally bubble up throughout Hancock Park, even under your feet. So, literally, "Stay Off The Grass!"

I did my probationary, volunteer eight hours sorting tiny fossils from small soil samples under a microscope. The goal was to separate out the flora and fauna from the soil in the hopes that a new organism might be discovered. I discovered the microscope and the sorting couldn't end fast enough.

Fortunately I passed that first chore and they promoted me to the next level.

Now this job was much cooler. I was still in a lab, but now I was surrounded by metal trays filled with ancient animal bones. Using oil solvents and a glue called Glyptol, I was trained and tasked with gluing pieces together to make a whole something, most of the time the bones were parts of some deer leg or a bird neck, etc. The paleontologists who sorted the bones out of the pits were charged with figuring out if the animal parts were ancient or modern. Small animals were still getting trapped in the tar and dying, drifting downwards. When they got a winner, often broken, my lab partners and I glued them back together.

The work was only mildly entertaining, but the knowledge was unmatched by anything else I would ever learn. There was one high point to my lab work. One of the broken bones was a saber-toothed tiger fang, cracked into several fragments. I showed the other lab workers who were all a little jealous and then spent an hour or so meticulously putting the puzzle pieces back into place. When it was complete, I had the greatest sense of satisfaction!

I was only going to be at La Brea through the summer; college was next. I had just about earned enough hours to leave the lab. Next stop would have been pit #91; the volunteer who was to mentor me had already taken me down into the pit for a close-up tour. But it wasn't meant to be. My summer had run out. I did return for a visit years later, after a new facility and museum were built, but now I was just another tourist.

This was but one facet of the life experiences a forensic comicologist must pass through to learn patience to make sure the job is done thoroughly and correctly.

I left the store and all the rest behind in the mid–'70s and went into other lines of work, including construction and cabinetry, before joining the San Diego Police Department.

Through mail order, conventions, swap meets and store sales, I've spent thousands and made thousands over decades of moving comic books in the marketplace. I've amassed more than 40 years of comic book business experience. I've owned and operated a large comic book store (Southern California Comics) since 1997. It's a specialty store that has consistently concentrated on the acquisition and sales of comic books from all ages. I've attended dozens of comic conventions over a span of four decades and more, many of them either as an exhibitor or as a friend helping out other dealers. My store is designed around my sense of comic convention exhibition, the way I set up my booths to maximize sales. It's unique in its location and fundamental stock sourced around the print aspects of our industry. Simply put, it's about comic books.

While other comic book stores offer somewhat of a template floor plan, we do things in an original way. Our emphasis is on vintage comic books and memorabilia. We excel in organization for a store that displays more vintage product diversity than any other I know. There are few games, very little manga or anime, no DVDs, no role-playing games, and no gaming tables. We are light on toys but heavy on Golden Age comics. We sell original comic book art but are strikingly barren of modern, variant-covered comic books. We are, in a word, unique.

I've developed partnerships and friendships with dozens of comic book collectors and retailers. During a span of several years, I retained membership in the "Network of Disclosure," a group of comic book dealers and collectors who pledged to disclose any form of restoration or enhancement known to exist on comic books when their ownership has changed parties. I retained membership for a brief period when its name and mission statement changed to the CBCA: the Comic Book Collecting Association. The CBCA granted itself a broader mission while retaining its standard of ethics. I discuss the reasons these organizations need to exist, and the problems of comic book restoration, in later chapters.

By 2010, I was invited to join the *Overstreet Price Guide*'s panel of advisors. The selection criteria center around candidates who make a difference in the hobby. The selection criteria invite advisors who can contribute their market knowledge in carefully crafted written reports. These annual reports are meant to convey honest appraisals of the comic book collecting marketplace from the points of view of national and even international experts.

My background as a retired San Diego police officer includes a three-year stint enforcing narcotics laws and targeting street gangs in some of the toughest neighborhoods in San Diego. That unit assignment propelled me into court, often three days out of the four I worked weekly. I developed expertise in narcotics and gangs through classes, specific seminars, and the rough-and-tumble streets. Court experience is valuable to a cop. Frequent appearances over my career force-fed me knowledge of the inner workings of the legal system. I became proficient at deciphering the laws of arrest, probable cause, the rules governing search and seizure, and evidentiary elements.

I taught other cops at the squad level. I exercised my expertise within my various commands when called upon. Unfortunately, I was less inclined to read or collect comics during a period of several years from the mid–'80s to the early 1990s. That interest was re-engaged sometime later.

Being a cop sends one into the lives of a lot of people. We try to either help them or stop them. It always seems to boil down to those two objectives. The law entitles us to stop bad behavior and protect those who are victims of that behavior. After 19 years of those encounters, I was inspired to help others in a hobby that has left some feeling victimized, while teaching them how to spot an unscrupulous player.

My comic book experience in the latter portion of my life evolved from the earlier experiences I've had in this hobby and my earliest interest in comics. Being an injured and retired police officer left me few options. Going back to college at 47 did not interest me. My hobby was relatively painless (I still suffer pain from joint damage) so I could continue to handle it physically. Friends and family supported me, so I became comfortable as a full-time comic book store retailer with a fixed business location.

In the Introduction, I wrote about the jaded mentality of my peers of the 1970s and later. With my return to the hobby years later, I expected to find a new generation that capitalized on lessons learned in the past by others. Instead, the simplest lessons go ignored by many. Rip-offs and hustles thrive in the Internet environment. Today's collectors seem unprepared or unwilling to protect themselves with just a little more education. The *Overstreet Price Guide* (*OPG*) seems abandoned by too many who could learn from a good read of the book. Gone are the days when everyone carried a copy to read or hold his notes.

It appears that instinct (often misguided) and the financial bottom line dominate decision making. Collectors are getting taken constantly. Buyers who don't ask enough questions are easily led by the nose. Unwise purchases are rationalized daily. These poor souls are paying wrong amounts for the right books or are buying the wrong ones altogether! How do we fix this? Where are the teachers, the mentors? What can be done?

The Birthing of the Forensic Comicologist

I was in a unique position to understand the value of scattered collections of comic books. Being a cop and an experienced comic book dealer put me right in between two worlds that barely coexist. Certainly one side does not understand the other. In general, the police are not adept at identifying one stolen comic book from another. For law enforcement, attaching value to stolen comics is speculative and often a complete mystery. Establishing value can go a long way to determine the severity of a theft crime involving comics. I knew a lot of police officers during my time on and beyond. My history as a "cop nerd to the nerds" got around the department. Periodically, I was asked by investigators to attach values to stolen comics or to try to identify victims when stolen collections were recovered.

After my career as a police officer came to an end, I won a well-fought battle with the city and gained an honorable retirement. That financial mattress gave me the comfort to regain my health and explore options for my future. The money is a sustainable resource thanks to the store. The freedom to do what I want allows my Forensic Comicologist persona to operate. The Forensic Comicologist is busy trying to set things right, and that plays right into the hands of law enforcement.

Not surprisingly, another aspect to dealing comics books is manifested when stolen collections come to me. A customer brought a list to me at my store. It was a list of comics from his burgled apartment. Singularly, the comics were common and would be hard to discern as stolen. Kept together, the variety of titles and issues was particular and unique to my customer's list. I had his list and agreed to help if I learned anything.

Only a couple of days passed and a skeevy parolee-sort lugged a large box of comics into the shop. My cop antenna, not fully dulled by retirement, started tingling (Spider-sense!). He was no comic book guy. I'd seen too many crooks of his caliber in my past to believe he read or collected comic books. He asked if I was buying, so I took a look at the contents of his box. Instantly, the indicators are there. Not only do they look to be in the hands of a bad guy, but they're my customer's stolen books! I excused myself and stepped out of his line of sight. I cornered one of my employees and had him locate and identify the suspect's vehicle parked outside our shop. I grabbed my customer's list and surreptitiously matched it against our "guest's" comics. I made the match and confirmed the comics were my customer's lost stuff.

I contacted the victim by phone as quickly and discreetly as possible. He gave me the phone connection to the investigative detective handling his case. Meanwhile, the suspect was growing antsy. Things were not advancing to his satisfaction. I tried to stall him while waiting for a callback from the detective.

The suspect glided over toward the door and saw my employee sniffing around his vehicle. With the events coming to a sudden close, I told the suspect I knew the comics were stolen. I bluffed that the police were on the way. I neither wanted nor knew if I could go toe-to-toe with the guy over comic books. Without a word, he turned tail and trotted outside to his car. Wisely, my employee backed away and let him escape.

He left us the evidence. That was an unpredictable outcome to a scenario where the situation could have gone awry. During those tense moments, I waited for the police to call me back. Finally, the detective called me. With all the information we had, including a cop-specific suspect description, finding this guy would not be a challenge. The license plate of the getaway vehicle led police to his name and his home. A search warrant was generated quickly and served the next day. The suspect was arrested and more stolen booty recovered.

The victim got back most of his stolen comics. Some items were still missing. He was more than happy at the speed he recovered his books. He was very pleased that someone cared enough to go the distance for him and for justice. Luckily for me, I have good employees to back my play, too. In fact, we'd generated a talent for crime-fighting that found a niche blending together the talents of our hobby and my previous career. I have my own "Avengers" and Southern California Comics is our "Bat Cave" (yeah, I know, deal with it). Being in the right place at the right time didn't hurt either. That's always been a karmic rule synonymous with police work.

On a side note, another man brought comics into the store within a week of the previous escapade. They were the rest of the stolen comics! This guy quickly got hinky and took off with the box before I could figure out how to stop him without force. My employees operated autonomously and bagged his car info with only a signal look from me. We passed this encounter on to the police for another day.

There are countless stories of comic book thefts that have been recorded for decades.

I know stories about ultra-safe storage facilities rented by comic book owners looking for some place to conceal their collections, only to return one time and find the contents gone. We experienced such a crime when we purchased an exhaustive comic book collection from Los Angeles. Once the collection of 27,000 comics was purchased, we hauled it down to San Diego in a 26-foot U–Haul. We'd made arrangements to temporarily occupy a vacant suite behind our store.

Upon our return, we unloaded the truck with the help of additional people and locked the place down for the night. The next day began with an early morning breakdown of the contents of the collection, moving the best stuff into our shop or to my house.

Processing 27,000 comics requires a one-at-a time itemization of every copy to get a handle on what we purchased. That takes days if not weeks to complete, and we only had a limited amount of time to occupy the temporary space. I knew I'd have to relocate remainders by the thousands until we could figure out what to keep, and what to sell off or give away. The only recourse was to rent a commercial storage unit and give ourselves the luxury of accounting for all the comics without a looming deadline.

I chose a facility near our shop in an area designed for manufacturing and distribution. There were not a lot of residents and the buildings weren't occupied 24 hours a day. The place seemed secure enough. The area was fenced, gated with entry codes, and had surveillance cameras and managers who lived on that property. I met the guy at the front desk, signed a month-to-month lease, and began the arduous labor of moving dozens of remaining long boxes into the new location. It seemed safe enough and very close to my comfort zone.

Within days one of my employees, Matt, showed up at the storage facility to begin the day's sorting, only to find the room had been broken into! Somebody had pried open the roll-up door and gained entry. What a bitch. The thief or thieves used a pry tool to force the door off its track and then lifted it high enough to get inside. Lucky for us, we left nothing of great value inside. We walked the property to try to find any sign of our stolen comics.

The facility was built above street level on the back side. The area was completely enclosed in Cyclone fence, but portions of the embankments had eroded, creating gaps along the bottom of the fencing. One such gap led to a concrete culvert designed to drain water to the street below. The bad guys obviously chose that point for exit, because we saw a pile of our comics strewn around the parking lot at the bottom of the steep drainage culvert. It appeared as though our thieves fled in a hurry down the embankment and lost their grip on some of our comics. We found *Alpha Flight*, *Thunderstrike* and *Namor* flung down onto the asphalt as though they'd been dropped by the bad guys in a hurry.

No big deal. But it taught us a lesson about the security of one of those public storage places: basically nonexistent. The worst-case scenario was that it was an inside job. How else would the thieves know to target us? We'd only been there a few days. Perhaps another tenant was involved. We will never know because we scooped up all the other comics and relocated them to our original location.

Do not trust public storage facilities with your valuables. We took lots of break-in reports at those places when I was a cop and they are still vulnerable.

The point of all this is to illustrate how vulnerable comic book collectors can be. There are no instructors, no classes and few mentors to teach collectors how to protect their investments. We all learn how to keep our stuff safe with war stories, hope and common sense. A void is just crying out to be filled with teachers willing to share their knowledge and experiences with other collectors. What if there were a tutorial on how to collect and protect comics, something collected together in one volume that collectors could refer to and learn how to save themselves from grief?

Police relate to these property crimes, like burglary, in a reactive mode. The crime was already committed and the investigation tried to play catch-up to solve it. What's needed is some entity that can teach others lessons on self-protection. Crimes can be solved with help and perseverance, and some prevention aid can stop the crimes. Somebody who has already experienced what crime can mean to comic book collectors. Somebody who can teach practical lessons learned from experience about collecting and protecting.

Enter the Forensic Comicologist

We suffered a large theft at the 2008 Comic-Con International. We didn't know it at the time. Too much booth activity and too much inventory allowed the enemy into our gates. It wasn't until weeks later that I received a call from an attorney in the Bay Area that we learned of our own victimization.

The attorney, also a collector, called because he checked our Web site and matched some books he just purchased with similar comics on our site. He called to validate his fears that he owned comics that might be ours and might be stolen. He was correct.

I flipped out when I verified the gap in our inventory. He explained how he ended up with the stolen comics and graciously offered to return them. We made arrangements to meet after I'd made a crime report with the local police department. That's the only way to handle a crime if the suspect is known and a victim stands any chance of getting justice. Make the crime report.

The attorney purchased the comics via a Craigslist ad. The physical transaction was handled in another city through an intermediary/friend of the attorney. The seller actually provided his real name, so we were all obligated to see this through and capture him.

A police sting was arranged here in San Diego and the attorney agreed to set up the suspect. The sting went operational roughly a week later and the bad guy was nabbed with additional stolen comics. But not mine. It seems our guy had been busy stealing comics from dealers at other conventions for quite a while.

The attorney and I met with police at the station where the suspect was being held. The bounty of stolen comics was stacked on a table in an interview room where we could look them over. Some of the books were still bagged with the identifiable price stickers, making it easy to identify other victims. When all was said and done, we could name four additional comic book dealers that were sadly now victims. We phoned those we could find and gave them the good/bad news. First thing we figured out was that all the comics the thief brought to town were stolen in other cities, specifically at conventions. In one case, the dealer knew he'd been ripped off, and he knew when and how. That little incident cost him several thousand dollars.

He related to us how it happened: the dealer had a booth at a con with his back to a wall. He used the space under his tables to store boxes of comics he had no place to display.

The space under most tables as at larger cons is kept hidden from most attendees with the enforced placement of cloth "skirts" along the aisle-side of any table. The skirt hangs to the floor and hides the area below the table. For some, it gives a false sense of security. We dealers will use that space to store whatever we can fit there, including things of value, while we are working. This particular dealer laid a small stack of Golden Age comics on a box under his table. The comics were masked from the aisle by the skirt. Time passed and he reached for the now missing stack. Perplexed at first, he admitted to himself the sad truth that the comics had been stolen, presumably by someone from the aisle side of the table. Very sad. Just a really nice guy trying to make a living, but he became complacent in his comfort zone, and he paid a price.

Back at the police station, I spoke with that dealer over the phone and matched some of the recovered stolen books with his losses. He was surprised and overwhelmed. He never expected this arrangement to occur (their return would occur later).

Comics from two other victims were identified. One remaining pile belonged to nobody identifiable and would eventually go up for public auction.

The thief passed all the requirements for prosecution except one: no witness to concur that he possessed stolen comics. Without a court-admissible statement from him and no witness, he was technically off the hook. The problem was that the thief can deny knowledge aforethought that he ever knew the comics were stolen even though he might be the thief. He can make up any plausible or implausible explanation denying the obvious and get away with it if no credible witness can present and refute his lies. The DA's office patiently waited for the police to produce a witness, but there just weren't any. The thief was let go, photographed and fingerprinted, but gone nonetheless.

We were fortunate. We got back almost $8,000 worth of comics. The attorney who steered us toward our returned books was out the money he paid for them. He took the blow well enough, but it was a bitter pill for him to swallow—losing money for doing the right thing.

Photographs of the thief were circulated among the dealers at Comic-Con International, the con that followed the above incident. The thief and an accomplice were actually in the dealers' room scouting the back-issue booths for opportunity. We dealers had planned for that potential problem and hired retired cops I used to work with to protect them from shoplifters. The tandem thieves arrived early on Thursday. The exhibitors' room was still sparsely occupied, making their identification quick. We set up several individuals in nondescript clothing in spots around the bad guys, thinking they would not be recognized. They weren't, so we allowed the two thieves to approach my booth to see if we could legally trap them. The goal was to catch them in the act of theft and find out how they were able to do it so easily.

Since we knew the identity of the larger man, we will refer to him by his first name, Oliver. Oliver and his shorter accomplice used a ploy whereby they would stand in front of the booth opposite the occupant (we left only one person in the booth to increase the sense of vulnerability). Oliver engaged the booth occupant, his partner alongside him holding a Comic-Con tote bag at his side, the strap over his shoulder. Oliver asked my booth employee a question about a comic book on our wall display. To answer the question, the employee had to turn her back to the two men. At that moment Oliver's accomplice used his right hand to lift a section of comics out of the front of a box on our table. He only partially removed them and then dropped them back into the box. My employee had foiled the first attempt by turning back to face them. The employee turned to look at the wall again, and again the accomplice lifted the same books out of the box. He nearly cleared the box when Oliver said something and he released them. We suspect that they "made" the spotters, but we will never know for sure. They turned and walked off.

We had security contact them afterward for an explanation. They were identified, and one of our guys blatantly took pictures of their faces. They got the message. One lesson learned was how they concealed their stolen booty. Based upon the positioning, they were using the Comic-Con tote bags to steal the comics. The accomplice would simply lift a random stack of comics out of a box and drop them into the hip-high bag. Those bags are dangerous because their size and construction style make it very easy to quickly hide stolen items.

We stymied their attempts to steal and essentially ran them off from our section of the dealers' room.

My employees are young, often much younger than me. I'm fortunate to have experienced, older people who have worked for me, which provides me with experienced alternatives in contrast to the younger, less experienced workers.

Since the beginning of our store's operation, the security apparatus of the store has been surveillance cameras and intuition with an occasional stroke of luck. I've done my best to identify places within the store where we are vulnerable to theft, taught my employees to look and listen, and warned them that the theft danger starts with the hands. But the instinct to hunt down a thief turns out to be a challenge for a lot of people. I want all my people to be tigers, but as often as not, they prove to be ill-prepared.

From a cop standpoint I want them to be cops. From a shop owner's point of view I want them to be observant and careful. I've trained most of them to be on alert and react appropriately. But I know the likelihood that somebody steals from us is still there. I understand that some complacency is involved, mine included. So the best form of defense is to secure the most valuable products. We use chains, signs, cameras, locked cases and line-of-sight to work stations to keep all that theft in check. It does work, but no store owner can ever afford to let his or her guard down.

It's as simple and quick as my employee demonstrated for the camera. Caitlin's quick theft/concealment illustrates the problem at virtually any comic book store.

2

A Brief History
of Comic Collecting

By the time comic book fans discovered the fun and potential of a convention dedicated to them, science fiction fandom had entered its fourth decade of organized shows. Those shows idolized science fiction and fantasy, sharing that world with people like Ray Bradbury and Forrest J Ackerman.

I can't begin a chapter on comic book fandom without dovetailing fandom's roots with science fiction (sci-fi). Sci-fi traces its lineage back to the 19th century with writers Jules Verne, Mary Shelley, and others. They were quickly followed by H.G. Wells, Edgar Rice Burroughs, and other prolific writers of their caliber. The imaginations of the 20th century were inspired by the science and exploration that emerged out of the Industrial Age.

These writers drew upon ancient history to find themes that had existed for centuries. Ancient Mesopotamian *Gilgamesh*, *Beowulf*, and Shelley's *Frankenstein* of old English literature all inspired fantasy and fiction; far Eastern proto sci-fi helped stimulate the writers of the Modern Age. There were plenty of science fiction-bred fans in a time when industry and science fomented discoveries of the previously unknowable. Writers and readers imagined sci-fi concepts in greater numbers as literature reached larger audiences. Access to little-known parts of the world was increasing. The world was shrinking and yet more mysteries were found. Writers found a wealth of newly discovered subject material to explore with their own minds. More people received quality educations in the early 20th century than ever before. More people were trained to read and more authors were there to feed them stories.

Sci-fi gained a regular platform in 1926 with Hugo Gernsback's creation of *Amazing Stories* (1926). This was the first regularly published English-written sci-fi periodical. Just one of the early pulp publications, *Amazing Stories* helped foster the creation of other magazines with cheap newsprint featuring sci-fi and fantasy. Fans quickly gobbled up the increasing number of "pulps" dedicated to their tastes in fiction.

By the late 1930s, die-hard sci-fi enthusiasts, many of them writers, formed the first society of unified fans: The Futurians. The Golden Age of sci-fi had arrived.

While British sci-fi fans made plans in 1936, New York fans gathered together in Philadelphia at the house of sci-fi fan Milton Rothman. Holding the first ever sci-fi convention, they were the progenitors of a cultural phenomenon—the fan convention. Subsequent "Eastern" events at meeting halls in Philadelphia and New York led organizers to designate themselves "The First National Science Fiction Convention" (1936). By 1939, the committee arranged for the first "World Science Fiction Convention" in New York. Known writers, editors, and guests adorned the proceedings. Fans from outside the circles of sci-fi writers could now meet their icons in person. Britain manifested similar get-togethers, but New York is largely recognized as the seedling that grew a dynasty.

Sci-fi clubs, such as The Scienceers, and sci-fi's first fanzine *The Comet* (1930), had already appeared by the end of the 1920s. Conventions and meetings were briefly on hold during World War II. Europe's fan movement was especially affected. They resumed in 1946 with Los Angeles hosting its first World Con. These World Cons had been presented in various countries, and they continue right up to present day. Science fiction had found its Golden Age.

Wikipedia reflects every definition of a fanzine that I found: A **fanzine** (blend of fan and magazine) is a nonprofessional and nonofficial publication produced by fans of a particular cultural phenomenon (such as a literary or musical genre) for the pleasure of others who share their interest. The term was coined in an October 1940 science fiction fanzine and first popularized within science fiction fandom, from whom it was adopted by others.

Comic books as we know them today were still a ways off while sci-fi was hitting its stride. Before there were comic "books" there were comic "strips." Comics in newspaper strip form began in America at the end of the 19th century. Recurring characters shared page space with many other comic strips in newspapers syndicated throughout North America. These popular strips were owned by the powerful newspaper publishers who printed them. They entertained millions of Americans. Ever alert for opportunity, publishers were always on the lookout for new talent and new ways to market their comic strip characters.

Throughout the 1920s and into the early 1930s, the producers of all that talent urged readers to sample the best of the expanding world's comic strips. In time, comic strips were repackaged to draw more cash out of the ownership of those lucrative comic characters. One ingenious new format was to take published comic strips and repackage them. Strips that had already been seen in hundreds of newspapers were subsequently bound together into sequential pages with stiff, cardboard covers. They were first manufactured in coffee table book format and then in magazine-sized editions. These early book formats quite anonymously introduced what we would later term the Platinum Age of comics (pre–Golden Age.)

Comic books remained a repository of newspaper reprints until new material was accepted by several publishers. The year 1938 saw the creation of Superman, whose creation reinvented comic books. Publishers, seemingly oblivious to the prospect of paying for new material for their comic books, suddenly raced to find stories to match the success of this costumed hero. Their contents became primarily new material virtually in short order. Suddenly, prewar kids and teens had something new to their generation that would dominate young Americans for the next decade.

Comics rode a roller coaster of success beginning with the war. Huge circulation figures were the norm, and all kinds of characters enjoyed varying degrees of triumph. However, postwar circumstances began to change. Superheroes were losing steam among

The Golden Age of comics was a rich time of quantities and varieties for every kid in the country. Who doesn't remember sitting around a magazine rack or newsstand reading comics back in the day?

an aging readership. Television began to draw away the younger crowd to its miraculous transmissions. Comics were struggling with the changing times. By 1956, comics and their contents had been watered down often to banal stories to placate adults with more orthodox views of fantasy for children. Superheroes were cookie-cutter in character and devoid of variety.

Enter DC Comics.

Batman, Superman, and Wonder Woman were all that remained of the "Golden Age" of comic book superheroes, along with a handful of backup heroes. Fawcett's Captain Marvel went the distance post–World War II, but fizzled out under unrelenting legal pressure from DC Comics and changing readership tastes. Translated into a timeline, the Golden Age roughly mirrors the "Golden Age of Science Fiction" (late 1930s through the early 1950s).

The comic book Golden Age starts with *Action Comics* #1 (1938) and is now generally defined as ending when DC revitalized its comic book line in the mid–1950s. That period began with a new version of *The Flash* that DC tested in an ongoing title called *Showcase*; issue #4 (1956) broadcast the arrival of a sleek, costumed lab scientist named Barry Allen. Utilizing a vehicle for the creation of future costumed men and women, the staff at DC

Comics conceived of an act of science as the genesis for powers. Barry Allen's alter ego was born.

Prodded by fans, DC recreated a host of their Golden Age characters. By the early 1960s, we had a virtual league of new versions of old DC heroes. Green Lantern, The Atom, Hawkman and others regained popularity through regenesis. Marvel Comics (earlier called Atlas) saw what DC had done. The future "House of Ideas" was languishing and suffered from a lack of growth.

Legend has it that the heads of DC and Marvel were at a golf course mixing discussion with play around the time *Justice League of America* (1960) was born. *JLA* became the topic of discussion, and publisher Martin Goodman (on the Marvel side) saw the need to have his tiny bullpen of writers and artists create their own super team. Stan Lee was Marvel's editor, and with the aid of Jack Kirby, he brain-powered up the Fantastic Four. DC and Marvel thus heralded in the first full decade of the "Silver Age of Comics."

Fans had publicly declared their allegiance, and had fielded questions and criticisms of their comic books for years. Letter columns had appeared in a few comic books for years. Amateur fan magazines, or fanzines, existed for some time, allowing comic fans to "talk" to each other from great distances. But the new age of comics propelled a new generation of readers to assert their comic book desires in more public and accessible forums. DC Comics began by printing the addresses of letter writers in their letter columns. Fans such as Billy Schelly, Jerry Bails and Roy Thomas created their own fanzines. Their homemade magazines for fans allowed comic book people to communicate with each other through letter columns and classified ads. These same types of columns and ads were also printed in comic books from DC and Marvel.

Where comics limited fan contact, the fanzines opened up the world of comic book fandom to future comic fan icons. Reaching tens of thousands of readers, the fan movement could marshal up forces outside of the restrictions monthly comic books inherently produced. DC's letter columns introduced the fans to each other, making the fanzine movement more accessible.

Fans met each other through the mail, over the phone, and finally in person. The template created by sci-fi conventions was now ripe for an adaptation by a parallel fan world: comic book fans. Kids and teens discovered not only others sharing their needs to trade comic book lore, but their discoveries of the generation of comics that preceded their universe.

Comic want lists and sales catalogues appeared in local papers throughout the United States and Canada. Amateur fanzines flourished among hard-core and curious readers. Comic back-issue sales lists filled pages of mimeographed paper. Xerox copies of a seller's lists could be ordered through an address in a tiny ad in the back of a comic book. Collectors sent away for the sales lists. Buyers sent everything from money orders and checks to coins taped to letters for back issues. All kinds of purchase payments zipped back and forth across the country, even Canada. Fans found hard-to-find back issues at then-reasonable prices in national catalogs and filled their collections through the mail. Loner collectors who once thrived only at garage sales and used-book stores were now national figures furnishing the needs of leagues of comic book collectors. Inevitably, these legions, this league of comic fans, would group together to enjoy the hobby en masse.

Early comic conventions started out in a style slightly different from their earlier sci-fi counterparts. Sci-fi cons sprang from the attentions of writers, editors, and super-fans. Comic cons, which began in New York and Detroit in the mid–1960s, started with the fans. The earliest fans worked in groups to find commonality in the importance of selling comic books. The standards that we live with now as guides for collecting did not yet exist. Price and grade uniformity were a little ways off. This first generation of comic fans began to lay down the groundwork for all sellers, traders, and buyers to work with.

Those early conventions brought tens of thousands of comic book back issues into the light. Serious collectors making the treks to shows discovered just how much stuff was out there. They saw with their own eyes that some comic books sold for more than their cover prices. A few comics in the mid–1960s sold for $100 to $200, such as *Batman* and *Superman* #1. For young collectors born in the baby boom years, these shows unearthed the comic books of their parents' time. For the first time, some kids held the big, thickly-paged comics of the 1930s and 1940s, comics that introduced Batman and Superman. These were magazines that in comic fandom's infancy were quietly becoming expensive. Comic fans were just beginning to see the value that could be gained from back issues that were selling for hundreds of dollars a copy by the end of the 1960s.

Comic book prices rose and collectors found reasons to spend the money. Adults and kids could be seen at shows buying and selling comic books as one. The significance of wage-earning adults spending money on comics was not lost on savvy sellers gazing into the future of our hobby. *Action Comics* #1 by the 1970s sold for well over $1,000, especially if in solid shape. Even the demand for back issues was creeping up, creating a supply-and-demand market. Dealers were exhibiting two forms of display at shows: their boxed inventory and their wall books. The boxed comics were usually commons that sold for fair or bargain prices. The dealer was less concerned for their welfare. Often as not, these boxed books were not bagged because that form of specific protection hadn't yet gone market-wide. The wall books, though, were the high-end comics that dealers needed to segregate. These better books would often have the highest prices at a dealer's booth.

They would also be the books thieves would most like to get their hands on. Dealers used to travel light without wall constructs, laying the comics out on tables provided by the convention hosts. Some dealers tired of the thefts of those tabled books and began building display walls that were out of reach of the passing crowds. Crime and time were evolving. The vendors who lacked the sophistication of a wall display (or the ability to transport such a construct) used flexible sheets of transparent plastic to create a shield over their tabled key books.

I've seen even more aggressive defensive styles, with dealers literally building wire cage tops over their comic book boxes. These cages allowed shoppers to reach down into the box only as deep as their fingertips, but not far enough to grasp a book and remove it.

By the end of my years in high school, the press was clearly enthralled with the comic book phenomenon. Local papers sought out casts of collecting characters to interview about their comics with the goal to seemingly shock the public with stories of extravagant comic book back-issue prices. The press used puns and the Batman TV show "Biff! Bang! Pow!" approach to have a little fun at our expense. Comic collectors took the news more seriously, ignoring the mockery and focusing on the bigger picture that comic book collecting was growing. Only the illuminated would truly cash in.

Neal Adams thrilled readers with his style of dramatic flamboyance that drove fans like me crazy for more Adams art. Adams's pull remains strong with back-issue collectors. The issues with covers he drew have especially strong collectibilty if Batman is involved. *Strange Adventures #215 (1968), Batman #232 (1971)* **(© DC Comics. Used with permission).**

Comic conventions started small. A few repetitive shows on opposite coasts developed into regional shows. Specialty comic book stores came into existence. Their owners, emboldened by the success of comic cons as business enterprises, were encouraged to open permanent locations. The comic book store concept developed at a steady rate across the country. Stores surrounded themselves with fans who promoted regular comic shows as a place to meet, make money and meet guests. Store owners and connected collectors felt experimental and created one-day and two-day shows, comic events that contained smaller elements of the mega-shows to come.

Guests and stars were paid to show up or came of their own volition, often to promote some project they were involved with. Much like the science fiction conventions, comic con fans included the very writers the shows were built around. Comic book writers and artists wanted to be a part of all the noise. They would roll up at the conventions on their own or with others to be a part of something they helped create. Imagine a time where you could meet Stan Lee without a line or payment. Or sit with Jack Kirby and his wife Roz at a hotel poolside while he drew sketches for fans, for free! You could meet Jim Steranko at his booth and pre-order copies of his artful *History of Comics Volume 2* (1972). Fans could line up to get an inexpensive sketch from Neal Adams at a table in any dealers' room he attended. Neal would stay put to draw and only relocate if necessary until every fan got a drawing, even if he went without sleep!

Neal Adams was always a good sport to the fans. He'd sit for hours and do sketches or sign his name. One such example of his tenacity occurred during a mid–1970s show at the El Cortez. Neal had a table in the dealers' room (located across the street from the hotel in their detached convention center). Neal sat for the fans until the dealers' room closed for the evening. Instead of quitting as well, Neal moved upstairs and had a table set up outside the ballroom. This was Saturday night and the grand masquerade contest was scheduled early evening in the ballroom. Neal's table was just to the right of the entry doors in the lobby.

At some point Neal took short breaks, but I never witnessed them. He did participate in the costume contest as a judge, which took about an hour. After the show, he returned to his lobby spot, where a line of fans had already formed. I wanted a sketch, but the line grew to lengths that precluded any quick work from Neal. I figured I'd catch him later that night.

I returned around 10 p.m. and saw that the line was still amazingly long. My friends had vanished and I had nothing better to do, so I looked for a distraction to kill time. I found that in the form of writer George Clayton Johnson. I knew George only slightly. I briefly dated his daughter's friend Lynn and got to hang out at George's ex-wife's apartment in Pacific Beach. George was sitting on the floor not far from Adams, engaging young fans in science fiction theories regarding the concept of "worlds within worlds" (if tiny atoms were planets). George always entertained.

For those of you who don't know George's background, he's the guy who wrote the original story that the Sinatra movie *Ocean's Eleven* was adapted from. He also wrote groundbreaking episodes of *Twilight Zone* and *Star Trek*. He co-wrote the cult favorite '70s feature *Logan's Run* (1976). George was already famous for his body of work by the time I got to briefly hang out with him.

George never ran out of energy, but I did. I peeked around a potted plant at Neal's line and finally found my chance. I knew the line would have to disappear sometime, but who would have thought 2 a.m. was that time? And Neal was burning out from that long day, so I made my move.

I was on a Marx Brothers kick back then. The rerelease of the Marx Brothers movie *Animal Crackers* (1930) hit the theaters earlier in the year after decades of litigious limbo. Most of my generation had little or no exposure to those movies. They just didn't pop up on local television. Since I was now into that stuff, I figured I would avoid asking Neal to do yet another Batman sketch and give him something different to do.

When my turn in line came up it was close to 2 A.M. I stood at his table and asked him if he could do the Marx Brothers for me … on a flying horse (I had no idea where that came from!). He said no problem for the horse, but the brothers would be tricky. He needed a photo or picture of the boys to get it right. Nothing was handy. Man, I waited all this time! But I had a plan. I asked him if he would stick around for a little bit. I told him I'd be right back with Marx Brothers images. The line was long enough to stall him, and he said "yes" anyway.

I ran to my car and raced home. I owned a copy of the Marx Brothers coffee-table book *Why a Duck?* (1971) with perfect Al Hirschfeld caricatures. I grabbed the copy and raced back to the convention. Neal was just finishing a sketch for a guy when I got back to his table. It was 2:30 in the morning. Neal was tired, but the man was no quitter. A deal was a deal, so I paid my $25 and got my quickie ink sketch. I was the last guy and a very tired Neal Adams took his bow and left for his hotel room and a much-needed rest.

I still have the sketch.

The 1970s brought more print attention to the surge in comic book popularity. Masquerade balls began as Saturday night routines at the bigger shows and featured all kinds of recognizable costumes. The creative, inventive guises some fans sewed together were often the highlight of any show. Full-sized Batmobiles and midnight showings of *The Rocky Horror Picture Show* (1975) were all the rage at budding conventions. Local radio personalities usually hosted the event. Yet, the national press, still mostly unaware of the growing comic book phenomenon, took little notice.

> I remember stretching out along some chairs in the movie room at the El Cortez one Saturday night at SDCC. Some movie called *The Rocky Horror Picture Show* was going to be on the screen, a show I'd never heard of. I was just looking for a dark place to catch some sleep. This would have been the summer of 1976. By that time there were followers on the East Coast dressing up for late-night showings, but nothing like that had hit San Diego.
>
> The audience grew in attendance the night I got to see it for the first time. Many of the uninitiated had never seen anything like this counterculture rock opera with cross-dressing tension and sexual satire.
>
> I was young and a little bit shocked by the blatancy of the movie. But it was raucous fun watching the true fans get into the spirit in costume and with rehearsed participation in the dialog and lyrics.

Mainstream journalism was becoming hip to the singular phenomenon of comic book collecting.

From a San Diegan's point of view, all the action started with our own comic book convention. An event that lasted a weekend expanded into 3- and 4-day events each summer. The con settled into its most famous venue by 1972, the El Cortez Hotel. The El Cortez was a 1920s historical landmark in downtown San Diego. Built on a hill, it overlooked the city and the bay. The hotel featured a glass elevator backed with neon-lit stars. The multi-floor ride up and the twinkling neon lighting gave patrons and San Diegans glorious views each night. The ocean beyond painted the open vistas in shades of blue and gray, giving the upper floors commanding panoramic shots of the reasons San Diego was settled. The presence of a critical harbor, the proximity to Mexico, and our wonderful weather are reasons enough to live here. SDCC/Comic-Con International are extra perks!

The Golden State Comic Con (later San Diego Comic-Con) was our convention, as my local friends called it. Our show drew increasing crowds with each year. By the late 1970s the venue had changed to absorb more exhibitors and attendees. The El Cortez had built an expanded convention hall behind it sometime in the past. But that quickly became inadequate for the needs of our con. Gone were the days of partying with the guests in just about every hotel room. No more jumping into the pool from second-floor balconies with hotel security in pursuit of wet bodies escaping through the hallways. The afternoons where anyone could pay to get his face done up in *Planet of the Apes* make-up by actual movie make-up artists in the hotel lobby were over. The San Diego Comic Convention had outgrown its first "permanent" location. The show had to hit the road.

Star-Trek Creature Galileo-Seven

Rob't "Big Buck" Maffei Plays The Creature

I worked at a drive-in movie theater in the mid–1970s among other jobs. The weekend manager was pretty laid back and he'd allow his friends onto the lot to hang out. One of his friends was a giant of a man named Robert "Big Buck" Maffei. Buck was a local character retired from acting. His large size and connections to friends in Hollywood like Dan Blocker pushed him into movie roles calling for large men.

Among other roles, Buck was cast as the boulder-wielding giant who menaced the cast of *Lost in Space* on one of that show's earliest adventures. The scene involving Buck was so dynamic that it was made into a model kit by Polar Lights.

Right: "Big Buck" Maffei was a bigger-than-life character on TV, in the movies, and in real life.

By the early 1980s, the San Diego Comic Convention had relocated to San Diego's Civic Center in the heart of downtown, the center of San Diego's political center. The move to the new venue accelerated other changes. San Diego's con was slowly evolving into a media con. Subculture themes within our comic/sci-fi/TV worlds developed. Shows like anime festivals and *Star Trek* and *Star Wars* mini-events found housing in the new center (they would develop their own conventions from the grassroots of ours). The new world of video machine games found footing in the newly christened Exhibitors' Hall.

Attendance ramped up commensurate with increased knowledge of the con's existence. The local nature of the event gave way to a national posture. And then international recognition followed.

The press finally took annual notice and fed the beast with lots of TV, newspaper, and radio attention. Curiosity seekers became crowds. The Civic Center managed to find room for all of us at first. Eventually, it succumbed to its own shortcomings. The larger hotels with meeting room spaces began taking on some convention events. These satellite locations relieved an overcrowded convention center of the burden of uncontrolled crowds. But it also indicated that the Comic-Con would have to move to a larger spot—and soon. The crowds encouraged, if not downright forced, our own con into its next phase of existence.

The early 1990s saw the opening of San Diego's new jewel: the San Diego Convention Center. Square footage galore! And just in time: Hollywood was just beginning to show

Badges of "honor" recording my attendance at conventions in the 1970s.

serious interest in the world of comic conventions. Simultaneously, comic stores were now numbering in the thousands, not limited domestically. Shops were established in numerous countries preferring their own inventories of local entertainment mainstays. Chain comic book stores grew in quantity from the single-store format that existed in the 1970s. Owners managed to sustain two or more stores by the middle of the next decade. The late 1980s extended those numbers even further. San Diego's own Pacific Comics chain numbered four different sites.

The prominence of varying locations to buy old and new comics made the hobby much more accessible. It seemed that everybody was buying comic books. Kids and adults were buying, collecting or speculating with equal fervor. Changes needed to be made in the way that comic book stores acquired their monthly comics. The old system foisted on stores by an antiquated and expensive magazine distribution system was inefficient and unreliable. Stacks of unsold comics could be returned for refunds. But the cost of doing business with those magazine distributors was just too expensive to allow stores to thrive on the sales of new comics.

The distribution industry started with returnable comics and small profit margins. New York's Phil Seuling spearheaded a national movement to get better discounts from publishers by going direct-market in the mid–1970s. Direct market distribution allowed specialty stores to become independent of nationwide periodical distributors. Now, stores could order with greater autonomy and variety. Returning unsold copies was no longer an option, but the discounts stores received were greater. This allowed comic book stores to

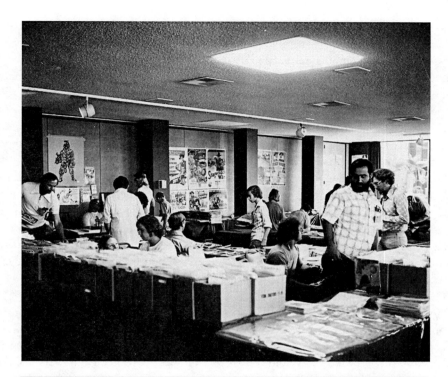

Top: The dealer's room at the El Cortez Hotel circa mid–1970s. That room held all the buy/sell/trading action a guy like me could want. I never wanted to leave the room! *Bottom:* Another photograph of the El Cortez Exhibitor's Hall.

generate enough income to actually thrive and grow. Trendy comic book publications expanded to reach larger audiences. Comic book ads buying and selling comics increased in quantity as want lists and catalogs went flying across the country. Classified ads that once peppered the ad space in 1960s comics now dominated the back pages of several comic-centric publications. The same publications saw an increase in larger ad space purchased to sell comic book back issues. Similar ads to buy and sell comics occupied greater space in daily newspapers and newsstand giveaways.

Locally, I watched the transformation of a city. My little hobby transformed slowly. Within twenty years, the metamorphosis validated comic-collecting legitimacy. The media wasted no effort in praising our hobby's impact while lampooning the fans. The mixed publicity nonetheless generated more attention. Comic-Con became an event for the press to praise and ridicule because it photographed well with all the costumes and craziness. The future of the hobby seemed to be predicated on the sane and the insane, the dichotomy of a hobby rich with cash flow and crazy characters.

Then Hollywood arrived.

My friends and I debated the future of comic books and the convention. Comic books were only a part of the big picture there. "Comic-Con" adorned the signs outside, but inside comics were being edged aside. Gaming, both role-playing and electronic, was coming up fast. Anime was as strong as ever, and the toy market was firing on all cylinders. As a result, back-issue exhibitor space was relinquished to provide room for expanded small and independent publisher set-ups. The gamers grew in floor size while the back-issue guys were shoved off to one end of the convention hall. We comic book guys saw our hobby written into the name of the show, but it began to feel like it was in name only.

Decent, big-budget comic book movies were a little ways off. Chris Reeve's *Superman* movies had climaxed and completed their runs. The *Batman* movies started out strong in 1989, but had little impact on convention development. For a time, comic book stores and retailers enjoyed super-explosive sales on all things Batman, but Batman paraphernalia and comics sales did not grossly impact Comic-Con. I remember several cons in California hosting a sort of traveling road show displaying a *Spawn* racecar at the opening of the same-titled movie. That was a cool curiosity, but said more about the egos of the people behind *Spawn* than it did about the character. The masses of movie and TV fans had not yet succumbed to Hollywood's advances into their domain.

The move to the new convention center opened floor space to do a lot of things. San Diegans could now see much of the event in the same room with plenty of space left over. New movies determined to appeal to comic book and sci-fi fans were in movie houses. Some of the movie life was dripping into comic conventions. Movie props from *The Time Machine* (2002) and *Mystery Men* (1999) created interest on the floor of the exhibition hall at back-to-back Comic-Cons. The massive Herkimer Battle Jitney from *Mystery Men* was followed by the intricate time machine that Guy Pearce used to move in time. Now, movie and television studio exhibitor booths took up space once occupied by comic book dealers, adding more pressure on back-issue guys trying to stay alive at the show. Huge monolithic displays gobbled up available display or sales areas. Comic book back-issue dealers were relegated to far ends of the hall that were once occupied by others. The next step in convention evolution had arrived.

The massive sales of the *Death of Superman* (1992–1993), the popular *Batman: Knight-*

fall (1993) story arc, and the advent of *Spawn* typify the motivations for increased numbers of comic book stores. Easy money brightened the prospects of store owners who had suffered through the recent black-and-white independent comic book implosion. Even guys without stores saw money to be made by hauling comics to shows from their own garages. Anybody could order new comics from any one of a small number of distributors and then cash in on a speculator craze not seen before in our hobby.

DC's name-brand characters were on fire. Recently formed Image Comics (1992) and Dark Horse Comics (1986) were riding tides on their own start-up success. Marvel's overreaching corporate acquisitions and a sense of financial invulnerability infused a feeling of new strength in the industry ... what could go wrong?

Well, something did. Marvel Comics seemed all but defunct under the weight of a corporate collapse. Simultaneously, stores were trying to level out their unsold inventories after years of buying on speculation. The salad days of selling to others in high volume dried up. Marvel's inept distribution system created discrepancies in the way comic book stores stayed afloat. Hundreds of stores closed in a direct cause-and-effect market shocker. Annually, comic sales dropped from over a billion dollars to less than a quarter of that figure. Hundreds of store closures left small regions of the country without comic book stores. Locally, San Diego suffered over a dozen closures between 1993 and 1995 (some say that figure is higher).

Comic collecting had influenced all kinds of people. Different generations had values for different genres. Old comics and new comics appealed to many for different reasons. Superheroes remained the dominant genre and Marvel ran that table. The 1990s exploitation and collapse of Marvel Comics disgusted readers. Many left the hobby behind.

Unsold mountains of current comics ended up in storage all over the United States. Dealers who once held distribution accounts and sold only at shows disappeared. Stores in financial arrears tried to find anyone to offload their tonnage. Many retrenched in public storage facilities, doomed to perpetually repurchase their inventories in the form of monthly rent. The comic book bonanza of 1991 ended up in the hands of liquidators by 1997.

Our little business depleted the stored contents of four or five defunct comic retailers during its inception.

Stores order their monthly inventories of new comics from Diamond Comics. If those comics fail to sell, they have a worldwide tendency to pile up in corners of comic book stores while the owners try to figure out how unload them and not lose money.

Through it all, one constant remained: those faithful to purchasing old back issues were still great in number. Back-issue prices held relatively steady in a changing market. High-end copies (high-grade or key books) continued to sell with regular price increases. The arrival of eBay and third-party grading altered pricing by the beginning of the 21st century. Comic book values went askew of the established numbers longtime *Overstreet* users were accustomed to. Collectors began to see more value in older comics. Some turned completely away from the comics on the stands and aimed strictly for the comics in the boxes. At least, the boxes in the shrinking number of stores that still carried quantities of back issues. The to-and-fro pitch of new comics sales were losing ground, and back issues were flooding the Internet.

Comic book stores, once the dominant location for old comics, gave way to floor space occupied by gaming and merchandise. Comic book catalogues printed on paper were erased by Web sites duplicating the same offerings. Buyers who were used to scouring comic book back-issue lists they mailed away for were growing content with the daily, random selections on eBay. For some people, shopping on the Internet, whether it was eBay or other Web sites, became the only choice. Techno-savvy people and dot-com business evolution developed computer-centric comic book buyers.

The possibilities of person-to-person Internet business told some store owners that this "wave of the future" eliminated their need to pay rent on a brick-and-mortar establishment. More store closures ensued.

Meanwhile, comic conventions increased in number and size. Dealers of all types sensed a gap in retailing. Internet-dominant customer bases could be relied upon to turn up at shows, filling the store void. The conventions were exciting, drawing in legions of fans. Now the remaining stores were competing with comic shows on a frequent basis, and with the Internet every day.

Beneficially, collectible comics could be accessed in greater quantities thanks to the growth of shows. Dealers who had no physical presence outside of permanent locations traveled from show to show to meet larger back-issue audiences.

At our level, our store lined up with the collecting behavior of a new generation. Our store was quite successful beginning with the new millennium. More and more people showed up to buy or make purchases online. Always looking to exploit our store's prominence, I asked questions. What all of us learned was that ten years after the industry's upheavals of the mid–1990s, many of those customers were returning.

Comics had pissed off some, bored others, or failed to hold onto a maturing readership. But in the mid–2000s, a lot of those people developed new criteria. College was complete, military service was over, careers were settled: these were some of the factors for the fans' return. Homes were purchased, marriages and families were in place, and disposable income was once again available. We had a returning crop of collectors yearning for the things that made their childhood memories happy.

The comic book industry's focus changed, as well. Adults are the primary targets for the comics produced in the recent era. I know that kids were the targets when I was a teen. The comics were geared for us. They did not grow with us. Today, kids are barely a consideration for comic buying targets.

By 2016, comic book sales were dependent on the annual story-arc events DC and Marvel created. These companies produced lengthy, interconnected comic storylines that dominate whole flocks of titles for a limited period. Cliffhangers and major character changes infused each of these max-events. Exploitation, a notion as old as the history of comics, thrived as comic book tales and fads filled issues that speculators would hoard. Then these fashionable comics were dumped back on the market for fast-buck profits before their popularity withered. The industry rewarded the profiteers with immensely popular variant covers designed to increase comic book store orders. These dealer-incentive covers encouraged store owners to order greater quantities of regular covers, since the cover incentives got better the more copies of the regular cover were ordered. This process rewarded Marvel in the 1990s, and Marvel, DC and the rest were sold now with increased order numbers to get those variants. The variant cover ordeal of the past was re-energized, igniting flocks of quick-turnaround fiends to fire up their computers for rapid sales on high-demand, flavor-of-the-week, limited covers.

Sure, it has that 1990s exploitative feeling to it. But there's an unmistakable fervor, an energy that is fueled by Internet chatter. Internet sites dedicated to current comics stir up the fans with glowing stories of happening comic events. Even purists soured on that whole speculator element must admit there's action and attention within the world of new comic sales. And that attention translates into back issue sales. eBay clobbers the comic community with the sheer volume of comic book listings for sale. There are tens of thousands of new and old comic books up for grabs. Web sites doing the same saturate the 'net. Comic collections are constantly up for sale all over the place, in newspapers, Craigslist, eBay, Web sites, swap meets, garage sales, auction houses, and anyplace that seems a proper spot to unload volumes of comics.

The successful sales of graphic novels and trade paperbacks in the new millennium has laid claim to new readership in comics. Store sales, show sales and Internet sales all have shown steady increases over the past 15 years. Even Walmart, sensing opportunity, has re-entered the world of comic book retailing by featuring graphic novels and trades for sale.

If our store is any indication of the vibrancy of the hobby, then the consistent buying and selling of comics and collections is the barometer of success.

Finally, our store gets at least one or two serious daily offers to buy comic collections. The results of the purchases enter our back-issue area as either bargain comics or something more lucrative. Those copies sell just as consistently as new comics. Our view is that the hobby is strong, and the business of comics, backed by self-replicating comic movies, is showing continued longevity and hopefully growth.

3

A Learning Curve

Running a comic book retailing business is profoundly educational. Business school or a business degree can only take you so far compared to what a comic book store owner needs to know. The hobby defines the knowledge necessary to sell comics better than others. I grew up with comic books. The aspects of comics were always parts of the whole; reading comic strips in the newspapers, collecting Big Little Books, buying original art: all part of the big picture. Toss in pulps and sci-fi books and you have a good portion of the life I grew up with. These were the reads that I collected with some determination by my final year of high school (go, Warhawks!). I employed the ability to visit more distant collections with my driver's license and a hand-me-down car from my folks. So I was always ready to check out someone's comic books.

> One peculiar customer was in our back issue bins on a typical store day around 2002. He was examining and sniffing the comic book bags we used in that area of our back issues. When I strolled past him, he stopped me and warned me that my bags were chemically toxic. He said he was a chemist and the bags were breaking down chemically. He claimed the active elements of the corroding plastic were producing toxins that were dangerous to people. He was serious, expressing frustration that we were unwillingly, or willingly, poisoning ourselves and our customers. Then he prodded his upper lip, emphasizing that his lip was numb from the chemical time bombs.
>
> I looked at him, trying to decide how not to make a scene. This was an atypical customer-relations issue for me. Should I try reasoning with him or bounce him from the store? I chose a third tactic: I stared at him silently with my "cop stare" until he acquiesced and beat feet from my store. Some battles are just not worth the engagement. Fifteen years later, I'm not yet dead from bag poisoning.

I gravitated to retail when I was just out of high school. Back in the wild and wooly days of my beginnings, I learned comic book retailing on the job. My first lessons occurred at the burgeoning network of conventions from San Diego to San Francisco. San Diego's Con was only slightly larger than shows in other cities. Anaheim featured a hyperactive show at a hotel near Disneyland. If memory serves me right, it was named the Casual Con and exhibited a dealers' room packed with back-issue retailers. That's a proper place to gain valuable market knowledge. These shows were typically held on one weekend in a small banquet room on the first floor of the Inn at the Park Hotel complex. Lots of back-issue dealers and a few celebrities attended. One of those celebrities was Joe DeRita, who played Curly Joe in the final version of the Three Stooges. Nobody but me ever remembers meeting a Stooge! Back issues were the big draw at that kind of small show. Everybody from the promoter on down was selling comics from a table.

San Francisco held the Bay Con. I remember crowding into a single-bed suite with three other guys at the Sheraton Palace on Market Street. That show was held another year at the Jack Tarr Hotel up the hill from the Sheraton. The Bay Con drew its foundation from the city it occupied. San Francisco brought in the counterculture set responsible for the hippie movement's more creative popularity. My first con at the Jack Tarr introduced me to the creative generation that just preceded mine. Underground artists/writers, and contemporary comic book people in their most energetic periods, schmoozed at Bay Con. Women in comics, something relatively unknown for a San Diego kid, were stars at Bay Con. Ladies like Trina Robbins and Cat Yronwode were fan favorites as they rode the crest of the post–1960s comic book revolution.

Oakland had a show back then,

In my day, skateboarding and comic book collecting came up the ranks of popularity together (at least in San Diego).

too, smaller than the others, but influenced by the hip comic book stores in Berkeley. Back then most comic book stores I knew were happy to share worlds with comic cons. I met many store owners and employees either working or shopping at cons up and down the state. With all of these shows taken in their entirety, a comic book enthusiast like me developed contacts and savvy right in the hobby's development era: my "Golden Age."

During this part of the 1970s, the earliest days, grading standards were past their infancy. Bob Overstreet and his collaborators pushed for standardization with their book, the *Overstreet Price Guide*, which debuted in 1970. Those standards were simple yet sparse (subsequent years and volumes would add more details to standards for grading and collecting). They were open for too much interpretation; I remember such simplistic terms as "Good," "Fine," and "Mint" being universally accepted. If you wanted to buy something with those grades attached, you sort of worked out the price with the seller in person. If you were shopping through the mail by catalog, you placed your fate in the hands of another, perhaps someone you found in the classified ads of a comic book. If you bought in this fashion, you risked learning about the skewed grading versions of others and probably got burned. The grade was just a viewer's choice. If you liked the look and liked the price, you bought it.

Back then it was not a disgrace to write the prices of comics right on the comic book itself. The theory was that if it was written small in pencil on the back cover or on the first page, no harm was done to the comic. Comic bags were not completely in vogue yet. Nobody complained too much, and only the fancy dealers were writing on stickers affixed to bags made just for comics. Everybody else was writing prices on pieces of paper or masking tape and sticking them on the polyurethane bags from back east (Post-Its did not exist until a little later nationwide). Dealers like Robert Bell out of New York were circulating comic book bags nationwide, and San Diegans were just beginning to order them.

Comic cons predated local stores in our city by about five years. The early shows took place in lodges and exhibition halls. Cash was king: no one ever approached with credit cards in those days. Large purchases were made by check without too much grumbling from sellers. There was no Fast-Check service to validate checks, so plenty of dealers got burned. Most of us took payment on faith with check writers. We all used checks in those days. Getting burned was inevitable.

On one occasion, I had a table at a show in Los Angeles. Just a small table set up in a typical exhibition hall arrangement. The guys around me all kind of watched over each other. For this show, I was fortunate to be armed with a new collection. Only recently, I owned a fat run of high-grade Golden Age *World's Finest* from issue #3 to issue #40-something. These included most of the issues when *World's Finest* had square-bound spines. I had a couple of boxes of random Golden Age and some Silver Age. We were living in the Bronze Age, so that tier didn't exist yet. The *World's Finest* comic books (1941-on) were spread out on the table for maximum effect. I sold a couple of issues along with other stuff.

My table neighbor introduced himself as an attorney and was selling his collection of comic book castoffs. Throughout the day, he eyeballed those *World's Finest* books. When he saw they weren't selling well, he pitched me an offer. I think it amounted to a few hundred dollars, fair by mid–'70s standards. I didn't want to return home broke, so I negotiated down a bit from sticker price and took the deal. Only rub: he wanted to pay by check. Now, I was young, about twenty, and only partially employed. Several hundred dollars would cover my $190 monthly rent and some food. He established his bona fides with proper identification and a good contact phone number.

None of us asked for more than that in those days. You either took the check to get paid or let the potential buyer walk. The Diners Club was for restaurants, not for comic con dealers. Maybe we'd ask for a Social Security number without really knowing how that could be useful. The guy seemed genuine and asserted in a very lawyerly way that his honesty and reputation were above board. So I took some cash and the rest by check. Within a week, the check bounced.

I freaked out! I had never experienced a bad check. I contacted my bank for an explanation and help. No help was forthcoming. I called the buyer's phone number, but it just rang. His address turned out to be a post office box in Los Angeles. I was not sophisticated enough to fight this battle. After a couple of more attempts by phone, it was pretty clear I got ripped off from the get-go. This was my first victimization as a comic book dealer. Now, I was officially a participant of the learning curve of the self-employed.

I established a regular retail stand at small conventions in Southern California. I packed cardboard boxes containing unbagged comics into my 1973 Toyota Carina and headed to each show with buddies. We set up together at these shows, being sure to place the good stuff laid out on the table top covered by a sheet of plastic wrap. Prices written on pieces of tape or random stickers applied on earliest versions of comic bags (Robert Bell bags!), refrigerator bags, Saran wrap, or whatever plastic(ish) wrapping was available. Archiving and decorum only existed in the upper echelons. My kind showed up locked and loaded, with no fancy set-up prices. Customer requests were answered with, "Sure, the prices are written on the inside first page, dude!"

Back then, prices reflected whatever the dealer interpreted as a grade. *Overstreet Price Guide*'s limited grading tiers of "Good," "Fine" and "Mint" left defects subject to interpretation. Missing a page? It's a Good. Coupon out—maybe a Fine? Some light spine stressing = Mint. If you were one of those East Coast mail order guys (Rogofsky!), you repelled all refund requests through the mail with responses like "tape is not a defect." Ha!

The Comic Book Rejects
By Michelle Nolan

In the 21st century, older comic books from the 1960s and earlier are almost never found at garage sales, since most non-collectors have long since cleared their homes of 50-year-old paper.

But in 2010, I finally found a Golden and Silver 13-issue lot—and it was a totally lucky discovery.

I stopped by a garage sale in my home town in the state of Washington, as I so often do on spring, summer and fall Saturdays, but I didn't see any books of interest. In fact, I didn't see any books at all.

But I did hear the words "Golden Age" from another shopper a few feet away. "I have a few," said the seller. "I'll go get them." I was prepared to be frustrated, since this rival shopper apparently was set to make a score.

The seller returned with 13 comic books—an intriguing mix of 7 issues from the 1940s childhood of his father and 6 Marvels from his own childhood in the 1960s. When asked how much he wanted, he told the would-be buyer, "$100—I know they're worth a lot more, but they're mostly not in great shape, so that's all I want." Much to my relief, the shopper rejected them as too expensive.

I quickly stepped in, asked to see the 13 comics, and immediately bought them for $100 (I thought bargaining would be bad karma, indeed).

The fair condition *Avengers* #1 and the fair *Fantastic Four* #3 more than made up for that $100 alone, but the rest of the comics ranged from fair to very good. I kept one of them (an early issue of *Target Comics* from 1942) and sold or traded the rest the next week at Comic-Con in San Diego for nearly $2,000 in value. They went to at least five different people.

I have found a few decent comic books at garage sales, such as a handful of near-mint copies of Star Trek from the 1970s for a quarter apiece, but I have never found such a lucky strike of comic books before or since. A "Lucky 13," indeed!

Selling was cheap and easy. A table might cost you $20 at a decent one-day show. Floor space was your second table top. The community of dealers was a disparate crowd of men with a variety of ethics. Whether it was buying, trading or selling, we all learned to do it "on the job." No school offered classes on how to collect and how to watch over your money while collecting. Many experienced comic guys ran the gamut of missteps as they established reputations, contacts and customer bases through repeat business. Customers learned trust. Trust was earned at repeat shows much easier than from mail-order purchases. Some of those dealers were just trouble from the start and virtually impossible to hold accountable. Others were operating out of their homes and storefronts, determined to make back-issue sales profitable through guaranteed repeat customers. Those guys lasted much longer but had to work hard to keep new material flowing in and out of their hands. If you didn't like a dealer, you steered clear the next time around.

I remember visiting local fans at their homes on several occasions, buying and selling comics (mostly buying). I met longtime comic book storeowner Greg Pharis in his garage when I was still in high school. Who knew that I'd be working with him in just a few years at Comic Kingdom, one of San Diego's first comic book shops?

I met one-half of the Schanes brothers at their house near the beach. Back before they became a 1980s publishing force, they operated out of their garage selling back issues.

My fondest memory was visiting Tom French for the first time. Tom was the Exhibition Hall coordinator for the San Diego Comic Convention from my earliest recollection right up into the early 2000s. Tom was one of the oldest members of the Comic-Con staff and was married to a very sturdy foe, Virginia, who you had to deal with if you crossed Tom. Tom was the local king of Golden Age and used to operate out of his San Diego residence from the living room. He'd turned a portion of their living room into a collector's laboratory with files for sorting paperwork, bright lights for examinations, and stacks of comics in various stages of inspection and collation.

Tom was easy to buy from because he was never in a foul mood, at least at his house and at shows while running both the dealers' room and his own back-issue booth. He was always positioned at the front doors of the dealers' room, which occasionally tried his patience. That was a perk that came from being in charge of the dealers' room, so he handled it stoically.

I met other comic book fans that I've long since lost touch with. If it's any consolation, home-based comic book sales activity is strong in 2017, with Craigslist and Facebook bringing everybody together.

My buddy Marty Rosen shares one of his collecting stories as a kid growing up in the early Silver Age:

It all began with my brother Jay. He is five years older and started reading comics before me. Back in the day, and we are talking about the late 1950s, no one knew comics would become such a valuable commodity. He had purchased the first issues of a number of the early 1960s Marvel pantheon including *The Fantastic Four*, *Amazing Spider-Man*, *The Hulk*, *Thor*, and *Iron Man*. Meanwhile, I was reading and collecting kiddie comics, such as *Walt Disney Comics and Stories*, *Baby Huey*, *Heckle & Jeckle*, and *Archie Comics*. We shared a bedroom and used to pile the comics in a closet we also shared. We never thought about them being future historic artifacts, and certainly neither did our mother. The books were periodically removed to the garage, where they collected for a year. Then the inevitable nightmare would happen each year … spring cleaning. The books were unceremoniously thrown out, never to be seen again. I salvaged a few books from the late 1950s to early 1960s and kept them in my closet after my brother moved out (finally!).

In high school I hung onto the books, but had stopped reading and buying comics. Then one day my best friend Ray decided to unload his comics. I was always a DC fan, just to be contrary to my brother. Ray wanted to give away his comics and asked if I would take them. His titles were *Justice League of America*, *The Flash*, and *Green Lantern*. I never knew Ray had been collecting these titles, but all of a sudden they were mine, mine, mine! I must have spent the next month reading all the issues, digging out the older books, including multiple *Superman* and *Batman* titles, *Rip Hunter Time Master*, *Challengers of the Unknown*, *Adventure Comics* featuring the Legion of Super-Heroes, *Blackhawk*, *Metal Men*, *The Atom*, etc. I realized that I now had an official comic book collection, and I have been lugging the books around for the last 50 years.

Mail-order catalogues for old comics were usually several pages of typed and copied lists. My friends and I placed occasional orders through the mail. Cash and coin was often the way purchase power traveled through the mail. We wrapped money in paper and stuffed it into envelopes as payment. Coins, too! We taped those to 3" × 5" cards to keep them from shaking around in the envelope. Strangely, it always seemed safe. Scams were infrequent and buys were often made on instinct. If the price looked right and the comic was halfway decent, it was a sale. Sadly, not much more thought seems applicable today for too many enthusiasts.

The standards set by concerned dealers, standardized in subsequent editions of the *Overstreet Price Guide*, helped define rules. Beginning in 1970, Bob Overstreet and others associated with his project set grading standards to limit pricing gaps. His publication became a tutorial for judging the structural value of any comic book through a designated tier system. I cannot emphasize enough what a big deal the *Overstreet Price Guide* was. It was our Bible of knowledge. It was worth waiting for each year to see what the prices were doing. *Overstreet Price Guide* provided the last word in grading and pricing debates. What third-party grading is now was *Overstreet Price Guide*'s finest hour. I have watched the maturing of *Overstreet Price Guide* for years and its increased focus on defining proper grading definitions.

Each grading tier adopted by *Overstreet Price Guide* defined the potential value of any comic book. As time went on, the *Overstreet Price Guide* added more tiers. Generally accepted grade levels limited the arguments over criteria. Now, some dealers found themselves in uncomfortable waters. As the hobby tightened its standards, buyers were carrying price guides with them into dealer rooms. Particular comics were scrutinized and matched against the wisdom of "the *Guide*." Unethical dealers felt new pressure. Many dropped out or struggled when the enlightened collectors grew in number.

Trade publications presented articles or essays addressing the changing climate. Other pricing guides, fanzines, or slick prozines (professionally published fanzines) routinely spoke directly to comic book consumers. Print institutions like *Rocket's Blast Comic Collector* (*RBCC*) and the *Comic Buyer's Guide* kept faith with fans through years of regular offerings and articles. You subscribed to them through the mail as they reliably shipped on monthly or other regular timetables.

Fans developed connections through articles and letters in fan publications and set new wheels in motion. Debates, opinions, and instructions were provided in print from many sources within our hobby. Mistakes were addressed in writing for others to learn from. Fans like me questioned purchases and prices we saw advertised. We used that knowledge to make careful choices when buying comics. We used data and information at our fingertips to figure out if a comic was worth purchasing.

Dealers shared price guides to compare and mull over the contents. We used the *OPG*, the only guide that mattered at the time. Other guides were produced but accepted with limited support. Pop-up debates on the dealers' room floor gave authority to those with the greatest understanding. It became increasingly difficult for the unscrupulous to fool an army of collectors armed with pricing guides. Those guides were early handbooks containing the kind of information that protected hobbyists from complete ignorance. Many of the questions of the day, such as the quagmire of grading comprehension, were raised among fans all informed with a commonality of knowledge. That knowledge grew with each year, especially in the 1970s. Those were my development years, as they were for a lot of Silver Age baby boomers. Tens of thousands of us came of age right alongside the merriment of collecting comic books.

Comic book stores sprang up all over the country by the mid–1970s. They were becoming ground zero for buyers and sellers looking to do business with back issues. These stores lured in collections off the streets, with more notable stores setting baselines for pricing collectors could agree with. Working at Richard Alf's Comic Kingdom in San Diego, I watched the store attract true comic book collectors and develop a pattern of sales consistency using the accepted grading standards and prices.

Richard Alf had a clear understanding of the hobby and had extensive comic collector connections. He was allied with the others who came together and formed San Diego Comic-Con (Golden State Comic-Con). Men within Alf's circle, like renowned collector Tom French, influenced many others to respect and enjoy old comics. They taught younger fans like me the process of comic collecting, inspired us to perfect our skills, and used them to attach values to those comics. We learned practices such as grading, what to offer to buy a collection, how to price them if *Overstreet Price Guide* was insufficient, and so on.

Tom knew what comics should sell for. He did not always agree with *Overstreet Price Guide*. I remember that he was always dubious of *Overstreet Price Guide*'s prices for *Wonder Woman* titles. I'm referring to *Wonder Woman* and *Sensation*

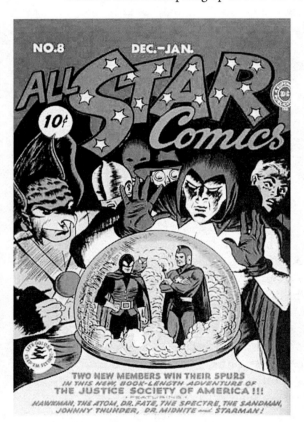

Wonder Woman makes her debut as a back-up feature in *All-Star Comics* #8. Her Golden and Silver Age appearances have always been in demand. Dealers in the past used to attach small price premiums to the Overstreet prices on Wonder Woman comics. We dealers always felt Overstreet's prices were too conservative against a strong demand and short supply. *All-Star Comics* #8 (1941–1942) (© DC Comics. Used with permission).

Comics. Tom always counseled that *Wonder Woman* titles were habitually underpriced and for a couple of reasons. He said there were fewer copies in circulation and they were originally meant to sell to girls. By the mid–1970s it was obvious that few girls saved them when they grew up. Tom's advice was to price them up 10 percent to 20 percent more than *Overstreet Price Guide* and that those price bumps were legitimate (Tom was proved correct all these years later!).

We did all this buying and selling when there were no computers and cell phones. We stayed in touch by telephone and through the mail. Conventions put us all together under one roof at a time. That experience expanded rapidly with the growing attendance of both men and women, young and old.

Fans were not satisfied by the process of dealing with each other from great distances, though. It was slow, cumbersome and impractical to travel long distances just to meet one fan and do business. It was especially difficult to convince your parents this was a perfectly safe opportunity.

We were all eager to get to the stores and shows where that real action was happening. We all needed to talk face-to-face. We wanted to see all the comics we could at one time and share in the energy that was gripping comic book fandom.

Everybody was getting a sense that we could all operate on a level playing field. There were important, influential fans chatting at shows and holding panels teaching their views on collecting. The information gleaned from these venues was rebroadcast in newsletters, fanzines and forums at other cons.

I worked for Richard Alf's Comic Kingdom for about two years. Richard floated his free store promotional to get the store's name out to the public.

My life is filled with odd synchronicities and coincidences. As the reader knows by now, I worked at Richard Alf's Comic Kingdom back in the mid–1970s. Richard promoted his store with a little homemade, four-page comic book called *Alf*. *Alf* was written and drawn with the help of two of Richard's friends, Steve Garris and Wesley Ford. I knew Steve but remember little contact with Wesley. Years later, *Alf* is fondly recalled by old fans of the store.

In between *Alf*'s 1975 publication and the present was my 20-year stint as a police officer. I was on the job around 1993 when I answered a radio call of a dead body in Ocean Beach. The location given was a small bungalow near the shore on Cape May Avenue. Two officers were dispatched separately; I arrived before the other. I was greeted at the door by a somewhat disheveled woman holding one hand over her mouth like she was trying to forestall shock.

She stepped aside as I entered to find a man's body, stripped to his boxer shorts, lying on the living room floor. I asked the woman what happened even though I recognized the scene and the man; it was Wesley Ford. I'd seen enough dead junkies to recognize Wesley's death was a heroin overdose. I'd known him around the beach as a low-level criminal, but never knew he was an addict. Recognizing a heroin death is no mystery to an experienced drug cop. The needle had disappeared (probably hidden by his addict friends, or stolen for their use). He had a fresh puncture wound along track marks inside one arm.

His boxer shorts were soaked, but with water, not urine. I asked the woman to explain. She said that she and a friend found him prone on the floor. In an attempt to revive him they removed ice cubes from the freezer in his kitchen (it was his rental) and packed them into his shorts to revive him. It's an old addict myth that the ice will shock an OD back to consciousness. The friend had fled before the police could arrive, but she was concerned enough to see this ordeal to the end.

I let police dispatch know so they could contact the coroner and I stood by with Wesley for about half an hour until a coroner crew arrived. My responsibility ended with the completion of a short report.

I didn't make the Wesley connection to *Alf* until years later after uncovering a copy of that comic. I don't shock easily, but that revelation is still a bit unsettling for me even to this day. Wesley lived in the same two worlds as I did: comics and cops.

In retrospect, it seems sad to me the tipping point for the happiest years of my hobby were probably the best years of Wesley's life.

I remember capitalizing on the shows I attended by sharing the stories with customers at Comic Kingdom. My fellow employees, a small band of rogues, held court at the shop regaling customers with our superior knowledge. We knew the big dealers and we knew the big guests. The comic book industry did not, as yet, take fandom too seriously. The only true face of fan zeal was Stan Lee, who promoted Marvel with unabashed salesmanship through Marvel Comics and on the road at conventions. He used his "Soapbox" column in Marvel comic books to stir up fan support and advertise his appearances at shows to meet the fans and lecture at panels. Stan Lee provided celebrity stature to his appearances. A lot of people were drawn to his showboat-attitude total up-sell of the comic book industry and all things Marvel.

Meanwhile, Neal Adams and Jack Kirby would draw sketches in comfortable corners of shows and talk about upcoming projects, never fearing the "spoiler" release of some cliffhanger story secret. Both men had reached celebrity status, but unlike Stan, it was about the hobby, their work and the state of the fellows they worked with. Collectively, these two giants owed no allegiance to any one comic book publisher, but every publisher benefited from their presence.

Neither Marvel nor DC carried the kind of room-dominating weight they carry now. Their personnel more or less spoke at panels, signed comics at booths, drew sketches wherever they could, or took part in discussions in small-group settings. The recognizable bosses were the editors like longtime DC editor Julius Schwartz, Warren Publishing's Jim Warren, and Stan Lee. Of those three men, I found Stan to be the most accessible guest and often the most active. These men spoke for their companies but addressed the fans' enthusiasm. They also enjoyed the more social aspects of conventions, and you could meet them if you were invited to the right parties. I was rarely ever that lucky.

Everybody just seemed so intent on knowing all there was to know about the preceding forty years of comic books. All the comic book creators who were within reach at conventions added fuel to the fan movement. We all wanted to play comics, cash in, and push the hobby forward to let the good times roll. We were surrounded by thieves, opportunists, speculators, super-fans and well-educated leaders who saw further than all of us. Collectors did seem to be getting smarter as more people entered the hobby and the business of comics. We didn't all know or like each other. But we were all in the same room together, a dealers' room where you could not hide (literally or metaphorically).

I can attest to the conditions of many comic book conventions growing up. They came in all shapes and sizes but seemed relatively formulaic in atmosphere and offerings. Most of the earliest shows were small, with the future glory of shows like San Diego and New York still far off. As the years of popularity went on, more shows began operation. By the 1990s there seemed to be shows in every major city, sometimes multiple shows. San Diego was no exception.

Some of those shows were less robust than others. My partners and I attended a show in northern San Diego promoted by a local character then known as Raven, who was a recognizable character at about six feet tall with fair skin and long, blond hair. Raven always wore well in black: black long-sleeved shirt, black vest, black pants and black shoes. Raven searched out a variety of venues to hold his small, one-day shows. He had them at lodges, meeting halls and even more remote locations. One such spot was a bowling alley in the northern portion of the county. The building held a second floor that contained a banquet room for rent. Somehow Raven found it.

Gino and I supported these small shows. They were cheap and simple, and comic book back issues were a viable way to make money. We set up at the event with maybe another 15 dealers including Raven and his selection of obscure movie and television recordings (VHS, DVDs). Setup was easy thanks to the single elevator at our end of the building. We carted our back-issue boxes to the second floor and were ready to go in minutes. At 10 A.M. the doors opened … and that was it. No throng, not even much of an attendee line. Just us dealers and support cast. This was not unusual. Some shows peak later than others and don't get gassed until late afternoon.

Another hour went by and the attendance was still weak. Raven kept us entertained with DVDs of the then new *South Park* animated show (which I had never seen but grew addicted to quickly). By noon it was clear that the exhibitors might be outnumbering the attendees. In fact, the only real business Gino and I saw was a father and his 12-year-old kid, James. We had the most serious back issue selection and that's what father and son were there for. James was a *Hulk* collector and found some issues in our boxes. The kid argued with the best of the adults, challenging our grades and prices. The kid was sharp and observant. You know, a real pain in the ass. He did make a purchase and wanted to come see our shop some day.

The show was a dud. Raven tried to make it real using a PA system to rev us all up. But without the fans, shows like this can't be considered as anything but a learning experience. As humbling as it was, Gino and I saw it as part of the dues-paying structure for any collectibles retailer. It's how we crawl up the food chain in the business. Start at the bottom and learn your lessons to success without forgetting your roots. That's the game. By the end of that day, Gino and I chalked up a pleasant experience making little money.

In hindsight, I would have done the show unless something more lucrative competed for my time. One good thing that came out of that show is that we eventually hired James, "The Hulk Kid," as we called him. He started out at our store as that ubiquitous teenager who haunts every comic book store until he ends up working there.

The sanguine feeling that the cowboy days of comic book collecting were modernizing for more sophisticated times was being proven in real time. Fans and collectors frequently asked questions their peers might not have asked a decade before.

Everyone tuning in meant fewer people were being ripped off by scammers and their own lack of knowledge. Unfortunately, this optimistic view of mine has not registered with a large following of others. Too many comic book people are too easily led astray by bad decision making.

It's as though we were rushing ahead of the hands of a clock, and now the hands are running backwards for many. I see too many comic book fans left in the dark, unable to finesse the right choices when collecting comics. It's as though the previous generations and their valuable information are not being passed on to the current generation. Too many people are skipping the lessons.

This was fertile ground for the Forensic Comicologist to step forward and right some wrongs.

Katie Leonard's random memory:

It doesn't happen often, but it does. Don't think I don't see it. The side glance, the prolonged stare. The shifting of weight as I come around the boxes to start searching through the one-dollar comics next to you. It doesn't happen most of the time, but I am aware when it does. Why, yes, I am a female browsing through the comics. Got a problem with that?

Yes, I'm mainly browsing for *Thor* comics. Yes, I did start reading around the time the films came out, but that's because I avoided them due to their incredibly inaccurate portrayal of Norse mythology: my ancestors' mythology—*my* stories. Sure, the boys in the movies are pretty, but that's not why I'm here. You don't know that it was a comic series that helped inspire me to delve deeper into the mythology and write my master's thesis. Why are you still staring?

So as I browse through these beautiful pieces of Jack Kirby art, treat me like a fellow comic enthusiast instead of a strange exotic creature.

And I need to look through that box you're standing in front of…

4

Deconstructing Comics (Part 1)

"Buy what you like. Buy what you can afford." This simple phrase defeats many collectors, but it is the collecting philosophy that I most adhere to. Like Uncle Ben's warning to young Peter Parker, "With great power comes great responsibility." The Forensic Comicologist believes that collecting comics should be simple. It's people who complicate the process.

"What do you collect?" That question guarantees all sorts of answers. Comic books cover a large trajectory of times and types. There's too much good stuff to choose from. For this, some collectors stare at vistas outside the scope of what they should or can collect. Money *should* be a factor, not *can* be a factor. Many people ignore their budgets and get into trouble. To understand how comic book people get into these financial and collecting predicaments, it helps to understand the history of comic book collecting.

I want the reader to understand why we collect. To do that, I'll give a little background explaining the unique history of the comics that are collected nowadays.

Over the years, the construction, printing and distributing of comic books has changed. Comics in the folded pamphlet style we recognize began in the 1930s: the art of storytelling communicated through four-color ink on newsprint paper. The maturation of comic books as a medium geared toward fanciful fiction and the absurd changed with the times. Those times included war, political upheaval and world-changing history. The world changed dramatically in just a few decades and comic books changed with the times, both physically and meaningfully. Let's start with the physical.

The dimensions of comic books changed quickly from their inception. Reduced page counts, reduced size and varied paper quality are attributes of the early days. I wanted to know why. As a collector, I always wanted to know everything there was to know about comics, including their physical nature. For this book, I researched across the Internet and used whatever books covered the subjects I needed to know.

Our appreciation for four-color print material starts with the paper.

In antiquity, prior to the invention of paper, written matter was recorded on sheets made from particular plants (papyrus) and animal skin (vellum). Manufacturers used wood pulp, utilizing chemicals to alter wood into paper from the middle of the 19th century onward. Alum and rosin were two of the chemicals mixed into the creating process (more on that later). This "ground wood" process was used for decades to produce cheap paper such as newsprint.

Chemical wood pulp is a process upgrade using purification methods. That form of paper creation yields the quality paper we recognize as stationery and other formats. By 1950, the pulping process eliminated certain chemicals that directly affected paper longevity.

In our hobby, the quality of paper is important. White paper is the holiest shade. Lesser paper quality reduces down to off-white, crème, tan, and brown. Any brown shade is frequently encumbered with brittleness. Brittle paper is the end of a comic book's life.

The chemicals alum and rosin were used in changing wood pulp to paper. They are also notorious for aging paper in quick fashion under prolonged exposure to air and heat. Woody acids are present in chemical pulps. The acids in comic book paper inherently add to the aging process. Ultraviolet light is another contributor to paper deterioration. Natural light and unfiltered indoor lighting will discolor newsprint and cheap comic book paper.

The bad news for comic book collectors is that the Golden Age of comics contain alum, used to treat paper, which eventually releases sulfuric acid. The acid destroys the paper. The decomposition of old comic books originates within them. External forces can hasten a comic book's demise, but the worrisome paper is there from the get-go.

The paper's chemical composition post–1950 eliminated alum and rosin. The belief was that alum-rosin combinations in paper manufacturing were the joint culprits in paper degradation. Alum was deemed necessary and cheap to bind the cellulose fibers together during manufacturing. By World War II, alum was thought to be the main perpetrator in the destruction of aging paper. Wood pulp remained the go-to choice for newsprint. Untreated newsprint remained the norm for comic books for several more decades.

For modern collectors who deal in vintage books, browning paper is a major detriment. The darkened page color indicates that the paper is becoming (or is) brittle. The brittle paper disintegrates, and that's the end of the comic book's lifespan. Tanning or browning edges can mean the paper is losing its flexibility and will chip or break off. Savvy collectors generally stay away from browning copies to search for issues with a greater lifespan.

By the 1980s, Marvel and DC Comics experimented with comics titles printed with better quality paper. Early versions copyrighted as Baxter and Mando papers gave select titles a slicker, whiter quality. Page colors were brilliant and there was no occasional newsprint bleed-through. Baxter was heavy stock, while Mando was a step up from newsprint. These upgrades lasted a short while in the market place. The paper cost was higher, so buyers did not accept them as the new norm.

Although those paper brands disappeared, the comic industry eventually upgraded the paper of most publications. Brian Hayes, writing on HayFamZone Blog in 2012, learned that Marvel and DC still use a paper that existed in the 1980s. Hayes termed it Hudson paper. This white, coated magazine stock has dominated comic publication as long as many collectors have been alive.

The coated paper adds to cost and partially is responsible for many new comic prices reaching four dollars a copy nowadays. Time will tell if the upgraded paper quality introduced in the 1980s will survive longer than the newsprint comics from the past.

Comics started out in the mid–1930s in tabloid dimensions with card stock covers and 36 pages. The comic book format with soft cover and 68 pages of newsprint, including covers (the Golden Age period), arrived by the mid–1930s. The dimensions are close to those of today's *People Magazine*. By the time *Action Comics* #1 (1938) hit the stands, a typical comic book contained 68 pages. By the mid–1940s and early 1950s the page count had been cut to 60 pages, then 52 pages. Finally, by the mid–1950s, comics were reduced to the present average page count of 36 including covers. Those same 36-page comic books of the 1950s ushered in the Silver Age of comics, with changes in direction for a new generation of readers.

Comic collecting cannot be done properly if serious collectors don't appreciate the importance of the quality of the paper. The impact of degraded paper can play havoc with the value of comics. There's always some question over how long comic book paper can last. The answer is "not long" if proper care isn't utilized. Keep those precious, old comics in a dry, temperate climate out of the sun and interior lighting. Use ultraviolet filters if artificial lighting can't be avoided.

Next, let's talk a little about the utilization of comic book paper for publishing purposes.

DC and Marvel Comics share a link in the Silver Age. From late 1957 to 1967 or 1968 they shared distribution nationwide (Independent News) and manufacturing (Chemical Color Plate). DC's parent company, National Periodical Publications, owned Independent News, and therefore exerted control over Marvel Comics distribution across the U.S. Marvel teamed up with DC's distribution in 1957 after an implosion within the company. Unfortunately for Marvel, DC controlled the partnership and limited Marvel with severe publishing restrictions.

With the growth in popularity of superhero comics by 1961, the two companies maintained slightly different paper dimensions coming from two different print shops. DC was slightly larger at 7" × 10¼" average, while Marvel measured around 6¾" × 10¼". DC and Marvel's comic book sizes standardized to fewer than seven inches wide to just over ten inches tall by the 1970s. The inconsistency in size is due in part to the size of the original art. Like publishers of magazines and newspapers, comic book companies didn't regulate artists' working preferences. Judging from Golden Age and Silver Age originals, the most popular production art size was 12½" × 18½", what we call "twice-up" page size.

David Marshall wrote for *The Art of the Comic Book* (college-level courses taught by Marshall) that the movement began at DC Comics. Murphy Anderson (artist of *The Spectre*) wanted to work smaller. Keeping the 2/3 ratio in mind, he chose 10" × 15" as a personal preference. Chemical Color Plate, engraver for all of DC's and Marvel's output and for most of the newspaper syndicates at the time, discovered working with smaller art:

—consumed less film per book (4 pages per plate instead of 2)
—was quicker to produce
—cost significantly less money

As long as artists adhered to the ⅔ ratio of the printed live art zone of 6" × 9", editors didn't care how big the art boards were. Eventually, art dimensions became standardized in the late 1970s.

Marshall continues, "With this new information, DC Comics made 10" × 15" their mandatory production size in 1967. When Marvel Comics followed suit in November, Murphy Anderson's individual preference became the industry standard."

Naturally, manufacturing comic books was very inconsistent, as evidenced by simply measuring any group of comics from the 1970s. Size differences can range as much as ¼" of an inch in height. I've measured width differences within Marvel and DC comics produced in the same month off as much as ⅛ of an inch. Standardization in the 1980s means collectors can buy one-size-fits-all comic book bags and boards to fit all companies from that era.

In the 1990s and 2000s, comic books shrank again, with the width narrowing to just under 6¾ inches. The height remained about the same at ten inches. The average modern comics are thirty-two pages in length, but the story content is not. Ads and in-house promotions have increased in the new millennium while story content has decreased.

For example: In the early 1970s, Marvel Comics featured 19 story pages out of thirty-two pages, plus covers, for twenty cents. By 2013, the pages were reduced to 28 (plus covers) pages, but 21 pages of story (and a promo page for the next issue that counts as a story page). The cover is included to correct the total page count to thirty-two, all for $3.99 per copy. DC went two directions by producing a run at $2.99 with 20 pages of story in a 32-page comic (including the covers), while simultaneously printing $3.99 titles with 32 pages, 22 of which are story (plus the covers).

Something as simple as the selection of inks used to print comic books is also impactful. They run, they bleed, and they fade. Ultimately, the age and behavior of ink affects how we collect comics.

Inks are either organic or inorganic. Manufacturers of ink have relied on plants, animals, and soils to concoct inks for thousands of years. Fruit juices, sea animals, and graphite mixed with liquids transformed the efficiency of man's written communication and art.

For our purposes, inks of the present generally consist of two classes: printing ink and writing inks. The comic books we collect are made using printing inks. The color-form of printing ink is primarily made from certain plant oils combined with petroleum solvents. Organic compounds comprise most color pigment oils in the printing ink process. Inorganic chemical compounds are used to a lesser extent.

Black ink is made using carbon black. Carbon black is produced by burning particular petroleum products. Various tars and a little vegetable oil are mixed and altered to liquid consistency. Writing inks used to be water-based until the 1950s. With the advent of ball-point pens, these inks became oil-based. Oil-based dyes tend to be non-smearing and quicker drying than water-based varieties. Newspaper ink is notorious for coming off on your fingers. Newspapers print product daily and allow the ink to simply be absorbed by the fibrous newsprint. The ink remains damp within the paper for much of its short life.

Comic books are driven through additional printing steps that allow the ink to adhere to the paper. Inks with alcohol or petroleum-based "vehicles" (solvents) dry by evaporation. An element of heating is usually involved.

By now, dear reader, you get an informed picture of the process that generates the short-lived fragility of 20th-century comic books. Papers that can disintegrate over time, inks that have half-lives if not protected properly, and older comics that were made with no forethought for longevity. Now that we've broken down the more important physical elements of comic books, let's figure out how the system has distributed those comics over the years.

Distribution Woes

Publishers produce their products, comics in our case. Printing plants receive the materials necessary to transmute comics from one format to another. The results are tagged (paint or ink marked) with their next destination, bundled as they were in the old days, or boxed as they are now. They go from the manufacturer to the next link in the chain: the distributor.

I'll step back in time to give the reader a reference point. First, there were no free-standing comic book stores until 1968 when Bud Plant, Michelle Nolan and several friends established a free-standing store. That group opened downtown in San Jose on March 3 of that year. The following month, Gary Arlington, famous in our hobby for his support of the underground comics movement, opened his store in San Francisco, calling it the San Francisco Comic Book Company. Gary is celebrated in 1982's *Underground Price Guide.* His shop was a meeting place and focal point for underground comic book talents when that genre was just organizing. In a 2014 article, Michael Yardley wrote about Arlington's store as a testimonial upon his passing: "San Francisco in the '70s was the Paris of the '20s for the underground 'comix' scene," he said in an interview. "I guess Gary's shop was a very sleazy, hole-in-the-wall version of Gertrude Stein's Paris salon by default. Gary was hardly an obvious magnetic personality, but he was an obsessive and he really genuinely cared about this subculture."

Before comic book stores existed, comic books were found at more common establishments: newsstands and small markets (magazine shops, military PXs, liquor stores, train and bus stations, etc.). In the old days several entities received a cut of the sale price of a comic book in the distribution chain. The distributors took their financial cut like others in the chain. This was demoralizing by today's standards when you realize everyone chipped away at the ten-cent cover price per single issue (twelve cents by 1962!). It's amazing anybody could make a living off the lowly comic book! Comics were often considered "loss leaders" at many locales. They were placed there to attract kids so parents would shop there.

The network started with the publisher and continued through the printing plant, the distributor and finally the retailer. The retailer could not sell comics without the distributor. The publisher had no way to gain the market without the distributor. The distributor was the major linchpin that held this network together.

National distributors oversaw movement of comic books filtered down to smaller distributors. DC Comics used Independent News as their distributor in the Gold and Silver Ages. DC formerly was known as National Periodical Publications. Conveniently, NPP was DC. The smaller, local distributors had dominance over territories, creating near-monopolies by location.

The national distributor allocated the quantities of comics to the various local distributors. These amounts included subscribers and "in-house" publisher needs. The print run was based upon these known distribution figures. Some publishers bypassed the national distributor and shipped numbers they found more acceptable directly to the indies (independent distributors).

All Negro Comics #1

Distribution woes plagued all the publishers (in a sense, a contemporary problem today). There were just too many middlemen in the chain. But some comic book publishers had it worse than others. Here's a sad example:

In 1947, a new publication was born. Orrin Evans, an energetic Philadelphia reporter, decided to try his hand at producing a comic book. Evans had been around the print industry since the early 1930s. He had exposure and contacts among cartoonists of the day. Evans knew that comics were a way of reaching an audience he had yet to reach.

Illiteracy was high in the urban Philadelphia area. His newspaper articles did not reach all of his constituents. Comic books could be a means to reach the others. Evans (who was African American) sensed that he could bridge an interest gap with black audiences. Comics of the 1940s featured few black characters. Fewer still were non-stereotyped. Evans felt he could change all that.

Evans collaborated with newspaper colleagues in Philadelphia and constructed an anthology of black characters in four-color stories (nomenclature for the four colors of ink used to create comics). With issue #1 printed, Evans and his backers looked for distribution (no information remains on the quantity distributed). The price tag of fifteen cents was a nickel higher than most comics and probably too expensive for a lot of kids. Regardless, Evans found ways to self-distribute. He was met with some resistance from retailers in Philadelphia. The theory is that retailers did not want to anger the local independent distributors by accepting Evans's self-distributed comic book. Most copies that were sold were distributed outside of town. Whatever the success rate of sales, Evans planned a second issue. All looked rosy until his newsprint sources refused to sell to him.

Evans believed that pressure was placed upon local wholesalers by distributors and other publishers. He felt they saw his comic book as an unwelcome intrusion on their turf. I find it sad and detrimental that Evans never self-published another comic book. A step forward for African American kids and comics could have been a step forward for our hobby.

All Negro Comics used to be considered a top-tier collectable because of its scarcity. Nowadays it's so rare to see one for sale, it seems to be an unknown to most people. I love the book because it has such a singular appeal on several levels. I hold onto my copy like a keepsake and have no idea if I'll ever sell it. After all, the Forensic Comicologist has a sentimental heart.

Other black-centric comic books were distributed in the late 1940s into the early 1950s. *Parents' Magazine* published two issues of *Negro Heroes*, while Fawcett put out three issues of *Negro Romance* and sports hero comics with Jackie Robinson and Joe Lewis, among others. Although these titles featured black characters, the publishers were white distributors through normal channels controlled by whites. Evans's only attempt featured all black characters by all black artists and writers. No future attempts to produce African American comics for blacks by blacks were made in postwar America. Distributors had had their say.

Comics were shipped directly to the independent distributors. Bundled together with twine or worse, the comics were not intended for minty-fresh delivery to the retailers. With binding creases and weather damage, comic books were a low-yield commodity. Once delivered, the comics were racked for display and sold "as is." If there were refunds given for ten-cent comic books, I'm sure it wasn't because the book was less than a CGC 9.8!

The unsold copies from the previous month needed to be dealt with. The independent distributor took the unsold copies from the retailer. In the old days, the returns went back to the publisher intact. The publisher could find ways to repackage and try another sales approach. To ease costs on shipping returns, changes were made.

First, comics could be stripped of their covers at the distributor's plant. That devolved into mailing a portion of the cover back to the publisher. For years the distributors made money by selling the comic book "remains" on the side. As a longtime back-issue dealer, I'm used to seeing comic collections come into the shop with the top of the cover neatly torn or razor-bladed free (the portion with the title called the masthead). Those copies were once intact before being returned back to the distributor chain. Somebody in the chain stripped the title off for credit from the publisher and resold the remains for pennies out the "back door." The fact that it freely happened without repercussions indicates that even retailers were privy to that option if nobody was enforcing returns.

> We've seen plenty of comics at our store that somehow returned to market after having the masthead removed at some point in the distribution/return chain. The fate of almost all those comics is the recycling bin. Occasionally we will have the right customer on hand at the store looking from some old reads. Those lucky fellows get any copies we're sitting on for free. Of course, the key issues are a different matter.

By the mid–1970s, distributors pressured the publishers to accept affidavits instead of partial comic book remains. These affidavit returns were simply invoices indicating a quantity was sold and the publishers were obligated to accept the note.

Meanwhile, the actual amount count could have been much less. The missing copies are historically known to have entered the underground market. Distributors prone to this behavior moved the missing product through unscrupulous or unknowing merchants without the publisher's being the wiser.

The whole return process destined comic books to be scarce in a secondary market. Those comics were torn apart so those early pioneers of comic book collecting had little to work with if they searched for comics that were on the returned lists. World War II amplified the potential scarcity as Americans took the immense inventory of comics out of the hands of citizens in the 1940s for the war effort. Millions of copies of comics were collected during the "paper drives" and pulped to help win the war.

By the 1950s, Americans' love affair with comics lessened. Superheroes were not in vogue. Returned war vets required comics with more vice and drama. Newly minted conservative thinking took prominence in government at the same time. Communism and crime were America's foremost fears with a rising concern over juvenile delinquency within our country. Anti–comic book crusades began by conservative apologists looking to blame the delinquency rate on comic books. Comic book circulation was already suffering a postwar decline in large part due to television.

Nineteen fifty-four saw mass hysteria centered around the mental corruption of America's children. These kids solemnly watched their future cash-cows go up in flames.

Exposes on comic books' perceived negative influence on young readers brought government inquiries into our hobby. The bad imagery seen daily in the press and even broadcast from church pulpits put the screws to comic book publishers. Comic books lost more readers and more ground. Increased television continually lowered readership as well.

Marvel Comics was another borderline victim of the distribution woes of the 1950s. Marvel Comics was called Atlas Comics from late 1951 to late 1957 (formerly Timely). Marvel had lost their previous distributor by the mid–1950s and had to sign with DC's distributor to stay in business following the implosion of 1957. Their sales declined to the point that they had to reach out for help. DC and its distributor NPP were happy to oblige— with restrictions. DC insisted that Marvel cut their title count from more than 70 titles in the first half of 1957 to 16 bi-monthly titles at the end of the year. A deal was struck and Marvel stayed afloat publishing a fraction of their once prolific monthly output. Marvel was forced into employee layoffs and a much reduced level of creativity.

Public pressure, changing attitudes and shady distribution practices forced many publishers and fans out of comics in the 1950s. A few publishers held on for several more years. The 1960s could have been a whole lot weaker if the distribution and sales problems for comics in the 1950s had continued. Fortunately, times were changing once again.

Marvel circulation figures remained lower than they could have been without ID (Independent News distributor) restrictions until 1968. Marvel regained publishing and distribution strength by 1968. Finding the means to separate from the NPP (and DC Comics), Marvel increased its title count and production numbers. However, the retailer climate was changing. Comics barely reaped a profit for magazine stands. Those retailers got their money from magazines, newspapers, and other products. Comics did not provide significant income. They found less display space or disappeared entirely from newsstands nationwide.

I grew up in one of San Diego's postwar suburbs. Back in the late 1950s and early 1960s, I could buy comics at supermarkets near my house. By the early 1970s my friends and I had to drive to a newsstand seven miles away to find the closest new comics in a city of over one million people! That newsstand was the only place for miles that maintained a decent selection of monthly comics.

Collecting anything requires that enough supply exists to provide the collector with realistic goals. The demand for old comic books ramped up with the decline in publishing and distribution. At first there was a thread of mostly guys filling in back issues from whatever source. Then, slowly, a collecting avalanche drove collectors to seek out hidden comic books everywhere. Pickers began to dig everywhere for collectible comics; an early realization emerged that there might be more buyers than copies.

It was 1973 and I was 18 years old when I got my first car. I was now free to drive wherever I wanted to buy comics. I needed a car because comic book stands were few, especially in the San Diego suburbs north of Interstate 8. The neighborhoods south of the Freeway 8 tended to be decades older than the properties north of the 8. To get a shot at a decent supply of monthly comics, I had to drive seven miles to North Park to a small newsstand called Paras News.

North Park retained a quaint, older San Diego appearance. Residential rent in that part of town was cheaper than my part of town, perhaps commercially as well. Paras

News was wisely situated in a business neighborhood at one of the busiest intersections in that part of town, 30th Street and University Avenue.

Paras News looked like it may have been built decades earlier and never upgraded or changed. It had a simple, no-nonsense display array for paperback books, newspapers, magazines and comic books. The adult material was arranged so the cashier could cover all points visually to keep the younger wolves at bay. Cigars, cigarettes and candy were kept behind the register and under glass.

Paras News was primarily new material with older comics for sale, like a few stores downtown. But they were on top of the monthlies. I never missed an issue because they didn't get a certain month or ran out of some titles. They were strictly local distribution-oriented, not direct market, so anything they bought was fully returnable. They picked up the comics they wanted from ARA, the local distribution arm of yet another, larger distribution network. ARA could always maintain a surplus, knowing they'd get their money back up the chain for unsold copies of comics and other periodicals.

From a historical perspective, I look back at the beginning of the 1970s as the time when comic fandom came of age. The *OPG* legitimized everything I believed in and justified my back issue expenditures. Suddenly the book's debut in 1970 created a new dual goal for collectors: to collect comics and make money. The years of public abandonment of comics, or the other pursuits that distracted people from comics, set the stage for their growing values. The more desired issues featured prices that actually increased with time. The idea of turning a profit from collecting gained momentum as some collectors treated comics as investments.

In the late 1980s, longtime comics fan (and Mylar supply guru) Ernie Gerber published an extraordinary project: *Gerber's Photo-Journal Guides*. The two-volume, tabloid-sized hardbound set constitutes an epic encyclopedic work presenting thumbnail photographs of about half of all comic book covers of the 1930s, 1940s and 1950s, along with the relevant information that accompanied the comic issues. *Gerber* has 21,000 photos of the approximately 40,000 issues published from 1934 to 1961, plus some other early 1960s cover photos as well.

Viewed as a comprehensive tool for collectors and researchers, the *Photo-Journal Guides* provide basic information significant to comic book collectors. Text includes Gerber's views on collecting, grading, and the relative value of comics. Gerber allowed that values of comics could be divined by comparing them against other comics, a novel formula at the time. His Relative Value Index demonstrated one method of pricing collectible comics. Although a lot of thought went into the utilization of RVI, little of it is discussed in today's market.

After decades of comic book publishing, we have seen tons of comic books end up in the hands of the public as collectibles. Many of those have changed hands more than once, gaining individual identities. A lot of comics have been catalogued like the most expensive diamonds. With recorded knowledge such as this, Gerber took a bold step in his *Photo-Journal Guides*: he coded known comic books for their scarcity. The *Gerber Guides*, in short, created a feature tool called the Scarcity Index (SI) for estimating the availability of any comic book predating the 1960s. Gerber's exhaustive research and inquiries allowed him to generate an eleven-point system he named the scarcity index. Nothing of this magnitude had ever been accomplished before. The SI attached a number to each issue of each title. That SI number was the best estimate Gerber and others could come up to let the public know how many copies existed of each. (Gerber was aggressive in displaying photos for popular genres and less accurate for less-favored titles like romance and humor comics. The same could be said for his Scarcity Index.)

As I discussed earlier, comic books tended to disappear in chunks from their inception on. A comic book was meant to have a short life and almost always did. Latter-day collecting saved many comic collections from harvest and drove many others out into the light. The SI numbers gave us a hint how few copies of the millions produced were possibly still out there. That does not take into account copies still disappearing and new ones being located, nor those locked away in collections.

Gerber traveled thousands of miles and spent thousands of dollars to write and take comic book photos for his comprehensive photo volumes. Five years of encounters with comic collections added to his knowledge of just how many Golden Age comic books were theoretically out there, by the end of the 1980s.

Gerber's Scarcity Index added another category, albeit often controversial, for collecting. Information about scarcity had often been supplied by those supposedly in the know who just estimated or just guessed at quantities. What's even worse, there has always been a concern among collectors that estimated quantities were toggled up or down to benefit a contributor's agenda. In any case, collectors started aiming for comic books to collect based upon their published rarity, a dimension of discovery that was less identifiable before Gerber.

Of course, I can tie the Forensic Comicologist into this chapter. The information here is crucial in the history of comic books. An FC needs to track down historical facts, precedents and urban legends. He or she must be ready to share that knowledge or educate the less-informed. Those who forget the history of comics are doomed to hear it from me again and again.

5

Deconstructing Comics (Part 2)

Scarcity

The Scarcity Index (or SI) theorized that every comic book that still exists can be categorized. In other words, the number of copies of any issue of any title can be estimated. At least general numbers of copies can be identified. SI numbers range from 1–11 with one being the most common quantity and 11 considered "rumored to exist." The first three numbers in the category chart speak in large, general numbers. Just about any comic book produced since the 1970s fits into these categories. Moving through the SI number ranges, we jump ahead to number 4, where Gerber now lists his tiers with specific numbers of extant comics. So a comic matching the number 4 tier would be estimated at being one issue of between 1,000 and 2,000 copies known to exist. An SI of 5 says 200 to 1,000 copies are around.

> SI 6 renders 50–200 copies as uncommon.
> SI 7 says 21–50 copies are considered scarce.
> SI 8 and SI 9 cover the spread between 6 and 20 copies.
> SI 10 states anything where fewer than 5 copies are known to exist.

I've attached a photo of a random page from the *Guides* displaying how the SI information is displayed, in conjunction with specific titles and issue numbers. In the below example I'm working with *Action Comics* from Volume One of the *Guides*. This is an example of the general layout of the contents. The chart on the right displays SI numbers next to each issue of *Action Comics*. The 4 indicates 1,000–2,000 copies known to exist at the time of prepublication research (mid–1980s).

The *All Negro Comics* #1 I wrote about earlier is a unique example of what the Scarcity Index brings to the table. Gerber attached an SI of 9 to the number of known copies by 1986. I own a copy, so I've taken part in discussions about its existence in quantity. The copy I owned I purchased in the late 1990s from a local comic book store. That store got it from the son of the original owner. We do not know where that owner got it. We do know that it was not part of Gerber's census. I've read that the print run for *All Negro Comics* #1 was 300,000. If this is true, then the drop in known quantities to below 20 is demonstrative of its scarcity.

After years of discussion, I believed that enough copies are known to exist that the SI rating of nine should be downgraded to 8. I personally know of two copies that surfaced, including mine, long after Gerber tallied his count. Gerber tried to stay accurate for his purposes, but time has added to the known supply. People have been digging Golden Age back issues out of the woodwork long after Gerber's estimates first appeared. For all of the research and time committed to the *Guides*, they lack the "evergreen" quality that follows print matter through Internet updates and supplementals.

My store buys collections almost daily with Golden Age being the era least likely to show up for sale. But in late 2015 through 2016 we were offered seven Golden Age collections, with half of those categorized as "regional owner." For some of the issues involved, the SI may have to make numerical adjustments upward.

When Comics Guaranty Corporation (CGC) grades a book, they add that book to their census data. CGC's data files have attempted to lock in the numbers of copies of every comic book submitted to them. Their statistics have added to Gerber's known quantities and present a more accurate picture of what Gerber only theorized. I submitted my copy of *All*

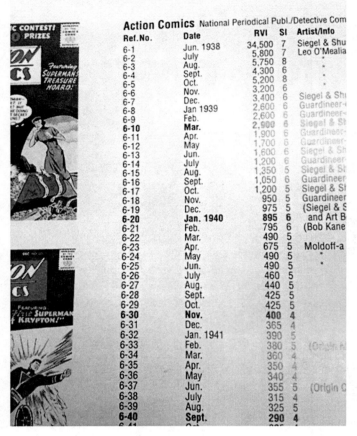

This sample page from the *Gerber Photo-Journal Guides* better illustrates the statistics available to collectors curious about the scarcity of particular comic books, *Action Comics* in this example.

Negro Comics #1 in the mid–2000s to CGC. It was graded a 2.0, which is a common condition with many known copies. Their census tabulated 22 copies in their database in late 2016. The SI dropped to a 7 on the *Gerber Guide* scale. It is still a tough book to find for sale.

CGC tabulates all of the received submissions that they successfully grade. Their census displays all copies displayed by grade and split into columns differentiating between restored copies and unrestored. CGC's data is continually refreshed, adding to the numbers count in real time. That accuracy is dependent on counting one book only once. Each grading company maintains its ever-growing census statistics.

The only hole in their systems is the repeated submission of the same books. An owner may remove a book from a graded container and resubmit it in the hopes of getting a better grade. If the submitter neglects to inform CGC that his submission is a repeat, CGC will mistakenly add it to their census without knowing it's a duplication of previous data. If a particular copy receives a better grade the second time around, then two grade variations of the same copy will exist together in the census (see later chapters for more on CGC and third-party grading).

The Scarcity Index was innovative. Many of my peers used Gerber's numbers to set collecting goals. Since scarcity is a factor in determining comic book values, some collectors used SI numbers to decide what rare or cool comics to collect. Others used SI numbers to inflate the prices of rare comics. Obscuring the numbers count with CGC's census also obscures the SI's numbers even further than the discoveries made in the last thirty years.

Presently, the CGC census is considered a more topical representation of known quantities. Where Gerber solicited surveys and counted the issues of comics available to count, CGC relies on known quantities only. Since CGC and the others individualize each and every book they grade, it is imperative the resubmissions be accounted for.

Scarcity can and does impact comic book value. *All Negro Comics* #1 is an example of a scarce comic book. Many copies of rarer comic books are locked away in private collections, skewing the numbers on how many scarce comics exist. Scarcity and age often go hand in hand. The 1930s comics often account for the largest percentage of SI 8s, 9s, and 10s. The 1940s and 1950s have weighed in with similar numbers, frustrating collectors. Many souls have scoured the country for decades trying to find copies of books that may no longer exist outside of current collections. *All Negro Comics* #1 was one of those prized rarities. There are copies in existence of every newsstand comic book published in the Golden Age.

So, scarcity as a component of collecting is as fluid as pricing. It is a solid factor in price fluctuation and desirability. As collectors, we can comfortably regard scarcity as a reason to collect. To find the one book nobody has and everybody wants is a blessing. Even today's market reflects customer determination to go rare or go home. One subsection of scarcity by existence (or lack thereof) is scarcity by production. I can sum that statement up in one word: variants.

Variants, or variant covers, relate to weekly shipments of new comic books to comic book businesses. Almost all comic book stores get their products from one distributor. Unlike days in the past, Diamond Comics owns contracts with all the large publishers to provide sole distribution for the products that those publishers ship to specialty stores. Those Diamond accounts represent comic book and gaming stores, both physical and virtual. Other types of stores carry comics and comic book–related products. Sports card stores, surf shops, alternative shops, sellers working from home, and others retain Diamond accounts to connect with weekly products.

Internet stores and Web site–based operations that function as stores also maintain Diamond accounts. All these accounts compete for markets spread out all over the planet, and these markets have all recently competed for large customer bases to raise eligibility for variant comics.

Variants and Scarcity

Comic books once were manufactured from their inception with a constant structure: one distinct cover per issue. With rare exceptions (early Gold Key *Star Treks*, for example) comic books stuck to that format until the 1970s. In 1976, Marvel Comics may have been feeling a financial pinch. All of their titles were cover-priced twenty-five cents. They debated price increases before settling on an experimental test. Six cities were selected. Up to five consecutive issues of Marvel's complete inventory that now displayed thirty-cent price tags were shipped to those particular cities. The rest of the country still saw twenty-five-cent cover prices. No noticeable decline in sale was noted for these "Marvel price variants." All of Marvel's titles went to thirty cents following the price variant market test.

Marvel repeated the experiment in 1977 and printed thirty-five-cent test prices ahead of a general price increase. History repeated itself, and Marvel's comics line increased to thirty-five-cent monthly titles. Collectors picked up on these exclusives years later. Jon McClure published articles in *Comic Book Marketplace* magazine in the late 1990s about these Marvel price variants. He brought attention to the scarcity of these Marvel pricing oddities and explained their origins. His article and other exterior forces brought the "scarcity hunters" into the market full-force to hunt down these previously barely known comic books. At least they were unknown initially by many in the unaffected cities. I did not even know about the price variants, or care, until McClure's article in a publication I used to write for!

There are a couple of significant reasons why one theme or group of comics may develop greater collectibility than another. Thirty-cent Marvel variants were sold in greater numbers than thirty-five-centers. Or at least, more of the thirty-centers have turned up. Thirty-five-cent cover prices covered up to five months of issues before the rest of the Marvel titles followed suit. The other factor of note is that there are key issues in the thirty-five-cent group, in contrast to the thirty-centers. Popular examples are *Star Wars* #1, *Iron Fist* #14, and to a lesser extent, *Iron Fist* #15 with the X-Men appearing (and the last issue in this series).

Since the 1990s, the values on Marvel price variants have risen with fervent collector desirability. The prices for these variants are vastly more expensive than their regular-priced peers. Utilizing the *OPG* for a baseline, we can measure dramatic price differences.

I remember the initial demand for these variants once the *Comic Book Marketplace* (*CBM*) article was published. We'd get inquiries at our store and requests at conventions. The most requested was the *Star Wars* #1 35-cent variant. We've owned three copies at various times at our store. The best copy was a raw Fine. We'd previously owned nothing better than VG(ish) copies that still sold for $500 and up. But the fine copy was like gold! We sold it almost immediately after purchase at Terry O'Neill's small annual convention in Orange County in 2014, well before the imminent release of the next generation of *Star Wars* movies. The sales price: an incredible $1,500! By 2017 the last recorded sale for a graded 6.0 was a whopping $4,400!

Nowadays the buyers for these variants are less public about searching for them. We've owned-lesser tier variants, and they tend to stick around our shop longer than in the past.

The 1976 *Amazing Spider-Man* issues 155–159 thirty-cent variant cover price is three times higher in NM- than their regular twenty-cent-priced counterparts. The 1977 run of *Amazing Spider-Man* issues 169–173 had thirty-cent cover prices. The thirty-five-cent variants in near mint minus sold for nine times more than the regular priced copies in 2016.

Star Wars #1 thirty-five-cent cover price (variant rate) was published in 1977. The 2013 *OPG* price in NM- is 38 times more expensive than the thirty-cent cover priced regular rate!

The market for Marvel price variants is relative to their scarcity, while strong collector desire continues to drive their values. Clearly demand is greater than the supply.

By the 1990s, publishers took a different path with the variant cover concept.

Initially, publishers saw incremental sales increases generated by the excitement built up around comic books. The late 1980s saw advancements in the development of characters and new comic book creator talent. More media attention was being directed toward comics. The 1989 release of the Michael Keaton *Batman* movie gave comic books blank checks to create more attention. Speculators saw the spike in interest and moved in for their cut.

Publishers saw the speculators and other readers as collectors buying for investments. The publishers created special issues and new titles to appeal to the market as collectors' items. Soon comic book completists were evidently buying everything, so publishers produced multiple covers to increase profits. Speculators interpreted the change as vast, open-ended opportunities to cash in. Publishers made more money and comic book buyers thought they would as well.

More variants were introduced, and "gimmick" covers were added to the lineup. Poly-bagged, die-cut, glow-in-the-dark, holograms over shiny covers, and color-varied variants represented just a portion of the direction the publishers were willing to go to exploit an artificially inflated market. Copies were sold in the millions with little concern toward readership.

> In the Modern Era, variant covers comprise a range of cover art. Comic publishers will publish the same comic issue with one or more covers to increase sales. The theory being that hardcore fans will buy everything their favorite company produces, or every vestige of their favorite title. Some variants are nothing more than equal numbers of the same issue: could be two covers, three different covers or more than that. These "alternate covers" are generally worth the same as their cover partners and tend to stall at any real long-term value gain. But these are not the "prey" true variant collectors are vying for. It's the rarer variants that are fought over by fans. The "Retailer Incentive" (or ratio) variants are the copies that come to market with built-in scarcity.

Some variants were produced in small numbers. These rarer copies left collectors scrambling to find copies. Wisely, publishers sought out retailer cooperation. Early retailer-incentive (R.I.) orders were offered to business owners. These R.I. covers were made available only to comic book retailers. They were generally offered in ratios to the retailers. A tier quantity was decided upon by the publisher, say one for every 20 copies purchased (1:20). Hitting this 20-issue minimum granted access to a single variant copy. The scarcity of the variants allowed retailers to price them above cover price. Demand for the variants by collectors and speculators promised retailers big returns on those covers.

The speculator boom in the mid–1990s strangled some of this frenzy. The exploiters tried to cash in when the new-comic market entered a depressed period. Comic stores suffered closures nationwide, with their inventories flooding the country. Prices on recent back issues and their variants dropped drastically as supply overwhelmed demand.

An adjustment period would arrive and allow the comic book retail world to reconfigure. Publishers stopped producing comics aimed at collectors. They concentrated on stronger content for readers and backed away from excessive variant production for a while.

In 2000, Marvel comics released their new comic book imprint: the *Ultimate* line. Beginning with *Ultimate Spider-Man* #1, a retailer incentive version was printed. This white cover variant was all the rage for a brief period—difficult to find, easy to sell for big bucks to collectors.

With a near-instant sellout, Marvel saw a possible return to the variant scene. Soon, Marvel began variant production for their other titles, followed by DC as well. Both companies energized the collectors' market once again with these different and rare covers. Subsequent reprints of sold-out titles were targeted with fresh covers (new art or different colors) that rose in value and collectibility. Even rarer covers with higher ordering ratios (1:100, 1:200) were produced to commemorate events.

Licensees such as Dynamic Forces produced variants that ended up for sale by hucksters on the Home Shopping Channel and QVC.

Comic stores routinely co-op with publishers to produce store-name variants to promote their name brand. Participating stores have to agree to minimum print runs they must pay for; these can run into thousands of dollars. Their emblem, sign or brand will grace the cover for an issue. And they get bragging rights that they've taken their business to the next level.

Diamond Comics introduced variant covers at their retailer summits held within different regions around the country. These variants, known as RRP, hit their stride with the introduction of Jim Lee's first artistic run on *Batman* comics.

Comic cons have produced variants as well. Most of the larger conventions create a selection of variants for their annual events. Collectibility is reflected through their immediate and consistent sales on eBay. In many cases, regarding variant comic book covers, there is a determined mentality among connoisseurs to take advantage of their scarcity—scarcity derived from an instant con-time flare-up of sudden interest in variants from a particular show. The demand is instantaneous upon release, with genuine collector drive to own them, at least for a while. As with many things variant, the thrill chills relatively quickly as fans move onto the next hot thing. Those once "necessary" variants are already forgotten.

The demand was often highest at the variants' release date. Profit was the motive and collectors kept abreast of the variant tempo to beat others for the purchase opportunity. An example of a typical variant concern works like this at our store:

We order titles two months before shipment to our store. We might normally order 40 copies of a particular Marvel title, say *Avenging Spider-Man* (40 copies of any Spider-man title seemed to be a norm at that time for us). With issue #1, Marvel is offering a variant cover drawn by a hot artist. The ratio to get just one of them is 1:50. An additional, rarer variant might be made available at a 1:100 ratio. Both variants have the same cover price and cost to my store is the same as the regular issue of *Avenging Spider-Man*. Our store may debate an order increase to qualify for the variant if we came up short on our initial order. We may be required to pre-order ten additional copies to qualify for the next-level variant. We have to balance the risk that those ten additional copies may not sell. Defunct comic book stores have littered the world with unsold comics for years because of the belief that they could always sell their inventory for profit. We are not willing to follow that path, having purchased the inventories of those speculative dealers on numerous occasions.

We debate whether the cost of ordering 50 copies of *Avenging Spider-Man* #12 to get

We were invited to Long Beach to look at the inventory of a closed comic book store. The inventory had been piled into a storage facility in a commercial area near downtown and far away from the store's original location. The original store owner still owned the inventory and paid monthly rental costs to keep the dusty comics in readiness for some imagined near-future sale. The comics were packed tightly into cramped shelves in about 200 long boxes. That equated to about 50,000 individual comics spanning the '80s to early 2000s. An affable, energetic sort, this older gentleman seemed unconcerned that he'd paid thousands in rent for years to house these comics.

He described the life he led and decisions he made to get to this point. It all started with a time when he felt those comics would sell. Each stored box held comics he had ordered new from distribution in the day. His nuanced buying habits changed around the early '90s with the advent of variants. He ordered heavy to get variants right up into the store's twilight years and stockpiled the regular copies … and that's where the problems began.

The owner assumed that the stockpiled comics would eventually reach the market in some capacity for at least what he paid for them wholesale. He thought that in some distant time they might even sell for retail. The same issue of Jim Lee's *X-Men* #1 with five different covers, for instance. He held onto hundreds of copies of an issue that ends up in bargain bins today. In other instances he chose to order large numbers of comics to get the scarcer ratio variants.

Twenty-four years later, that turned out to be a bad call. Ratio covers were just in their infancy and there were few opportunities to over-order copies to get them. To get in the game, he made the choice to order heavy to get those variants. They were long gone, of course, by the time I met him. The commons he ordered to get those variants crammed the boxes he held in storage. They resembled the thousands of puffy boxes of comics I've seen everywhere in this business. I witnessed the quantities in overage and knew there was no way he made enough money to compensate for all those unsold, regular covers.

I offered him nickels on the dollar for those unsold copies, knowing even I would be challenged to unload over 100 copies of an issue no longer popular. The deal was never made.

the 1:50 variant will be a wise decision, instead of the 40 copies we normally order. We know that the variant has to sell for a base margin to offset the number of regular copies we may not sell. That variant price in this case has to great enough to offset those ten extra copies if they don't sell. There is a 1:100 variant of *Avenging Spider-Man* #1 that is not within our range. No amount of clever math will up-sell another 50 copies of a title that may not survive cancellation within a year. Marvel likes to cancel titles.

Once the issues of *Avenging Spider-Man* #1 ship to our store, the single variant is culled out. We inspect it for defects and then scan the Internet for the current going price. That and common sense set our asking price.

Typically, we open the store on Wednesday to a trickle of early buyers. Most early morning guys scan our "new variants" racks first. They want to beat out the competition city-wide to hoard the variants that are considered most desirable from week to week. By the end of the day, most of those covers are sold. Some buyers will hold onto their copies; others will put them on eBay. Still others will submit them to third-party grading companies. If a substantial grade is attributed, 9.8 or higher, that issue is maybe considered to have reached the minimum value necessary to generate a profit. Stores always have the option of grading variant submissions for the same goals.

In every instance, scarcity drives the variant market while demand lasts. There are almost always more customers than copies. As they filter through the system and demands are met, the next round of variants arrive at the stores and the cycle repeats.

As ye sow, so shall ye reap.

More often than not, the most common variants lose appeal within mere months. Their desirability diminishes and so does the value. Heavier hitters like rarer Sketch variants will tend to hang on longer. The "Remarked" or "Sketched" variants, with actual original cover drawing art, are the top of the food chain. They can only be surpassed in sales numbers by the third-party graded versions of the same books (third-party grading will be dealt with in another chapter).

Grading companies authenticate signed comic books. Comics books can be purchased already signed (i.e., Dynamic Forces) or collectors can have them signed at conventions and store signings. Unfortunately, a certificate accompanying a signature is not enough validation for a third-party grader to pronounce it authentic. Third-party grading will witness a signature and then pronounce it valid with an accompanying label sealed in with the comic book. The label is tagged with the words "Signature Series" to validate the authenticity. Some companies will hire signature experts to validate non-witnessed signatures to achieve Signature Series labels. All this comes with a price.

As I mentioned earlier, the variants that draw the best chance at value increases are the ones that feature sketches—original art. DC, Marvel and other companies have caught on and obliged comic customers by producing virgin white blank covers. These covers are meant to be used as canvasses providing a convenient art board for customers to collect original drawings.

Comic conventions are the magnet for these blank covers. Attendees buy the blanks at whatever outlet carries them and zoom on into the shows that feature accessible artists doing sketches. Sketches range anywhere from free to various charges after that. The artists are under no obligation to provide free sketches, although some do.

The witness program (no, that's a different witness program) requires the on-site comic book grading companies to see the artist sign the copy or do the art. This is the main form of validation to gain a Signature Series label. Witnesses can be either grading employees or "deputized" persons approved by the grading companies. In either case, that variant or sketch variant must be witnessed. That can be a challenge at a crowded con where witnesses might be in short supply.

As a comic convention retailer, I see no lack of fans searching out variants for their own particular reasons.

My Ahab Complex, or Old Shazam Strikes Again!
by Michael Copeland

Every convention, I have a "Captain Ahab" comic. Not a comic about Ahab or his beloved whale, but a comic that I obsess over during conventions. Even if I find everything else I'm looking for; just doesn't feel like it was a successful convention. One particular year, my comic radar was set on *Marvel Super-Heroes* #12, Captain Marvel's first appearance.

I should point out that this was not the Captain Marvel of the 1940s. That character had been out of comics for many years. In the meantime, Marvel Comics acquired the rights to the name, Captain Marvel. So, the character created to use the Captain Marvel name was not a young boy who shouted "Shazam!" and became a super-powered being. This person was a Captain in the alien Kree Navy whose name was Mar-Vell. Captain Mar-Vell. Captain Marvel. Get it?

I had set out to this convention to obtain a copy of Mar-Vell's first appearance. Amid obtaining issues of *Iron Man* and *Tomb of Dracula*, I found this particular issue extremely hard to find. The comic was not in bins. It was not up on people's walls. It was nowhere to be seen! It was soon the last day of the convention and I reached the Death Valley that all collectors eventually fall into: I asked dealers if they had it. Most shook their heads, not at all sympathetically, no. Some laughed. One looked at me like I had lobsters crawling out of my ears. I resigned myself to the idea that maybe this was the one book I would not be able to find. Like Ahab, it was going to get me in the end.

As I was walking in a daze, I spotted a smaller vendor I had not visited before, for one reason or another. It was getting late in the convention. One of the vendor's assistants was asleep, leaning his head on a comic box. He was drooling a little. Another had red teeth, due to, no doubt, a steady diet of Red Vines and soda. It was loud and crowded, but figuring I had nothing to lose, I squeezed into the massive throng of people surrounding this booth and began to look. Suddenly, a piercing white comic cover caught my eye.

Could it finally be? Could my hands finally be resting on the one book that eluded me all these … uh, days? All of the endless hours of frustration and disappointment were, at last, totally, at an end? *Marvel Super-Heroes* #12, the very first appearance of Captain Mar-Vell, was about to be in my hands … and for a mere $14! The find of the day! Heck, maybe the find of the convention!

I quickly raced back to my hotel room. I held my four-color beauty in my hands and stared at the cover through the plastic covering. Older coverings always made comics look bad, and this was no exception. I carefully undid the plastic tape holding the two flaps of the plastic bag together. I was immediately overwhelmed by the dusty, musty smell of vintage newsprint, so powerful it actually caused my knees to wobble. This pungent smell, rumor has it, has caused curious behavioral issues. One stated that a guy, upon detecting fumes of a Golden Age comic, lost his mind, started barking and chased a dog up Fifth Avenue into a tree. Another rumor, told in hushed tones of convention goers, speaks of an ugly argument that nearly led to a breakup of an engaged couple when he admitted he liked the smell of old newsprint more than his fiancé's perfume. But these are just rumors.

The plastic was now off! The cover, showing Mar-Vell in all his glory, looked pristine. I inhaled once more, and sat down to read this comic beauty. I took a deep breath, savoring every moment, and opened the comic. A table of contents! Larger books and annuals in the Sixties had these. I quickly scanned it, looking for the story introducing Mar-Vell. I didn't see it. No matter. I scanned the table of contents again. Still nothing! Well, I am excited, I thought. Maybe I'll find it quicker by thumbing through the book. Okay, here is the *Spider-Man* reprint with the Golden Age *Human Torch, Sub-Mariner*, and a monster story. No Mar-Vell. Did I miss it? I paged through the book again. Where is it?! Then I looked at the small print at the bottom of the title page. The answer hit me like a bolt of lightning! The interior of the book was not *Marvel Super-Heroes* #12! It was *Marvel Tales*! Someone had switched the covers! Was old Shazam himself taking revenge on me for daring to read about a mortal who was not his creation? I sank down into the seat and buried my head in my hands. It was Sunday around 6 p.m. The convention was over. Nothing else could be done.

6

Demand

Demand is the second part of the "supply (scarcity) and demand" formula. Without demand, the values of comics would be meaningless. Without demand, lots of comic books have little or no value. Plenty of comics from the past to the present are of no interest to buyers. They're comic books that sold for better than cover prices ages ago before sinking in popularity and value. They never regained the higher values again. To name a few examples, 1970s *Warlord*, 1980s *Moon Knight*, 1990s *Superman*, and perhaps *Fantastic Four* are all titles that have seen better days. They sit stacked in boxes on store floors or convention tables waiting for buyers who may never come for them.

Modern comics with no shelf-life in the used market are abundant. Whatever value they can obtain is often reduced to pennies on the dollar in the resale market. Quarter bins at stores and conventions are the last stop for these books to find new homes (at Comic-Con International, no one can afford to sell bargain comics because those cheap prices won't come close to offsetting booth costs). Gloomily, our hobby has seen modern comics open on eBay listings with minimum bids of a penny.

Golden Age and Silver Age comics offer examples of the same depreciation. There are scarce comics from those ages that don't connect with any collectors. It might be the title; it might be the genre. It could even be that the last interested buyers belong to an outgoing generation, no longer purchasing with vibrancy. Some comics can only thrive at a particular grade level. A higher-grade copy of the 1970 centennial issue of *Fantastic Four* could be sold at CGC's 9.8 for over $1,200. A low-grade copy at 3.0 will either sell for less than ten dollars or not at all. Although it has some key-worthy status as a centennial issue, the *Fantastic Four* title has lost some luster over the years, and therefore some value. Centennial issues are usually heralded by the publisher as milestones and sometime come into the world of collecting as minor-league keys. Nowadays, a highly-graded copy of *Fantastic Four* #100 would be the primary reason somebody would go after this book. A 9.8 is fairly uncommon.

Demand for old comics did not exist as we know it now until the 1960s. The genesis of popularity, as discussed earlier, for comic book collecting started with fans all over the country during the Golden Age. But it was a new generation that pumped up the demand to new levels. Scarcity helped drive demand as we already know. But what else set the field on fire?

As a kid, my friend and I had our favorites. Our standards for collecting were simple:

1. Favorite Characters: We were at the age of infancy for Marvel's launch of the Fantastic Four and Amazing Spider-Man. DC's superheroes were in their stride and most of us were hung up on Superman family titles, the Flash, JLA, and others. Characters remain a strong influence on demand. Marvel's new creations in the early 1960s highlight demands that exist into the present. For example, characters from other companies like Doctor Solar and Archie had less appeal to my friends than Batman and Spider-Man. The fans who grew up 10 and 20 years before us enjoyed a wider variety of characters, many of whom we'd never heard of until we caught up with the burgeoning fan movement. Those older readers collected a wider variety of titles because of their earlier exposure to hundreds of titles that were gone by the time my friends and I started reading comics.

2. The Publisher: The comic book companies of the Golden Age covered many genres. Their choices of titles and characters offered variety that appealed to almost everybody. There were superheroes for the masses, funny animal comics for cartoon enthusiasts and little kids. There were westerns for fans of B-movies starring Lash LaRue and Roy Rogers. Horror, science fiction, and even educational comics were produced. If your friend was a sports jock and didn't read much, there were sports comics for him or her.

In the Silver Age, the number of publishers was drastically reduced. DC and Marvel resurrected the popularity of superhero comics, while smaller companies dabbled in them. *Archie Comics* dominated the field of teen comics. Dell and Gold Key produced comics adapted from current television shows and movies. Dell created Walt Disney titles in the Golden Age that ended up in the publishing hands of Gold Key and lasted into the 1980s (with everlasting popularity in Western Europe continuing into the present day). As kids, we read whatever was handy. *Richie Rich* from Harvey Comics was at virtually every doctor's or dentist's office in my childhood. I encountered them so often in waiting rooms that I never felt the need to buy my own. I would have preferred the more mature stories of *Green Lantern* or the *Atom*, though. But any port in a storm to combat the apprehension of a doctor's office visit!

3. Favorite Artist or Writer: The Golden Age saw a concentration of artists and writers come of age, albeit anonymously for many. Only a few gained credit for their work right on the cover or page one. Men like Bob Kane and Will Eisner alerted fans that they were the talent in charge right on the covers (even when creators like Kane had long since stopped drawing and were using uncredited people to do the work). Fans could rarely identify an artist they found appealing. It was up to the fans to single out a particular style they could identify as one artist. Dell Comics published *Donald Duck* stories in the 1940s by several artists. One artist, Carl Barks, stood out as an especially talented cartoonist. Even today, Disney Comics are prized if Barks did the art (he was known as the "good" duck artist). On the other hand, EC Comics credited the stories to almost each artist right on the first page of each story. Standouts like Frank Frazetta and Jack Davis honed their skills for successful futures within those pages and then beyond comics.

Fans were truly blessed in the 1960s. They saw Marvel glorify the talent of their personnel ("Bullpen") on the story pages and in letters columns. Great fanfare was a part of Marvel's seduction, bringing celebrity status to its Bullpen. DC Comics led the way with letters columns where fans mentioned the names of artists (DC did not go out of their way to appreciate their artists publicly; the fans would do that for them within the letters columns). Marvel's Stan Lee promoted his Bullpen (artists, writers, colorists and letterers) in editorials and announcements in each book. Stan took credit for anything he was attached to, unabashedly displaying pride for Marvel's cutting-edge comic books. For years it was just a few artists who received written recognition on the title pages of comic books. Writers, too, saw general credits by the 1960s (they were even less likely to have their names printed in a story). Fans could now discern the name of the artist whose style was most to their liking. They could hunt down monthly titles solely on those credited names alone.

Artists labored behind the scenes or under assumed names as they worked freelance for rival comic book publishers. We all recognized their styles but wondered why Ross Andru's art at DC looked like Mickey Demeo at Marvel, only to find out later that Ross was using an alias. Both DC and Marvel wanted either the best or fastest artists for the cheapest prices. Comic books from the 1960s provided younger fans like me with Jack Kirby, Steve Ditko, Neal Adams, John Romita, Gil Kane, Jim Steranko, Murphy Anderson, Joe Kubert, and many more. As my teenage years reached the midway point by 1970, I had too many favorite artists to choose from.

4. Cover Art: Let's face it: some covers just grab readers as the sole reason for ownership. Covers are designed to grab and hold the attention of prospective customers. Some covers work better than others. A particular artist may only be responsible for cover art for pure marketing reasons and rarely do interiors. For instance, I remember when Neal Adams seemed to be doing every cover for DC in the late 1960s but rarely drew the interior pages. He was the go-to cover artist for DC for that brief period, with art that displayed a dramatic flair not normally present on DC covers.

The cover art was designed to sell a comic even with interior art that did not necessarily match the exterior style. Some comics gained cover popularity because of some later story or Hollywood event. The work of contemporary artists like Glenn Fabry and Tim Bradstreet is generally only available as covers for *Preacher* (1995) and *Punisher Max* (2004), respectively.

The garish covers were a form of maturing realism for an industry that once felt it was only catering to children. Comic covers were originally built to fire up the imagery required to lure in the young readers of the prewar and war years of the 1940s. Those comics flourished in World War II with covers ranging from the benign family dynamic to the outrageously violent. War made comic books shine with action, patriotism and drama.

Favorite tastes changed with the 1950s. Violent and salacious covers appealed to an older audience that had changed with war's end. The Korean War ratcheted up the carnage and fear on comic book covers to hook all readers, but mostly older teens and men. A perceived increase in juvenile crime and reduced inhibitions found places to roost in comic books.

Photo covers became more prevalent, grabbing fans of the movie and television shows that spawned them. Celebrities on covers spoon-fed their fans and grew a populace hungry for more. Comic books exploited what the Hollywood fan magazines had been doing for years and added the photo cover niche to their litany of genres.

By the 1960s, superhero dominance took two paths. DC used word balloons, coupled with a character's actions, on its covers. Marvel placed compelling phrases on their drama-filled covers to induce buying, such as *Fantastic Four* #43 (1965): "Lo, There Shall Be An Ending."

Standout covers attained their own collectibility and rose in value on separate terms. Intricate pencils, prominence of a protagonist, or the intro of new characters gracing the cover resonated with readers. Buyers became collectors and injected the significance of these images into the hobby.

Some comics from the past gained and retained collectible status almost solely on the basis of the cover drama.

5. Quality of Comic Books: The quality, or grade, of a comic book determines value. Comic collecting has built cottage industries around the attachment of grades to any comic books within purview. As businessmen and women, we've learned to appreciate quality and capitalize on the best-looking copies of collectible comics. We recognize that high grade is sometimes synonymous with high price. Collectors buy what they like and what they can afford, but they often like the best.

The scarcity of a certain title's issues can be guessed at. Most of the superhero comics from the past 50 years exist in abundance with plenty of copies to fill demand. Less common are the highest-graded copies, and demand is correspondingly higher as well. Non-superhero comics, especially from Marvel and DC from the 1960s and 1970s, are somewhat scarcer. These include romance and western titles. It's likely that those issues are contrastingly in lower demand.

Some of DC's horror titles have crossover popularity with great covers, trendy new artists like Bernie Wrightson and Mike Kaluta, plus key first appearances. One great example is *House of Secrets* #92, the first appearance of Swamp Thing.

Get a nice copy of a scarce comic and you may be able to cash in later at a profit. CGC takes it a step further with archived census numbers that specify the quantities of comics in each grade. With that knowledge available, we generally know just how many or how few high-grade copies are around. Some copies are not known to exist in Near Mint categories, while even lower grades are uncommon. Here's an example: *Atom-Age Combat* #1 (1952) is registered with only 4 copies in the CGC census (and a small number of raw copies that filter through eBay). Fortunately, one high-grade 9.0 exists. Issue #3 also shows four copies with nothing higher than 8.0. Issue #2 does not show any copies at all. This is an uncommon title to find for sale and these census figures illustrate that fact. Their scarcity can be attributed to collectors who have locked them up for years.

For my particular collecting habits, I have to have copies that are no lower in grade than VG (at least I did until it became impossible to afford an *Amazing Fantasy* #15 in VG!).

The comics I collected had to merit ownership structurally; they had to hold their pages together by design and not through restoration or some bad patch job. Condition and appropriate grading are important.

I encountered a store customer recently who thought otherwise. In a conversation over a particular copy of *Avengers Annual* #10 (1981) we had for sale, this customer wanted a cheaper copy we did not have. He felt the $100 copy was too expensive. We explained that was an achievable price at the grade we posted. He didn't care about the grade, only the price. Ridiculous. Some balanced factoring between price and quality has to be found to prevent total chaos.

I agreed with him that a lower-grade copy would be suitable to save a little money. However, I countered by acknowledging that the higher-grade copy may continue to hold its value or even increase because of the Near Mint grade. He asked, "Is grading really that important?" Flabbergasted that this was even an issue, I ran an analogy past him about getting ripped off by unscrupulous Craigslist buyers who welcome naïve guys like him into their webs of sin. He was unimpressed in his defense of just getting a "good deal" (meaning cheap and not caring if he overpaid because he would never learn enough to know this).

The vast majority of collectors I've known use condition as a filter for picking out the books they want.

The following is an excerpt from Bob Bretall's ComicSpectrumBlog regarding his pursuit of an *Amazing Fantasy* #15. His article includes a statement regarding his appreciation of my store's standards. His experiences mirror many of the challenges we all go through to figure out how to find and purchase particular comics without feeling bitter about the performance. I've reprinted this with a few minor grammatical adjustments to keep my editor happy. Bretall's opinions definitely reflect mine:

[E]arly issues of *Spider-Man* have been on display in my comic room for many years. I get daily enjoyment out of looking at them. And in case anyone is curious (people have commented about this before), the windows they are near are sealed double-pane glass with reflective and UV blocker coating. Heat does not transfer through them. The wood shutters are typically about the same ambient temperature as the rest of the room, even when the windows are getting direct sunlight.

So, I had every issue of *Amazing Spider-Man*. But I was missing Spider-Man's first appearance, *Amazing Fantasy* #15. This is the true "Holy Grail" for any lover of Spider-Man and is also currently the most sought-after Silver Age comic, even more so than *Fantastic Four* #1, which started the Marvel Age of comics. As such, it also carries a pretty hefty price tag, and I was pretty much resigned to never getting my hands on a copy.

That was until I went to New York in October 2014 to be on *Who Wants to Be a Millionaire?*

I visited friends while I was back there and everyone seemed to have a copy of *AF* #15. Lenny had a copy. Tony had one. Rick (my co-host on the Pop-Cult Online and plus-one lifeline on *Millionaire*) had one. When they asked what I'd do with the money if I won, one of the things would have been "buy a copy of *Amazing Fantasy* #15."

Then I started to notice articles on-line about Wall Street types investing in key Silver Age comics, because the perception was that they were outperforming the stock market. Did these people actually care about comics? I'd say mostly probably not; they cared about money, but their actions were causing the prices to increase month-over-month. It became clear that the longer I waited the more it would end up costing me, if I was ever going to get a copy. But this was a substantial expense and not something to just jump into, so I had to do my research if I was really going to get serious about buying this comic.

The first step was talking to several friends who were big time into buying graded comics and also interested in the concept of investing in comics. I also talked to Dinesh Shamdasani (CEO and chief creative officer of Valiant) when I was at Stan Lee's Comikaze Expo. I'd chatted with Dinesh a number of times in the past and knew he was also big-time into getting his hands on key comics; talking to him, it seemed like it was for the love of comics with a side interest in the investment potential of these books. He gave me a lot of great advice and stressed that I'd need to do some legwork. I also talked to several comic dealers at Comikaze (an annual California convention) about the market for key books and their insights on buying/selling CGC books and key Silver Age books in general. All of these people told me about GPAnalysis for CGC'd comics and CGC Collector Society message boards.

Why CGC? For key books, particularly Marvel first issues/appearances from the early 1960s, pricing gets crazy. These are the books investors are gobbling up: the books were rising in price month over month. It's absolutely crucial to know exactly what you're getting and make sure you pay accordingly.

I'm cool with buying a comic for a couple of hundred bucks and rolling the dice on condition and whether or not it's restored. For super-key comics, the price/value differential for every half grade and the huge hit that restoration provides to the price/value means that knowing a precise grade and whether or not the book is restored makes a huge difference. I can judge grading myself if I'm buying in person, but I'm no expert on identifying restoration. If you are opening yourself up to online buying, there's a huge incentive for sellers to knowingly or unknowingly inflate the grade of a book. For non-key books this isn't that big a deal. I judge what I think the grade is based on the pictures and typically put in a high bid that's below guide value for a book a grade lower than it looks just to be on the safe side. I'm not going to overpay by any significant amount. Assessing if a book is restored from a picture is typically going to be difficult unless it's really amateur/obvious restoration.

GPAnalysis for CGC is a paid service that offers sales information, trend analysis, and other info on what CGC'd comics are selling for at a lot of the top online auction and dealer sites. This allows you to get a feeling for the minimum, maximum, and average price (by specific number grade) that the comic you're interested in has been selling for. This cost me $10 per month, and I subscribed during the months I was seeking out and buying *AF* #15. It was well worth the price, because even taking into account that prices are going up, it let me know when someone was asking for a ludicrous price based on the realized market, and also when a book was actually a pretty good deal compared to the current market (like the one I ended up buying).

The CGC Collector Society message boards are pretty typical for internet forums. There are a lot of really knowledgeable people there, but also a lot of folks who seem to get off mostly on bragging about what they have and acting superior to people who are new to the hobby (in this case, the subgenre of comic collectors who buy CGC'd comics). The forums also seemed to be very heavily trafficked by dealers who are there to buy low and sell high.

The next step in my personal journey after talking to friends and a variety of people (including dealers) was reaching out to dealers and Internet sites that specialize in Silver Age keys. I touched base with several dealers who had been recommended to me via Personal Messages on the CGC boards, but struck out there. A couple of them didn't have any copies in stock; the others were asking for more than I was willing to pay. I think most people are aware that you are rarely going to get the best price if you let a dealer know you want something really bad. That has a strong possibility of setting off $-signs in their eyes as they think they can get absolute top dollar from you because you really want what they have. This is where I needed to be disciplined. Armed with the CGC census data and GPA price analysis, I knew how many copies were out there and what they were selling for. There were plenty of copies out there: if I didn't get the one Dealer A was trying to sell, another one would be along from Dealer B tomorrow, or the following week. The bottom line was that you should take your time, set the parameters for what you want to pay, and wait until the right deal comes along. Be an informed buyer. In the end, I only ended up looking for about six weeks before I found the right book at the right price and pulled the trigger.

When I talked to Dinesh, he made the point to me that comics are one of the few forms of art where professional restoration is considered a major detractor. "Fine art" is professionally restored all the time and it's seen as a plus, preserving and enhancing a rare object. Personally, as long as the price is right, I'm perfectly fine with a restored book. That is, I'm OK if I'm paying a fair price factoring in the reduction the current market dictates for a restored book.

Back to the hunt: Since I had no luck with sellers from the CGC boards, it was time to move on to other Internet sites and dealers.

For the sites that I liked upon first examination, I set up accounts (where applicable), added the book I was looking for to my want list where that capability existed, and sent e-mails to the site owners introducing myself and describing what I was looking for. Four sites never bothered to respond to my e-mail, so they were removed from consideration. Five sites responded to my e-mails. Three of them within a couple of hours (and this was on a Sunday afternoon), the other two by the following morning (Monday).

I got some nice notes back from each of these guys, but unfortunately none of them had any copies of *AF* #15 for sale. They mostly let me know that they'd keep an eye out, with the exception of Jamie Newbold, who had several copies, none for sale. It turns out that he had decided to buy up key Silver Age comics for investment purposes, building a nest egg for retirement. While this wasn't going to do me any good for the purposes of buying *AF* #15, it was great for another reason. Southern California Comics is in San Diego less than an hour's drive from my home. I drove down there the following Saturday with my wife and we talked to Jamie. He's a great guy, extremely knowledgeable, and willing to share his experience.

Jamie is probably the most important factor in my now owning a copy of *Amazing Fantasy* #15, even though he didn't sell it to me himself. By speaking to my wife and me at length about the investment potential of these key Silver Age books, as well as the fact that he himself was buying these books as an investment, it really drove home for my wife that while I don't primarily consider comics to be an investment, and I would not buy them solely as an investment, it sure is nice to know that any money spent on them is not money wasted on some ephemeral object of my affection. There is a tangible value associated with these books. You won't lose money on them, and they are an actual asset.

So, I had put out all kinds of feelers. I had done my research. Now it was time for the waiting game of examining the copies of *Amazing Fantasy* #15 offered for sale at the various venues, deciding which ones were good deals, and making offers or bids on them as appropriate. Believe me, I didn't come close to getting the first comic I took a try at. I was outbid on a number of comics by people who obviously wanted those specific comics more than I did because they were willing to pay more money. No harm, no foul. I knew more would come along, and they did, almost every day. *AF* #15 is a very heavily traded book. I mentioned before it is probably the hottest Silver Age book out there. I put in offers on "Buy it Now" listings that had a "best offer" option. I didn't low-ball anyone. I put in offers strictly based on a fair price according to GPA and added notes to the sellers explaining my rationale. I had a lot of these rejected with the sellers deciding they'd like to set a new high price. This conflicted with my personal criteria which were to pay *at least slightly* under the existing high. While always desirable for the seller, as a buyer I didn't want to be setting any records for price paid.

And then I saw it. A really sharp-looking copy that was restored, which meant it looked a lot better than the price I'd have to pay for an unrestored copy in the same condition. Plus, it was a certified Signature Series book signed by Stan Lee. As a Signature Series book, it got a yellow label from CGC, with a much smaller purple band along the top indicating the restoration. This meant it would not be screaming restored from across the room.

As desirable as an unrestored book? No, but acceptable, given that I thought I could get it for about what I would otherwise have paid for a book in 2.5 condition looking considerably more beat-up, and I really was looking for some eye candy to put on display. It was not just a book to be squirreled away in a safe deposit box.

I decided to make a run at this book. It had a Buy It Now price and a "Best Offer" option. With a bit of negotiation back and forth via Personal Messages, the seller and I came to an agreement on price. They told me to put in a "Best Offer" at the agreed-upon price, which I thought was very fair while still being what I considered to be a great deal. The offer was placed as agreed, accepted, and I had just bought my Grail book. (Please don't ask me to tell you the specific amount paid. I'd rather not say, but the ballpark price can be figured out easily enough using the techniques I've described here.)

Editor's note: "Slabbing" is the vernacular term for the container third-party graders use to encase a comic book after grading.

6. Age: Old comics are just plain cool. Owning them now is like traveling in time. They are weird and cool and different, so therefore worth owning! Over the years my friends and I have elevated this principle to put 1930s and pre–World War II comics on a pedestal.

For us the oldest comics, often the scarcest, are the comics we tend to keep. Eighty-year-old comics just don't pop up that much in the wild, but primarily in the hands of dealers. They're built differently from those of ten years later. They look different and the characters often acted differently.

Quality comics are not necessarily finite entities. Modern Age comics exist everywhere in high grade. Older comics can be found in high grades. New collections of pre–Silver Age stuff surface all the time. Grade hunters know this, with some holding out hope that they will finally find their white-paged Centaurs or some such antique in prime grade. Grade hunters have scoured collections for the best-of-the-best and found them. Some Golden Age comic book owners had innate desires to keep their comic books tidy. They protected the quality of their possessions. Still, more readers inadvertently kept comic books in storage under ideal circumstances. Those collections often resurfaced in like-new appearance and obtained pedigree names to highlight their tremendous appeal.

Many high-grade copies of comics from the Gold and Silver Ages have been brought to market since the 1960s. *OPG* speculated on prices for copies of vintage comics that may not exist in high grades. They theorized early on that there's a reasonable certainty that some examples exist in the world. With the creation of third-party grading, collectors hunt for the grade over the title, knowing that imagined top grades do actually exist. Outside of a handful of obscure copies, super-high grade 9.9s and 10.0s do not exist and are rarely up for sale. The more modern releases do contain 9.9s and 10.0s. The goal of buyers geared towards those examples is to own the "Holy Grail" 9.9s and 10.0s, whatever the title may be.

I did a little research to find the statistics for two random Modern Age books. I figure a few demonstration models will help illustrate what's in store for buyers looking for high-grade keys. My criteria were CGC grades at 9.9 and 10.0. The two books I chose were *Spawn* #1 from 1992 and *Spider-Man* #1 (McFarlane series) from 1990. They're plentiful with comprehensive statistics to draw from to complete a picture. There's also an almost mystical reverence for these comics by fans of the Modern Age.

First, I went over the original sales figures to see how many copies were printed. *Spawn* #1 saw a distribution of 1.7 million copies. This was Todd McFarlane's first project as part owner of Image Comics after his era with Marvel. *Spawn* #1 was comics' first glimpse at this perennial character and McFarlane's celebrity rose with this title. CGC census statistics totaled 4,342 copies in 2015. Six copies were 10.0s while 63 were 9.9s. 9.8 hit at 2,304 copies. eBay sales listed at thirty days' archive no CGC sales above 9.8. An average price for a 9.8 copy is $80.00. Tracking statistics through another website, GPAnalysis.com, documents the following from sales figures:

10.0: sold once (2008) for $616.00
9.9: nine copies from 2011–2015 with the last recorded copy selling for $810.00 (June 2015)

9.8s are much more common with 2,304 copies documented to present (late 2016) against 9.6s at 987 copies and 9.4s at 490. I would have expected to see those numbers somewhat reversed with the lower grades more common. The fact that high-grade 9.8s are five times as likely to be available than 9.4s tells you that vying for a high-grade *Spawn* #1 is not a battle worth fighting. The last recorded sale for such a high-grade 9.8 copy was only $75.00 in 2016. Heritage Auctions, one of the largest repositories for information on CGC sales, recorded no *Spawn* #1s with universal blue labels selling above the grade of 9.8.

Spider-Man #1 was a new title written and drawn by McFarlane two years before *Spawn* got started. Marvel expected prominent sales based upon his popularity as a Spidey artist on *Amazing Spider-Man*. 2,350,000 copies comprising several variants (11 in total) were printed of the kick-off issue. Sales were over the top with multiple reprints (featuring their own variant covers) also issued. All told, 2,650,000 were believed to be distributed.

McFarlane's *Spider-Man* #1 records the following stats: a month of eBay sales displayed no copies higher than 9.8 (June 2016).

CGC census figures list 14 extant copies in 10.0, 83 copies in 9.9, and 2358 copies in 9.8 (as of June 2016). You can add another 19 copies in 9.9 for the Gold Variant (which was a second printing). No 10.0s were graded after 2015. It does seem incredible to me that between 2015 and the middle of 2016 no 10.0s were graded out of roughly 220 submitted copies that were at least 9.8. Where did all the future 10.0s go?

GPAnalysis notes two copies in 10.0 have traded hands in 2013 and then nothing since. The most recent sale in 2013 was for $417. Clearly, a book of such distribution magnitude could have generated more 10.0s, but only the few exist. So when they come to market, a feeding frenzy would follow. 9.9 saw 17 copies sold beginning in 2014 with a recent copy selling for $389 in mid–2016. The three years encompassing 2011–2013 displayed 50 copies sold in 9.9. A portion of those 9.9s were the same copies selling more than once. Few owners were selling their copies.

Heritage Auctions shows the following:

10.0–3 copies sold since 2008, ranging from regular copies at $287 to $374 and a silver edition at $657 (as of late 2015).

The bottom line for these statistics is that both *Spawn* #1 and *Spider-Man* #1 were heavily sold and collected at first, but they lack real significance in the back-issue market of the new millennium. They are heavily touted as key books, but they're keys from a "glut" period of production. The scarce quantities at the top of the scale give these items a high demand, driven more for the grade than the comic story or art importance. Saturation at 9.8 and lower indicates supply and demand have met somewhere in the middle. These books are not "key" enough to go out and splurge on raw copies for grading submission. The chances of getting better than 9.8, a $62 book at best, are slim to none.

In contrast, they are favorites to get signed by either Stan Lee or Todd McFarlane. They are easily and cheaply bought and look good to many collectors in a slab with a Signature Series label. My store still gets calls weekly from comic book owners offering to sell their collections. More often than not, they have either "the hot" *Spawn* #1 and/or "the hot" *Spider-Man* #1 as their lead-off issues to tease potential buyers. It used to be funny.

7. First Issues: Number ones are all the rage, or at least they were until the last ten years of publishing buried us in #1s. *Spawn* #1 and *Spider-Man* #1s are glommed onto because they were firsts, mostly for heavy fan favorite McFarlane, but primarily because they were #1s at a time when that really mattered. They have spectacular art, but they're not scarce. The covers are gorgeous, but then so are most of McFarlane's covers.

The market is most exciting when a key first issue is up for grabs. From *Action Comics* #1 to *Savage She-Hulk* #1 (1980), first issues are targeted for the challenge and the likelihood that they will always be collectible. Many number-one issues have entered the halls of collecting history. They are once and always "chosen" comics on the lists of buyers before issue #2 even becomes a consideration. The only changes are value and availability. Number-one issues have great demand, which decreases availability. There's scuttlebutt aplenty on social networks ridden with posts boasting or posting about #1s. The fires to buy are fueled by consistent talk about number-one issues of potentially "hot" comic books.

There are plenty of worthless number-one issues, but don't tell that to the speculators caught up in movie hype. Every number-one issue is considered a project that might get picked up for a show, so many quick-buck artists are holding onto the dream that their bargain-bin "number one" purchases will pan out one day.

As a young collector, I went for DC and Marvel #1s because, frankly, there were a finite number that had been published prior to the 1970s. After that it became more or less repetitive, with characters starting over again periodically in their own premiere issues. There's always another number-one issue just around the corner for the *Legion of Super-Heroes* and *Teen Titans*.

I looked for the issues that came before me. I thought those were the most collectible and still do. The Forensic Comicologist retains a deeper love for the ancients.

8. Keys: Number ones can be keys as well as first appearances and so on. Keys can be the first appearances of a particular artist, writer or character. *OPG* helps immensely with key identification. Every source of information about comic books leads readers to comments and analysis of key comic books.

A lay person can log onto eBay for comics to buy or sell and quickly discover how key comics are valued. Any key on eBay draws moths to flames as the bid histories rise in number. The same will not be true for the non-key issues in the same run.

A pure example of this observation can be summed up with a typical listing for *Incredible Hulk* #181 (1975), the first full appearance of Wolverine. It's listed as a NM- and had 79 bids by the closing of June 2, 2016. Closing price was $2,800, well below GPA value for a graded copy, but still strong money for a raw copy. That's the fire in the belly of key issue buyers hard at work!

Issue #180 featured Wolverine in a cameo panel on the last page. It's technically Wolverine's first appearance, but its key status can't compete with #181. I found a copy on eBay within the same timeframe as #181, also graded as a NM-, raw. The owner of this semi-key book found his auction stalled at $374. No one was biting. That's a little better than half the value of a CGC graded copy. Perhaps the condition was in question by viewers, but the long game is that it's not a strong enough comic to reach key book status. Fans have designated #181 as the real McCoy, while #180 is second fiddle.

Here's another conundrum within the key world: Spider-Man's first time at bat. We know *Amazing Fantasy* #15 was his first appearance. We know it has colossal demand and extreme prices. But it's not his #1 issue. That falls to *Amazing Spider-Man* #1, following the success of *AF* #15. To prepare a comparison on their mutual key statuses, I'll use both *Overstreet Price Guide* and GPAnalysis for prices. I'll use an average grade of Fine/6.0 between the two to match values:

> *AF* #15 June 2015 (most recent sale) CGC 6.0 = GPA $38,246
> *OPG* =$20,000 (2015–16 volume)

Current market value plays havoc with *OPG*'s somewhat limited ability to keep up with changes within a given year, but these are heavy numbers for a grade that went for six or seven thousand dollars years ago.

Now, doing the same chart comparison with *Amazing Spider-Man* #1, we see:

GPA 2016 (most recent sale) = 6.0 $8,600
OPG 2015–16 = 6.0 $5,400

Amazing Spider-Man #1 begins a series that ran nonstop from 1963 to 1998. That's a tremendous, historical run considering how often titles were canceled and restarted over the years. *ASM* did start over, and then continued its old numbering with a second series, confusingly carrying it into the new millennium to issue #700.

I've outlined a hierarchy of key status for certain comics. A character can only appear first once. But he, she or it can appear in number-one issues any time it suits a publisher. All those #1s do not make them key books in the sense that they are worth investing in. *Amazing Spider-Man* #1 is the less expensive alternative to an *AF* #15 for those who are willing to accept *ASM* #1 for its lesser-tier key status.

Some key books remain out of reach for collectors. I found money in the early 1970s to buy keys as I took comic collecting more seriously. Some issues like *Fantastic Four* #1 (1961) stayed out of reach for years as its key status continually outshined *AF* #15. I had to resort to low-grade copies in many cases of keys I wanted to own. Nothing has changed 40 years later as those old keys are still expensive, some-

Charles Atlas ads targeted comic book readers for decades. There were so many variations of these ads that I was able to wallpaper one wall at Richard Alf's Comic Kingdom with them. No two of those ads on the wall were alike!

times barely within reach. But new keys are generated periodically thanks to Hollywood. There are enough affordable key books of something or other for all collectors to enjoy the hunt.

As we learned earlier, my copy of *All Negro Comics* #1 (1947) fits several bullet points for collectibility: scarcity, age, and quality of the copy (it's a nice 2.0 Good grade with a corner of the copy missing, but the rest of the copy looks nice).

Other factors for collecting comics drive some people. More extreme search criteria might include themes. I sell to a lot of golfers with golf-cover fetishes, for instance. Themes and fetishes can be categories for collecting. People are looking for graphic crime or sexual innuendo covers/contents. I had a friend who was a big war comic buff. He was hooked on flame-thrower covers. We both joked about it because the graphic use of a flame thrower is somewhat grisly and repulsive. That was really what he was aiming for. I've catered to surfing cover fans, bowling fans, the classic "eye injury" fans, Christmas fans, and more. Of course, the sexy woman covers appeal to an even wider audience than just the fetish enthusiasts.

Occasionally people search for comics they once owned and want them for nostalgia. If you can stretch your imagination into collecting realms more obscure, I'm sure it's already been done by somebody.

The Forensic Comicologist has experienced many awkward requests for weirdly-themed covers. There are collectors who search for ads, like the Charles Atlas muscle-gain ads run on the backs of comic books for decades.

Those ads were out of touch with comic book readers in the 1970s. Clearly the advertising world couldn't separate the readers of the 1940s from the readers of the 1970s. We still appeared to be easy targets for a little mental manipulation by whoever thought they could make a buck off us. Comic book people seemed to still be considered "outsiders" by mainstream standards: weaklings, antisocial bookworms, or just plain weird. We thought differently and looked at stupid marketing ideas like those posted by Charles Atlas and others as laughable. Many of us were raised on the satire of *MAD Magazine*. The Forensic Comicologist loves that type of sardonic humor, both wry and silly.

We were all maturing beyond the reach of a commercial society that didn't understand us.

7

Fast Forward

As a store owner, I get daily callers offering me comic collections. Most of the stores in San Diego get these frequent offers. Every store, craigslist.com, buyer-listing, and print advertiser for comics gets these calls—often daily, sometimes hourly. All told, we get as many as 1,200 calls a year to buy comic collections. Sounds good, right? Maybe.

Sometimes the sheer volume of product still out there can be a burden to purchase for resale. Just because a comic book is old doesn't make it rare, valuable or even desirable. Sometimes the market is less for those books than book values claim. Sometimes comics are no longer popular or fans are used to buying them from dealers who make a living selling comics for a quarter. You never know.

In the land of supply and demand, lots of issues have too much of one and not enough of the other. I figure the best instrument for discussion is laying out some figures so the reader can put into perspective just how many comics are out there.

Take a look at some circulation figures I've inserted. These are randomly selected sales figures comparing the circulation numbers (from Comichron.com) of popular titles from 1969 versus their 2009 counterparts. (Note: These are average figures for any one month within the given year. These are figures gathered through reference sites online that collected and retained these statistics.)

Batman 1969 = 356,000 copies per month
2009 = 76,936 copies per month
Superman 1969 = 372,352 copies per month
2009 70,118 copies per month, with a significant drop toward the end of that year to 62,517 monthly copies

That time frame shows how popular comic books were a generation or two ago. Compared to today's circulation figures, we Modern Age comic book fans are not pulling our weight! The disparity in circulation figures also illustrates just how many potential copies may still be out there. Certainly the 1969 models I used for *Batman* and *Superman* are prominent reminders of what successes comic books were back then.

Consequently, pulling in those 1969 issues of *Batman* and *Superman* may not be that big an achievement, since they may still be all over the place.

I dug a little more and found stats that were less separated by time. In this case I chose *Wonder Woman* beginning with 1985. That year she drew a circulation number of 84,500 copies. By 2013 she was reduced to fewer than 35,000 copies at market. Again, I'm showing the reader just what was printed at the time and possibly still exists in quantity today. Not rare, not even uncommon, like some eBay listings would lead you to believe.

The drop in figures for all three titles is a pure example of a nationwide drop in the interest of comic book readers for three name-brand DC Comics characters. Drawing back a bit to look at a bigger picture, 1969 saw a total distribution number for all DC titles at 5,285,131 copies. Marvel enjoyed a larger number with 8,042,000 circulated comic books. This totaled a whopping 13,327,131 copies for the Big Two companies for a year in the heart of the Baby Boomer generation. However, the major social upheavals of that segment of the population were to change the sales of comic books.

Even more telling are the general total numbers from the mid–1980s, a bridge point for two generations: 1985 saw grand total numbers of 10 million copies distributed for all companies, versus 6.6 million in 2002.

Obviously, the good old days of the 1960s produced whopping circulation counts for many comic books. Yet those figures are small by 1940s standards: *Action Comics* alone sold 900,000 copies a month in 1941!

Various external changes in American habits diminished the desire to buy comics by the 1960s. Television attracted an audience growing away from comics. Newsstands that barely supported racks of comics were slowly removing them for other retail products. Teenagers who were impressionable in the 1950s were now parents in the 1960s. These families still felt the turn-off toward comics that they grew up with. The comics once entertaining on adult levels were all but gone.

Back then, parents tended to ignore any intrinsic value comics held, seeing them as a distraction for children. They spoke to their kids about how "stupid" or "bad" comic books were. In the 1950s and 1960s, baby boomers were inclined to "discover" comic books that were coincidentally written for their evolving tastes. I'm a baby boomer. I was raised by a doting dad who loved comics and thought they were a great way to teach kids to read. The comics he bought me were written with more sophisticated plot devices and dialogue than the comics of the 1940s (for the most part). I would get a hold of *Batman* circa 1968 and feel the writer was speaking to me, not talking to a little kid. Conversely, I read reprints and worn copies of the old 1940s and 1950s *Batman* comics and felt that they were written for little kids. They were not necessarily my cup of tea and I found them silly.

By the 1970s, comic book circulation was at the lowest ebb since their inception. Comic book specialty stores began to grow in numbers as a way to enhance profit. Plenty of comic book fans owned large collections. Comic cons expanded the collective knowledge that comic books were in fact "good." Comic book store owners filled the gaps left by slowing newsstand and supermarket sales. The advent of direct-market sales changed the very nature of comic book retailing. Now, comics could be purchased directly from publishers and shipped without interfacing with troublesome distributors. Comic book stores could order copies without limits and be reasonably assured to get them (at better discounts).

When I worked at Comic Kingdom, Richard Alf, the owner, was a forward thinker supportive of the Comic-Con beginnings in San Diego (and was part of the founding membership).

Richard began his tenure as a comic book store owner with the second store in town. Both stores were limited when it came to buying new comics at wholesale prices. The only option was ARA Distributors out of their multi-thousand-square-foot warehouse.

Comics were about twenty-five cents a copy back then, which doesn't sound like much by today's standards. But Richard managed to pay us from the income gained from selling those twenty-five-cent comics and still support the store.

Richard bought what he needed for our store with a minimal twenty or twenty-five percent discount, maybe five cents off cover price for most comics. Not much. He could return the unsold copies for credit, but there was no leverage to get better discounts. Richard soon glommed onto the rising distribution fad of "direct market" distribution. He was still picking up comic books at ARA, the local periodical distributor, to fill our normal minimum orders. ARA distributed to chain grocery stores, newsstands, liquor stores and the like. Nobody at their end was concerned about quality control or preparing for some upheaval in a comic book storyline. Soon he was able to kiss ARA goodbye.

I accompanied Richard and then-store manager Greg Pharis on at least two trips to ARA to pick up comics for the week ahead. The massive repository for all periodical distribution in the city had to be about 20,000 square feet in size. The magazines of all types and titles were stacked in bins or on shelves neatly lined in rows throughout the building. Comic books were segregated in one area for easy shopping.

I don't remember how they were originally packed at the printing plant, but by the time we got to them at ARA, they were freely stacked on the shelves. Our job was to count the number of copies we wanted of each title and then cart them over to a conveyer belt that ended with a cashier. Once they were paid for, we hauled them out to our vehicle and back to the shop. I thought the process was kind of fun. I was dazzled by all those stacks of cool new comics, and we could take as many as we wanted! Just thinking about the stuff that I would have seen back then makes my mouth water. I mean, just think about it—that would have been 1975, the year that *Giant-Size X-Men* came out. If I was there accompanying Richard or Greg that week, I would have helped count out a handful of copies from a large stack of *GS X-Men* #1s. All the copies would have been in generally pristine shape at only twenty-five cents a copy minus our discount! Forensic comicologists and all other fans get weepy over memories like these.

When Richard shifted over to direct market, he placed his orders for comics for our store through the distribution network built up by Phil Seuling, progenitor behind direct marketing and a comic book guy. With occasional exceptions, all our weekly comics came through the direct-market process, meaning they were shipped to the store. There was no pick-up spot in town; it was all done through the mail.

As employees, Richard allowed us to take advantage of direct-market orders. We could piggyback quantities of comics we wanted to sell later on top of his orders. Our additional numbers helped him to improve the discounts he received from Seuling. Direct market did not allow the unsold copies to be returned anywhere for credit, so Richard owned what he could not sell. Conversely, Richard had instant inventory at better order discounts for back-issue and mail order sales. He could have done the same with ARA—purchased more wholesale copies than he expected to sell immediately—but that was risky back then. Nobody knew if a comic book store had long-term sustainability in San Diego at that time. Hoarding new comics for later resale was not considered a safe bet. At least Seuling's ideas provided a better discount, say 50 percent, and took some of the sting out of retaining unsold copies.

Store owners like Richard could guarantee a healthy selection of back issues by having control over their monthly orders at more affordable prices.

As I was saying earlier, Richard shifted more of his store orders to direct market. He allowed his employees (three of us) to place secondary orders for our own purposes. By piggybacking our wants on his orders, he got a better wholesale discount. We'd sell our copies at Comic-Con. An historical example was the 1976 release of *Howard The Duck* #1 (discussed earlier). Richard calculated the store's needs and how many copies filled a case. One full case measured out to so many copies and met a tier discount Richard aimed for. We bought the excess copies from the store and hoarded them for outside sales. Issue #1 was cover priced at 25 cents. I remember the demand ramped up with the growing popularity. This was a character that spoke to, or for, a generation jaded by war, politics and a generation gap. In the post-hippie era, Howard was considered hip.

Within weeks, *Howard the Duck* was on fire. Comic Kingdom sold through the first lot of #1s. We held copies back to exploit the demand and raised prices. Before we were through, copies of #1 were selling at $40.00! This was a relatively new phenomenon for us. When Comic-Con came around, we turned huge profits off our copies of Howard, matching the store's sales success.

Richard seemed okay with our side sales, but after a while he was annoyed that we were selling to people he felt he should be selling to. Eventually Greg, part-time employee Hans and I were fired. This was a time after Richard opened up a mail-order warehouse miles from the store. He used the building to store large numbers of back issues, and he had me and others file the books and keep them organized. Greg ran the store and I shifted back and forth between the two locations. Oddly, Richard paid me cash to work the store and comics to work the warehouse.

I definitely took advantage of the work-for-comics plan by fishing out the best stuff, like Neal Adams comics, in lieu of cash payment. Those books then went downtown to Comic-Con. Those were the hot books then, the *Batman* titles, *Avengers*, *Green Lantern*, *Green Arrow*, and the like. Those comics were so in demand that the store couldn't keep them in stock. Greg had me bring copies to sell at the store whenever I was at the warehouse. Of course, we were selling them at Richard's store for Richard. This was part of our job. The comics I got paid with were for me with Richard's blessing, but he got buggy over taking others to sell for the store. That's where the terminations came in.

Richard's excuse was that we were taking money away from him, stealing as he put it, even though we were simply selling them at his store for him. He cried that the mail-order side of the business needed those hot books more, that he couldn't meet demand. He fired us and even fought us over our unemployment insurance. At a hearing over our unemployment claims, he again accused us of stealing. The unemployment department arbitrator didn't buy his line and granted us our unemployment checks.

In reality, the reason for the firings was a little more sinister than false accusations. Richard had hired a warehouse manager, a former Colorado comic book store manager. That guy wanted the store and convinced Richard to give it to him to run. But first he needed to get the three of us out of his way. Richard bought into this BS and fired us with trumped-up charges.

That would be the first and only time the future Forensic Comicologist would ever get fired.

This kind of thing was happening nationwide. Comic book stores grew in popularity and numbers. Distribution of comic books rose in volume, and people in the business were making decent livings. Comic book circulation was on the rise again.

The publishers enjoyed the increased business and began experimenting with their output: better paper, miniseries, gimmicks, and expansion of character titles ensued. These alternative formats added to the flood of comic book sales. Circulation figures were on the rise. Independent comic book producers added to the pot, too. The black-and-white, independently-published comic craze of the 1980s swept through the States. Small publishers took root and fared well for at least a few years. Soon, the 1990s would have its boom of comic sales as well.

DC's *Batman* and *Superman* crossover events dominated their superhero markets. Superman was killed and Batman's back was broken. Two of the most exciting villains introduced for these stories, Doomsday and Bane, are still the best bad guys to hit DC comics in twenty years. The "Death of Superman" and "Knightfall" story events were extremely popular, seemed to go on forever, and are still read today.

Marvel struck gold (and platinum) with *Spider-Man* #1 (1990) and *X-Men* #1 (1991). Prodigal Marvel sons Todd McFarlane and Jim Lee were given carte blanche to do what they wanted as long as they were making Marvel a lot of money. Copies of both titles were flying off the shelves, encouraging more gimmicks and printings. Unfortunately for Marvel, Todd and Jim would be gone very soon.

Todd, Jim and other hot Marvel artists all jumped ship and began their own comic book company. Image Comics came on strong in 1992 and floored the country with top-notch art and "in your face" stories; art and action "Powed!" the competition. The former Marvelites now had complete control over their own projects and didn't have to put up with the demands of an overbearing company.

Smaller companies like Dark Horse Comics thoughtfully attended to licensed movie projects. *Aliens*, *Predator*, and *Terminator* adaptations extended lifelines to their movie fans. Guys like me who couldn't get enough of the movies could get our fill through the comics. Dark Horse produced *Star Wars* sequels, prequels, and spin-offs, which dazzled the dedicated.

Sales figures began climbing to new heights. Just as an example, *Amazing Spider-Man* printed over a half-million copies in one month in 1972. By 1992, Marvel recorded 660,958 copies. The trend, as often as not, was down instead of up until this new highpoint in sales and distribution.

The sheer volume of comics produced was heightened by rampant speculation. Anybody could buy tons of comics and sit on them for a supposed payoff at various venues like comic conventions. The industry was watching, so they exploited everything new as "Collector's Items!" and too many buyers bought into this farce. Copies were literally being manufactured in numbers greater than actual readers or buyers. Stores were stockpiling copies they intended to sell at a later time of their choosing. Retailers with unlimited access to distributor accounts bought and sold from small conventions, mail-order catalogs and garages.

Home computers were about ten years old and quickly finding acceptance nationwide. Computers provided another method to reach customers. Everybody was gearing up to make large amounts of money selling relatively new comics to the public at large. But sales to whom?

It had to be too good to last.

There is a reason my store claims to receive 1,000 comic book collection offers a year. There are millions of comic books out there, many of them from the speculator/hoarders of two decades ago. It's the story of an exploited market stuck with thousands of boxes of comics when the bubble burst in the mid–1990s. All the comic book publishers at that time were praying for the overindulgence of fans (read: speculators) and enjoying circulation increases not seen in a while.

Marvel was the top retailer, as it has been ever since (with a brief respite for DC when they hit it big with a couple of story events and the changes to New 52 in 2011, and then again with DC Rebirth). Marvel churned out titles under the long-held attitude that if some character(s) is selling well, print more. Marvel helped lead the way to overindulgence, but they were not the sole culprits.

Marvel enjoyed boom times as they went through ownership changes that happened more than once. When Marvel ended up in the hands of Revlon's Ron Perelman, growing pains were induced. New ownership tested the waters with price increases and title multiplication beyond anything Marvel had seen since the early 1950s!

At first, Marvel's shotgun approach spread across comic book racks and made money. But Marvel put together other slick business moves that ultimately led to financial collapse. The impact of Marvel's succubus-like behavior resonated with comic book people. Marvel's greed and arrogance impacted comic book stores as well. By 1993, fans were experiencing cover price increases across the board. And it wasn't just comics: the sports card hobby grasped in every direction and formulated its own future hurdles by running a hobby known for its longevity into the ground.

I remember walking through a Sears once and passing a kiosk in the store, selling sports cards. "Collectible" sports cards! Talk about exploitation! Sears in the collectibles business: ridiculous!

Comic book stores were everywhere, too; all over San Diego. It seemed there was a store in every ZIP code; sometimes two and three, way more than those communities could logically support. At one point, I counted five stores within

(Left to right): Employees Ray Monte Holmes, Rob Mediavilla, and Bob Capoocia unloading boxes of comics purchased on some road trip is a common occurrence in our business, ca. 2016.

two miles of each other! That doesn't even count the hobby stores, sports card stores, and whatever other stores carried comics (Walmart, Target, etc.).

I walked through a Sears department store in San Diego's East County as a shortcut from the parking lot into the shopping center proper. I was walking along an aisle reserved for kitchen stuff and household wares when I spotted a kiosk crammed in between appliances and dishes. The sign above said "Collectible Sports Cards." I didn't register the name of the booth or if it was in fact a Sears-owned feature. It simply looked like any small booth I might see at a swap meet or a fair. Not grandiose like a large convention setting, but certainly an oddity for a department store chain. I looked closely at the cards under glass. They were honest-to-God individually priced collectible sports cards, the kind one would expect to see at a true sports card store or a sports card convention (or on the Internet!). It all seemed so shallow to me: like if Sears is going into collectibles, how will collectibles stores even survive?

And please don't get me started on the prospect of Walmart sensing blood in the water and going vintage retail!

We already deal with Amazon.com and a slew of corporate sites that attempt to remove small stores from the equation. By the way, Sears is still at it. They offer collectible sports cards on a Sears web site. Sheesh!

Finally, there was the quality of the comic books by the early 1990s. Cookie-cutter artists and uninspired writers ground out whatever the commanders above required. Readers construed that as declining effort, and saw the constant new titles and price increases as the publishers stacking the deck against them.

Even the back-issue market blackened the realm with prices over retail—as if hundreds of thousands of boxes of near-new comics were scarce, but with unlimited demand.

Collapse was destined.

And when collapse came, it figuratively swallowed up stores whole, seemingly in an instant. I have friends estimating that 30 stores closed over a two-year period starting in 1993. This San Diego County shutdown even included businesses that carried comics on the side. Many people suffered. Others survived and struggled, while even more people simply put everything into storage to wait for another opportunity, while paying storage fees.

My friends and I looked around at the devastation: shuttered stores and a shortage of places to buy decent back issues. One had to drive up to Los Angeles to find stores with decent runs of back issues (Comicmania in Orange County was the closest at that time, with great back issue selections going back to the Golden and even Platinum Ages).

I was just getting back into the hobby through successful and successive San Diego Comic-Cons. Selling was a snap at the shows if you could afford a booth (many could not). The hang-up was gathering replacement inventory.

Finding collections requires effort and knowledge that penetrate the somewhat confusing vastness of comics printed since the 1980s. Dealers like me learned how to breed discretionary prowess, to differentiate the best from the rest after piles of purchased comic book collections. It made sense to respect some frugality when it came to acquiring collections. It made no sense, for instance, to buy out a storage room of common 1990s comics in bulk so the owner could get out of the monthly rent, then turn around and rent another storage room ourselves. Off-loading thousands of comics purchased cheaply can be troublesome. I think bulking them out while paying rent on them may not be lucrative over time. The alternative to getting rid of them fast and cheap is to live with them, bring them into your house or apartment to minimize offsite rent. Good luck finding love with that lifestyle.

Back in the day, comic collections surfaced with owners bringing them to comic conventions for a once and only appearance. They knew about the shows and reasoned they could get the prices they imagined, selling directly to attendees. Some just wanted to get rid of their collections but didn't want to deal locally with strangers. At the conventions, little did these collection owners know the dealers would see them as prey and mount assaults before the attendees even entered the building.

If you wanted old issues at prices guaranteed to make money, your chances were good at any convention. The people who wanted to off-load some relative's comics could easily get into any convention. Booths were available, or attendees could just walk in with a collection and march from dealer to dealer to try to hook a buyer. The San Diego Convention masters (owners, promoters, the city) had not yet learned they could squeeze exhibitors beyond their financial capacity. Example: Comic-Con International cost me $5,800 (2016) for two end booths ($6,300 for 2017!). That's a lot, but the San Diego show does not have union labor that charges a per diem to forklift exhibitors' merchandise into the exhibition hall with no move-in fees. At the New York Comic Con, you must pay union rates to forklift your stuff in. It's just more overhead and more grief.

But it all got junked as comic buyers reset the standards for value. In the mid–1990s,

A snapshot of our booth at Comic-Con International 2015.

the storage of unsold comic boxes seemed to make sense; rent a storage unit or push your car out of your garage. Just store those comics for a rainy day. But that rainy day never came. It became clear eventually that no one was jumping to buy unsold comic book store repositories of forgettable comics with any ferocity. Ads popped up in newspapers to sell comics by the thousands—whole stores even! These were the swan songs of dying and dead comic book stores. Comic shops that once thrived at comic cons were now encumbered with quarter bins to make a buck trying to get any cash for their inventory. Boxes of cheap books were stacked on top of tables, under tables, and behind tables, show-stock that would barely make expenses even if all of it sold. The conventions themselves lost the ability to attract new back-issue retailers. Or I should say they forced those local guys out of the exhibitor halls with overly expensive dealer rates for booths. That typified the end of the 1990s and the beginning of the new century.

eBay was just beginning to fill the Internet with more and more of the same: unwanted and unloved wholesale boxes of *Ghost Rider*, *Micronauts*, *Superman*, and *Alpha Flight*. Hundreds of thousands of comic books sat around, anchoring down their owners. The once imagined quick riches from large stashes of semi-old comic books turned to mush when they hit the Internet.

Buyers were choosy and selective, more interested in getting select books cheap in high grade. The heyday books from 1990s phenom publishers like Valiant, Image and others were suddenly negligible when offered for sale online. I don't think many people realized just how many copies were out there until they all showed up for sale at eBay's inception.

There was a theory, more of a prediction, that come 20 years later those discarded comic books would find collectibility. The presumption was that the people who bought them the first time would become nostalgic and buy them back at the 20-year mark. Close to the opposite has happened, with most of that material still worth little, even nothing, by 2016.

I ran local print ads to buy comic books in the 1990s and into the new decade. Scanning garage sales and swap meets was hit or miss, and there were plenty of people to compete against. Usually swap meets involved dealing with other guys doing what I was doing. I needed comic book owners looking to unload collections without the hassle of other resellers picking alongside me. The ads in papers were successful.

I ran ads in free local papers that were in racks in front of virtually every grocery store in the city and county. I posted my phone number in those listings, receiving about a call a day. The pickings were small at first, mostly recent comics. Occasionally, I reacted to offers for older books with key issues included, the sales of which would provide more seed money. I advanced my tactics a bit and created a business name, acquiring a business license. The upgrade in style enticed sellers to choose me for the legitimacy. A business license also gives the impression that one can be held liable for negative actions. Clearly if you're held accountable because of a public persona, it's harder to hide bad doings. Of course, that's a guise put on by the unscrupulous as well, but not me. I started getting referrals and repeat business once the word got out. I handed out business cards at conventions and met dealers ready to quit the hobby. Slowly, good things were happening.

I "briefcased" it to shows if I did not have a booth and did comic book business in the aisles. "Briefcasing" is the term we use for sellers wandering the aisles of any convention looking to offload a small number of comics. We love briefcase dealers because you never know what comic book gems are inside. In fact, at a recent comic book show, I saw a friend of mine carrying his briefcase. I watched dealers prowl him with their eyes, hoping for the chance to get at what was inside. (Nothing. He was hoping to fill it with comics at the show.) One dealer stopped him to beat the others to the punch. He was actually rude to my buddy when he learned the case didn't hold gems for resale, snidely commenting that he should have worn a backpack instead. Goofball dealers.

At one show I met an old gentleman and his wife. He held a battered leather briefcase that he set up on top of my display boxes. He opened the case and pulled out a short run of Golden Age *Batman* comic books beginning at #1, maybe six or seven copies in all. I know he had #1–4 and then spotty after that up to #10. All the issues were battered, with one and two held together at the spine with an old type of brown cellophane tape. This took place around 2002 when Gino, Bob and I had made the exhibitor transition from two spots in the hall to just one large end cap.

The gentleman's name escapes me so I'll call him Rob Caine. Rob didn't target my booth specifically. He had purchased Comic-Con attendee badges at the door back in the days when you could, so he and his wife could sell his comics. He wandered up to our booth randomly and it was his first stop.

Rob asked if I could look at some comics and gently laid the briefcase on top of my tabled boxes. The contents of the briefcase were wrapped in a paper grocery bag, so that came out next. He reached into the bag and slid out several magazines which were the approximate size of comic books from 1940 and spread out the comics like a fan. I was speechless looking at *Batman* #1. He was pleased with my reaction and asked me if I was interested. Yeah, sure I am (I said, trembling).

This opportunity came along before any of us had that kind of money, even though the earliest copies were covered with spine-reinforcing tape. Yikes!

What it boiled down to was the suggestion that Rob Caine should keep them and invest in restoration to get the tape removed. Professional comic book restorers had exhibitor booths back then and there were a couple set up in the room. I told Rob that I was unprepared to buy his books (I did not have a money guy to back me up for these things yet). In all good conscience, I felt he owned two or three copies in the stack that could increase in value and desirability if they were fixed.

We discussed all that would be involved in restoration, including potential costs, and he agreed that might be the best course. So I walked him over to an art conservationist.

Soon, my garage was loaded with comic boxes filled with back issues. I didn't have to tie up a lot of money at this point. The comics I acquired just didn't cost that much. It was all pretty easy and fun.

By the late 1990s, three of us formed a partnership. Bob, Gino and I had known each other a few years, mostly as competitors. We liked each other and thought alike, so a team-up was inevitable. We worked together at small conventions while still remaining separate at the bigger San Diego show. Our alliance matured into a partnership at conventions, removing any barrier between us and taking it to the next level. We formally took the name Southern California Comics with our three names as a partnership. Although incorporating was discussed, we felt it was too soon to make that call (a meeting with a lawyer did occur much later, but it seemed more of an unnecessary expense then).

The strength of that alliance allowed us to open a store. The store was designed at first

to be a part-time venture among the three of us. The theory that it would take time to gather a customer base was solid. It did take time! We had scouted for affordable storefronts, but there were none on our meager budget. None of us wanted to borrow money, so it would all have to come from out-of-pocket change. So we chose a nondescript warehouse suite in an industrial park with really cheap rent to set down our roots. With that done, we displayed ads in the Yellow Pages. The calls to sell us comics were increasing. Local established comic book sellers recognizing opportunity began calling. Now the floodgates for new inventory were opening.

My partners and I ran the store equally, but I had more free time to buy comic collections. I was under the misconception that the size and quality of offered collections were relatively similar to those I'd encountered in my previous experiences. I was still playing catch-up with the state of comic book retailing, but the store's presence changed that mindset dramatically. Since the word was out there that we spent good money for comics, the bigger fish were beginning to bite. Soon, I had meetings with former retailers and dealers all over San Diego County. We met at storage facilities and in homes, garages and apartments. I stood in living rooms and motel rooms. Where I once carried one or two boxes to my Ford Bronco, I was now struggling under the weight of 20, 50 … 100 boxes and more! I didn't even feel like I was competing with anyone because there was so much material to buy.

Top: **The organization that goes into displaying bushels of comics when it's "feast" at the store. I don't even want to think about those shelves in a "famine."** *Bottom:* **Sometimes we need outside help to deal with the boxes of comics we purchase. The author with Spider-man, ca. 2016.**

One early call responding to my "free advertising" beginnings was one of those dream calls all dealers pray for. I had a mysterious woman ply me with a copy of *Incredible Hulk* #1 (1962) and *Superboy* #1 (1949). That's the Golden Age *Superboy* #1. That's a comic book I've not owned to this day!

The caller insisted that these two books and two other heavy-hitters were the real deal and she wanted to sell them to clear a debt. I told her I was most interested and asked where we could meet. She was a little standoffish about meeting directly. She was concerned about having strangers at her house, so she asked me if I would mind being escorted to meet her. That sounded a little ominous, but she said it was for her safety so I said yes.

The next part of this is where it gets a little weird. My directions were to meet two guys in a dark Chevy in a Carrows Restaurant parking lot off an exit in National City, an industrial town just south of San Diego.

Off I went.

It was dark when I arrived, so I backed into a parking stall in the restaurant parking lot and waited. My escorts arrived as described and backed in next to me. Now these two Hispanic gentlemen set off my cop alarm just by their appearance and tough-guy demeanor. I debriefed them a bit about what we were about to engage in, seeking reassurance about my safety. I agreed to follow them to a small house a couple of blocks away. They met me at the front door and opened it to introduce me to the woman who phoned. I don't remember her name, but for identification purposes I'll call her "Maria." I followed Maria into her kitchen and saw the *Hulk* #1 and the *Superboy* #1 on a table along with a *Journey Into Mystery* #83 (1962) and an *Amazing Spider-Man* #1 (1963). There was a fifth book I no longer recall. Maria asked me to give her a price for the books and told me a story about them.

She once did a favor for a family friend and loaned him several thousand dollars. She insisted on collateral, so he put up the five comic books and gave her a high value to ease her worries. She believed him, but the friend never came back so Maria could collect on the debt. She was forced to sell the comics to get restitution.

I looked the books over very carefully. They did look real nice, maybe too nice. They looked so nice that I suspected restoration could be a possibility.

They were restored. After a few minutes of careful scrutiny, I judged them all to have color-touch: well-placed spots of acrylic ink to fill in creased areas on each cover. The added colors filled in places where the fold or crease would have broken the printed art, leaving a white line. This was not the news they wanted to hear, certainly not when she was counting on the value of these items.

I broke the bad news to Maria and could feel a chill come over the room as my two escorts appeared decidedly angry. "Don't kill the messenger," I thought as I explained restoration to enlighten and perhaps diffuse the tension growing between us. Maria was nervous and upset. I had to revalue the comics, obviously much lower. That news forced her hand. She realized upon discussion from the other two that they would have to go after the guy she loaned to and return the collateral for real cash. Not an easy task, because I actually knew who the guy was. His Pog business, the business he started with the loaned money, had recently failed. He was possibly also "in the wind," as was I was after dispensing the bad news and effectively ending the deal on a sour note.

I'm just glad it wasn't me stuck in that mess.

There was no Craigslist in the 1990s and few buyers seemed willing to pay for want ads in the local press. Brief freebie ads did appear in conjunction with mine in *The Reader* (a free, weekly publication), the *Pennysaver*, and the *Ad-Visor*. I never crossed paths with those other buyers while out in the field buying collections. The competition from speculators and other buyers has always been active. eBay and Craigslist opened avenues for more competition. Those guys didn't even have to leave their houses. They could conduct business from their house or over the Internet. They helped widen the gaps between reality and fantastic prices. We tried to anticipate that and kept our pricing models up-to-date for comics spanning all decades. We wanted a stable pricing platform that regular collectors could believe in. That meant perennial bargain bins at our store, staying realistic to how much or how little value was in the bulk 1980s-1990s comics. That became tricky, as we learned later while attempting to stay topical with recent comic book values.

The store was now receiving the phone calls that provided us with serious legitimacy. The calls were also pulling me farther out of town. Now I found myself in Los Angeles, Orange County, Riverside, and even the deserts. The size of the box count was reaching new limits as well. Hundred-count boxes were turning into 200-count and higher, more comics than I had truck space for. I was reduced to surrender at one facility where the owner had over 1,000 boxes. He wasn't even the original owner—he took possession from a defunct comic book store that didn't even sell him the entire inventory! At that time 1,000 boxes was more than we wanted to handle without partnering with others. No potential San Diego partners were within our area, so we let that collection go. We did know that a lot of the contents were of no interest to us, so avoiding the collection was not that big a worry. The collection looked like store inventory that had been picked through and these were the least interesting remnants.

The desert collections could be challenging in my youth. Nobody I knew owned a truck, and I never knew if the trip was going to be a waste of time. The deserts were wide open east of San Diego, so we combined work with play. My girlfriend and I found ways to make the trip worthwhile, such as target practice in the badlands.

The disappointing aspect of these opportunities was the repetitive nature of the comics. We saw thousands of copies of the same comics over and over again. Every former 1990s retailer seemed to be floating in a morass of DC and Marvel flotsam. The same titles and the same issues at every stop, store after store, garage after storage unit of hastily stacked boxes of sameness: quantity over quality. Strangely, none of the possessors seemed concerned that their mountains of comics would ever hurt them. They saw no signposts of a boom-to-bust landscape.

I understand the immensity of the problem that closed down so many stores in past years. I saw the magnitude of loss so many retailers had suffered by ordering more than they could ever have sold for profit. If many more collections like what I've seen exist, then how is anyone going to recover and make money? Maybe never.

As of 2016, my business has been buying collections for two decades. That doesn't include the meager back issue buying I did in the 1970s and early 1980s. I've seen tens of thousands of comic books that my peers and competitors only imagined were out there. Utilizing the Web site Comichron-The Comics Chronicles, I decided to research just how many comic books were published (Comichron gathered stats for the print runs of past and present comic books).

The first lesson learned is that comics were produced in the billions—almost 7 billion since 1997, to be more precise. Wow! I had no idea, and these were figures just for North America. Who knows what the rest of the world would contribute? Comichron listed estimated circulation for all comics, trade paperbacks, and related magazines between 1997 and 2012. These were estimated stats, so I decided to work with the low figures for each year.

A second category on the site narrowed the list down to the number of comic book copies from the top 300 list. This category was also stacked year-by-year from 1997 through 2012. I read that 1997 accounted for over 100 million copies alone. The total copies produced through 2012 amounted to over one billion copies. Folks, many of those copies are still out there in some capacity. The thought that almost any of that production quantity is scarce defies logic.

The legacy of all that print material I sum up with an analogy: a whirlpool. The comic books exist in huge numbers. The copies that have reached the resale or secondary market must be in the millions. I think the odds favor that count. These copies move from storage to market, swirl around a bit, and then get restocked for sale when the buying community reflects on what they own and then turns them out en masse. The swirling enlarges and evolves into a whirlpool as more material is dumped back onto the market. All the material condenses into a few areas where they are marketable (cons, stores and social media). More attempts to clear out storage and reduce rent propels more copies into the ever-widening maelstrom. The whirlpool swirls around at greater speeds as more people check out the supply, add to the pot, or check and reject what's out there. All the while, the centrifugal force keeps twirling the comics around with such force that they never disappear; they just keep spinning around, and the whirlpool keeps growing larger as more comics are sucked in.

We caught up to the whirlpool ages ago. Making surgical strikes, we got better at reaching in and making selective back-issue purchases that were collectively smarter. We seized quantities of comics we had faith in as sellers or just good material for perennial sales. We left the larger mass of unsellables with the owners in many cases. In the past, we might have tackled everything if the price was right, but not any longer. We figured that owning and collating thousands of undesirable comics was a money loser, especially if we paid people to sort comics. The flood of offers to buy seemed inexhaustible. Our patience has rewarded us with opportunities to buy for resale in consistent, joyous amounts. The continual, almost daily arrival of collections at our store illustrates how much material is available.

In July of 2016 we hauled in 50 boxes of comic books. My staff and I had not examined the contents prior to moving them to our store. Instead, I told the owner I would make the offer after an exhaustive inventory. Within one day we knew it was about 75 percent drek. I called the owner and gave him my spiel about wasted effort and he was good with it. Out of all the boxes, I could only commit to a $400 purchase. To ease any discomfort on his part, I offered to donate the comics on his behalf. The timing was perfect because San Diego's Hard Rock Café was holding a comic book drive for the United States Marine Corps. This was the week of the 2016 Comic-Con International and everybody was looking for an angle.

The owner was grateful we had a noble end for his comics. He was convinced the money was not there, as well. In the end everybody was satisfied.

To be fair, we do end up with thousands of less desirable comics every year. Rather than wrestle them into our boxed inventory knowing they may never sell, we do something different: we give them away. We started early on by donating them to local charities and facilities that housed children from troubled families or worked with kids who were hospitalized. They were donated to the Veterans Hospital for recovering war veterans. We left them with YMCAs and Boys and Girls Clubs. We donated to schools and the military. Even after all that, we still had boxes of comics left over.

Our new approach was to add them to the Free Comic Book Day comics we received from the publishers each year for that event. Even though it says "free," we still have to pay for them. The publishers' costs and expensive shipping make it formidable to order heavy for all comers. The answer was simple to that predicament: we used the accumulated bulk books and added them to the pot. Now, instead of hundreds of copies to be handed out for free, we let thousands go.

After years of FCBD participation, we routinely see a couple of thousand people dutifully line up at each year's event to get their cut of free comics. We all know what they're getting is nothing special, but the fans appreciate free comics and our massive parking lot sale that supplements the event.

The market was flooded with modern age comic books. Sellers held out maybe too long to return their comics to market. Most certainly, a lot of inventory entered the market after the 1990s implosion. I see much of it in a relatively short amount of time.

The arrival of eBay followed a nationwide reduction of viable comic book stores. Back issues were being dumped on the open market at a horrendous rate as stores toppled and got rid of their inventory before it crushed them. More often than not, the gains of once-successful stores devolved into loss tiers, with just giving away comics to unburden one's storage fees as an acceptable bottom tier. The massive numbers of modern comics still swamp the Internet, stores and social media. Comics find their way back up for sale constantly by readers who got what they wanted on their initial purchase. Now they put them online or elsewhere to get some financial compensation to avoid long-term storage. Or they sell them to us.

Still, quite a few collection owners are hopeful there's a market for their comics. We regularly field inquiries about purchasing 1980s-1990s comics. A little education is often required to gain the owner's trust. We offer a verbal discourse in "over-supply and low demand" marketing awareness. But often to no avail. Our encounters with "quantity-over-quality" back-issue buyers are just too frequent. There are too many uninformed or uninterested comic book people out there. Buying bulk comics is just too appealing to them. The appeal is the ease with which anybody can buy old comics. Getting them cheap doesn't seem to concern people that perhaps it's too easy. "If it's too good to be true…" does not register with a lot of back-issue marketing hopefuls. And now, with the proliferation of Hollywood presentations, every first appearance in a comic book is considered a potential investment. This is true to some degree, especially for core characters. Of course, the surprises the movies and television bring us enchant hopeful collectors when they see the likes of Groot and Rocket Raccoon forge new inroads in first-appearance value increases. Now any character is up for grabs, such as a potential future *X-Men* movie's villainous Mr. Sinister. Or perhaps Cable gets a role.

In 2016 we dealt with comic books that feature every DC permutation of the *Suicide Squad*. I'm still kicking myself because I sold a really nice, very fine copy of *Strange Tales* #110 (1963) in 2013 for $3,500 before I knew there was a targeted movie date for *Doctor Strange*. In July 2016 it was selling for almost $8K!

Whatever ignorance and hype do to propel purchases can always be alleviated with a little education. Even a good grasp of comic book terminology can produce desired results, in contrast to the poor job others are doing to compete for the resale prize money. We will address some terminology in the next chapter. The Forensic Comicologist is big on terminology.

8

Pedigree Comics

Merriam-Webster defines pedigree as: "The origin and history of something, especially when it is good or impressive." The pedigree noun accurately denotes the "best-of the-best" in our hobby.

There are comic books termed pedigrees and there are accessible statistics-gathering lists of pedigreed comics. Almost anyone serious about collecting quality books can own pedigrees. GPAnalysis lists sales figures for pedigree sales.

Pedigree comics, like pedigree status in other walks of life (for example, prize-winning domestic animals) indicate an upper caste, or class of specimen that is considered the finest in its category.

In our hobby, pedigrees are often older comics of higher quality. The degree of difficulty in finding high-grade vintage comic books allows for the few to be considered special. If those few turn up in larger collections with many of the copies in high grade, they are on their way to pedigree status. But the pedigree status is selective and not easy to come by. For argument's sake, I'll proffer that vintage means 1960s and older. The 1970s generated a collecting mentality that encouraged comic book readers to take care of their comics.

I've seen countless comic book collections whose contents were a mixture of 1960s to 1980s. While the 1960s comics may look well-read, the newer issues often look great, maybe too often to justify pedigree status. There is just nothing that special about recovered copies from the 1970s and 1980s. I see them all the time and they almost always look high-grade.

To qualify as a pedigree certain criteria must be met:

Origin

A pedigreed collection must have been accumulated by one individual during the time the comics were new.

The comics meeting this criterion will often retain certain sameness in paper quality and minimal defects. Marks on the covers will all have the same similar period identities. For example, our hobby is rewarded with notable pedigree finds.

Most are offered by survivors of the collection owner. Others are guided publicly by first contact with a connected comic book dealer (one who is dialed in with other dealers). Some finds are lucky enough to be in the possession of the older citizen who first bought them.

The proliferation of comic book stores and national dealers gives pedigree owners places to shop their stuff. If the dealer is intuitive, he or she will recognize a pedigree opportunity from the get-go. Those finds are so rare that once they surface, the news travels fast, and demand synchs up with the availability of the books when it's time to sell.

We've purchased several of these original-owner collections without yet feeling the "vibe" of pedigree.

Quality

A pedigreed collection must primarily consist of high-quality comic books.

Analysis of known pedigrees shows the average copy has been graded at Very Fine or better. Not all pedigrees are submitted to CGC/CBCS where the VF stats are located. But all pedigrees must contain a large quantity of high-grade copies. The books may look nice, but the status of a pedigree requires a third-party consultant to lock the status down. Just having nice old comics isn't enough. Extra effort has to be initiated to carry a collection to the next level.

Some copies will remain raw against third-party grading submission costs. The cost of submitting the entirety of a collection can be daunting to the owner. Let's say a 500-unit collection of VF or better vintage comics from the 1960s runs an average better than VF. In fact, the average value of a common issue in the collection is $125. The submission cost to get all of them graded could run upwards of $20,000 and higher. If the pedigree-necessary keys are present, the submission costs will greatly increase. That could cause a lucky owner to shiver with fear over the financial responsibilities of selling the collection.

We all know that graded copies are more desirable to most collectors than their raw equivalents. But if you're the unemployed son of a recently deceased comic collection owner, you may not have the income to take the collection to the next level. It is certainly troublesome to meet the responsibilities of pedigree acknowledgment.

This copy of *Detective Comics #27*, the first appearance of Batman, illustrates points I made about comics from pedigreed collections. Their quality has to be high to be a qualifier, there must be a certain quantity of key books within the collection, the book should be relatively uncommon (as is true with many Golden Age collections), and the collection itself must be unique. Here we see the *Tec 27* example from the Pinnacle Hill Collection. *Detective Comics #27* (1939) (© DC Comics. Used with permission).

Completeness

A pedigreed collection must contain a substantial number of key or rare issues, or represent a significant portion of a particular genre, company, period, or classic title/character.

- Golden and Silver Age pedigrees are successfully measured by the size of the collections. They must have a qualifying number of comics. Opinions differ on what a qualifying number of copies means, but I leave that up to the people assigning pedigree status.
- Key issues must be present. If we're talking a typical 1960s Marvel collection, the decision-maker for pedigree status wants to see plenty of number-one issues and first appearances.
- Most issues produced by at least one of two companies: either Marvel (Timely) or DC Comics. The difficulty of putting a pedigree collection together without comics from either company is almost insurmountable.
- Presence of rare issues. This is not always a necessity, but it will help push the pedigree status forward.

Market Acceptance

CGC and CBCS and the collecting community must continue to recognize the pedigree name of a collection past the point of initial sales.

The buyers must accept the above-average prices pedigrees command. Comic book buyers must continue to acknowledge the named significance of a pedigree collection. Many pedigrees exist. The Edgar Church Collection was the first, established in the late 1970s (also known as the Mile High Collection). The awesome nature of that immense Golden Age collection determined its reign in the pantheon of comic collections.

When a collection is discovered and hits the streets as a pedigree, the chatter is enormous. If CGC or CBCS label the collection a pedigree, the chatter increases, as does demand to see and own a piece. The buying market is generally open to newly identified pedigrees. The label is not acquired without some debate. Once the label is assigned, only a small minority may challenge it. The rest will jockey to buy it.

Edgar Church (1888–1978) was a comic collector and artist who worked independently and eventually for the telephone company in Colorado illustrating commercial telephone book advertisements, the precursors to *Yellow Pages* advertisements.

Church kept thousands of miscellaneous periodicals in his Colorado home to use as references for his art. From these magazines he would clip images which he would store in one of hundreds of labeled boxes. The collection of comic books that he amassed, later known as the Edgar Church Collection or the Mile High Collection, is the most famous and valuable comic book collection known to surface in the history of comic book collecting. The collection consisted of between 18,000 and 22,000 comic books, most of them in high-quality grades, and was discovered and bought in 1977 by Chuck Rozanski (Mile High Comics). About 99 percent of it was later sold by him to various collectors. The collection is famed for holding the highest-quality copies of many Golden Age comic books, including the best known copy of *Action Comics* #1 (his copy was believed to be a 9.4 or a 9.6, but the current owner refuses to get any of his books graded).

Collectors tend to attach more value to something special. Edgar Church copies quickly began to sell for more than regular prices and do so today. The collection topped categories for the high sale prices spurred on by the white, supple paper quality and huge demand. Edgar Church copies tend to be exquisite examples of what new comics looked like in the 1940s.

A couple of examples involve 1940s issues of *Flash Comics*. Scouting though GPA sales stats, I found a recorded copy of #1 that sold for $450,000 as a CGC 9.6 in 2010. The closest in quality to the Edgar Church *Flash Comics* #1 (1940) was a 9.2 copy that sold in 2014 for $182,000. That's a testimonial to the fantastic quality of that pedigree collection.

A graded copy of *Flash Comics* #2 was sold and recorded by GPA for over $40,000 in 9.4 in 2010, also the highest-graded copy sold. The next highest grade was again a 9.2 from 2005. In many of the examples I researched on GPA, the highest graded Golden Age comics were from the Church Collection. The collection set standards not benchmarked before and encouraged others to match Rozanski's success with their own "barn finds." Our store has owned Edgar Church copies. The affordable issues we owned were the lesser interesting titles such as DC Comics' *Gangbusters* and *Mary Marvel* from Fawcett. Even those issues come in nice shape and sold back in the day for about three times their *OPG* value because of the Edgar Church qualifier.

Other collections fitting pedigree criteria have since been named. The uniqueness of any subsequent collection was measured against the Edgar Church pedigree. Criteria settling any disputes over what constituted pedigrees were established. Many really fine collections have been tagged pedigree. Names like Dave Crippen, Allentown, Mohawk Valley, Rockford, Crowley and Denver occupy pedigree spaces on census sites.

Establishing a pedigree tag to a collection requires a CGC/CBCS determination. Before CGC, market acceptance determined a collection's status. The objectivity of others and their willingness to pay more than *OPG* granted collections pedigree status. There were a few experts like Rozanski and collector/dealer John Verzyl who could stand up for a Church copy based upon their intimate history with the copies. Many attempts to pass off ordinary copies of Church books have occurred.

We suffered from possession of one of those false copies early in the store's life. It was sold to us locally from a reputable owner who passed it off as a Church. We submitted it to CGC and they concluded it was not. I got hold of the seller and he made claims that he bought it from Rozanski himself in the basement of his Colorado home. I thought maybe CGC was mistaken, so I called Mile High Comics and spoke with Chuck. I described the book, but he didn't remember. I figured he was close to the dealer from the story I was told, but Chuck was unimpressed. He wasn't about to let that possibility sway his concern that it wasn't a real Church. He just replied, "That [expletive] can say whatever he wants. I don't think it's one of mine!" I corresponded with at least one other Church expert, but he was also noncommittal. Without a proper trail of provenance, the book could not claim a Church pedigree. I dealt with the seller later and received proper compensation.

With CGC/CBCS available for grading, collectors depend on their involvement to certify pedigrees. CGC or CBCS and pedigree identification are synonymous. Simply put, owners of newly discovered comic collections must meet the four requirements for pedigree designation. The collection will need to be examined by CGC or CBCS for pedigree consideration. Buyers will seek out CGC or CBCS certified pedigrees because CGC or CBCS approval usually means universal acceptance. That level of acceptance will often drive up demand and price. Any collector can identify his own comic book collection as a pedigree, but gaining valid renown as such is the trick.

In 2013 I took a trip to Los Angeles to view a comic collection. The collection was in a storage facility owned by the estate of the collection's inheritors. Their story was unusual because of the distinctive aspects of the collector.

The collector was in her late teens or early 20s when she showed an interest in collecting comics. For anonymity's sake, let's call the owner Lana Fuller (a slight change to protect the family). We know Lana started collecting in 1952 because the earliest date attached to near complete runs of titles was 1952. At that time, superhero comics were sparse in publication. She was obviously much happier collecting *Tarzan* and other jungle titles, as well as anything featuring horses, based upon the contents of the boxes we searched through.

That changed with 1956. DC's superhero comic book lineup outlasted everybody else's. Fawcett, with its Captain Marvel titles, was gone, and Atlas Comics (pre–Marvel) failed to re-energize their old Timely publishing lineage. Lana collected some of the Atlas *Sub-Mariners* but skipped virtually all the other superhero titles of the day. DC continued with two Batman titles, several Superman family titles, and the team-up title *World's Finest*. Even Wonder Woman maintained consistent publication through the superhero doldrums of the 1950s.

The Super Book Find
By Michelle Nolan

On a warm autumn day in the mid–1990s on the San Francisco Peninsula, I spotted one of the best bargains I will ever see in book scouting sitting on a shelf inside the fence at a church rummage sale.

It was, indeed, a super bargain—the scarce 1942 *Superman* novel by George Lowther, illustrated by co-creator Joe Shuster with 10 full-page illustrations, including four beautiful color plates, protected by the rare dust jacket.

I also spotted my super nemesis, an older book scout with an unsavory reputation, about 10 people behind me in the line, which would wind through part of the church when the sale opened.

I could not take the chance: I had to get to that book first and fully protect it with my body. He may not have seen it, but he was good. Good enough, in fact, to recognize potential value.

Even on warm days, I wore a sweater at sales, so that I could cover the books I might find. That would not, however, stop him from lifting a volume or two while my back was turned.

Three elderly ladies stood behind me, chattering away. I asked if they were church members, and they were. So they gave me the directions I needed and, as soon as the door opened, I whipped off my sweater and asked one of them if she would hang it up for me in an appropriate spot on this warm day. Confusion reigned just long enough to delay them at the door for the few seconds I needed to scoot to the shelf, snatch the book and stuff it under my blouse.

The scout entered the book area of the sale and uttered an obscenity at me, for which he was summarily ejected. Lois Lane would have been proud!

A year or so later, I motored down a nearby street early on a garage-sale Saturday, looking for an intriguing sale I had seen advertised, featuring "old paperbacks." For one of the few times in my long collecting career, I found that the seller's use of "old" really meant "old"—as in the 1940s and 1950s, the first full decades of the modern American paperback.

There were about 20 boxes in the driveway, filled with a motley mixture of oldies of all types and conditions. I could see at a glance that there were at least several dozen of considerable value. When informed they were 10 cents each, I offered to buy them all for $100—since there likely were not more than 1,000 books.

The woman in charge accepted the $100 bill I carried for such rare occasions and halted the paperback part of the sale, giving me the time I needed to fend off the competition. A few moments later, the aforementioned unethical scout showed up and began to look through the boxes, when the woman promptly informed him that they had already been sold.

"You [C-word]," he shouted at me. "You [B-word]."

"That's OK, Frank, you can buy all the books I don't want," I calmly replied, for I had told the woman that I would quickly return the vast majority of the books but would not ask for any refunds. I had offered the $100 for what I wanted, but was glad to give her the chance to make more money.

Not only did I find books I wanted to keep and others I made plenty of profit on, but the day was also a most satisfying payback. Not many years before, this book scout sent me off on a wild goose chase on the next block with his word of "hundreds of old paperbacks"—all worthless romance novels!

Lana's collection in Los Angeles yielded a shockingly nice copy of super-key *Showcase* #4, a slightly warped copy. We combined our efforts with a pro and pressed the book into a much higher grade and sold it to another party. Lana's collection, which we named the Southern California Comics Collection, contained a near-complete run of the Silver Age *Flash*. Lana originally purchased the *Flash* right up until her passing in 2012. She also collected most of the DC hero titles that followed the *Flash*, including *Justice League of America* (1960), *Hawkman* (1964) and *Atom* (1962). She did the same with Marvel's newly minted heroes beginning with *Amazing Spider-Man* #1 (1963) and *Fantastic Four* #3 (1962). She bought full runs of virtually all the DC and Marvel heroes.

Lana's family remained only vaguely aware of her buying habits. She clearly bought all of her comics new from childhood, with the exception of some she picked up at comic conventions she attended with her niece. She kept a small notebook to check off filled holes in her list. I itemized the collection while examining the contents of the boxes in a Public Storage franchise. I counted 170 banker boxes with a total of over 27,000 comics. Sorting through them, I made piles of comics based upon their ages just to begin the process of evaluation. I repacked boxes containing all modern comics and kept separating out all copies pre-dating the 1980s. After five hours of exhaustive repetition, I had culled out about 4,500 comics dating from the 1950s to the 1970s.

The goal of this research was to provide the inheriting family with an overall value to the collection. I explained that the vast majority of the value would encompass less than 20 percent of the books. I reasoned that much of the inventory was modern comics. I considered the modern books to begin in the 1980s (Copper Age) and continue right up to the present (2016). As discussed elsewhere in this book, the modern-age books generally have such little individual value that collectively their financial impact can be minimal. The family who inherited all this described some of the storage history to me. They said Lana led a sort of hoarder's life. She didn't normally challenge herself with conservation qualities. Bags and boards were rarely used and tailored comic book boxes were nonexistent. Only orderliness was evident, as most of the books in a run were in numerical order. That's an upside in my business. The downside was that the comics were not always in the boxes as identified to me at the storage unit.

No, unfortunately Lana lived frugally in a trailer home with little proper storage space. She used the entire space she lived in to store her comics and other collectibles. She stacked the comics throughout the windowed trailer home. The comics were piled in bedrooms, hallways, and even a bathroom. The earliest comics were unprotected and often within reach of a window (the modern comics were also stacked but never removed from their shopping bags). Sunlight did reach a number of the older books. Light bulbs are one thing: they can discolor or fade comic book paper. But sunlight will tan or even brown the paper, turning it brittle. Unfiltered sunlight is Kryptonite to old comics. And this collection had been exposed for decades. The inheritors arrived too late to box them up for storage and retard the degradation.

The comics were stacked with the spines all facing the same direction. So the edge of one book in a stack close to a window faced the same potential damage as every other book in the stack. Some stacks were removed from a window's proximity while others, like those placed in a bathtub, saw no escape from the sun for years. Inevitably, some of the best books in the inventory were sun-damaged. Because the collection was put together numerically for storage, I assumed Lana piled them up around the house that way. This meant that if *Amazing Spider-Man* #1 had a tanned edge, then issues #2 and on probably did as well. I was correct. Though the collection contained full runs of DCs and Marvels from the late 1950s to the 1970s, quite a few of them saw sunlight and displayed tanned edges. I documented the collection through the afternoon, cycling through one tightly stacked box after another. I itemized the key books and those most likely to carry extreme value.

This was an extravagant collection. Lana spent money for comics that she really could not afford, at least not in these quantities. To her credit, she bought much of it new from local markets. The stores of the day were not concerned about the purity of condition. Comics in those days were sold pre-creased and dented because that's how distributors treated them. This remarkable collection lost points because those original defects and sun damage slashed through a large percentage of copies. We determined that 75 percent of the DC and Marvel key comics were present. Some fat runs possessed all the issues and their keys—the keys that are integral to "pedigreeing" a collection.

The four criteria I mentioned above for establishing a pedigree collection are reviewed below in the context of how the Southern California Comic Collection (our label for the Fuller collection) fits in:

- Origin: Pedigree status thrives on original-owner collections from vintage years. Lana's collection fit the requirement: a single owner bought vintage books new and used and built the collection over a 60-year period.
- Market Acceptance: Does the market routinely crave the books in a particular collection? That's one factor that determines the viability of pedigree status. Our find was the kind of collection all dealers live for, a comprehensive group of the most desired titles from

the two most popular companies of the Silver Age. The quantity was not an issue. There were several thousand DCs and Marvels, but also Dells, Gold Keys, Archie Publications, and long-defunct smaller publishers. Many comics were worthy of weeks of grading, pricing, and cataloging. There were many comics that would sell quite easily to a wide range of buyers.

• Completeness: How complete are the sequential runs? Are a significant number of issues missing? If, for instance, the collection included a run of *Amazing Spider-Man*, did it have most of the key issues? A pedigree tag would follow the collection if the run was at least nearly complete from the first issue forward. The pedigree status would depend on the presence of dozens of titles in numerically complete runs, including a majority of the key books from those titles. Lana's collection was all of that.

• Quality: Pedigree requirements loosely translate into VF or better conditions overall. We made inquiries with our peers, people more familiar with CGC pedigree standards than my staff. The paper discoloration was more of an issue than the creasing the comics were "born" with. Some comics had tan, or even brown edges, while others did not. Some copies had wide bands of vertical or horizontal tanning edges, while other edges were narrowly shadowed. Time had tattooed many copies with a singular band, or bands of tan different from every other copy. The only way to brand the collection's quality was to bring in more experts. With some inquiries, I received visits from people I considered grading experts. Their firm belief was that the average grade of the books that mattered needed to be better than what we presented. Our quest was to align grading standards with CGC's to project the minimal pedigree needs.

We round-tabled the various discoloration issues in discussion. Without tanning, many of the copies would have measured off at "Very Fine" or greater. With the tanning, we downgraded the copies to an average of Fine Plus (6.5) or Fine/Very-Fine (7.0). Some of the keys did grade higher, but their weight was not enough to pull the entire lot into pedigree territory. What a shame. Ultimately, we acknowledged the significance of this collection by simply paying homage to the original owner. We created a simple certificate of authenticity, a tribute to Lana's accomplishment, and enclosed a copy with each comic book.

Like "pedigree," other terms such as "slabbing" and "CGC'ing" did not come into our vernacular until well into the richness of this hobby and the multiple generations who collect. I'm addressing quite a few terms throughout this book, but many more are out there. *OPG* and various Internet sites provide exhaustive glossaries of defined terminology. Every dealer is aware of the bonuses that come from discovering a pedigree-worthy collection. Demand is greater, prices are often better, and for a while, at least, the owner gathers a lot of attention within our hobby. Meeting all four requirements is no easy task.

We've come close on several collections. One collection in 2005 matched all the requirements, but the owner was the problem. He wanted his son to take control and get the best deal from a dealer. The inexperienced teen opted to keep half the collection and sell the other half to us in bits and pieces, making the pedigree process difficult. Maddening. As we did later with Lana, we named this particular collection (our half) the Hollywood Hills Collection, without any fanfare or hoopla—or pedigree.

The 400 or so books we bought from Junior were all Marvels spanning 1965 through early 1968. The kid's father bought the comics off the stands in San Francisco. He loved Marvel superheroes so much he tended to buy multiple copies of each issue within that three-year time frame. He stored the comics in no particular archival fashion for 40 years. When I visited their house, the comics were just being removed from old, browning Saran Wrap and bagged in comic bags. To say I was initially disappointed is an understatement. I saw the crappy plastic wrapped around old comics and figured they would be brown as well. Peeling off old plastic wrap from old comic books is not that easy. The plastic tends to adhere to itself, and at any moment a wrong grip can tear a comic book. It was slow going, but the surprising results were amazing: the covers were bright, shiny and vibrant with deep color. But the interiors, after decades of haphazard storage, were an even bigger shock. The margins of those pages were white! Bright white like it was 1965 again! That was a real credit to the luck of the owner. He protected them without more of a thought than keeping them safe and flat.

We've all seen really nice comics come from large collections in which many copies do not have the appearance of having ever been read. The toppers that indicate potential pedigrees seem to have more to do with the owner's love of his or her books rather than efforts to keep comics in investment grade. We know that the comics of the past did not see practical resale potential until well into the Silver Age. The greatest pedigree collections come from the Silver and Golden Ages. It's love that brings them to us years later.

With the Hollywood Hills Collection (HHC), we teamed up with notable comic collector personality Mark Zaid to pay for the comics. Once in hand, about half the books went to CGC. Of those we nailed down an average grade of 9.4. There were maybe 50 9.6s and a dozen 9.8s. Conversely, we ended up with equal numbers of 9.0s and 9.2s, but with white pages. These were outstanding copies. Could this half of the collection been successfully pedigreed?

Maybe. The problem was that the time period of 1965–1968 yielded fewer key books from Marvel than one would think. The depth of the issues in both quantity and quality most certainly was appropriate. The market desirability was plainly there. But no run was complete from beginning to end. We were not about to spend a fortune of encapsulating the entire 400 books only to be judged pedigree-worthy by CGC. We knew that titles such as the Marvel reprint titles (*Marvel Tales, Marvel Collector's Item Classics*, etc.), *Sgt. Fury* and a few others would not grant sufficient profit after encapsulation against the costs of submission. In addition, 9.4 is a great grade for Silver Age, but we would have needed all 9.6 and higher to score with those books. As it stood, we did well enough during retail to make sufficient profit off the books we did slab. Many of those went to dealers and pressers to see even greater profit elsewhere.

Providing our own certification of authenticity (COA) does not provide an automatic market enhancement. It does provide the benefit of drawing attention to select collections within our inventory. Both the HHC and SoCalComics collections were outfitted with COA cards in each comic book. In those two cases, we tracked the sales of those books and noted that buyers tended to zero in on them if they liked the sample they purchased in the beginning.

I'll mention our third and final attempt at identifying a pedigree collection within our midst. It was 2005 when a particular collection of back issues arrived at the shop. A gentleman identifying himself as a caretaker for an elderly man brought in a box of Golden

Age comics to sell. The owner, whom we will identify as Benny K., was in his 70s and suffering from Alzheimer's. Benny was actually in the car in our parking lot, but apparently was not mentally fit to deal with strangers. His caretaker explained that Benny was a long-time resident in one of San Diego's beach communities and had lived in the same house since the early 1940s. Benny's house was now up for sale and he was destined for relocation to an assisted living manor. The caretaker was tasked with cleaning out any value in Benny's house to help defray the costs of Benny's future home.

The caretaker described the house as cluttered and wanted his job to be over. He said he felt he had exhausted the value in the place until he found a box of comics in the garage. He worked in rapid succession to grab Benny, load the comics in his car and go to the first comic book store he felt was appropriate—us.

I'll cut to the chase and list the better contents:

Batman: beginning with a broken run from #12 to #40-something.
Early *Superman*s.
Early Fawcett *Captain Marvel*s.
Plastic Man and other Quality-published titles.
Spirit comics, a few miscellaneous titles, and a fat run of *Walt Disney's Comics & Stories*, starting with issue #31.

There were other odds and ends, but the comics all had a couple of unique factors in their favor: they all started in the early 1940s, and they all had white pages or off-white to white. Bone white in some cases! It seems Benny lived within the moist coastal air for 70 years and somehow managed to store his comics in such a manner that weather never impacted the comics.

One factor that was negative was Benny's desire to subscribe to each issue of *WDC&S* after the issues reached #45 or so. As many collectors know, readers could subscribe through the United States Postal Service to their favorite comics from a few of the companies. Back then, the comics were mailed folded in half vertically. Dell folded its Disneys in half vertically with the exterior (usually the front cover) stamped with the recipient's mailing address. Many of Benny's Disney copies bore the vertical creasing from mailing that reduced too many copies with ice-white pages to the realm of VG grade. Fortunately, a select few had flattened out over the years and bore no color breaks. This included a few key copies. The issues numbering in their thirties were store-bought and unaffected. Nowadays they would be perfect candidates for pressing.

Ideally, this was yet another shot at naming our own pedigree collection. We had a significant quantity from the right period from the original owner with possession for about 65 years. The initial copies of each superhero title were low-grade. It wasn't until Benny's books hit about 1942–1943 that he took better care. The manner in which he stacked them contributed to their survival. And many of the books from that time featured some first appearance or other, so they had key or semi-key official quality to them: *Batman* issues included the first appearance of Alfred the butler, the only Joker/Penguin team-up, and a cover featuring Hitler. *WDC&S* issues featured early Carl Barks art. Overall quality was once again our worst enemy. We got close again, but no cigar. Discussions with others sounding out about the bullet points of pedigree-ness suggested the submission costs of all the books would ultimately lose money to even try to gain pedigree status. It was better for us to return to the COA formula and let the sales of the books ride on that promotion.

The prospect of getting a collection pedigreed requires the cooperation of an acknowledged grading company accepted by the public for that sort of thing. It is not easy to find collections worth pedigreeing. We've come close and have been celebrated by fans of our collections that were so near to that goal.

About three years after the Benny K. collection purchase, I was contacted by an acquaintance with a few comics to appraise. Tom brought the stack of comics by my shop one fine day. We laid the comics out on top of one of the shop's glass cases. First out was a surprisingly good run of old Timely *Marvel Mystery Comics*, about 20 copies beginning at issue #20. That was a shock. Timelys just don't show up at comic book stores. The copies were a little rugged in the low numbers, but got better in grade after that. Nice white pages, too. He displayed a couple of low-number *Batman*s beginning with a high-grade #3. Then a VG copy of *WDC&S* #1. Whaattt! What kind of collection was this? There were some Fawcetts and early issues of *Spirit* from the 1940s ... now wait a minute.

"Tom, who owns these?"

"The bank does," replied Tom.

Filling in the blanks, he explained that he was now working for an estate sales outfit. The owner of these comics just died with no family, so everything went to the bank, which had power of attorney over the owner's finances. At that I got an itchy feeling at the back of my neck that I knew who the owner was. I asked Tom and he said he thought the guy's name was ... Benny with a last name starting with the letter K! It was more Benny K. stuff!

Tom was tasked as an employee of the estate sales company to attach values, and the comics were the last things on the list: Benny's books. The ones that were not found by the caretaker and we didn't know existed. The final pieces that would have sealed a pedigree deal those few years ago.

To spoil the surprise, Tom said they weren't for sale and would probably not be for awhile. Cagey Tom knew the relative value of those comics, but just wanted expert confirmation and quick grades. I hedged my bets that I would be on the short list when the time came, since I had helped out. Pretty clearly, Tom had ideas of his own, and they probably did not include me. I tried to jump-start with an offer. There were about 60 books, but Tom's "middleman" status roadblock left me stymied. Tom, the bank, and Tom's bosses were all in the way of putting a period to the end of the Benny K. Collection story. Tom packed the copies up and blew me off after that in subsequent encounters at a couple of events. I still dwell on what could have been.

The Forensic Comicologist hungers for the opportunity to capture his own pedigree collection and granting his own name to the collection. Like finally getting a 10.0 from CGC or CBCS, catching a collection worthy of pedigree status seems elusive but not impossible.

9

Eras and Genres
Platinum Age, 1897–1938

Funny books, as they were once called, aren't necessarily funny at all. The 1930s grafted newspaper cartoons into four-color, 64-page comics (68 if you count the covers). Newspapers of the day had every type of story theme, filled with action, adventure, comedy and mystery. Violence was commonplace and daily strips often ended with imminent danger or cliffhangers … to be concluded in the next strip!

Animated cartoons found their origins in comic strips. Cartoons returned the favor by appearing in comic books. Popeye, for example, leapt from the comic strip *Thimble Theatre* onto the movie screen in cartoon form in 1933. Fleischer Studios adapted *Popeye the Sailor* into theatric shorts for Paramount Pictures and saw worldwide movie house distribution. In 1937, *Popeye* appeared in comic book format for the first time. Available only as reprints, *Popeye* did not appear as new material until 1946. The strip-cartoon-comic book drive train is clearly linked when tracking the lineage of these early characters. My history with the genre couldn't possibly extend any further back than my earliest memories of comic books, cartoons and newspaper strips of the late 1950s. My father was the source around my house. He bought the television, brought home the comic books, and subscribed to the newspaper. He relished his childhood memories of the happy times, surrounding me with the reading material he cherished as a kid. He got me to appreciate the old black-and-white, slapstick 1930s cartoons. He taught me to appreciate the history of those forms of pop culture that came before me.

Other researchers have traced comics history far back into the nineteenth century, but we won't. For our purposes, we want to bring our readers into the age that represents the beginnings of comic books: the Platinum Age. I feel it's important in any discussion about comic book collecting to review a little history. As a forensic comicologist, I want to establish my take on the history of comic books, validating to the reader that I know what I'm writing about. A little history goes a long way to establish authority in the matter.

I make a living off retailing comic books from all eras. I do this successfully because I understand comics from the past and their current fans. I've read thousands of comics and I still read comics. Knowing why people buy and read comics old and new is crucial for collecting and selling. Knowing the origins of comics gives me expertise many others don't or won't possess.

There is an early twentieth century quote (George Santayana, 1905): "Those who cannot remember the past are condemned to repeat it." I believe that those who won't learn from the past are doomed to miss it.

Comic historians pinned 1897 as the inception date of the invention of the comic book. That year, Hearst Publishing gave G.W. Dillingham Company permission to resell *The Yellow Kid* comic strips in book form. The earliest book actually had the phrase "comic book" printed on the back of its cardboard cover. That is the first known use of those two words in conjunction with the new format. The book itself was a square-bound, black-and-white affair with 196 pages. It measured 5 × 7 inches and cost 50 cents.

Success followed this first foray into the new way to read comic strips. William Randolph Hearst, a mighty man at the end of the 19th century and into the next, permitted other strips to be reprinted in book form. Hearst was always keenly aware of the competition from rival *New York World* newspaper publisher Joseph Pulitzer. For both men, comic strips sold newspapers. By 1922, the first monthly comic book saw print. Embee Distributing Company's *Comic Monthly* mimicked the earlier style. They opted to capitalize on the growing comic mania, so they started their own project. Slightly larger in size than the previous books, *Comic Monthly* tried to keep a regular publishing schedule, but ceased printing one year later.

The prolific publisher Cupples and Leon began its comic book offerings in 1903 with collected strips featuring such timeless characters as *The Katzenjammer Kids* and *The Happy Hooligans*, so their published construct was made up in similar fashion for the time: flexible cardboard covers that opened to black-and-white reprints. Cupples and Leon tackled more characters, bringing *Little Orphan Annie*, *Mutt and Jeff*, and others to book form. Still, the magazine format we recognize as the classic "comic book" was so far nonexistent.

I've been a purveyor of this early comic book format. I started buying and selling these old comic strip rereleases back in the 1970s. The market was small, but active; plenty of seniors who grew up with those books were still around shopping. By 2017 the market was clearly drying up.

In 2016 I met a fellow at my shop with a small stack of about 15 Cupples and Leon cardboard-covered comic books. They were worn and some were stained; not unusual for 90-year-old books. The gentleman wanted to sell after all these years of ownership. I did a little pricing research with him looking over my shoulder. I expected the books to be cheap, based upon both condition and desirability. The dollar figures weren't very enticing to either of us.

I knew they would be hard sells, so my buy-in was low. He was disappointed and still maintained an emotional attachment. He wouldn't relent when I made my offer, so the books walked. I can't denigrate the man; I still own things from my childhood of little financial consideration. If his intent is to pass them on to others for profit later, I think he's going to come up short again. His inheritors within the family will more than likely find they own historical curiosities. I find it hell getting old in this hobby.

Then in 1929, George Delacorte's Dell Publishing produced the first full-color periodical called *The Funnies*. Its 16 pages resembled a newspaper insert, but it was sold on newsstands as its own entity. *The Funnies* ran its course by 1930.

In 1933, Maxwell Gaines (M.C. Gaines) pioneered the periodical prototype we know as the comic book. Gaines was a publisher in need of a new product to sell. He devised a simple four-color saddle-stitched pamphlet that reprinted popular newspaper comic strips. Within the Platinum Age, Gaines brought us one step closer to the form we identify as a comic book. Gaines's idea was based upon the source material. His content was a simple newsstand page folded into equal quarters. He multiplied the number of quarters into 64 pages printed on both sides. A slick cover was added, and the now-recognizable comic book format was born.

Gaines's introduction of the world's first comic book was in collaboration with Dell Publishing's release of *Famous Funnies: A Celebration of Comics* (1934), 36 pages of newspaper strip reprints believed to have sold through Woolworth Department Stores for ten cents. Eastern Color Printing, the company Gaines represented, parted ways with Dell and ran their own comic book titled *Famous Funnies*. Beginning with issue #1 in 1934, the title continued the market norm: it carried reprints. This first issue was 68 pages for the price tag of a Depression Era–friendly dime a copy. Within a dozen issues, the publisher started showing a profit, proving the new invention was hot.

The public wanted more, but fresh newspaper strips for reprint material were shrinking in availability. The comics contained so many pages that they could chew up a year's worth of strips in just a few issues. Something innovative needed to be added.

New material began to appear in comic books. The publishers soon understood that the public enjoyed these new features, characters that had never seen publication in the newspapers. Publishers were hungry for new material to fill their pages and add more comic books to distribution. DC Comics in its infancy was known as National Allied Publications. Malcolm Wheeler-Nicholson was a relatively new publisher. Following World War I, Wheeler-Nicholson found work as a pulp fiction writer. He was familiar with the periodical system and felt he could capitalize on the comic book craze. The rights to all the popular strips were owned by others, so he couldn't flourish in that world. He took the final evolutionary step and created *New Fun—The Big Comic Magazine* (1935), breaking ground in a new arena.

New Fun #1 was filled with newly drawn and written humor and adventure strips. Wheeler-Nicholson's writing talent backed some of the new characters. Wheeler-Nicholson understood the risk trying to sell any oversized comic book with original features. *New Fun* #1 was the first comic book subsidized by advertisements and not sold through a sponsoring business. The thinking was that ads would offset costs and the comic book might pay for itself in a short period. The thinking was on target; the country ate it up! Wheeler-Nicholson added a second title in 1935 called *New Comics*. The first issue was smaller in size than the large, tabloid *New Fun*. Its dimensions now closely resembled the classic size of the comics of what we now refer to as the "Golden Age."

Distribution woes quickly followed Wheeler-Nicholson's products. Newsstands were reluctant to carry comic material with new, unfamiliar contents. Unsold copies mounted and the cash flow wasn't sufficient to put out issues on a consistent schedule.

National Allied publishing created one more new title: *Detective Comics* (1937). Released later than Wheeler-Nicholson planned, *Detective Comics* was his final shot at making his comics profitable. He was now experiencing chronic money problems. His only out was to take on partners. His choice for partner was Harry Donenfeld, a fellow publisher. Conveniently, Donenfeld was also a "bigwig" with a major magazine distribution company. That company, Independent News, would become entwined with the future success of comic books for decades. Donenfeld, a strong personality in his own right, slowly pushed Wheeler-Nicholson out of his partnership business, forcing him out through courtroom antics. Donenfeld took control of the comic book publications.

Left and right: New Fun Comics was a progenitor of the Golden Age of comics helping to form DC Comics. The *New Funs* turned into the legendary *More Fun Comics,* paving the way for new characters such as The Spectre and Dr. Fate. *New Fun Comics* #6 (1936), *More Fun Comics* #61 (1940) (© DC Comics. Used with permission).

Wheeler-Nicholson took a percentage of *More Fun Comics* (1936) (formerly *New Fun*) upon his departure. Donenfeld, with Jack Liebowitz, renamed the company Detective Comics, Inc., abbreviating the name to DC Comics. Jack was the son of a Julius Liebowitz, an old union hand from the Bronx and an acquaintance of Donenfeld. Jack had become an integral part of Donenfeld's publishing/distribution network and settled in as a partner in Wheeler-Nicholson's old company National Allied.

Comic books inched forward toward the 1940s. More comic book publishers surfaced, all searching for more and more new material.

The Platinum Age of comic books was now approximately forty years in the making. It would take two young DC creators to find the hook that would usher in the next era: the Golden Age.

Just about any 1930s comic book should be considered collectible because of the age and the "cool factor"; they're so old and rare that it's doubtful the world will continue to see many more undiscovered 1930s gems.

Looking backward, the collector mentality today stops at the point where the Golden Age starts: *Action Comics* #1. Many contemporary fans see the Golden Age as springing from just the one title. A generation has passed away that would otherwise educate us all about what came before. I talk to many about the old days of comics, but especially Millennials, the dominant crowd in my business.

From a forensic comicologist angle, I tend to lecture about comics, and I'm fascinated with their history. I try to teach those who are patient enough to listen, but that seems rare. My less-informed customers tell me of their belief that *Action Comics* with Superman started it all. The truth only bores many of them because the era's beginning is not all about *Action Comics* #1. From the known historical perspective, the 1930s were closing now in our *Reader's Digest* version of the comic book's origin. The world was about to get slammed with cultural change from within and fear from without.

It was 1938 and the storm clouds of war were building over Europe. China had already suffered Japanese invasion and Eastern Europe felt the heat of German tension. Heroes were hard to find. America was hungry for Depression distraction and entertainment. Movies were at the height of their popularity, with science fiction, pulps and comics growing. The only thing missing was a new hero for the ages to take the American public on their next incredible ride. Enter Superman!

Jerry Siegel and Joe Shuster's seminal character arrived in *Action Comics* #1 in June 1938. The world needed a hero, even a fictional one. Siegel and Shuster were science fiction fans. They had read the exploits of pulp heroes growing up and wanted to create their own. Superman was their latest attempt to get an original character published. Both men were inspired by science fiction and comic strips. Their invention of Superman drew inspiration from the wonders of space and otherworldly fiction. Flash Gordon, Buck Rogers, The Shadow and others underscored the prominence of pulp fiction entertainment for kids and adults alike. Newspapers, movie serials and radio shows filled Siegel and Shuster with the fantasies of what could be.

The "Superman" character was repeatedly offered to publishers in their attempts to get him into print. It took several years until Major Wheeler-Nicholson hired Siegel and Shuster to write for his fledgling comic book company. They worked on the Major's three comic book titles, writing and drawing their own inventions. When the Major solicited them for new content for a fourth title, they presented him with Superman. *Action Comics* #1 carried Superman's first story, birthing the American phenomenon, the Golden Age of comics.

Our hobby's Golden Age encompasses hundreds of titles and millions of copies, leaving a rich history for its legacy. But before we leave the 1930s entirely, I'd like to fill in some blanks. Other genres of the Platinum Age formed their own branches on the familial tree of American pop-culture fiction. One of our store's more obscure possessions happens to be dated near the beginning of the Golden Age.

Big Little Books

While I'm on the subject of Platinum Age comics, let's address the two other genres from the 1930s: the "Big Little Books" and "pulps."

Comic books, the original cardboard-covered strip reprints, saw diminished sales in the early 1930s. Twenty-five and fifty-cent cover prices were less affordable in the early years of the Great Depression. Publishers looked for money-making alternatives. Of course, the comic magazine was born, but so was a second option for readers.

Big Little Books originated with the Whitman subdivision of Western Publishing. Western published children's books that were often sold at Christmastime. Once Western learned that racks of children's novels would sell at department stores year-round, they established the Whitman line to develop new lines of kid books. For ten cents a copy, Whitman offered smaller versions of kid books, but printed in kid size. BLBs featured newspaper strips, novelized adaptations paneled with one-page illustrations taken from the published art.

The typical BLB was built around more than 300 pages wrapped in colorful, flexible cardboard covers. The intriguing dimensions of BLBs at roughly 4 inches by 4 inches by ½ inch or greater made them ideal for kids. While the interior illustrations were black and white, the vibrant covers advertised the adventures of popular newspaper characters. *Dick Tracy*, *Little Orphan Annie*, and *Mickey Mouse* were three of the earliest BLB hit titles. BLBs sold well, and soon Whitman reached agreements to print other characters under license. Titles were released adding movie stars and radio programs to the growing selection of genres.

Walt Disney Studios allowed their stable of cartoon cast members to appear in BLBs. Westerns, spy dramas, crime, and action heroes found life in the pages meant just for children. The ten-cent cost was palatable to parents. Whitman produced at the rate of six titles a month in their glory period, the early to late 1930s.

Whitman experimented with various size formats and came up with an invention called the "Big Big Book." BBBs were roughly the size of today's graphic novel but contained a BLB's interior layout. The larger size does not show up often in the collectors' market, leading me to believe the distribution was somewhat muted for those copies. Other variations on the BLB theme included nickel book spin-offs. Soft-cover BLBs were given away as premiums and promotional items. These "giveaways" were distributed by gas stations, with food products such as cereal, and through radio programs.

Whitman's competitors surfaced with their own brands of BLB titles. Whitman remained the popular choice with ten- and fifteen-cent cover prices. BLBs saw much action right up until mid–1938. Whitman continued in the same vein with "Better Little Books" until 1950, but their Golden Age was dominated by the arrival of comic books. (Marvel briefly put out their own version of BLBs in the 1960s and 1970s. They consisted of color reprints, more of a curiosity than an investment in today's market.)

BLBs retain a small corner of today's collector market. *OPG* maintains a BLB section in its annual publication. That section came along late in the publication's history, later than it should have, since the BLB generation has all but moved on. The list that *OPG* compiled of known BLB books is large and comprehensive. The pricing displayed for three grades for each book may not be reflective of what a determined seller will really get.

Unfortunately the sales of BLBs have dwindled to the sparsest opportunities yet. We carry them at the store because the Forensic Comicologist likes them. His father liked them so he likes them. The same cannot be said for our store's customer base. BLBs are most certainly curiosities. Their sales are driven more by a title or two rather than the genre as a whole. Even at comic book conventions, the small central core for buying and selling such things as BLBs can make sales seem grim.

We took all our BLBs to the 2016 San Diego Comic-Con for a full six days of exhibition. They were placed prominently along the front perimeter of our 200-square-foot booth. We prepared proper signage to drag attention to them and waited. We waited and we waited. I'm a firm believer that within our hobby, everything will sell at least once. BLBs are no exception. I do remember when their action was vibrant; I even collected them for a while in the 1970s.The 2016 show demonstrated the rarity of BLB sales. We sold about seven BLBs to three people in the midst of 130,000. I probably won't be taking them to the next show.

Pulp Magazines

Although pulp magazines or "pulps" have less to do with comic books than BLBs do, I will address their connections. Pulps have been in circulation since the late 19th century. Named for the cheap wood-pulp paper they're printed on, pulps were ten-cent successors to dime novels of the past. Pulps appealed to readers attracted by the lurid, action-packed covers and racy adventure stories. Pulps often presented stories by honored writers, and the covers were painted by artists who would often see fame in comic books. In fact, pulps were a natural part of the comic book audience. Comics were partially inspired by pulps and shared common sales space on newsstands or wherever both were sold.

When the 1940s raged with war, the use of paper became restricted. The superior sales of comics, the shortage of paper, and increased popularity of better-quality magazines hurt the future of pulps. Noteworthy pulp publishers such as Street and Smith, Dell, Fiction House, and Martin Goodman's Marvel Publishing saw the writing on the wall and moved into the comic book game. For a quarter or less, pulps gave us heroes like The Shadow, Doc Savage, and the Spider as they swept across the covers. Villains made their mark, too. Doctor Death and Depression-era gangsters invited readers to enter their worlds.

The Holy Grail of Pulps, *Weird Tales*
By Mark C. Glassy, Ph.D.

During the late 1950s and into the 1960s I grew up reading *Famous Monsters of Filmland* magazine, and "Uncle Forry" (editor Forrest J Ackerman) made all those monsters seem like family; I too am a monster kid. From time to time Forry mentioned in the pages of *FM* the "legendary pulp, *Weird Tales*" and many of the authors published in that pulp magazine, chiefly H.P. Lovecraft. During the 1960s I lived in Sacramento and downtown was one of my favorite hangout spots, Beer's Bookstore. This was a used bookstore (long since gone) and I can still remember the musty and moldy smell as I entered the store. The shelves in that bookstore sagged and groaned from all the books. One entire back section was devoted to pulps, and as soon as I discovered these I was hooked. Back in those days you could get issues of *Weird Tales* for 10¢ up to a whopping 25¢ each! In this way, I was able to complete about 80 percent of the initial run's 283 issues.

My fraternal grandmother, whom we all affectionately called Grandma Glassy, immigrated to the United States from France in 1918. At the time she spoke very little English. She soon settled in Tacoma, married, and began her family (my dad was first born). To enhance her English skills, she took to avid reading, and her house was filled with all sorts of reading material. While visiting her house as an adolescent, I marveled at all her books and magazines, some of which, believe it or not, consisted of issues of *Weird Tales*. During my junior and senior years of high school, when I was actively buying *WT* at Beer's Bookstore, I was able to convince Grandma Glassy to let me have all of her copies of *WT*, some of which were the ultra-rare early issues.

Fast forward a few years, after much diligent searching, I finally found someone (Robert A. Madle; thank you, Bob!) who sold me his early "bed sheet" issues, the impossible-to-find 1923 and 1924 issues (good luck to those of you out there searching). And with those I now have a complete run of the *Weird Tales* pulp magazine. It is estimated that only 8 or 9 complete sets of *WT* exist!

Pulp collecting is an active hobby, though pulps are generally scarcer than comics from the 1940s. The Internet continues to provide active pulp markets. It is a shrinking market much like the one for BLBs, though. Pulps were created for earlier generations. They appealed to readers since the cover bore the only color art a pulp collector would see. A generous number of famous writers owe some of their fame to pulps. My shop owns a bookcase full of pulps for sale. Just a scan shows some of the covers advertise Ray Bradbury, Edgar Rice Burroughs, H.P. Lovecraft and Dashiell Hammett, all legends within the world of fiction.

Pulp themes have hierarchies with their own cadres of fans. Classic pulp heroes, early stories by world-famous authors, and the more racy titles are fan favorites. Their covers range from wild space aliens endangering sexy damsels in bondage to gangsters with Thompson machine guns blazing. Any collector entranced by cover imagery would be rewarded with glimpses of pulp art.

Like their kissing cousins the comic book conventions, pulps have their conventions too. Unlike the flourishing comic cons which number in the dozens annually, there were only two large pulp magazine conventions in 2016. I don't use that count to dismiss pulps. There are numerous book shows across the country, and pulps are most certainly a feature within the exhibition halls at those shows.

In 2015, I brought select pulps to the San Diego Comic-Con and did quite well. I didn't have any extra display space, so we hung some eye-grabbing copies on our wall display, situated between high-priced comic books. That did the trick. We turned those customers onto boxed copies kept under a table and made some good coin from those sales. However, I still wouldn't redesign my booth to display more pulps by sacrificing comic books. The comics are still more lucrative at that venue.

Pulps do suffer from one malady that affects their desirability. Because of the cheap quality of the paper, high-grade copies are scarce. The copies I've seen most often are ragged with brittle edges. Great care must be taken with the handling of pulps. Pulps in that format lasted until the late 1950s before being replaced by a smaller, slicker digest-size periodical. Pulp and BLBs competed for shelf space with comics. The public's hunger for comics turned them away from BLBs until that format became unsustainable in the late 1940s. Comic books (and newspaper strips) continued the lineage, just as *Homo sapiens* evolved from among several hominid species to become the sole being known as man.

I grew up with a friend named Ed Farrell. Ed loved all things science fiction and fantasy. Our timelines started at roughly the same time where we both started seriously collecting comics in high school. Ed and I started attending San Diego Comic-Con (then Golden State Comic Con) in the very early 1970s, although we didn't yet know each other.

We met at a pinball parlor near my apartment. Ed ran the place at night and I'd hang out before going to work for the local newspaper as an early morning delivery driver. Our collecting discussions brought us together at Comic-Con and drew other fans into our circle of friendship. Within a few years, Ed began dealing heavily at shows and through the mail with pulps, books and all nature of science fiction collectibles.

Ed and I lost touch in the late 1980s and didn't reconnect until around 1993. In that time Ed had gained a nationwide reputation as a classy and classic book dealer. He was good at acquiring collections in the sci-fi/fantasy vein, finding less competition than expected for that genre in a big city like San Diego. He traveled to seek stuff out and spent fair money on other people's collections.

By 1994 I had paired up with Ed at that year's SD Con and sold a bit of my old inventory from his booth. I made a surprising $1,500 at the five-day event. That may not seem like much, but I thought I would do much less. I had no idea how my collection would resonate after all those years in storage. Ed made money because Ed knew his audience and knew what to bring to that show. Years passed, and Ed and I lost touch again as Ed found it less and less profitable to sell sci-fi and books at the evolving SD show. After 1999 I never saw Ed again.

In 2015, Ed's relatives contacted me and told me he had passed from cancer. He left a house and a garage full of property, and the relatives were desperate to sell it or get rid of it. Needless to say, Ed had left behind a massive collection of all kinds of science fiction and fantasy memorabilia. All of it came up for grabs. The details of the contents are vast, too vast for this paragraph. Suffice it to say that pulps were a big part of his collection.

Ed spent the year leading up to his death selling some of his pulps on eBay. I ended up owning boxes of pulps Ed never let go. I purchased several hundred pulps, including rare *Short Stories* from 1905 onward and the larger "linen"-size pulps of the late 1920s. Early stories by Robert E. Howard, Edgar Rice Burroughs and H.P. Lovecraft dotted some of the earlier pulps, leading them to be some of the most desirable in Ed's collection.

I have some expertise with pulp retailing, but nothing prepared me for the breadth and scope of Ed's gigantic stock. I think the most notable fact about Ed's pulps was that that a large number of them were in the best shape I'd ever seen for any collection of pulps. "Astounding" (also a popular pulp title!) would be the term I'd use to describe a large majority of the rarely-torn spines on his copies. It was a truly outstanding collection filled with plenty of complete covers that drew me in every time I looked at them.

Thank you, Ed.

10

Eras and Genres
Golden Age, 1938–1956

A letter was printed in issue #42 of DC Comics' *Justice League of America* in the mid–1960s. The writer, a fan named Scott Taylor out of Connecticut, commented on DC's repetitive reprints of their older comics. He used the term "Golden Age" to describe those stories and noted that a generation later would refer call their generation's comics as "Silver Age."

Silver followed Gold in awards ceremonies, so comic book fans quickly adopted the "Age" terminology. Comic dealers began tagging their selections with the precious-metal identifiers.

The *Overstreet Price Guide* began its publication in 1970 at the end of the Silver Age and formalized the term "Age" in print. Fans adopted the Age terminology and accepted Gold and Silver as givens. Of course, nobody living in the 1940s called that era the decade of the Golden Age of comics. For many the pre–World War II years and the beginning of the war were thought of as the "First Heroic Age of Comics" (a phrase not often used in present times).

Golden Age comics are familiar to just about every comic book guy or gal. The Platinum Age tier is a time frame relatively unknown to today's avid collector (hopefully you read the previous chapter!). The Golden Age is the furthest back in time current comic collectors can imagine traveling. At least, most of my customers are aware of the existence of 1940s comics. The people today are firmly indoctrinated into the existence and importance of *Action Comics* #1, the comic book contemporary collectors are told is the beginning of it all. This most celebrated icon of genuine Americana opened the door to a firestorm of four-color imagination. In our mind's eye, the inception of comic books began with DC's seminal heroic character in *Action Comics* #1 and then exploded with characters and genres, companies and titles, seemingly almost at once.

Writers experimented with far-flung plots and ideas. Many were science fiction fans or even established writers from that world. Artists, some coming from the pulp magazine element, used their pencils and color choices to suck in readers with outlandish costumes, otherworldly panels, and slam-bang action. This new age for comics worked without a net. Anything wholesome was fair game. Working within the values of the period, our comic book ancestors placed our pop culture on a future-track.

Incidentally, the term wholesome brings tame, child-friendly entertainment to mind. With the war beginning and America's Jim Crow laws still in effect, wholesome might not be the best description to everyone living back then. Plenty of Americans' values and self-esteem were ignored by comic books in the Golden Age. Comic books are indicative of the times, but what's not within their pages is fair treatment for people of color and religious faith. Homosexuality was only marginally portrayed in the heavily censored movies of the time and never permitted in comic books.

What we got were stereotyping, racism and blatant violence in comic books, offending many adults. We can attribute that to a less-elevated culture, excusing comic books for belonging to that time. Even though we sell comics in the enlightened 21st century, that makes it no less uncomfortable to sell racist art to buyers who could justifiably be offended. Will Eisner's Spirit was an otherworldly detective-hero fighting crime in the inner city of his hometown. As was typical of the 1940s, *The Spirit* comics featured a sidekick. The Spirit's sidekick, an African American kid named Ebony, was a stereotype from another time in comics. The "Stepin Fetchit" behavior of Ebony was typical of a black character designed to entertain a white audience. Fortunately that typecast in comics began its descent as the growth of the civil rights movement gained steam in the latter part of the 1950s.

Violent smash-up covers, energized by gratuitous torture scenes, were great propaganda tools for the comics in wartime. Violence in that form offended many in the 1940s. Despite the war, plenty of Americans were devout believers in peace, and not every parent was amused by the vicious images in four-color. Parents began to show concern about the violence and cruelty that comic books exposed to the children. Pressure would mount in the Golden Age to subdue outrageousness in comics.

Timely's entry into superhero comics included the first issue of *Marvel Comics* (listed as issue #2 in *Overstreet*) featuring beautiful cover art by Frank Paul. Paul was a popular cover artist for *Amazing Stories* and added comic books to his repertoire with *Marvel Comics* in 1939.

Comic book heroes of all costumed hues were invented with every super-power permutation the writers could conceive of. Some floundered, many succeeded, and many of those survived into the following decades, with production often interrupted. Characters like Batman and Captain America have lasted for more than seventy-five years. The comic book circulation of the early Golden Age was huge, with copies of some titles selling in the hundreds of thousands. Today's comics don't get to brag about similar circulation, but characters like Cap and Batman are no less popular.

Most collectors are dialed in on Batman's true age of origin, along with Superman and Captain

Everyone knows *Detective Comics* #27 featured the very first appearance of The Batman—or did it? *Action Comics* #12 posted an in-house ad promoting Detective Comics #27 "on newsstands now" with a picture of The Batman. Both comic books are dated May 1939, but *Action Comics* #12 arrived on the stands one week prior to *Detective Comics* #27. We owned the featured copy of *Action Comics* #12 pictured on this page. Time will tell what will be its financial fate. *Action Comics* #12 (1939) (© DC Comics. Used with permission).

America. But what about Marvel Comics' seemingly Silver Age creations "The Vision" and "Ka-Zar," and their actual Golden Age beginnings?

DC's *Justice League of America* sprung from the 1940s' *All Star Comics'* Justice Society of America counterparts. Some stars disappeared (Star-Spangled Kid and Stripsey), others found new versions of themselves (Sandman), and still more lost their sidekicks (Green Lantern lost Doiby Dickles in the next generation). Then there's the multitude of small, long-gone publishers that filled the newsstands of the 1940s with titles and themes of all sorts, forebears of the coming comic book eras.

Harvey Publications, later those fine purveyors of *Richie Rich* and *Casper the Friendly Ghost*, hammered out dramatic stories of the Green Hornet and Kato in the Golden Age. Archie Andrews tested teen spirit in *Pep Comics* #22 (1941) before landing his eponymous title and spin-offs.

The Shadow made the transition from pulps and radio. *Shadow Comics* ran for one full decade through magazine publisher Street and Smith. Will Eisner's *Spirit* started out in newspapers before being granted full comic book status in 1944. Quality Comics' *Plastic Man* leapt forward from the 1940s into each succeeding decade; *Blackhawk* as well.

The Lone Ranger began in 1939 comics with the rest. After stops and starts, he lived again in the pages of Dynamite Entertainment's *Lone Ranger*.

The previous list demonstrates the perseverance of comic book creators today and the staying power of these legendary comic book heroes of the past. *The Shadow, Spirit, Green Hornet, Lone Ranger* and even *Blackhawk* have moved into our publishing present, all courtesy of the Golden Age.

Archie Comics publishers have the distinction of being only one of three companies to continue into the present. DC and Marvel continue with immense fanfare, but Archie has somehow hung on to their smaller empire against all odds. Founded in 1939 (then called MLJ Publishing), they shared their opening salvo with many companies that vanished by the first half of the 1950s.

Archie has been a family operation from the beginning. Even today, Archie is run by CEOs linked to the original men behind the company. Archie's fortunes took a modernized turn for the better in 2017 when *Riverdale* arrived on scene as a television show.

Magazine Enterprises created the original version of Ghost Rider, a western hero dressed all in white who found his way to Marvel Comics in the 1960s (as both Ghost Rider and Night Rider.) Ghost Rider is a name that doesn't necessarily share lineage with its Golden Era doppelganger, but the character Marvel calls Ghost Rider continues on in film and television.

The history of comics is the history of several early 20th century newspaper and magazine publishers. The popularity of comic books seduced several magazine publishers to move over into that realm. We looked at the influence of pulps earlier. The Shadow, Buck Rogers and Flash Gordon started with newspapers and pulp magazines. Their transition to comics followed the desires of their publishers to make money in comics. Notable magazine publishers capitalized on their library of fictional characters already in print. Others created titles with new names just seeing print. Of all those publishers, a few reached the top.

Martin Goodman was a pulp and magazine publisher already established by the beginnings of the Golden Age of comics. He found game in 1939 with comics as a profitable medium and entered the fray. Goodman partnered with publisher Funnies, Inc. to produce *Marvel Comics* with issue #1 (*Marvel Science Stories* was one of his ongoing pulp publications at that time). Goodman's new comic book company was quickly named Timely Publications and saw Human Torch, Sub-Mariner, and others greet the light of day in 1939. Goodman hired new talents Joe Simon and Jack Kirby, who co-created Timely's third big character: Captain America. Goodman hired more new people and tasked them with increasing Timely's stable of new comic characters. He also brought on an eighteen-year-old Stan Lee as an assistant in the office. The dates are mired in age and poor memories, but Stan was hired in either late 1940 or early 1941.

Timely was just one of Goodman's publishing arms. He saw the money in comics and urged his comic book company to grow. Captain America appeared even before the start of America's entry into the war. Cap joined the fight with the Human Torch and Sub-Mariner. Timely's aggressive, over-the-top covers pulled in thousands of buyers. But their overall sales were low compared to the "Big Three" of the day: Quality Comics, DC Comics, and Fawcett Comics. In regards to Ka-Zar and The Vision: Ka-Zar first appeared in a short series of Goodman's pulps starting in 1936, while The Vision arrived in comic books in *Marvel Mystery Comics* #13 (1940). I didn't know any of this until well into my Golden Age collecting days.

Quality had success with *Plastic Man* and Eisner's *Spirit* comics. However, DC throttled the competition with around 900,000 copies of each issue of *Action Comics* at its peak. Timely's output was less than half a million with each issue. Walt Disney's cast of characters saw four-color print in Dell Publishing's *Four Color Comics* and *Walt Disney's Comics & Stories*.

Before there was Disneyland, there were Disney cartoons and Disney comics. Walt Disney Studios hired craftsmen to produce the best art and stories for their comics through Dell Publishing. Disney comics were extremely popular and maintained newsstand appeal into the mid–1980s. Disneys have seen intermittent publishing since then.

Dell's *Four Color Comics* title brilliantly allowed Dell to try out licensed characters without committing to producing new titles for each. Westerns, funny-animal comics, and Disney products dominated issues of *Four Color Comics*. Dell responded to the success of each tryout with either additional new titles or continuations of one of the new titles following the public's acceptance. These successes were granted their own titles, eventually gaining sequential issue numbers. Overstreet would come along and tag the first *Four Color* appearances as #1s side-by-side with the *Four Color* issue number. Example: Woody Woodpecker made his first eponymous comic book appearance in *Four Color* #169 (1947) after appearing in *New Funnies*.

Dell Publishing kept releasing new issues of Woody in *Four Color* until the end of 1952. *Woody Woodpecker* was now independent of *Four Color* with issue #16. *Overstreet* lists the previous 15 issues of *Woody Woodpecker* with the documented *Four Color* issue numbers collated as issues #1–#15 in Woody's timeline as a self-titled comic book.

Four Color Comics also has the distinction of being the title that ran up to #1,354, the highest numerical run in comic book history! Some of the later issue numbers in the *Four Color* run were unpublished and appear as numerical gaps in 1961–1962 in *Overstreet*.

The name Captain Marvel has existed in comic books since 1940. DC Comics' incessant litigation forced Cap's publisher out of the market in 1953 and left our stalwart hero in limbo. Marvel resurrected the name for their purposes. DC returned the 1940s version to comic books in 1973. To keep peace with Marvel over possible copyright infringement, Captain Marvel's name would not appear on the covers. *Captain Marvel Adventures* #113 (1950). *Captain Marvel Adventures* #123 (1951) (© DC Comics. Used with permission).

The granddaddy of all titles was Fawcett's *Captain Marvel Adventures*. First introduced in *Whiz Comics* (1940), Captain Marvel went on to capture massive amounts of attention. Fawcett (later a successful paperback book publisher) competed in the comic book market with Captain Marvel and his entire retinue of related characters (Mary Marvel, Captain Marvel Junior, and the Marvel Family). Sprouted from *Whiz Comics*, *Captain Marvel Adventures* powered up circulation to an astounding 1.3 million-plus copies per issue by the middle of the war years, truly a heroic age.

The good Captain was extremely popular in the back-issue community through the 1970s. Again, there was still a preponderance of first-generation fans looking for copies. By 2016 the thinning of those fans relegated ownership to true Golden Age Captain Marvel fans. The character is still produced in comics with the belief that he will one day see the big screen. Sales of the Captain Marvel titles are slow but consistent. I don't shy away from buying them in collections for resale.

By 1941 there were nearly 700 issues across 150 titles, as determined by comic book historians Dan Stevenson and Michelle Nolan. Each issue generally sold from 150,000 to well over 500,000 copies. But of the 29 publishers, only a dozen firms produced at least 24 issues.

The wartime comics handled that real-life crisis in different ways. Timely confronted the war in direct clashes with the tyrants our soldiers battled overseas. Timely covers exploded with over-the-top violence and diabolical cliffhanger scenes. Germans and Japanese were reduced to barbaric misanthropes. At DC, the contact between good guys and bad guys was more benign. They taunted the despots and glorified American patriotic commitments. Comics saw themselves as propaganda tools. The creators behind the scenes wanted comics to contribute to the war effort on behalf of those who could not go. Just like Hollywood, comics could be used to entertain the troops and boost morale while occupying the minds at home with badly needed distractions. But comics had another, more patriotic duty to perform for the war.

As the war costs mounted for America, supplies grew scarcer. America's shipping lanes were imperiled, making the importation of goods difficult. Metal and rubber made the war machine march on, but paper made it run—lots of paper. The military's need for paper increased with the war. Simultaneously, the paper suppliers felt all aspects of the war. Manpower shortages at every level of paper production lessened our country's ability to mill lumber and make paper, since laborers were now in uniform. Labor issues affected mill work when lumberjacks went on strike at one point. They wanted a greater rationing of meat when food output was curtailed; more meat provided more protein to work harder with fewer available men. Fewer lumberjacks meant less paper.

World War II took a massive bite out of American morale in its early stages. Comic book creators combated the morale issue with their own brand of Realpolitik justice for our enemies. *World's Finest #9* (1943) (© DC Comics. Used with permission).

Publishers found reduced paper allotments forced them to manufacture books and magazines with fewer pages. Paper was thinner for newspapers. Even the unprinted margins were narrower to maximize every inch of printable space.

Paper drives were the answer. Communities were encouraged to reach out for scrap paper donations. Organizations like the Boy Scouts of America put together paper drives with support from the war production board. Within the first eight months of Japan's attack on Pearl Harbor, the contribution of donated paper flooded that market. A temporary moratorium on paper donations was short-lived, and 1944 again saw an acute shortage that remained till the war's end.

The paper came from every walk of American life: newspapers, cardboard, packing material, books, magazines, and yes, comics. Millions of comic books, that most disposable of kid entertainment, were left in heaps in every town and city to be trucked to mills for pulping and reuse for a paper-hungry military. Few publicly raised an outcry. Young comic book readers felt it was their duty to help gather scrap paper together for the war effort. The numbers of copies repurposed must have been staggering. The combined sales numbers at the beginning of the war numbered in the millions monthly. Tens of millions of copies by year's end! Involuntarily, comic books sacrificed themselves for the war.

DC Comics and Superman were in the war to win it! *Superman* **#18 (1942) (© DC Comics. Used with permission).**

To understand how the paper drives of the war years impacted comic book survival, let's look at a couple of statistics:

Golden Age sales peaked in 1942. As written earlier, *Superman* was selling an outstanding 900,000 plus copies per issue. Let's take a random issue number from that period, *Superman* issue #16, to understand how copies of 1940s comics have diminished in quantity. The *Gerber Photo-Journal Guides* listed the scarcity of that book as an SI = 4. That's somewhere between 1,000 to 2,000 copies existing. That accounting was in 1986. By 2016, CGC only registers seventy-eight graded copies. I'm sure many more raw copies exist, but it's a stretch to believe they number in the thousands.

Another example is Timely's *Captain America*. We'll take issue #10 (the last Simon and Kirby issue). Gerber lists SI = 4: again, 1,000 to 2,000 extant copies. However, CGC acknowledges they've certified 52 copies (as of 2016). Cap managed to sell a million copies an issue even after a rough start with issue #1. (Some people voiced objections to the prewar militarism of its content. Protesters included members of the American Nazi Party!) Cap outsold almost all of the titles within its own company.

Finally, I'll tackle the title with the record for highest sales numbers: *Captain Marvel Adventures*. With Captain Marvel (nicknamed the Big Red Cheese) hitting all-time highs of a million-plus in 1942, there must be huge quantities of copies still around. Issue #12 has Captain Marvel joining the Army, so this issue must have sold well at the time. Gerber says a common SI = 4, the same as the previously discussed issues. CGC listed only 28 copies that passed through their grading service by late 2016.

Obviously, I cannot account for the true numbers of copies of any of these books. Raw copies in the hands of collectors will account for many more. But still, travels over the country to various shows do indicate that the retailers most likely to have copies simply do not. As we've learned, scarcity can be a component of desirability. It's seriously doubtful if more than 500 copies of these comics exist today.

I believe that there is no authority that can account for all extant copies of Golden Age comics. But if there was an authority, it would probably be the back-issue dealers who sell Golden Age comics with the greatest frequency over the longest period of times. A successful Golden Age dealer with national connections will probably be the likeliest source for a good guess at the number of extant copies of most Golden Age comics. My theory is that one owner may sell an old comic book, say *Captain America* #12, to a dealer. The dealer sells to a buyer and mentally or physically adds that copy to his or her mental bank. Later another copy of #12 ends up in the hands of the same dealer.

Years of sales have allowed numbers of copies of *Captain America* #12 to pass through the same dealer's hands. That dealer accounts for copies new to the market and copies that have passed through his or her domain more than once. Our dealer shares this information with other dealers, sharing even the same copies. Nationally more dealers learn of the sale of copies of *Captain America* #12 and can corroborate the number of known copies. There are plenty of dealers nationally, but fewer who could tabulate even a wild guess as to copy-counts of *Captain America* #12.

The sources for the accountability of known copies of comics, such as *Captain America* #12, are shared between national dealers, grading companies and their census statistics, and (auction) markets like eBay that have sold copies of *Captain America* #12 not accounted for by the others.

Gerber's scarcity index was invented before the grading companies and eBay existed. Many of the national dealers in business now were not yet in business when Gerber began his quest. The conclusion I draw is that decades after Gerber gathered his statistics, we are still unsure of how many copies of most Golden Age comics are out there.

Now I'll take that statement one step further: scarcity does not always drive desirability. The issue of *Captain Marvel Adventures* I used will be my example. Fawcett Comics, publisher of *Captain Marvel Adventures* (and a host of other Marvel Family titles) sold phenomenally well in the 1940s. The war years' sales were strongest for their superhero titles, as well as for most of the popular costumed characters. Captain Marvel's self-titled comic and sister title, *Whiz Comics*, ended when the company closed down its comic book line in 1953.

> The best answer for Fawcett's termination of its comic book titles was a decline in comic book sales coupled with 12 years of litigation by DC Comics' parent company: National Comics Publications. NCP sued Fawcett over Captain Marvel. The lawsuit was motivated by greed: NCP felt the heat of the competition that the good Captain's sales generated over Superman titles. NCP wanted what they considered a title that infringed on their trademark off the stands. Fawcett fought well but relinquished their hold on the comic book market for sound economic reasons in 1953.

At the same time paper drives were eliminating millions of Golden Age comics, there was national concern about the content of the comic books. Adults and non-readers viewed comic books differently from kids. Mothers to this day are still chided for throwing out their kids' comics in previous decades, because the parents found the contents foolish, or even incendiary to impressionable minds.

Comics of the 1940s occupied kids' short attention spans much like television and video games do in the modern era. Parents (mothers especially) are notorious for tossing comic books in the trash. Even after the war, the feeling spread that comics merited no redeemable qualities and were not worth saving. In frightening fashion, parents, educators, and politicians saw this more controversial reason to dispose of comics: the protection of their children.

Peter Jones, local collector and friend, tells his tale of the acquisition of a copy of *Action Comics* #1. Some of you may know Peter from encounters at comic conventions or association with the old national club American Association of Comic Book Collectors. Here's his story in his own words:

It goes without saying, but I'll say it anyway, that *Action Comics* #1 is a "Holy Grail" for many comic collectors, and the ever-increasing prices for that book keep it out of the hands of most. In the past I've attempted to take a cheaper route and collect poor man's copies of some of the big keys. I call books that are assembled from parts of more than one copy "Frankenstein" books. They are also known as "married" copies, which make them sound ever so … genteel. Sometimes I fill in the missing parts of an incomplete copy with color Xeroxes to make a readable book; these I call "cyborg" books.

My overall success rate in this kind of endeavor has been extremely low, and I've essentially abandoned such projects over the years, but I've had some requests to share the following story. My memory of some of the details is a little vague, but it goes something like this: I put out feelers for a low-grade incomplete copy of *Action Comics* #1. I reckoned that in the best case I could assemble a complete copy, and in the worst case I might only end up with a coverless and incomplete *Action Comics* #1, at least with the Superman story intact, which would still be pretty cool. To me, having the world's worst copy of *Action Comics* #1 was still preferable to having no *Action Comics* #1.

A few separate *Action* #1 wraps sold for decent money on ComicLink recently (editor's note: this story took place years ago), so I guess there are other collectors who feel the same way. This was pre-eBay, so that meant putting occasional ads in *CBG* (*Comic Buyer's Guide*) and calling dealers and other collectors. It's difficult to find parts, and empty covers are scarcer than coverless copies. I also wasn't surprised to find that a seller's radar goes up when I ask for an incomplete book or just a centerfold or a cover. They rightly surmise that I'm trying to complete a comic, and they adjust the price upward if they even have a part that I need.

Comic collectors can be a suspicious and cantankerous lot sometimes, and the other Dr. Frankensteins out there zealously guarded their scraps of key books. Typical conversations inevitably veered towards what they might get from me rather than what I could pry out of them. It really didn't go very well. Somehow I heard of an antiques auction, not even a comic book auction, somewhere on the East Coast, where an *Action Comics* #1 missing the cover, first wrap, and centerfold was offered. I called the auction house and they said it had already been sold, but I managed to track down the buyer and ask if he was interested in selling it. He wasn't, but he wished me luck. I heard that a lot.

Eventually, one of my ads in CBG got me a phone call from someone who had a copy that was missing one page but was otherwise solid and fairly attractive. The inside cover of *Action Comics* #1 offered a contest where kids were encouraged to carefully color the first page of Chuck Dawson (a black-and-white strip), tear it out and mail it to National Comics. The best colorists would get some sort of prize. It made me wonder if there are more than a few copies out there that are missing that page. Anyway, this copy was not inexpensive, but it was heavily discounted. I agonized and passed on it, but on further reflection (and some manipulation of my financial resources), I called the seller back and went for it. Any regrets I had evaporated when I held the book in my hands. I couldn't believe I truly owned an *Action Comics* #1, even with a page missing.

I had moved into the eBay age by now, searching for an incomplete copy with the page I lacked. Finally, a hideously trashed one surfaced. It was missing the cover, at least one outer wrap, and the centerfold, pretty much the most crucial parts that any other bottom-feeder like me would want, but it had my needed page. There were indeed a lot of other bottom-feeders out there, and the competition was more ferocious than I expected. I was very determined, though, and I won it. It turned out the page I wanted was in decent shape, too. With a little reluctance I took a razor and cut it out. The spine was already split about half-way down, so the extraction didn't take much effort, although I offered a silent prayer for forgiveness from the comic book gods for desecrating even such a wretched *Action Comics* #1 corpse as this one. I laid the page inside my first copy and beheld a complete *Action Comics* #1. A Frankenstein book, yes, but unrestored, and likely the only one I'll ever own. I barely refrained from shouting maniacally, "It's alive! It's alive!"

In case anyone wonders what I did with the rest of the second incomplete copy, I used my *Famous First Edition* reprint of *Action Comics* #1 to make color Xeroxes of all the missing parts and assemble a readable cyborg book, which I sold to another collector (with full disclosure; he knew what he was getting). That almost entirely paid for the cost of obtaining the page.

The Forensic Comicologist is not one to shy away from a good story. Two good stories are even better! Here's science fiction/monster/comic book fan addict Mark in his own words:

By Mark C. Glassy, Ph.D.

As a baby boomer I grew up on Superman. I watched the original George Reeves TV show when it first aired and have been hooked ever since. Though I remember the TV show, to this day, I still do not remember the first *Superman* comic I saw, though it must be from the 1950s. That is buried in the strata of time. And I still vividly remember the morning in 1959 when my dad broke the very sad news to me. "Superman is dead," screamed the newspaper headline. I was crushed.

Since those fondly remembered 1950s, I have been a fan and collector of the Man of Steel. Throughout my formal education, which ended in a Ph.D. in biochemistry, my tenure on the UCSD faculty (where I still am), and my forays into the world of cancer immunotherapy, I still enjoyed my journeys into the land of Superman. After founding a few biomedical companies along the way, I had the resources to realize my dream, a complete run of *Action Comics*. Slowly I began to dig deep into the run and was able to add issues #2 to #10 to the collection; I had all the other issues subsequent to them.

Then I focused on the real target, *Action Comics* #1: the Grail of grails. Wanting one and finding one are two entirely different animals. I did search for a while, but nothing was available. As it eventually turned out, during the 2008 San Diego Comic-Con, I visited the booth of Bob Underwood, a producer and writer, most famous for writing and producing the 1980s TV show, *Night Court*. On his table, sort of hidden among other items, and not singled out, was just what I was looking for: *Action Comics* #1. I forced myself to keep cool as I nonchalantly inquired about that particular issue. As soon as I held it in my hands, I could actually feel the electricity and goose bumps aplenty. We negotiated a price, and as it turned out, we both had accounts at the same bank, so it took just a couple of minutes to transfer the money to his account. Immediately after the successful transfer, Bob said to me, "The book is yours." Believe me, that was magic to my ears, and instantly washed away many years of longing and dreams. The actual price is not important, but I will say it was the last *Action Comics* #1 that has sold for under $100,000. I would grade this copy in the 6 to 7 range.

I have not slabbed my copy of *Action Comics* #1, nor do I intend to. Every couple of years I put on the cotton gloves and actually read the issue! The thrill and excitement in turning the cover and seeing the first page is a joy beyond words. I now have the pleasure and honor of saying I have a complete run of *Action Comics*, the pinnacle of comic books and the Superman saga. Truth, justice, and the American way.

We know people who know people who love the opportunity to share their extreme possessions. This *Action Comics* #1 is the real deal, displayed in our shop for Free Comic Book Day 2017. *Action Comics* #1 (1938) (© DC Comics. Used with permission).

The Golden Age of comics was a period of imagination, creativity, and experimentation. Covers illustrated with racist overtones, scantily clad femme fatales, and sensationalized violence made many adults nervous. What was all this gratuitous art and storytelling exploitation doing to the kids?

Crime comics were in vogue with early police heroes and agents finding voice in the

1930s. Crime was always an urban blight and crime comics were entering the marketplace. Crime comics sensationalized cops and crooks alike. Unlike the superheroes, crime comic books brought an edgy, gritty fictional realism to their stories. These comics were not necessarily for kids, but there were no restricted comics in those days. There were no rating standards that prevented kids from buying certain comics. They followed the headlines of the day and emulated movies with archetypical criminal figures.

In my mind's eye I picture a windblown newsstand somewhere on the streets of Brooklyn during the war years of the 1940s. The streets are teeming with kids all looking for something to do in the inner city streets. Crime is everywhere and the kids who live on the grimiest streets can seldom escape it. I see a kid about 10 years of age stopping by the newsstand to catch a glimpse of the new comics that week before the operator shoos him away. This poor kid can barely scratch ten cents together, but he sees what he wants: the newest issue of *Crime Does Not Pay* (Lev Gleason Pub.). He debates the price but can't wait to see the dirty crooks inside get theirs, so he pauses to scoop out his change and offers it to the man behind the counter. Pretty soon he's sitting on the curb reading about Dillinger and his gang coming to a fiery end. In his world, the comic book metes out the kind of justice the streets rarely see in real life.

Soldiers returning from the war loved comics, but they had matured in combat and were less interested in superheroes. Trends were changing: crime, Westerns, war, horror, and science fiction–themed comics were the heirs apparent to comic book readers.

Cartoon comics, funny-animal comics, and movie/television-based comic books reached out with more wholesome reading. *Classic Comics* (later *Classics Illustrated*) revisited classic novels and abridged them by using comic panels to retell the stories, shortening the time a student would have to spend reading the book. Virtually every genre under the sun was available. Adventure heroes ranged from Frank Buck and Tarzan to Westerns with Roy Rogers and John Wayne, and even sports comics with celebrated retired ballplayers like Babe Ruth and Lou Gehrig!

Everything was placed into comics. If a trend started to form, like Korean War–era comics, then a dozen publishers would grind out cookie-cutter war comics. If a company like EC Comics increased readership with violently graphic covers, then somebody else would try to match them. By 1952, the covers on newsstands featured a plethora of bloodied, chopped, bullet-ridden, hanged, and salacious subjects on covers each month. Built-in attempts to produce kid-friendly material went head-to-head with *Chamber of Chills*, *Shock SuspenStories*, *Frontline Combat*, and *Vault of Horror*.

Post–World War II, comics had seen better times. Circulation was lower than wartime levels. Publishers were looking for ideas to capture attention. The lurid characters of the early 1950s comics matched the fascination of their smaller audience. The adult nature appealed to many, but helped to alienate parents, educators, and politicians. Talk of censorship turned into action.

A psychiatrist named Dr. Fredric Wertham force-fed the public the fear that comics were corrupting America's youth. His book *Seduction of the Innocent* (1954) explained the crisis and used pseudoscientific "facts" to underline comics' negative influences. Wertham already had the attention of many Americans. Quotes like this one impacted parents' concepts of comic books: "Badly drawn, badly written, and badly printed—a strain on the young eyes and young nervous systems—the effects of these pulp-paper nightmares is that of a violent stimulant. Their crude black and reds spoil a child's natural sense of color; their hypodermic injection of sex and murder make the child impatient with better, though quieter, stories." Wertham went on to inflame readers' senses with, "Unless we want a coming generation even more ferocious than the present one, parents and teachers throughout America must band together to break the comic 'magazine.'"

What started out in the 1940s as a combination of praise and criticism of comics devolved into downright denigration of an American pastime. Full-blown revolt was brewing, and Wertham induced our government to kick the beehive. Fortunately for me, my father had a bit of the devil in himself and a thick skin for the outrageous horrors and violence in comic books; he didn't feel the need to protect me from the worst of it when I hunted down old comics in the 1960s.

Once again, comics were being destroyed, only this time it was both metaphorical and physical. Parent groups encouraged the censorship of "dangerous" comics and sent many an issue to the dump. No comics were safe. Dr. Wertham, ever the concerned professional, targeted all comics. He badgered the animal-on-animal violence in Disney Comics, Wonder Woman's overly powerful feminism, and even the Dynamic Duo for supposedly being gay!

So comics were thrown away or burned. No paper drives this time—just good ol' American unnecessary repression. Senate hearings commenced, chaired by Estes Kefauver of Tennessee. Kefauver was a zealous politician with eyes on improving his political station. Kefauver was a hard-nosed bureaucrat who had cut his eyeteeth in a Senate committee investigation of organized crime in 1950. His multi-city road show put the screws to organized crime figures on camera as he pushed to uncover what we know today as the Mafia.

Dr. Wertham's pressure against comic books ultimately enlisted the attention of Senator Kefauver, whose Senate subcommittee held hearings on comics' influences on juvenile delinquency. With Wertham as a witness, the U.S. Government's Senate hearings tore comic books apart, linking crime and horror comics to the delinquency of teenagers. Comic books were so thoroughly bad-mouthed that the remaining publishers of the 1950s either adopted a code or closed shop. There were few exceptions. *Classics Illustrated* opted to operate without unnecessary restrictions. They published renditions of literary classics. If they were good enough for American libraries, they were good enough in comic book form. Of course, Dell Comics were never part of the Comics Code. Dell believed their comics were family-friendly and could continue thriving outside of Code intervention.

The committee never established a link between teen violence and comics. Recommendations were made to publishers to tone down the content they were printing. Publishers got the message and developed a self-policing authority to govern comic book production. All but several top publishers agreed to adopt the principles of the newly-formed Comics Magazine Association of America. The seal of the CMAA was affixed to the corner of most comics. The seal guaranteed security to distrustful parents already prone to dispose of comic books on sight.

But by 1954, the damage was done. Comic books were damaged goods in the public eye. Circulation dropped and several publishers quit.

11

Eras and Genres
Golden Age Part 2: The Atomic Age!

Paraphrasing Charles Dickens: It was the best time for comics, it was the worst time for comics—the Atomic Age of Comics!

As discussed earlier, World War II was a low point for humanity but a high point for comic book sales, specifically superhero comics. These colorful characters slowly fell out of favor after the war and were replaced with romance, science fiction, jungle stories, crime, funny animals (including the Disney cast), and westerns, among others.

And then the Soviets detonated a nuclear device that rocked the Free World. Suddenly, America's sole position atop the atomic food chain was being challenged by its mortal Cold War foe. The first Soviet nuclear test in 1949 was followed within one year by the North Korean invasion of South Korea. America and its allies rallied behind the nascent Republic of South Korea and branded the North as the new enemy, an enemy backed by powerful communist interests. The United States was back in a war magnified by its global participants.

The American population was ideologically at war with communists and has been since World War I. Atomic weapons raised the ante at the end of World War II, and comic books sensed American readers' mood change. United States marines, soldiers and sailors had fought and won one war only to enter into a new conflict within five years.

Americans were feeling the impact of anti-communist hysteria. The fear of a communist takeover was always present, churning up the concerns and paranoia of an American populace still consumed with bitter memories of the recent past. The knowledge that the Russians had "the bomb" heightened fear and mistrust. Movies filmed with lighter fare during World War II, such as Busby Berkeley musicals, were being edged out by crime noir and war dramas. Communist infiltrators replaced monocle-wearing Nazis as B-rate bad guys. Novels were replacing pulps, and with greater quantities of spice and violence.

Comic books represented this age of the atomic bomb with their own brands of story and art, exploring and exploiting each reader's fears. Editors were always looking for trending themes and found them in the fear and hysteria taking place worldwide. Titles like *Atomic War* (1952), *Atom-Age Combat* (1952) and *World War III* (1953) gripped newsstand shoppers with covers blasting nuclear clouds in four-color imagery. War comics mixed hand-to-hand combat with all-out city-killer bombings. Science mixed with science fiction and produced comic books with alien attacks entering the fray. Every week newsstands pulverized comic book fans with graphic horror, sex and violence. The new way of things would hook returned soldiers and those craving edgier comics.

Science fiction was a generally fresh movie genre with the advent of 1950s entertainment. Classic sci-fi already existed with Fritz Lang's *Metropolis*, Universal's *Frankenstein*, and the *Flash Gordon* and *Buck Rogers* serials of the 1930s. Inevitably, aliens and atomic bombs worked their way into comics as metaphors for the worsening fears of a potential World War III. A favorite movie of mine, *The Day the Earth Stood Still*, arrived in 1951 amidst the undercurrent of imminent world destruction. Brilliantly written, the film answers the question: "Is God watching?" with a metaphorical "Yes!" Communists were one thing, but now Americans needed to watch the skies for space-based peril.

Comics were on board simultaneously, drawing upon the talents of sci-fi scribes both in and outside the world of comics. EC's *Weird Science* (1950) portrayed arms-laden aliens in spaceships over Earth in nuclear bombing runs. Charlton's *Space Adventures* (1952) went for the pre-emptive and took the fight to the aliens in their homes.

Horror comics came into their own during the Atomic Age of comics. Classic horror, once evoking the fable-like fiction of Dracula or Frankenstein's monster, metastasized into grotesque stories of gore and vengeance in the 1950s. Horror comics grabbed readers with shocking art not seen in movies or the developing years of television. EC, the best of the best, utilized the talents of Graham "Ghastly" Ingels and Jack Davis to draw horror as it had never been drawn before. Both Ingels and Davis illustrated corpses and rotting flesh with mortifying detail and hooked buyers on sight. But EC shared infamy with Harvey Comics and their brand of horror.

EC Comics has a rich history spanning two generations of publishing family. Max Gaines and his son William took turns running the company after a twist of fate forced William to take over the reins from his father (dead in 1947 before his time). Max was instrumental in getting much of what we know as DC Comics off the ground in the 1930s and '40s. He left that company and formed his beloved Educational Comics, producing *Picture Stories from the Bible* (1942) until his death.

William Gaines started with additional titles to get the company moving in a new direction. *Saddle Justice* (1948) and *Crime Patrol* (1948) are just two of the titles suggestive of the genres William (Bill) was eager to produce. Although the name of the company was Educational Comics, the titles that were making money were the ones he and his creative staff had invented after Bill's ascension.

Bill canceled the educational titles and went for the more dramatic fiction. The results were the now legendary and wildly popular horror, sci-fi, crime and war comics that inspired a brigade of imitators.

Often imitated but almost never replicated, EC's output challenged readers with innovative, plot-twisting stories and amazing art.

The caliber of artists Bill chose from remains famous. They raised the bar in the early 1950s with unique, iconic styles. Gaines celebrated his artists publicly in his comics, gaining them fame while most artists in the comic book industry remained anonymous. I collected ECs from the moment I actually owned one around 1975. I read the stories and boasted about the artists as though I were the first one to notice them! Actually ECs were popular from their first moments on the stands twenty-five years before. I was astounded at how the stories and art just seemed to get better in the four years of EC's heyday. The back issues were relatively expensive in nice shape even after just ten years of national comic book fandom. ECs were being shared by more and more people as I competed with others to find copies.

Today, EC remains famous as the Atomic Age publisher that set standards for excellence. The titles have been reprinted many times, most under the auspices of the grand EC fan and scholar Russ Cochran. Those reprints have watered down the ability for dealers like me to sell ECs as readily as we once did. It is certainly a challenge to get full *OPG* for them. I've learned over the years that to move them, at least the lower-grade copies, I have to offer discounts greater than 30 percent. That's not a surprise because of the generational gaps involved, but it is a shame that demand in the 2000s is not as vibrant as the past.

Harvey's horror titles and art were often violent and graphic, even by today's standards. Horror titles like *Witches Tales* (1951) and *Chamber of Chills* (1951) pandered to the mayhem with sadism, bondage, and torture as editorial recipes to sell comics. Latter-day collectors still seek out some of Harvey's better-known issues for the covers that inflicted the most pain. Truly, these remain collectible comics!

Attention was diverted to war comics with the advent of the hot war in Korea. War was on the minds of many, including those who were in combat and those who wondered about it. Millions of war vets and war buffs hungered for tales of combat from World War II. Publishers catered to their desire for war stories with multitudes of combat stories, both real and imagined. Korea burned with combat between two opposing forces, good and evil. Comics placated the curious with quick, violent lessons of combat against the same determined enemy that could blow up our cities. Comic book publishers discovered that the godless Commies were good to go in 32 pages every month. Commies were little better than stereotypical villains, replacing Nazis as the villains *de jour* of the Cold War 1950s.

Often times, the quality of the stories in lesser-known horror and war titles did not match the exciting covers. This was a time when publishers were experimenting. They knew they were producing for two generations: the war generation and the early Baby Boomer kids. These two groups of fans contrasted against the time between wars and the advent of atomic fear.

The Atomic Age (or Atom Age) is considered an era within an era. A debate about the segmentation of the Golden Age era still gathers essayists. The Golden Age formally ended with the arrival of the new version of *The Flash* in 1956, but it most certainly seems to encompass two different eras. Much like the differences between the top and bottom halves of California, the Golden Age seems to diverge after World War II.

I've written about the endangered comic book industry of the 1950s. Parents, officials, and politicians clamped down on comic book creativity that they labeled as excessive and explicit. Censorship threats put pressure on publishers to tone down their comics, while governmental hearings threatened enforcement. Distributors saw sales reductions while communities across the nation saw local magazine burnings reminiscent of Nazi book burnings of the thirties. Comics had been destroyed in the previous decade to generate raw material for the war. Now, they were being destroyed out of fear and hate. Comic book companies would be reeling soon under pressure from external forces, but the money being made induced companies to stall on self-censorship. After all, they were just comic books! Companies like Quality and Harvey were used to making cash from comic book sales and didn't concern themselves with the changing attitudes at the turn of the decade.

Larger publishers such as DC Comics and Dell had always put out products that reflected more kid-friendly content. They supported ordinances and boycotts, albeit with no fanfare, that impacted their edgier competitors. DC supported the appointment of some sort of authority that set codes of behavior for comics. Dell felt they did not need to be "stamped" with outside approval. They received a minimal amount of fringe criticism for their content, but by and large they produced the kinds of comics parents approved.

With television's early success, Dell Comics was inspired to produce comics based on cartoons and live-action TV shows. Dell whipped up wholesome comics with virtually no controversy. Dell stuck with a formula and licensed Disney characters as well. Under single owner George Delacourt, Dell Comics never accepted the Comics Code. Delacourt felt his giant share of the retail market (one third of all circulated comics) would ensure he could dominate sales without Code constraints. He was outside of the grip of the billowing market forces that were developing into a public firestorm.

The results of gathering scrutiny over the "evils of comic books" forced a code of conduct onto comic book publishers. Leaders and parents bought into the fantasy that a perceived rise in juvenile delinquency could be tracked back to the influence of comic books.

One of my store customers, Gary Johnson, told me a story about parental concerns regarding kids and comic books. He lived in the San Diego community of Point Loma in the 1950s. Somewhere around 1955 at the age of about 10 he made a trip to a small shopping center near his house. The small mall held several shops, including his father's shop. Next door was Leo Volzes Drugstore.

Volzes sold old comic books for a nickel a pop with no particular concern for display. They were left unattended on racks for the kids. Gary once found an old copy of a *Wonder Woman* comic book for a nickel. Gary said he dwelled only briefly on the bustier and bare legs; he just wanted to read the story.

He brought the comic home to the chagrin of his mother, a devout Catholic (100 years old in 2016!) with ultraconservative sensibilities. She took one look at the *Wonder Woman* cover and was she mad! She scooped up the comic and her son and drove back to the drugstore. Mom walked Gary up to checkout and demanded to talk to the manager. She then scolded the manager for selling that kind of "objectionable" material to a child and warned him that from now on, "My son can only buy western comics at your store. You make sure he doesn't buy anything else. If he buys more *Wonder Woman*, you tell me."

The manager got the message and so did Gary. He only bought westerns from that point on. To this day Gary shops for comics, always looking for ancient westerns.

Government witch hunts for hidden domestic enemies caused many to swallow common sense and opt for restrictions nationwide to allay fear. Restrictions in movies, restrictions in the press, and restrictions in comics were supported by Eisenhower–era politicians as the country seemingly yearned for relief from the stress and violence of back-to-back wars.

Campaign slogans and power plays among bureaucrats made comic books easy prey. The contents of some comics were ready-made to stimulate battle with conservative-minded zealots with agendas. Their constituents followed suit when they were called to arms to censor what was thought to be a genre of entertainment that heightened societal problems.

Late in 1954, the Comics Code Authority was enacted, with its label first printed on the covers of participating publishers in 1955. This Code was created and paid for by cooperating comic book companies. They hoped the powers-that-be would stem their tirades against comics once they saw this commitment to family cooperation. Comic book publishers, distributors, and retailers all measured the wisdom of the Code against a general boycott and reduction in sales.

Smaller companies like Star Publications, Toby Press, and others quit the comic book business. Fawcett and Avon already published paperback novels, so they got out of the less profitable, troublesome comic book world. Eastern Color, the granddaddy of comic books, closed up shop late in 1955.

Bill Schelly's book *American Comic Book Chronicles* (2013) noted how censorship in the 1950s was the final straw for many Atom Age publishers. Declining profits was the bottom line for companies forced to make hard decisions. The book continues with statistics informing readers that 1952 saw an "industry high of slightly more than 3,150 issues published," while "only about 2,300 were produced with 1955 dates" (statistics patiently gathered by Michelle Nolan) and "only fifteen companies produced as many as a dozen issues in 1957."

The end of Golden Age and Atom Age comics depleted the talent pool of writers and artists once so numerous. Many writers and artists were driven to find work elsewhere in their chosen fields or leave the environs of their given talents behind for good. The dark clouds of censorship and failed business reduced comic book production to a few superheroes from DC, cartoon characters, westerns, and watered-down science fiction and mystery books. There were few publishers left. Some, like DC and Dell, often took the TV and movie approach and built comic book adaptations around the likes of Bob Hope and Bozo the Clown.

Prior to the Comics Code, horror, war, and crime comics smothered each other for shelf space while sharing profits with *Mickey Mouse, Mighty Mouse, Super Mouse* and every other kind of mouse. Funny-animal comics, westerns, television and movie comics, and educational-themed offerings were now staking greater claims. Comic books even dabbled in the music scene with Martin Goodman's (Atlas) *World's Greatest Songs* (1954). Singer Eddie Fisher was featured along with the lyrics to a Frank Sinatra song.

War comics with watered-down action and characters emphasized American victory at the end of each story. Comic book publishers were struggling to keep up with advancing foes and declining readership. They searched for any benign format that would continue to sell comics. The violent and graphically glorious destruction of our enemies via comics was no longer tolerable for parents. Everything that was the most memorable about Atomic Age comics was gone after the institution of the Code. For today's collectors, the "Pre-Code" horror and crime comics are highly prized. Eye-injury covers, torture covers, headlight covers and just about anything grisly that found its way onto 32 pages of fun is considered collectible today. These copies in high grade commonly sell for several percentages above *OPG*. They are not common, and buyers can expect to find them in lower grades, if at all.

When I gained true competency as a collector in the late 1970s, I worked within a culture populated by collectors from two generations. The older people still collected the comics of their youth, maintaining the popularity of companies like Gilberton (*Classics Illustrated*), Dell and Gold Key (and their licensed Disney comics), Archie, and other less lucrative sellers in today's back-issue market. The second generation of fans, my generation, was often less inclined to put money on some of those genres when the current happenings at Marvel and DC made the superhero market more interesting.

It's roughly forty years later now. The folks who went after the *Classics* and the Disneys of the past are mostly in the past as well. I see a few at conventions and at my store. They still surround themselves with comic book vestiges of the bygone era. They are about the only people I can sell those old genres to. I know that the pricing guides have not kept up with the decline, allowing prices to remain the same or increase marginally when the reality is much cheaper. Those titles, along with westerns and funny-animal comics, get really lean numbers and often have to be heavily discounted against *OPG*.

Forensic comicologists everywhere lament the loss of the Golden Age non-superhero market. The collections of *Classics*, teen humor, kid comics and the like are still surfacing, but there's no one to sell them to. I can't offer original-owner collections of *Daffy Duck* and *Cisco Kid* the kind of money they often expect. They don't want to hear my thoughts: that there's no money to be had selling them. When I deliver that kind of bad news to them, that induces them to feel cheated. I have to go into a short discourse about changing times and tastes. They're just impossible to market unless they're at super-cheap bargain prices. If the buyer were to contemplate buying them for resale, I wish him or her good luck. If the buyer wants them because they are old and cool, then go for it. They're still fun to own.

In their day in the first half of the 1950s, Dell and Gilberton were still just two of many companies that survived the 1940s. Some reduced their page counts to the universal 32 pages. Others like DC ramped down from 52 pages to 44 pages on some titles, and then finally 32. All still for a dime. One word of note about DCs in the early 1950s: the superhero titles like *Batman*, *Superman* and *World's Finest* are not considered scarce, but you wouldn't know that if you were looking for them. A lot of those comics did not survive the test of time, and many collectors who desired full runs of such titles had to work hard and long to find some of them. *Gerber's Photo-Journal Guide* volumes list their scarcity indexes at 4s and 5s, but the reality is they're much tougher to find than indicated.

Since most of my focus on collecting will always remain on DC and Marvel, I can't leave this chapter without marveling (!) at Atlas Comics in the early 1950s. Publisher Goodman's firm adopted the name of his distribution company in 1951 and changed the name from Timely to Atlas. They entered the Atomic Age with a selection of teen and glamour comics and some funny-animal stuff. Not long after the most creative company, EC Comics, shifted its format from benign animal fables, Bible stories and westerns to the grittier stuff they are famous for, Atlas followed suit.

I found this excerpt from a Wikipedia page that I also read somewhere else in the past: "As Marvel/Atlas editor-in-chief Stan Lee told comic book historian Les Daniels, Goodman 'would notice what was selling, and we'd put out a lot of books of that type.'" Stan was referring to Atlas following EC's trend-setting titles and their popularity. Atlas produced dozens of similar titles, all with short, forgettable stories from talented, low-paid artists.

Atlas did away with their superheroes by 1950 (with a failed attempt to revive them a few years later). In the absence of superheroes (again from Wikipedia): "Goodman's comic book line expanded into a wide variety of genres, producing horror, westerns, humor, funny animal, drama, crime, war, jungle, romance, espionage, medieval adventure, Bible stories and sports comics. As did other publishers, Atlas also offered comics about models and career women." Other companies like Harvey Comics, St. John and Ajax/Farrell followed the trends, but nobody did it in volume like Atlas.

I've known lots of collectors who've spent time and money collecting and filling in runs of Atlas titles. Most of the copies I owned (and I've owned a lot!) are generally much-read and not expensive to own. For a hobbyist, it is fun to hunt them down. Atlas titles were targets of mine during my collecting years and I still feel true comic book fans should give collecting those titles a try.

One story of note: six years ago I received a call at my shop from a woman asking if I was interested in buying old comics. She went into a little detail but surprised me with her name: Nancy Maneely, the daughter of Joe Maneely! Joe was a popular Atlas artist until his untimely death.

Nancy was the youngest of three girls, too young to remember her father well because he passed when she was just two. The story she told me when she arrived at my shop was that she grew up wishing her dad had been a part of her young life, so she collected copies of comics that he had worked on, almost all of them with Atlas Comics. This was her way of connecting to her father. She'd been doing this for years and had amassed duplicates she no longer wished to keep. She offered the duplicates to us because of our reputation for dealing in old comics.

She brought in roughly 350 comics with two things in common: they were all Atlas, and they all had her father's artistic work on the covers or in the stories. These dupes were her lesser-graded castoffs, and I eagerly fit prices to them to make Nancy an offer. She was easy on me and didn't offer much of a challenge, so we concluded the transaction successfully.

She mentioned that there was a book in the works about her father, but as of 2016 I found nothing about that on the Internet.

I did not own any original art. I saw it, liked it, but couldn't really afford it. The comic books cost me enough of my minimum-wage salary I earned working at Richard Alf's Comic Kingdom. Comic art was a pace change I couldn't make—that is, until I saw a Russ Heath cover for sale in the dealers' room at Comic-Con.

One of the dealers at this show had a loose stack of original comic book art piled on top of his table. Comic books in boxes sat on the table against the art and kind of helped keep the art straight. I couldn't miss the art while going through the somewhat redundant selection of comics for sale. I feathered through the art pages out of curiosity and saw all kinds of random pages, cover art included. Tucked into the stack was the cover art to *Astonishing* #9, an Atlas title. The cover art for a story called "The Little Black Box" was by my favorite: Russ Heath. *Astonishing* #9 was released n 1952, a few years before my collecting target date. The price was only $35.00, a little steep for me, but it was Heath, it was Atlas, and I could always sell off some comics. So I bought it: my first original art purchase.

Once home, I pinned it to the wall of my living room. I used pushpins with their flanged shape to hold the art to the wall, without actually putting holes into the paper. And there it resided for months, properly mounted in my living room near my pet cockatiel and her cage.

As often happens with the best of intentions, my prominent and protectively placed tribute to comic art became a target of the bird. She managed to wing her way over to the furniture just in reach of the Heath cover and then found her way back to the perch while I was gone. Upon my return, I immediately saw the results. My bird had meticulously nibbled on the right corner of the page, leaving a pile of tiny paper fragments on the carpet below. The bird's disastrous need to chew on my art removed about a 3" by 4" corner of valuable Russ Heath artwork. My $35.00 investment was ruined. I love animals, so my bird's fate was never in doubt. A wing clipping was in the works, however. As for the art, I thought about disposing of it, but like all obsessive collectors I just packed it away with other stuff and basically forgot about it for 25 years.

It was 2002 and I had come into some hard-earned money. My collecting habits were in full force, but my comic book hobby had long been replaced by comic book original art. My tastes led me to covet art from the 1950s to the 1970s. That was a good cross-section of Gold, Silver and a little Bronze Age art reflective of my age. I sought out art of all kinds, just as long as it represented work done by artists I grew up with.

My art collecting began in the 1970s, lightened up in the 1980s, and regained momentum by the late 90s. Art was plentiful thanks to conventions, Web sites, and eBay. I composed a list of artists I wanted, which covered virtually everyone from a three-decade period, including the long-immortalized EC creators. I thought it would be great to count EC artwork among my collection of generational talent.

I put out some feelers and shopped cons for EC pages. Brother, they were (and are) not cheap! But now I could afford it. One of my contacts asked me if I'd like to own a complete EC story: all seven pages! I asked "who," "what," and "how much." I was put in touch with art dealer Tom Horvitz.

Tom lived north of Universal Studios. He was renowned in my circles for the large, exotic collection of art he maintained both as a dealer and collector. I got in touch with Tom by phone and followed up with a subsequent trip to his place.

Tom's selection of art was impressive. There was so much good stuff, it was overwhelming. He seemed to have everything! To this day it is hard to remember details when you're enraptured by the Fort Knox of art. Just a couple of standouts come to mind: the original Jack Kirby cover art to *Captain America* #100 and a full-page Sunday strip of Hal Foster's *Prince Valiant* (his stuff was also wall-mounted, but no pet bird!). And of course, a full 7-page EC story by Jack Davis. The story was from *Frontline Combat* #5, the Stonewall Jackson story.

Jack Davis was comfortable working in any genre. When his prolific tenure at EC ended, he segued into commercial art doing covers for magazines, *TV Guide* and movie posters. I remember seeing his art adorning sports magazines. He worked everywhere! (I was sorry to hear of his passing in 2016.)

Tom and I negotiated on the EC art while he carefully opened drawers of specially made wooden cases and pulled out more cool art. While we talked, he laid out Russ Heath art. I admired the pages but told him that I had already filled that need. Then I told him about the unfortunate fate of my cover. Tom took my tale with only a slight grimace and then informed me that he was Russ's art agent. He asked if I wanted to meet him. He said Russ lived nearby and could make the trip over if desired. I took the offer. Duh!

Tom called and Russ was over in 15 minutes. He brought some of his art over to share with us. As cool as that was, I didn't really have the money for that on top of the EC story. I politely declined, offering that I had the mostly intact example of one of his earliest works. Russ asked, "Mostly?" I sheepishly told my tale of bird woe and tried to change the conversation. Russ asked if I had it with me. When I said it was at home, Tom told me it might be repairable. He looked over at Russ and suggested that maybe Russ could fix it. Russ asked if perhaps I had a picture. I didn't, but I bet I could get one fast!

I called my wife Kim, who was fortunately at home. With quick directions to a stored suitcase, she found Heath's *Astonishing* cover. She quickly emailed us a scan. Russ and Tom looked it over and quietly discussed the cover's repair needs. Russ said he could trim the rough, bird-beaked edges and redraw the missing corner, using a published copy of the original comic book. I told him I would be more than happy to find a copy, like pronto.

The arrangements were made. After business was concluded with Tom, I returned home to San Diego and packed up the damaged cover art. My instructions were to mail the art with the comic copy I found and send it all to Tom Horvitz. The rest was up to Russ Heath.

Russ took possession of the art and worked his magic. Within a matter of a few months, the missing corner was redrawn to spec. Horvitz said Russ could create the replacement art but not reattach it to the cover correctly. For that we would need the expertise of one Roger Hill.

Roger Hill is a comic art historian, consultant, and collector. His unique history with this hobby couples with his talent for limited restoration of original art pages. Tom Horvitz introduced me, indirectly, to Roger. He explained that Roger would provide the second half of a two-part process to repair my Heath cover. The cover, by the way, was missing the title and panel art along the left side. All stats (photo copies affixed on the cover) were long gone when I first bought the art. Remember, I paid a measly $35. You get what you pay for.

Roger possessed the talent and expertise not only to recreate the missing stats, but to attach them properly to my Heath cover. Additionally, I hired him to attach Russ Heath's newly drawn replacement piece with seamless precision. The price tag was fair for the unique talent Roger could provide in returning my art to its previous glory.

A restoration job of this nature takes time. Months can go by, if not longer. Roger kept me updated since we didn't know each other. He admonished me that the new art was shades lighter than the 50-year-old original paper. Shading to match could be accomplished for extra cash and more time. I optioned out, reasoning the restoration being done would always be acknowledged, so no attempts to disguise it need be made.

The months did go by. Eventually, Roger called to let me know the job was finished. We completed the financial part and the art was shipped from Roger's Kansas home. My artwork returned within a short period of shipping time. I cut the thin, wide package open and unveiled my refurbished Russ Heath cover for the first time in a year.

What a breathtaking change! What was old was new again. All the missing pieces were recreated to exact copies and attached with tight, artistic precision. My art was beautiful—maybe even better-looking than when it was first drawn. The uniqueness of the team effort not only defeated the best offense my bird could provide, but rebuilt a mostly awesome creation by one of America's living legends of comic book art. More interesting was the fact that Russ Heath had drawn the cover for *Astonishing* #9 fifty years earlier for Atlas editor Stan Lee. Fifty years later, he drew a piece of it for me to bring the part back to full life. It was 80 percent 1952 Russ Heath and 20 percent 2002 Russ Heath with a solid performance by Roger Hill to tie it all together. Holy cow!

Appropriately, my Heath cover art bridges two eras in comic book collecting, sort of: It's true Golden Age by *OPG* standards, but from the Atomic Age.

DC managed to stretch a few name-brand superheroes through the last years of the Golden Age. Atlas (Marvel) tried to reengage readers with three of their best by returning Captain America, Human Torch and the Sub-Mariner to comic books briefly in the mid–1950s. They failed to catch on and disappeared for another decade or so. Superheroes were seemingly a vestige of the past. The finale for comic books in the mid–1950s needed a prayer, some form of resurrection, and a silver lining to follow the gathered storm.

What will happen to them next?

Only the Forensic Comicologist (and everybody else) knows.

12

Collecting Gold

DC and Timely (Marvel Comics) characters continue to be published in newsstand and specialty markets today. Batman, Superman, Sub-Mariner, Captain America, et al. generate tens of thousands of current comic books, keeping their legacies alive and in the public eye. The wonder years of the Golden Age are very well collectible because of that legacy. Collecting Golden Age comics just requires a simple understanding of what fans have recognized as reasons for selective collecting.

Publishers

Take titles like *Action Comics* and Timely's *All-Winners Comics*, for example. They have retained collecting popularity for a number of reasons.

Their age alone appeals to comic book collectors. Timely and DC brought the Human Torch and Batman into the world. Those characters exist today and resonate with collectors of the past. There's a mystique to the comics produced in that era, and not just DCs and Timelys. Several other publishers still generate fierce loyalty in today's fans. Thirty some-odd publishers made comics at one time, but not all enjoy desirability now. Centaur is one example of a niche publisher in high demand. Centaur only existed for a short time (1938–1942). Centaur was a small-press company created by comic book men producing titles that lasted only a short while. Their short-lived existence made them popular among Golden Age collectors of the obscure. Titles like *Amazing-Man* (1939), *Amazing Mystery Funnies* (1938), and *The Arrow* (1940) barely found room on the newsstands thanks to poor distribution.

Timelys in particular are collected because their publisher stands for an archetypal Golden Age experience. The covers often scream: "More of everything!" The legend of Simon and Kirby's original Golden Age work extended to others, creating a Timely Comics "house style." That means their comic cover orientation was designed for maximum impact. Timelys are on the tongue of any serious Golden Age buyer I've ever met. They are common enough, but are almost always priced above *OPG*. That pricing bump is considered acceptable.

The collector's desire for particular publishers has evolved beyond what was popular even 20 years ago. The once super-popular Fox Feature Syndicate started production at the end of the 1930s and offered primarily superhero and humor titles. After World War II ended, Fox optioned to milk profit from action and crime themes, the latter known for its notorious use of sex and violence to sell copies. Nicky Wright, noted writer of *The Classic*

Era of American Comics, writes that Fox's books easily "competed well in the most sexy, sadistic, and violent category." Fox's cover artists were encouraged to take their "good girl art" styles to the max, drawing their female characters with the sexiest imagery comics could get away with. Gorgeous ladies in skimpy costumes adorned the covers of such titles as *Rulah* (1948) and *Phantom Lady* (1947). These titles were once highly prized until pricing and some fan indifference gradually lowered their demand. Nowadays it is challenging to find avid Fox collectors. Either the back issues are too expensive or the collectors are fewer in number than in the past.

My father obviously was unconcerned about my exposure to comics of controversial content: he kept copies of *Mad Magazine* around the house. *Mad*'s sass and satire were not necessarily for young kids, but I'm talking about my dad, a man who loved watch me set off fireworks!

Fiction House published comics from 1938 through 1954, encompassing most of the Golden Age. They used studio artists and cheap paper to produce sensationalistic comics with covers that centered on shocking action or a woman in a bathing suit, or something else tight and clingy. I remember collecting them in the 1970s when they were much more popular. Titles like *Wings Comics* (1940), *Jungle Comics* (1940) and *Jumbo Comics* (1938) spun cookie-cutter stories of dubious written quality with art that was less exciting than the cover. By 2016 most Fiction House titles were likely to sell at half-price or less. That's a pity for a company that spanned all of the 1940s.

Conversely, Centaur Publications has seen a marked increase in collector demand. It was originally owned by a Harry "A" Chesler (and published as same), but Centaur's owners took control of the parent company under their publishing name: Centaur Publications Incorporated. With only four years of publication, Centaur still managed to create dozens of original characters. Their talent pool included Bill Everett, Carl Burgos, and Paul Gustaufson (also a veritable who's-who of early Timely Comics work). Centaurs are scarce and more so in high grade. The demand is fierce among a cadre of hardcore American collectors. Higher-grade copies seemingly don't exist in quantity and are prize catches when they surface.

Cover Appeal

DC's often docile, kid-friendly covers were drawn with simple, hero-in-action poses, displaying the feature characters. Superman and Batman titles subdued the shock value of a perilous event with their heroes often in control. War-inspired covers were infrequent and rarely stigmatized the enemy with racial undertones. Postwar comics adopted lighter fare and were often humorous. Other companies seemed to embody the frenetic nature of Timely's covers, generating their own style of "shock and awe" to grab readers.

Timely's titles faced buyers across the magazine stands with a frenzy of action and violence. Their comics attacked our enemies with a kinetic force of last-second rescues, tortured victims, missiles, gunfire, bondage, and bad guys who behaved and looked subhuman.

Golden Age comics rarely used cover art to relay a controversial message. The covers were to attract young readers and lovers of fiction. Covers were designed to appeal to men and boys, but there were comics for girls as well.

Archie (MLJ) Comics Publishing, inspired partly by the Andy Hardy movies popular among teens in that time, beginning with the title *Pep* sold goofy teenage characters to both sexes with covers promising dating tips, do's and don'ts. Girls liked the titles designed just for them, like *Katy Keene* (1949), with covers advertising new clothing patterns submitted by the readers themselves.

Outstanding covers from the Golden Age are still collectible with many Alex Schomburg, L.B. Cole and Lou Fine covers held up as quintessential Golden Age work. These were artists extraordinaire whose covers sold the copies instead of the other way around. Check out Schomburg's cover to *Suspense* #3 (1944) or *Guns Against Gangsters* #1 (1948) by Cole. Schomburg's *Captain America Comics* war covers were often more desirable than those of the artists who followed. Lou Fine's intricate pencil work combined with his dramatic flair is best illustrated in *Science Comics* #2 (1940) from Fox.

The theme of that particular cover is built around danger and the sexy damsel in bondage and distress. For years collectors zeroed in on bondage covers and "glamour girl" foregrounds. Fox Publications capitalized on raw emotion and sex to groom buyers through their covers. *Phantom Lady* was one of their more popular postwar titles that inflamed male senses with the sexy femme fatale in skimpy outfits. Issue #17 is considered the most classic of the *Phantom Lady* bondage covers. This was a time where the boundaries had not yet been pushed too far. *Jo-Jo Comics* (1945) from Fox not only illustrated women and danger on covers, but were an example of studio artists at work.

Will Eisner, comic book creator of *The Spirit* (1940), formed a comic art studio in partnership with Jerry Iger and hired artists to work for them. They farmed out comic artwork (covers and stories) that were sold to other companies like Fiction House, Quality and Fox. They drew covers and interior art under contract to Eisner Studios sticking with themes that the publishing clients asked for. Many of the collectible covers from that period were from Eisner's shop and propelled artists like Matt Baker to fame.

Glamour covers captured male customers with little class and a lot of lurid. Many covers were the hook for readers and considered collectible for that art. *OPG* identified them by theme in decades of its guides. Bondage covers, eye injury covers (all kinds of injury covers!), drug use covers, Hitler covers and so on were typified as collectible by the cover art.

The war years fancied a certain amount of propaganda. Racial overtones and enemy degradation were popular art themes for soldiers and the home front as well. Comic book editors let almost anything slide in those 1940s years in an effort to capitalize on the war effort and sell piles of comics. Many covers are ridiculously collectible for the vivid pictures. Often as not, however, the interior art and story were quite subdued compared to the story unfolding on the cover. The art inside could appear more primitive and the story simple and insipid, with none of the promise that the cover displayed.

Semi-nude women were drawn as heroines, victims and villains. They graced comic book covers for a complete decade with little thought towards censorship. The changing postwar era introduced a more fashionable type of cover art: the "Good Girl Art" style. Titles like *Tessie the Typist* (1944), *Joker Comics* (1942) and *Torchy* (1949) featured beautiful women in "cheesecake" poses with sultry "headlight" cover appearances. These covers are still very collectible, although often hard to find. The more lurid covers continued to exist in titles like *Crimes By Women* (1948) and *Dagar* (*Desert Hawk*). However, they were competing for magazine rack dominance with a whole host of crude, stereotypical and ghastly covers that stand up today as collectible. The sheer volume of comics for sale on a newsstand forced retailers to limit some due to display constraints. There just wasn't enough space to sell them all. Retailers had to figure out demand or what they thought their customers wanted and avoid the others. I have to figure that the more lurid or action-packed (i.e., violent) the covers, the more likely the retailer placed it for display, thinking it was a sure seller.

Cover art considered collectible today is often from the wild years of the Golden Age generation before the harsh changes the 1950s were about to heap onto comics.

From the simple positive messages of Superman (1939) in *Action Comics* to the horrific Graham Ingels covers wrapped around *Haunt of Fear* (1950) from EC Comics, the transition from one decade to the next was clearly emphasized in the comics. Novice collectors can cover-shop

Phantom Lady comics illustrate the titillation that comics were reaching for after World War II. The dangerously drawn "headlight" covers were reaching their zenith in the early 1950s. The travesty of censorship to come would put her and other pin-up girls into remission for decades. *Phantom Lady* #13 (1947) (© DC Comics. Used with permission).

for all kinds of comics for the sake of exotic collecting and find others in their midst are doing the same.

Topical covers dealt with the social situations of the period. Each comic genre paid some attention to the war to stay relevant on the newsstands. For wartime comics, nothing was a bigger draw than a picture of Hitler, Mussolini, or Japan's Tojo being taunted, teased, and subdued by the good guys. DC occasionally worked them over, such as on the cover of *World's Finest* #9 (1943), making them visceral targets for America. Other companies dealt with the war in varying graphic degrees. These "reality"-based covers debasing an enemy are still popular as collectible themes, giving them a key importance.

Torture and bondage were common themes in war comics. There was always the imminent cliffhanger moment to seal the fate of the hero or villain. Hot dames in constant danger titillated the male population from front cover to back page. Timely's covers set the bar high for their explicit violence and anti–Axis vibrancy. Standard Comics followed Timely's examples with their attacks on Nazis and the Japanese through cover layouts of the war. By the time of America's entry into the war, the enemy was a completely conceptualized target, demonized by artists and editors into something less than civilized, or human. The Black Terror was a lead hero in Standard Comics' bullpen. The title *Black Terror* (1942) exemplified Timely's cover response to the war effort, with the hero going about his grim work with violent gusto. He was energetic in his use of any handy weapon to slaughter an overwhelmed enemy.

Topics of the day dealt with fear more than fun. Silly comics like funny animals and kid comics rarely bothered with topical influences. It was all basically "cat chases mouse with hammer" slam-bang fun. The war years' influence was major, but it didn't last forever. Eventually, the hot war of the forties was replaced by the Cold War of the fifties. Communists and fifth-column saboteurs became the foreign enemy. Now Captain America had to shift gears and fight former allies on the covers in his brief pre–Code run in the 1950s. Unfortunately for collectors, these copies are increasingly difficult to find.

The end of the war presented challenges to publishers. They continued to produce superhero comics, but the buyers were reducing their intake. The war's end turned out crops of readers who turned away from the costumes. With the war over, other themes inspired covers of a topical nature. Crime was seemingly on the rise as crime comics became in vogue. Crime comics exploded in popularity with crude renderings of "true crime cases," bloody bodies and bullets flying. Some covers became collectible for their sheer gore and menace. EC Comics' *Crime SuspenStories* (1950) horrified parents and chilled kids with ultra-shocking covers to issues 16 and 17. To this day the kind of crime covers EC produced remain fan favorites. Other companies preceded EC's graphic visions with their own kind of grisly crime covers. Lev Gleason's *Crime Does Not Pay* #24 (1942) is an example of a timeless collectible because of the gritty cover, a woman's face held to the burner of a stove. Nasty!

By the end of the 1940s, graphic covers became the norm geared to men and boys. Many were GIs returned home with a lost sense of innocence. They required harsh, more adult themes in comics to be entertained.

What about the fairer sex? Girls had teen comics, romance comics and funny-animal comics to choose from, with very few considered eye-catching collectibles today (aside from the Good Girl and glamour tease covers posed by voluptuous women discussed earlier!). Based upon years of buying and selling, I feel that more little girls read comics in the Golden Age. Their appetites did seem to range from the silly to the girly, teen types. I've met plenty of women who owned those kinds of comics in the past.

Westerns, war, science fiction and adventure genres grew in popularity among the returning soldiers. New young readers joined those audiences. But it's the pre–Code covers of the late 1940s through early 1950s that generated the highly developed collectible covers that stand to this day. Today we call those early 1950s horror and crime comics pre–Code, signifying the best scary, sensational and dirty stuff sold before the watered down-comics required by the Code.

Hosts of collectible covers have entered the pantheon of fan-nation picks. The demand changes with the age groups dominating the current market. I've always advocated for buying cool covers for that reason—coolness. But if a buyer is hell-bent to buy for resale, then discovering what's popular over and above the few covers I've discussed requires time on the Internet. You can attend many good back-issue conventions and can learn quick lessons by seeing how dealers display their comics. The best covers, the ones we all consider collectible, will be mounted on the exhibitors' wall displays.

First Appearances

Just about everything from the early Golden Age era was a first. First appearances are always the best bet for drawing the biggest bang for a collector's buck. The first Batman appearance, the first Superman, Captain America, Captain Marvel and on and on and on … many characters in comics today began in the Golden Age. These are characters today's readers imagine no further back than the 1960s. Characters named The Angel, and the aforementioned Vision from Timely (Marvel), existed in the 1940s. So did Red Hood and Aquaman from DC. There are so many firsts for so many discretionary investors. The heroes are well-known, and serious collectors have that market dialed in pretty well.

Many of the villains who plagued Golden Age heroes are still reaching out to attack the good guys in today's comics. Villains like the Joker, Penguin, and Riddler began in *Batman* and *Detective Comics* of the 1940s. The Red Skull showed up on the cover of *Captain America Comics* #3 (1941). But there are lots of villains who have yet to be exploited. Who's to say that a future movie or television project won't rejuvenate some forgotten villain for a screen appearance? These are the kinds of questions that collectors are trying to answer with cash as they attempt to locate and own first appearances. Today it's easy. Just look into a well-stocked store's inventory of back issues and hunt for firsts in the bargain bins. As often as not, those boxes get played out, so further investment cash is necessary to afford more expensive firsts. And that's just for the villains!

Comic book heroes' first appearances from the Golden Age are highly touted and often supremely costly. For example: DC's roster of superheroes reads like a who's who of firsts: Spectre, Flash, Green Lantern, Atom, Sandman, Hawkman and more. The whole Justice Society of America started out of one of the publishing names that would become DC Comics. *All-Star Comics* (1940) featuring the JSA would begin. Wonder Woman (part of DC's Big Three, with Batman and Superman) rolled out in *All-Star Comics* #8 (1941–1942) before being rewarded with two of her own ongoing titles: *Wonder Woman* (1942) and *Sensation Comics* (1942). Her first appearance will run you well into five figures in less than average condition!

For Golden Age firsts, it's going to cost collectors a lot of money. First appearances of characters from companies not likely to show up in a contemporary film are usually affordable, but not necessarily considered collectible (from an investment point of view). Many companies created characters who did not make the transition into the Modern Era.

First-appearance collectibles are not limited to fictional characters. Our hobby tends to award status to the first appearance of the men and women behind the comics as well. First stories by particular writers or first art by particular artists can draw collector attention. The Golden Age produced Jack Kirby and Stan Lee, two blockbusters in the comic book world. Bob Kane, Siegel and Shuster, Will Eisner, and a host of talented names that bear as much importance as those already mentioned, all showed up in the early days of comics. But are they collectible?

Paging through *OPG*, I looked for well-known artists but with less well-known firsts in comics in the Golden Age. I started with Joe Kubert, made famous in my time by his work on DC's selection of war comics, plus Tarzan and Hawkman. His first credited art assignment was in the Golden Age in Holyoke's *Cat-Man* (1941). He was assigned work on a new character, Volton, with issue #8. The dollar values *OPG* attaches are slightly greater than the preceding issue. The book describes that issue as Kubert's first work. What's not stated is whether the slightly elevated book value is due to his art or to the new character introduced in that issue, a character long forgotten by most in our hobby.

I tried another popular name not associated with the first creation of any character: Stan Lee. Lee gets his first *OPG* credit with *Captain America Comics* #3. As a writer, his talents were less apparent, since writers were rarely credited back then. The book is expensive, but it is unknown if *OPG* adds value because of Lee's first work, since any early issue of *Cap* is phenomenally expensive due to *Captain America Comics'* collectibility in general.

I looked for comic book creators who got started later in the Golden Age by searching the Internet and *OPG*. I decided to research a personal favorite of mine: Russ Heath. Russ was an asset to DC for his portrayal of war and its machines in some of DC's war comics from the 1950s into the next millennium. Russ is a legend in our hobby. I figured Russ should have a key beginning worth a few more bucks. I found Internet references to his first work in Atlas Comics (Marvel) with a Kid Colt story in issue #4 of *Wild Western* (1948). He gets a footnote mention in that 1948 issue, but there's no direct increase in listed value due to Heath's work.

I did a little more research for other examples, but the collectible market for first appearances in the Golden Age by staff members just does not resonate like the fictional characters.

Artists

The Golden Age invented practically everything in comic books, from Will Eisner's cinemagraphic styling on *The Spirit* stories to Jack Kirby's fluid work on early Timely covers. Reed Crandall's *Blackhawk* and Jack Cole's *Plastic Man* were the marks of true American illustrators. *Prince Valiant's* Hal Foster and *Flash Gordon's* Alex Raymond were both products of metropolitan art studio educations. Their talents are renowned not only for their classic styles, but for inspiring other artists down through the decades.

Golden Age comics are remembered as much for the characters as they are for the art. Natural artists, art school graduates and classically trained illustrators all found work in comic books at the end of the Depression. Many artists transitioned from other mediums such as newspaper strips, pulps and commercial illustration to work in comic books. The written content of the story was rarely as exciting as the story the pictures told, especially to younger readers. The art is the draw(!). Every Golden Age fan remembers the art. Collectors will tell you that they select their interests from this category. Art is as important as cover and character. In fact, one artist can dominate the popularity of one character more than any other artists who shared work. Carl Barks and Simon and Kirby stand out as creators with such prominence.

Barks was just one of many Disney animators until called upon to do comics in 1942.

He took on full comic book responsibility shortly after and continued his Disney duck run until 1966. Ever faithful to the duck family of comics, Barks commanded the attention of the duck faithful. His breezy, articulate renderings motivated fans to label him the "Good Duck Artist." His desirability as a Disney comic book artist makes him the most sought-after Disney artist of his time. Although Disney comics once commanded high prices, the stories told by Barks are about the only Disneys still claiming significant value.

Joe Simon and Jack Kirby had a hand in much of the development of the Golden Age genres. Both men could conceptualize, write and draw comic books. Together and independently, they tackled superheroes, romance, westerns, and crime. Both men were on the ground floor of Golden Age history, adapting and displaying their own art styles to satisfy hectic demands. Work was plentiful among studios. Kirby worked with Simon in Timely's infancy and delighted collectors with Jack's art on the first ten issues of *Captain America*. Simon was a breakdown artist, but Kirby applied the muscles and fleshed his panoramic panels and fluid sketches of motion with action that personified Timely Comics. Only Alex Schomburg came close to matching (or surpassing) Jack Kirby as the seminal Timely cover artist. Timelys that feature either cover artist are collectible must-haves. Buyers should appreciate Schomburg's talent to fill every corner of a comic cover with action pertinent to the story with slam-bang art.

Comic artists can be counted in the thousands. While there were lots of stars, many others were studio hirelings who may never be identified. Studios like the Eisner-Iger Shop employed over fifteen artists and writers in their modest studio by 1939. Many artists came and went, but a few luminaries were produced. Men like Lou Fine, Reed Crandall, Alex Toth and Wally Wood (four of the brightest stars) drew art fans to their work on their own merit in the 1940s and early 1950s. Other studios generated their own bullpen of future celebrity artists or briefly housed freelancers.

Fiction House Comics rarely credited its artists, but a couple of special men have celebrated recognition anyway. Matt Baker (introduced earlier), an African American artist, made his bones with his smoldering renditions of sexy heroines on previously discussed titles like *Phantom Lady* and *Sheena, Queen of the Jungle* (1938). Baker's women often wore little more than thin, gauzy lingerie that barely restrained these very buxom young beauties. Often labeled "headlight" covers (car buffs call them Dagmar bumpers!), Baker's drawings eventually added to the comic book scandal of the 1950s. His covers and interior art are highly prized today.

Jack Kamen addressed a simple approach to female drawings. His art placed the All-American Girl into harrowing peril while wearing near-revealing, shredded clothing. Scripts were purposefully written to flatter his ability to draw damsels in distress. Kamen's work is best identified by the long, comb-like arcs of eyelashes he drew to accentuate their eyes. Kamen's work extended into the colorful period of the 1950s EC Comics, where he was given more latitude to illustrate crime and suspense stories.

As a long-time EC fan I was always amazed at the sheer talent employed at EC, both written and drawn. I had and have favorites. The art styles were so diverse each artist was a standout. I do allow myself the luxury of picking one I enjoyed the most: Wally Wood (Woody, as he preferred). Wood's use of Zip-a-tone, Craftint products, shading and paper choices were literally crammed into every available space in every panel he drew. His EC work, including *Mad*, made him my guy. I just loved the *Mad*-ness in his stories, the almost frenzied layouts giving the impression that he didn't stop drawing until he ran out of space or ideas. To me, he's still highly collectible.

For art's sake, I want to give one more shout-out to Golden Age artist L.B. Cole, one of my favorites. Cole's cover work dominated certain collector circles right through the 1990s. Cole utilized basic colors to produce covers with a poster-like quality. A lithographer by trade, he drew with a formidable flair for the dramatic. He split his art duties between comic books and wildlife magazines like *Field and Stream*, where he drew the most accurate animal illustrations I've ever seen.

His attention to detail, especially with wildlife, was evident in his time-consuming pencil work. He eventually moved that talent into the field of realism, doing the art for non-comic outdoor magazines. Cole's gripping cover art could never be equaled by the stories inside those comics. Titles like *Suspense* took melodrama to new places with covers like the eerie spider cover with issue #8. He uncovered unspeakable terror utilizing light and angle to emphasize the helplessness of the scene.

Renowned American illustrator Frank Frazetta has been a comic book art superstar for years. His painted paperback book covers and awesome barbarian/fantasy posters of the 1960s and 1970s were the hottest items of the day. Frazetta started in comics as a kid working as an assistant to adults. After comics in the 1950s he worked on comic strips *Li'l Abner*, *Flash Gordon*, and his own project, *Johnny Comet*. He gained celebrity status for comic book collectors as soon as *OPG* was first printed. Novice collectors and veterans alike found references to Frazetta's work itemized in succeeding *Overstreet Price Guides*. These reference notes aided the challenge in hunting down Frazetta in Golden Age comics.

Frazetta's early work in comics in the late 1940s graced pages with fine penciling that overwhelmed the quick art drawn by studio guys who sandwiched his work. Frank's art definitely brings up the value of any comic book he's associated with from the Golden Age.

From the Society of Illustrators' Web site I caught this accolade:

> Frazetta's career exploded when at long last the perfect subject matter was given to the perfect artist to depict it. Starting with new editions of Edgar Rice Burroughs's *Tarzan* adventures, Ace Publishers were ecstatic with the success of their series brandishing Frazetta covers. Lancer Books enjoyed similar success with their own *Conan the Barbarian* series.
>
> The Society of Illustrators gave Frank Frazetta an Award of Excellence in their 15th Annual Exhibition of American Illustration.

We comic book fans can take pride in the knowledge that Frazetta was always "one of us" first before the world caught up to him.

There were some projects and publishers that presented art that was more house-style than unique. *Batman* and *Detective Comics* artists deviated only slightly from templates that were set by Bob Kane and DC Comics. Art shops hired artists to work fast and relatively cheap. Style was reduced to keeping within the panels and little fancy stuff. A lot of gifted artists floated from one project to another. Unsung artists kept their companies' favorite characters afloat, replacing other notables and receiving little or no credit. Guys like Syd Shores and Al Avison followed Simon and Kirby on *Captain America*. The over-the-top action on the covers followed suit, making for eye-exhausting visuals. But their art as collectible is overshadowed by the title on its own.

The end of World War II brought a lot of talented artists home to look for jobs. All kinds of artistic talent were available to publishers in the second half of the Golden Age. I used examples to highlight what fans consider defining representations of collectible art. Quite a few 1940s comics are worth looking into because of a particular artist's work. A prime example of a gifted comic book artist in postwar America is Johnny Craig. Johnny served time in the military and returned to take up comic art. Craig got picked up by EC Comics after the company was inherited by William Gaines, son of the owner, M.C. Gaines, who died in 1947 in a boating accident. Bill Gaines brought his own "clean, crisp" style of penciling to EC's bullpen.

Craig was prolific for EC during its three phases of comic book production. Craig helped set the tone for EC's new emphasis on cliffhanging horror and gore with stories that had fable-like endings. His art is collectible for the sheer delight of its graphic nature, but prices for his work do not involve higher dollar figures.

EC Comics started in the 1940s with simple, non-superhero projects. Funny animal, romance, westerns, Bible stories and crime titles made up the bulk of Gaines's Educational Comics selection. William Gaines wanted to take his company in a new direction. He revamped the company name, changing it to Entertaining Comics, and added drama, grit and horror to a more poignant line of comics. Fans have referred to that period beginning about 1950 as the "New Trend," making the previous generation of EC comics the "Pre-Trend" period.

Following the turmoil heaped upon EC in the mid–1950s by censorship-prone organizations and individuals, EC took steps to stay in the comic book game. They revamped their image a second time by softening the content of their work, attempting to stay within the new rules forced upon them by the Comics Code Authority. EC trumpeted this change as their "New Direction." Sadly, the titles were not up to snuff, and the company left comic book publishing.

EC invented what we all know as *Mad Magazine* in 1952 as one of their comic books. The satire was a first of its kind in that medium and a sure-fire success for EC. Shortly before the comic book line folded, *Mad* was reshaped into a magazine format in 1955, no longer subject to the content restrictions placed on comic books. This was a wise move for them because *Mad Magazine* is published to this day.

Collectors and investors have plenty of reference material at hand to decide a comic book's value. Artists are easily identified for their work and the market long ago established desirability for particular artists. For collectibility, a lot of time has passed. What artists made comics more valuable may not hold true after all these years. Newer generations have little connection to that world and feel differently about where they are going to put their money.

Condition

Golden Age comics are inherently fragile. The wood pulp paper of its time was cheap and flimsy; the construction of that pulp newsprint was built to fail. Light, heat, handling, and pollutants all trigger the corrosive nature of comic book paper. Papers manufactured 60-plus years ago are lucky to survive at all, let alone retain any supple qualities and bleached whiteness. When deciding what to collect, buyers should be aware of the condition pitfalls of comic book paper.

Since the paper is old by our standards, it's likely to be sensitive to handling. Obviously, the whiter and more supple the paper, the likelier the longevity. Conversely, the darker the paper (increased tanning or browning), the greater the evidence of environmental or acidic damage. That browning paper generally indicates trouble as it devolves to brittleness, which is the kiss of death for a comic book. Collectors want their comics to last, so the whiter the paper, the longer its life span.

Comic books were manufactured with little regard for production consistency. The uneven cut of the paper, non-linear staples, and uneven coloring are common defects in many newsstand comics of the day. Collectors need to understand how those manufacturing defects can affect the value of a comic book.

Golden Age collections are still surfacing. A national back-issue dealer, Ed Robertson, told me a story about such a collection he uncovered in 2013. The owner of a vast DC collection from the 1940s was institutionalized and his caretakers needed money for his care. His belongings had long ago been placed in storage. The storage unit was unloaded to pay down debt, and hundreds of this gentleman's comics were discovered (the owner bought them as a kid but forgot about them). The collection was stored under ideal conditions, so paper quality suffered browning cover exteriors, but only tanning interior page edges. Plenty of life was left in those comics, even though light will play havoc on pulp paper. The ultraviolet spectrum in daylight or artificial lights tans paper or fades ink 100 percent of the time.

The Los Angeles (Southern California Comics Collection) group we picked up in 2013 mirrored that problem (discussed in an earlier chapter). The owner bought the comics new but had limited storage options. She stored many of them in piles or on shelves throughout her home. Items stored lower than the reach of the sun through her windows suffered little or no light damage. Those within reach of the non-filtered light got nailed daily for years on end. The leading edges of those copies were tanned by the direct sunlight permanently.

Golden Age comics were manufactured with higher page counts than today's books, making them heavier. That kind of weight can cause tears around the staples. Careful inspection for those tears from cover-to-cover is necessary. Tape has been used for years to fix tears before tape became a no-no and drastically affected comic book values.

The rarest of the Gold can often be expensive in even the lowest of grades. As these old gems disintegrate from handling, parts of the comics tear off and disappear. Enthusiasts will often build them back together using spare parts. A front cover from somewhere online, a back cover or incomplete copy from another source; there are ways to complete a comic book. Unfortunately, a rebuilt copy will be considered restored. Restored Golden Age books do not carry the same values as their unrestored counterparts (see our later chapter on restoration).

All kinds of restoration are identifiable. The adding of a little tape here, a little color-touch there, occurred in the Golden Age without regard for the fate of the books. It's not uncommon to see covertly inked creases to enhance a comic's appearance without necessarily trying to fool anyone. Collectors owning up to their own idiosyncrasies "fixed" their prized comics even in the 1940s. It's up to today's collector to make note of this when examining a potential purchase.

I bought a collection of comics out of Orange County near Los Angeles in 2010. The owner was the son of the original owner. The father bought his comics from the 1930s to the mid–1940s. The son knew almost nothing about his father's fascination with those comics. What I saw stretched out in a dining area of the son's home were four boxes containing about 360 comics and Big Little Books. There were pre-hero DCs, early *Superman*, Centaurs, Harry "A" Chesler comics, *Famous Funnies*, Disneys and a small host of less familiar publishers.

I examined a good portion of the earlier comics, noting that many were heavily read. Their covers and spines were either barely there or barely functional. Also, the original owner had a habit of cutting out favorite panels from random comics for reasons unknown to his family. The father did make serious attempts to hold his battered comics together with tiny pieces of adhesive tape.

Given time, the type of tape available in the 1940s, clear cellophane tape, will surrender to age, literally falling off a comic book repair job. Unfortunately, "our" owner went to the post office and acquired specific USPS mailing labels that were available in short strips. Those labels could be separated from their backings and applied to paper to hold pieces together. Our owner was quite prolific in the application of those labels to hold covers together on some of his earliest (and potentially most valuable) comics. He used the labels like stitches across split spines to keep covers attached front and back, and the interior pages when the staples were no longer adequate.

Those labels, unlike cellophane tape, held their adhesive nature and remained firmly in place for seventy–plus years. Restoration is all about making a comic book look better, so in a way he restored his comics while stripping them of later value when he clipped interior panels.

Condition means much to more people. Any buyer looking to invest, or collect with an eye towards future sale, needs to appreciate how important grading is. Golden Age comics often come with pretty stiff price tags, and nobody wants to get burned by a not-as-advertised copy.

One prevalent irritation for many is comic book restoration. Golden Age comics tend to wear a blend of restorative additions, making the search for unrestored Golden Age copies a challenge. Common aspects of restoration that appear in Golden Age issues include glues and adhesives. There are fairly sophisticated adhesives that are applied to seal tears. In the old days, simple dabs of wood or paper glues were enough to hold a comic book together. Years later, those glues hardened to the consistency of a crusty rock. More sophisticated glues are utilized for much the same repair work. The chemistry of specific adhesives or "flex-adhesives" allows the glue to bend with the paper it's adhered to. The glue is applied lightly and retains a supple quality for years. Although glues are doomed to mark those old comics as "restored," they do allow decomposing copies to retain a few more years of intact life.

The goal of a Golden Age collector is to acquire comics that please. The pleasure of ownership requires that copies last during the period of ownership. Restored copies promote longevity, but not value. Covers can be reattached and repaired. Tape can be removed, tears can be sealed, and color can be reapplied. The one critical defect that cannot be corrected is page color.

Page quality, or color, starts with "white" pages at the top of the chart. Color degrades through darkening and loss of the original suppleness of the thin pages of wood pulp paper. White ages to off-white, then to cream or tan, and finally to brown. With each color change, the flexion of the paper can lose the supple quality that extends its life. The aging nature of the paper changes to brittleness. Brittle paper is a frequent problem with Golden Age books. Brittle paper is the death of a comic book. They just were not produced to last through the decades.

Professional paper conservationists have science on their side and can retard paper's aging process. Tanned paper can be returned to white. Brittleness can be extracted from aged paper, returning it to supple. The life of almost any comic book can therefore be extended. But it is still labeled restoration. Third-party grading companies can identify lightened or whitened paper since it's always produced through artificial means.

Golden Age ownership often requires accepting a comic book that has undergone some form of restoration. There are just not that many unrestored copies of many of the more choice titles to satisfy all collectors. Restoration is pervasive with many Golden Age books.

A great example is the iconic *Batman* #1 (1940). Following Batman's success in *Detective Comics*, National (DC) published his self-titled comic book in 1940. As our readers are aware, only fractions of quantities exist of the hundreds of thousands manufactured in the 1940s. Our reference for surviving copies takes into account the number of certified copies in the census numbers of the various third-party grading companies.

Batman #1 undoubtedly sold well over 200,000 copies. *Gerber's Photo-Journal Guide* estimated the number of survivors as of the mid–1980s at 200–1000 copies. Third-party grading company CGC has certified 219 (as of early 2016). Out of that figure, CGC identified 125 copies as being restored. More often than not, the best graded copies of *Batman* #1 are restored.

Here's an example: the highest graded copy is a Near Mint minus 9.2. There are seven in this category with six listed as restored. A second category, 8.0, lists 15 copies that have been CGC certified, 11 restored. 6.0 = 15 certified copies, 13 restored, and so on. The unrestored copies of *Batman* #1 are scarce and will come with a premium because of demand and a small supply.

Cost

If you want to buy a Golden Age book in order to own a curiosity, there are plenty to choose from. The values of 1940s comics have been maturing for decades. There is reluctance within the formal pricing guides to devalue these comics. Pricing guides created years ago prefer not to set the clock back. The reality is that prices are conditional and easily identifiable through real-time Internet displayed sales figures.

For instance, buyers can study posted sales figures from eBay's short-term sales histories. International auction houses post their archived sales numbers for members to research, while third-party grading companies and GPAnalysis.com record sales data and publicly publish the statistics (sales data is updated routinely as new numbers become available).

I addressed condition as a serious reason to decide if a book should be purchased. Now, I'd like to demonstrate some examples of pricing differences. I'll use the NM- 9.2 tier for *Batman* #1 discussed earlier and extrapolate on costs. The CGC census recorded 7 copies going through their system as of June 2016. One was unrestored and six survived at various levels of reconditioning. The unrestored 9.2 sold for $567,625 in 2013. Two copies repaired at various levels sold for $37,000 and $66,000. The most recent copy as of 2015 sold for $47,500. Almost certainly these high-end books are traded within a small group of people and are not often seen by others. The six restored copies are also expensive, but to the tune of one fewer zero.

Batman #1 in 6.0, a grade of fine, exists in that grade with more certified copies than the 9.2. While no unrestored copies were with GPA's records covering 2011 to late 2015, an extensively restored copy sold for $25,000. The next lowest, unrestored grade tier showed that a Universal blue label 5.5 sold for $74,000.

Even if you have that kind of money, you will find it difficult to find unrestored copies. They tend to sit in collections for lengthy periods, with the owners acknowledging the unlikelihood of upgrading, so keep the copy you have. Restored copies are the fallback choices and are more affordable. In other words, buy what you like, but buy what you can afford (and find!). We pried a collection away from a local owner several years ago. The owner had dutifully put together a near-solid run of *Batman* beginning with issue #1 and complete into the 1990s. His #1 was a CGC labeled 7.0 with moderate restoration. Although we paid one lump sum for the first 100 issues, the #1 was negotiated separately. We agreed on a purchase price of $7,000, which was below market value at that time. Three weeks later, we sold it to another dealer for $10,000. Restoration only lowered the price, not the desirability!

For more comparisons, we will look at other pricing standards for *Batman* #1. Typically, these prices reflect the varying prices many Golden Age comic books sell for in grade and condition, and this segment is all about grasping the significance of condition.

Heritage Auctions Archives often provide information for specific comics in grade. They record both encapsulated and raw sales figures from years of in-house sales. They've crossed paths with *Batman* #1's many times, making it easy to do comparisons. Heritage lists no 6.0s and no raw "Fine" grades. Two restored 6.0s have sold for over $10,000, while a CGC 5.5 once sold for $55,269. As noted earlier, a CGC 9.2 (NM-) copy once sold through Heritage for a remarkable $567,625 in 2013. Heritage also reaches a worldwide audience, so that massive exposure helps them achieve large sales numbers.

By comparison, the 2016–2017 *OPG* grants a more modest value in 9.2 at $550,000 (for a raw copy, not encapsulated). A 5.5-graded (fine minus) copy registers in at around $74,000. That's pretty close to the price a CGC copy currently commands.

Occasionally, eBay sees *Batman* #1s for sale. Looking eBay over, I found a recent sale of a copy restored to a 7.5 and graded by CGC. The heavily restored copy sold for $60,000. Perhaps the level of restoration held back other prospective buyers, but the same graded copy sold for $23,000 just two years ago! The copy had been restored with added pieces and masking color. Below I've listed three price comparisons in identical grades for three different grades over two years apart:

2013	2016
Restored 7.5 = Sold $49,000	Restored 7.5 =$60,000
R 6.0 =$21,000	R 6.0 = no change
R 3.5 = $12,285	R 3.5 =$23,000

The author, his son Michael, and granddaughter Elise: three generations of Newbold comic book fans, circa 2016.

In each case, the sellers calculated that their *Batman* #1s would sell for about ⅓ of *OPG* unrestored. Each copy was CGC graded and identified with extensive restoration. In any case, when we deal with Golden Age comics, collectors can appreciate the kind of dollar figures for the more sought-after marquee comics.

The bottom line is that condition can and will dictate collectibility and price. Condition matters to most collectors. Collectibility, like the other bullet points above, is a major consideration for serious collectors. Comic book back-issue retailers who don't respect this point are doomed to lose business.

There are other themes and reasons to collect Golden Age comics (flamethrower covers, golfing covers, every permutation of the bully-kicking-sand-in-the-guy's-face "Make a man out of Mac" Charles Atlas ads, and so on). People still collect one title with the goal to complete a run. I'm from that generation, but those guys aren't around in large numbers any longer. No theme, just a title or two. Collectors create a spreadsheet with plenty of empty boxes. Then they hunt all over the country to find comics and check off the boxes.

The Forensic Comicologist gets excited when he speaks of the Golden Age. That era represents heady times that became a vision quest for Baby Boomer collectors back in my day. Golden Age comics are forever cool.

The points I make above are relevant to the next era of comic books as well, but Golden Age buyers will find camaraderie with others collecting for these reasons.

13

Silver Age
Last of the Ten-Centers

Out of the gate, Barry Allen got a slow start. The "Fastest Man Alive" began his fictional life as the Flash in #4 of DC Comics' *Showcase* (1956). *Showcase* provided exactly what its title suggested: tryout characters for DC to introduce for potential serialization. DC was focused on the comic book norms of the day. They produced CCA-friendly material while respecting the desires of their 1950s audience. They offered nothing too sensational or pathos-filled in their titles.

In 1956, DC was exploring the market for new features. *Showcase* and a sister title, *The Brave and the Bold* (1955), were perfect spots to experiment with new ideas. DC used these ongoing titles to avoid paying postage upgrades with new titles for each idea. Dell Comics had been doing this for years with their *Four Color* series. Dell's *Four Color* title began in 1939 and is labeled in *OPG* as Series 1. The long-lived Series 2 began again with issue #1 in 1942 (as stated in an earlier chapter, this series ended in 1962 with a whopping 1,354 issues. (The last issue is listed as #1354, but some of the previous issue numbers did not get produced.) So far this record number of synchronous issues appears to be unbreakable. More than likely we will not see the likes of that again.

Any TV/movie adaptation or new character could be showcased in a random issue of *Four Color* (except for a few numbers never printed in 1961–1962). If it stuck with the audience, Dell would contemplate its future, often providing its own title).

DC's first three attempts with start-up ideas in *Showcase* did not light up the readers. Issue #1 featured firefighters in their action-based element. For DC, this was the least financially risky way to test the marketability of a new comic title. Issue #2 followed with animal stories, and then wartime "frogmen" in #3, by Russ Heath. Their stories have largely been forgotten. Issue #4 heralded the hero who would give us the next comic era: the Silver Age. That hero would be the Flash. Although conceptually unique as a first, there was another version…

All-American Publications, sister publisher to National Publications, created the Flash in 1940, featuring the self-titled speedster as another member of the DC universe of superheroes. The Flash had super-speed and would become a member of DC's Justice Society of America. This original version of the Flash was named Jay Garrick and had little in common with his future doppelganger besides the speed. As I discussed earlier, only a few DC superheroes survived the postwar transition in comics. Jay was not one of them; he disappeared from comics in 1951. Jay as the Flash would not reappear in comics for 10 more years.

Interestingly, the writers for both versions of the Flash were published science fiction storytellers. Gardner Fox got Jay Garrick off the ground with his lighthearted plots in the 1940s, while John Broome sprinkled science into Barry Allen's world of speed.

Detective Comics traditionally led with Batman tales followed by back-up features. Characters such as Pow-Wow Smith and Robotman occupied the comic, along with other back-up heroes. By the mid–1950s, costumed heroes were virtually gone from the stands. DC held on with Superman (and Superboy in his own title), Batman, and Wonder Woman (Aquaman and Green Arrow stayed on as back-up features.) But the rest were missing. *Detective Comics* bucked the trend, helping to keep Batman alive while introducing a new character for the new age.

The Southern California Comics Collection's star acquisition: *Showcase* #4. This book started a new generation of comic book fans, if you believe the first appearance of a new-gen Flash changed the direction of comic books in the 1950s. This book remains a red-hot commodity and is nearly out of financial reach for many collectors. *Showcase* #4 (1956) (© DC Comics. Used with permission).

It was late 1955 when DC adapted a one-shot, prototype character from *Batman* #78 (1953.) The "Manhunter from Mars" was reintroduced in *Detective Comics* #225 as the "Martian Manhunter." The new superhero predated the acknowledged kick-off point for the Silver Age by about a year. This is an important issue. It predates the exact point in time we recognize as the beginning of the Silver Age, but is a highly collectible book due to its proximity to the dawn of a new era in comics. A high-grade copy is rare and will set you back several thousand dollars. In 2017, this book seemingly couldn't get any hotter (like *Action Comics* #242, the first Brainiac).

DC was antsy about the sales success of *Showcase* #4. They had tooled it to introduce an updated version of the old Flash, but with modifications for a new generation. This was a risky experiment to see if America was ready for new heroes; no other company was entertaining new costumed characters, so DC was on its own. The issue featured a "flashy" red suit for the new hero and sported streamlined art from DC veterans Carmine Infantino and Joe Kubert.

The issue hit the stands with

greater than expected fanfare, so editor Julius Schwartz banked more new Flash stories but did not publish them until the middle of 1957 (about nine months later). DC knew the character was a hit when the sales figures were tallied.

Issue #8 of *Showcase* was to be Flash's second outing after a significant wait. Issue #8 was followed by two more *Showcase* appearances in #13 and #14 before DC finally granted the Flash a self-titled comic book series in 1959. All four of his *Showcase* appearances are prized by collectors today, helped along by the character's presence on TV and in upcoming movies.

DC utilized *Showcase* to try out subsequent creations. The *Challengers of the Unknown* were brought to market in issue #6 of *Showcase* (returning in the following issue). Jack Kirby drew these adventures predating the Fantastic Four by almost five years. Both groups have important placement in today's market and perhaps reflect Jack's affinity to a quartet of heroes that either behave like family or are a family. Space Ranger, Rip Hunter: Time Master, and Lois Lane (adapted from the Superman titles), all saw daylight in further *Showcase* offerings.

The *Showcase* title was shaping

DC struck "silver" at the end of the Golden Age with the emergence of the new Flash. His seminal appearance in *Showcase* #4 is considered the birthplace of the Silver Age, but is it? Many fans argue that Martian Manhunter's on-scene arrival within the pages of *Detective Comics* #225 marks the beginning of the Silver Age of Heroes. The extreme collectibility of both issues says the fans can go either way on this matter. *Detective Comics* #225 (1955) (© DC Comics. Used with permission).

up to be an exciting place to premiere ideas once DC realized the potential. Green Lantern was the next revised biggie with *Showcase* #22 (1959). Originally created for All-American Publications, Alan Scott's *Green Lantern* showed up on the scene around the same time as *The Flash* in the 1940s. Both Green Lantern and the Flash were later regular members of the Justice Society of America in their team title *All-Star Comics*. Gil Kane's lavish art style gave the new Green Lantern (Hal Jordan) a modernistic sleekness with his two-toned costume. Readers responded with thumbs-up over DC's less-cartoony art styles for their reimagined heroes.

I can just imagine that the editors at DC at this time were pumped with the success each revamped Golden Age character was seeing. They saw Hawkman, the Atom, Aquaman and more become accepted by a new age of readers. The DC writers and artists were all creative people doing jobs they were hired to do, but the feeling that all their work was rewarded with reader excitement must have been tremendously satisfying.

These were tough times for comic book people, however. Closing publishers and layoffs affected a lot of talent and warned others that peril could be just around the corner. To see the steady output of new characters and comics must have been a great relief. For talents like Julius Schwartz, Gardner Fox and John Broome, the inclusion of more sophisticated science in their stories gave them outlets that hadn't been available 20 years earlier. These were my favorite writers and their titles were my favorite comics. I wanted none of that infantile Superman family stuff; give me *Green Lantern*'s science-based, spacefaring plots!

DC continued to produce war-themed comics with titles begun a few years earlier. DC rolled with the stiffening rules towards violence and managed to keep the war action clean enough to survive the new Comics Code. DC kept the action in titles like *Our Army at War* (1952) and *Our Fighting Forces* (1954). DC acquired *G.I. Combat* (Quality Comics from 1952 to 1956; DCs from 1957 until its end) from defunct Quality Comics and refitted *Star Spangled Comics* (1941) into *Star Spangled War Stories* (1952). DC morphed the western title *All-American Western* to *All-American Men of War* (1952) and let their stable of war titles total five. The war-themed comics found popularity among kids and adult men alike. The message of war was salted with irony, but the earlier antiwar feeling that EC Comics broadcast was not part of DC's program. DC was clear on the fact that war brought pain, so their stories did not shy away from writing about suffering.

GI Combat #87 has the distinction of being a really stylized war cover, a sharp example of a grey-tone cover and a key first appearance: the first Haunted Tank. War comics lack the huge collector popularity of a generation ago, but this baby is still in demand. *GI Combat* #87 (1961) (© DC Comics. Used with permission).

DC's war comic success almost guaranteed that talented creators Joe Kubert, Robert Kanigher, and Russ Heath would strike hero gold if the right soldier was created. The war titles were strong sellers for DC. The writers knew that they could tell the stories they wanted, if they could invent important, recurring characters. That happened with Sgt. Rock in *Our Army at War* #81 (1959). Issue #81 is considered prototypical. In other words, DC had a character that could have been Sgt. Rock, but was not yet identified as such. Issues #82 took us closer to Rock, and then #83 birthed the character as we know him today: Sgt. Rock of Easy Company. The other hot war key from DC was the Haunted Tank, first seen in *G.I. Combat* #87 (1961). These popular ten-cent cover firsts are at the top of the food chain, as DC war-comic collectibles go.

DC tried other concepts: an American Indian fighter pilot, Johnny Cloud, debuted in *All-American Men of War* #82 (1960). I give credit to DC for generating an American Indian hero during the western movie era when Indians were often portrayed as villains. Another DC hero mash-up was Gunner, Sarge and Pooch in *Our Fighting Forces* #45 (1959), but in hindsight I can't remember those issues ever being in demand as collectibles. They were mostly picked up to fill runs.

War comics, mystery, and sci-fi anthologies rounded out much of DC's inventory. The other companies that continued through the 1950s producing the same genres saw the Code water down their contents. Several folded, while Charlton and ACG continued with their own brands of sci-fi and mystery. For collecting purposes, few significant key issues occupied any of the remaining output of science fiction and mystery titles until the seventies.

Gray-tone covers, or wash-tone if you prefer, arose in an experimental period in the late 1950s and DC's early 1960s titles. Cover artist and colorist Jack Adler, and pencils by Jerry Grandenetti, took a new, temporary direction with cover art designed to stand out against all the other titles and companies. The gray or wash-tone element for comic covers was derived from mixing an amount of black and white with pure color to "wash out" the finished art. That "gray tone" gave DC's covers a distinction that has been virtually unmatched in comic books.

There are some exceptions: DC's horror line, titles like *House of Mystery* (1951–52) and *House of Secrets* (1956) produced a few wash-tone covers in the early 1970s.

As a collector, I remember those covers were highly sought after in the 1970s, especially the war covers. Grandenetti's gritty, tense war covers were all the rage with my generation. I didn't remember seeing them when they first hit the newsstands; I was just a small child. By high school I was a DC war comic buff, and those wash-tone covers were the most desired for looks alone.

OPG assigns greater value to those issues, and die-hard collectors will not challenge the price difference between wash-tone covers and standard covers. Unfortunately, the best and most consistent wash tones (Russ Heath *covers*) had quite a run, but the drama and sale remained mostly in the war titles.

The war comics are not in vogue with as many collectors in the new millennium, and were much more desirable even 20 years ago. The grey-tone covers were still a big draw for collectors a short generation ago, but war comics do not resonate with the Millennials and today's young readers.

Charlton had scored it big when they landed Steve Ditko as the talent for *Captain Atom* (1965), which started out in an earlier title called *Space Adventures* in 1960. Many of those issues, especially the earlier appearances in *Space Adventures*, are still in great demand. Steve Ditko still commands that kind of admiration. His stark view of right and wrong, an Ayn Rand view of life, breathes through the work he wrote. His art, with a psychedelic bent, continues to draw in Silver Age collectors.

Silver Age first issues are expensive and always have a market. By the late 1950s, the stories and art became formulaic for virtually every new title and bereft of collecting "oomph!" factors (outside of Atlas Comics, which morphed into Marvel and began its series of post–1957 implosion titles).

Charlton was the only large company that printed its own comic books. Their fascinating uniqueness provided a lower-paid haven for comic book artists and writers who wanted less editorial control than DC and Marvel. Charlton held the rights to characters that DC coveted, like Captain Atom, The Question and Blue Beetle. Charlton folded its publications by the early 1980s and sold those characters to DC.

Interestingly, Alan Moore set his eyes on those Charlton characters when he was writing *The Watchmen* (1987). DC didn't want to see the characters die, which would have been their *Watchmen* fate, so they refused to let Moore have them. They were not A-list players, but DC had put money into them, so they still had to pay out.

Like Atlas Comics, Charlton copied the successes of other publishers. Atlas and Dell were producing westerns, so Charlton did. DC was producing romance comics, so Charlton did. My years in this hobby have turned up dozens of Charlton romance titles. They continued publishing them right up to the end. Their romance comics were a little spicier than the stuff DC was putting out. Referring to Vince Colleta, inker for Jack Kirby at both DC and Marvel, an article on ComicVine.com compares the DC and Charlton romance titles: "Colletta in particular excelled at implying a subtle eroticism to his figurative posing that meant Charlton could count on the appeal of some of these titles to easily excited adolescent boys as well as the books' intended audience, young girls."

Charlton has never been known as a hot stable of collectible back issues with worrisome prices. They are completely affordable but difficult to find at the store level. The Internet and conventions are about the only consistent sources for Charltons. I don't see them often in collections brought to my store. The paper was cheap, the inks were poorly applied during manufacturing, and Charltons didn't have the powerful circulation the Big Two had.

Michelle Nolan and Dan Stevenson count an industry-high 1,420 Charlton-published romance issues from 1949 to 1983. Whatever worked or kept the presses going sent Charlton into production overload.

The war kids of the 1940s grew up with superheroes. Favorites who thrived before the 1950s had evaporated by the Korean War. The new generation of ten-plus-year-olds was raised on comics that followed a new, non-costume path. Only DC published capes and cowls of any longevity. Companies like Ace Comics and St. John were content to go with short-term success that non-superhero comics presented. Nobody else appeared to be getting rich on costumes, so why experiment? DC had the heroes that mattered, written and drawn for young kids. Nobody was inventing new heroes, not even DC in the early 1950s, so the market was content to remain stagnant when it came to innovation. The concern was to stay afloat under mounting public pressure and draw out profit until everything folded.

Archie Comics, Dell and Gilberton were confident they could ride out the storm, publishing their lines of comics without drastic changes or new directions. EC Comics and the others stood to lose the most. Fortunately for EC, they had the comic book *Mad*, which became *Mad Magazine* with issue #24 in 1955 to avoid the Comics Code. Both *Mad* and EC's short-lived Picto-Fiction magazines were immune from the Code in magazine format. Picto-Fiction was another EC attempt to keep their titles afloat. Pages were printed with one to four story panels and overlaid text. Picto-Fiction was ignored by the readers, but *Mad* sailed into legend, still published today by DC Comics.

The introduction of next-gen DC heroes for next-gen kids helped invigorate decisions the company made. These kids were tantalized with characters "born" with them, something designed for them, and not just at the right moment. DC understood this when enthusiastic letters about the new Flash and Green Lantern reached their offices. The historical connection between their older counterparts and the new was easily communicated between two generations. DC understood young readers wanted their own heroes because every generation wants their own thing.

DC fielded letters about the obvious: would more heroes be revamped and inked into print? DC was still experimenting with new titles. The short-lived *Phantom Stranger* (1952), *Frontier Fighters* (1955), and *New Adventures of Charlie Chan* (1958) came and went. *Congo Bill* (1954), from the pages of *Action Comics*, tried his own title and failed (all four titles are scarce and maintain a respectable level of collector desirability). DC continued to skip around, inventing more heroes in varying genres while contemplating their next caped costume.

Adventure Comics #247 is typical of what DC was doing at the end of the 1950s: new characters and new ideas. Issue 247 is the first appearance of the Legion of Super-Heroes, still a hot collecting key. Adventure Comics #247 (1958) (© DC Comics. Used with permission).

DC did keep the *Adventures of Bob Hope* (1950) going as one of its few humor titles not associated with cartoon animals. Hope's title spawned another comedian, or in this case, comic duo with the *Adventures of Dean Martin and Jerry Lewis* (1952). Dean left in 1957, and *Jerry* continued on his own into 1971. Towards the end, Neal Adams was even doing *Jerry's* covers.

Adventure Comics had been Superboy's haven for years. Science fiction writer Otto Binder wrote a story that sent future comic teammates The Legion of Super-Heroes back in time to meet Superboy. What started with *Adventure Comics #247* (1958) as a one-time story eventually returned in #267 in their second of many appearances. Like Flash's *Showcase* appearances, DC was slow and deliberate when it came to superhero sequels.

Adventure Comics #247 is distinct for being a collectible "heavy hitter" without being a try-out issue or a number one. As of June 2016, a common CGC 4.0 sold for over $1,631, while the highest recorded GPA sale for a 9.2 went for almost $18,000.

Bizarro, Superman's backward doppelganger, was hilariously stupid. The Bizarro stories remain bizarrely popular with collectors and very affordable in lower grades. *Superman* #169 **(1964) (© DC Comics. Used with permission).**

DC took their time reprising the Legion until they were certain they could work in solid stories. Superman co-creator Jerry Siegel wrote the team's second story for issue #267. Simultaneously, DC writers followed the sci-fi theme with the oddity Bizarro in *Superboy* #68 (1958) and Brainiac in *Action Comics* #242 (1958). The Bizarro World opened up a new vein of humor for the Superman Family, while Brainiac turned into a world-class, serious baddie for Superman. Both issues, hard to find in high grade, are big on want lists. Strangely, both the names Brainiac and Bizarro have transcended the comic book characters. The term "Brainiac" has come to symbolize supreme intelligence, while "Bizarro" is still used to denote something weird.

While *Showcase* explored new characters, DC's *Brave and the Bold* title ran anthologies with fictional, non-costumed heroes. Robin Hood, Viking Prince, and Silent Knight all split time in the title with art by the likes of Kubert, Heath, and Golden Age artist Irv Novick. DC's Superman titles continued to innovate with the introductions of fresh members to that mythos. *Action Comics* #252 (1959) saw the arrival of Supergirl.

Again, Otto Binder, a veteran of Fawcett's Marvel Family characters, went back to the well, returning with a themed version of an established legend.

Action Comics #252 was always a key that has seen minor fluctuations in value, but it was not at the top of many collector lists for DC keys. It's Supergirl's first appearance. She saw her popularity increase with the promotion of a new TV show in 2015. Looking at GPA and a few random grades, I see a 4.0 went for a high $1,867 in 2015, while a more desirable (and equally common) 6.0 went for $3,850.

But fame is fleeting. The TV show was on summer break by mid–2016. The 4.0 was now selling for $1,463 and the 6.0 deflated to $2,868, frightening for owners who lost about 25 percent of the value.

These are two examples of how wobbly the market can be when collectors treat comics like fads. We all need crystal balls to see into the future, not somebody else's say-so.

Left and right: **The Superman editors and writers continually added members with the dawning of the Silver Age. Braniac became one of Superman's most dangerous otherworldly villains, while Supergirl joined her cousin on Earth as an ally.** *Action Comics* **#242 (1958) (© DC Comics. Used with permission and** *Action Comics* **#252 (1959) © DC Comics. Used with permission).**

The reader acceptance of new characters to augment solid favorites reinforced editors' decision to collect a team of their new creations into one purposeful supergroup. The success of the original form of the idea was "The Justice Society of America," which ran for a full decade in *All-Star Comics*. The retro versions of Flash and Green Lantern were direct links to Barry Allen and Hal Jordan. Editor Julius Schwartz pushed for the creation in 1960 of a new "JSA." He saw reasons within the growing stable of new DC heroes to form a team much like the old one. The Flash joined with Green Lantern, Martian Manhunter, Wonder Woman, and Aquaman, along with Superman and Batman (charter members in 1960). The Justice League of America was born. The Atom would soon join the nucleus of DC's biggest team entry to date.

The Justice League (JLA) started in *Brave and the Bold* #28 (1960) and ran for two more consecutive issues. As it had done with *Showcase*, DC was allowing another ongoing title to become a place to try out new ideas. The rampant popularity of the series pushed ahead DC's plans to give them their own book. October of 1960 saw issue #1's debut in the *Justice League of America*. It was the beginning of hugely influential fiction in comics and nearly the end of the ten-cent cover price. Issue seven was dated late 1961 and was sold with the last ten-cent price tag, matching all of DC's other titles. DC increased its cover price tags across the board to twelve cents.

Both photographs: **One month the comic books at DC were still ten cents, then the next month saw the first price increase in the history of comic books (Dell had alternate 15-cent cover prices). The sticker shock from 10 to 12 cents sent shock waves through the hearts of many young readers. This was the Silver Age of Inflation, just for kids.** *Justice League of America* **#7 1961, #8 (1962) (© DC Comics. Used with permission).**

Purchasing new comics off the stands at ten-cent price tags predates the memories of most guys my age. For those older than me, the two-cent price increase to 12 cents was the only price augment for comic books they had ever seen. My father's generation never knew another price. Comic buyers older than me must have experienced sticker shock. For more than 25 years, comics were a dime. Sure, the page counts had shrunk from what now seems a fantastic 64 pages to 32 pages. But still, the dime cost persisted.

DC felt buying pressure. To curtail the potential loss of readers, DC published an open letter to readers in early 1962. The letter was printed on the inside front covers to appease readers' concerns. DC gave a brief tutorial on inflation, introducing the concept to young readers. Instantly kids knew that distributors and retailers all feel inflationary pinches and increased costs to stay in business. The DC editorial spot-checked other comic book companies and pointed out that "some of our competitors (over at Dell) are now charging 15 cents for the same size comic magazine that we produce." *Classics Illustrated*, published by

DC's Silver Age mentalists repeated their Golden Age team success with a Silver Age teaming of most of their popular costumed heroes. The result in *Brave and the Bold* #28 was the formation of the Justice League of America. Their *Brave and the Bold* home lasted for three highly collectible issues until they fired off in their own self-titled comic book. *Brave and the Bold* #28 (1960) © DC Comics. Used with permission and *Justice League of America* #1 (1960) (© DC Comics. Used with permission).

Gilberton, is the only other line that increased to the higher price point. The letter offered the notion that turning it up to twelve cents was a fair price and a better value to fans.

The twelve-cent price tag was printed on the cover of every 32-page DC comic from there on in (80-page giants would span the 1960s with quarter price tags, but were usually reprints). Since DC distributed for Marvel and had some say over their marketing, Marvel followed suit at the exact same time (*Fantastic Four* shifted to twelve cents with issue #3 in 1962).

DC held the major role as superhero producer, though Archie Comics offered a limited number of their own costumed inventions. With the help of Jack Kirby, Archie published the successful *Adventures of the Fly* (1959) and two issues of *The Double Life of Private Strong* (1959). Success was minimal, but it got them into the superhero game ahead of Marvel. This was pick-up work for Jack while working for Marvel grinding out the non-hero anthologies. Marvel's fledgling title *Fantastic Four* and its success were still two years out.

Legends abound about the impetus for Marvel's re-entry into the superhero genre. The version I heard for years surrounded the frequent golf outings between the owners of DC Comics and Marvel Comics. Marvel owner Martin Goodman listened to one of DC's principals boast about the success of their new team-up title *Justice League of America*. DC's sales on that book were exciting and encouraging. Once again, DC had struck gold with superheroes. Goodman thus met with his editor, Stan Lee. The legend goes that he told Stan to create something to rival the *JLA*. Stan approached Jack Kirby for help on this project, and the result was the 1961 release of the *Fantastic Four*; more in a bit on this subject.

Fantastic Four #1 was published with a ten-cent cover price. DC was already phasing out that price point, so the newly celebrated Marvel supergroup only lasted two issues at the cost of a dime before following DC into the twelve-cent arena. Marvel's *Amazing Fantasy* #15 (1962) popped onto the market with the new cover price of twelve cents. All the succeeding titles Marvel started or continued are legendary at this point in the Silver Age, and all bear the Silver Age standard price of twelve cents. *FF*'s uniqueness for the first two issues at ten cents just adds to the luster of those comics as collector's items.

Stan Lee has told several versions of the idea for Spider-Man over the decades. Most of the stories start with Stan and end with Jack Kirby and then Steve Ditko.

Kelly Konda wrote an article in *Comic Book Marketplace* (2014) delving into the creation story behind Spider-Man. There are few articles about the subject that are as insightful as Kelly's, so I reprint it here:

> The problem with Stan Lee's story about how he created Spider-Man is that by his own admission he's told the story so often not even he knows if it's true anymore. The actual origins for Spider-Man likely go back over a decade earlier, and don't involve Stan Lee at all. Joe Simon and Jack Kirby had created Captain America together for Timely Comics in 1941. By 1959 they had split up as partners, Simon going to work in advertising and Kirby catching on with DC Comics. Then Archie Comics approached Simon about creating a new superhero for them since DC was having success reviving old superheroes. Simon enlisted his old partner's help, and they revisited an old idea of theirs about a young orphaned boy living with an old couple. He wishes upon a ring he finds in a magical spider web, and is transformed into the adult superhero Silver Spider, fighting crime with a gun which shoots webs. Kirby nixed the name Silver Spider, suggesting Spider-Man instead, which they briefly ran with before ultimately re-working and re-naming the character The Fly.
>
> By 1962, Stan Lee, who'd been with Marvel since its Timely days in the early 1940s, was now editor-in-chief, and Jack Kirby his go-to artist. Stan Lee wanted a teenage superhero, cutting out the middle man of the DC model and just dropping the adult hero and making the sidekick the main character, but who actually created the character?
>
> The version that seems to have the most validity is that Lee approached Kirby to help come up with a teenage superhero. Kirby pitched him the version of the Silver Spider he and Simon had co-created before adapting it for the Fly. Lee liked it enough to request some artwork, but Kirby delivered something which looked far too much like a re-worked Captain America. So, Lee gave the project to Steve Ditko, who immediately noticed the similarities between Kirby's proposal and The Fly. As a result, Lee allowed Ditko to change things up. He dropped the web gun and whole magic ring premise, and threw out Kirby's original design for the costume, instead creating from scratch the now-beloved and iconic Spider-Man costume.
>
> Both Lee and Ditko agreed that Lee thought up the name Spider-Man while Kirby maintained he did (only for Simon to later disagree and argue that actually way back when they created the Silver Spider together it was he, not Kirby, who created the name Spider-Man). Lee probably thought of having Spider-Man get his powers from a radioactive spider bite instead of a magic ring, but not even that is known for sure.

I concur that it seems we may never know the absolute truth. Time, death and age have muddled the memories of Spider-Man's creation, so the Forensic Comicologist must learn to live with it.

My earliest comic book memory extends back to the very early 1960s. My father worked late nights at the college library on Mondays. Typically, he'd be home just about my bedtime. Occasionally, he'd bring home a comic book and read it to me before I fell asleep. On a Monday in early 1962, he brought home one of those DC war comics with the dinosaur covers, which I distinctly remember. Like other issues of *Star Spangled War Stories*, GIs were imperiled by dinosaurs. This particular issue displayed my favorite: a T-Rex, who was menacing GIs stuck in a tree. I was only six and delighted at the imaginative fantasy that could pit army men against prehistoric monsters. From a more practical perspective, I remember the black-and-white box at the top corner of the front cover. Unknowingly, I fixated on the stark ten-cent cover price. It contrasted sharply against the soft pastels of the cover art. It also heralded the end of the ten-cent age of comics. (I enjoy the fact that I'm tenured [old] enough to remember owning ten-centers right off the newsstands.)

Issue #99 of *Star Spangled War Stories*, my fondest comic memory, was the last ten-center for that title, cover date December 1961/January 1962, as it was for all of DC's titles, other than the seasonal 25 cent square-bound reprints. Both DC and Marvel offered annual 25-cent comic books. These issues almost always contained reprints of stories from ten and twenty years before. The story I read was that they were released in the summer when it was theorized kids had more money to spend. Editors expected kids would have summer jobs or allowance increases to occupy them on school break. The kids would be bored and naturally steer towards comics: mowing lawns meant more comic book spending, so why not squeeze them for more money? For 25 cents a kid could buy 80 pages of old Batman stories, old Superman Family stories, or reprints of Marvel's earlier products. The sales must have been brisk because I'm forever seeing those square-bound comics show up in collections at my store. They are not the lucrative sellers they once were; today's collectors are less interested in buying reprints.

This was the point in my life where I unknowingly entered the Silver Age, right in time to see the birthing of the New Age of Marvel Comics and the first price increase for comics anyone had ever experienced. I read the letters columns in comic books as I got older. Many of the letters were distracting because they were more focused on pointing out coloring goofs or lapses in logic in the action. But I didn't have any idea how revolutionary those letters would become to fandom. Back then, little kids shared their comics with their friends. As kids, we gave no thought to proper handling and storage. It was also a time when a kid's parents were just as likely to throw out old comics as their folks had been a generation earlier. The comics were disposable. We knew other readers were out there, but we were not yet collectors. We didn't know that someday soon we would want to make contact with some of those letter writers. We didn't know that searching for back issues would become a sport.

Ten-cent cover prices carry a mystique in today's market. Most comics were cover priced ten cents for a generation that passes further into history every day. The kids felt the excitement from working all day recycling bottles or doing the neighbor's yard work to scrape together pennies just to buy one comic. During the war, those ten cents could buy 64 pages of four-color entertainment, which was meant to be read over and over again.

Our ancestors led the way into our hobby by spending billions of dimes on comics for close to three decades. The Golden Age of comic books is practically synonymous with ten cents.

In Dick Lupoff's great sci-fi fanzine *XERO* (1960–63), a series of published articles celebrated comic books of the 1940s. Individual submissions were included in each issue under the installment title *All In Color For A Dime*. This well-received publication paid homage to the comics of yesteryear, keying in on the soon-to-be extinct ten-cent cover price.

Ten-centers from the mid- to late 1950s represent a "changing of the guard" from the Gold into the Silver Age. There's definitely a "cool factor" surrounding all those DC firsts and Atlas Comics prototypes.

Some of Marvel's pre–Atlas horror and mystery comics somehow survived the 1957 implosion (more on this in another chapter) brought on by their distribution woes. Stan Lee, his writer, and several artists hung on with simply crafted, cookie-cutter story templates for their horror and monster fiction. They ran formulaic fables through such titles as *Tales of Suspense, Strange Tales* (1951), *Journey Into Mystery* (1952), and others. The writers wrote dozens of short vignettes with less-than-shocking moral outcomes. Some of the characters in these stories bore similarities to later Marvel characters.

Besides Archie Comics, ACG and Charlton followed suit with the increased cover price to twelve cents. Dell was experimenting with fifteen-centers before settling on twelve cents. Gilberton's *Classics Illustrated* comics were already at fifteen cents. That was upsetting if you depended on *CI* to shortcut school assignments requiring reading classic fiction with the inevitable follow-up book report.

Every age group in comics knows *Classics Illustrated* for their faithful, fully drawn adaptations of classical fiction. Classic novels such as *Moby Dick* or *Crime and Punishment* had been adapted to comics for nearly three decades by the end of the 1960s. But most of us from my youth remember just how accurate those comic versions were, dutifully following the original story in comic book form. Those stories were so well-adapted to young readers that many saw no reason to read the novel version. Especially if that version was to be turned into a book report over the weekend!

Golden Age, the Atomic Age, the comics of the 1950s, are resoundingly popular with today's collectors. Discovering a collection of that material that hasn't seen the light of day for decades is the best part of my job. There was so much material and so much variety that even today someone is still collecting it. It certainly takes a booth at a convention, a store or a well-attended Web site to find those customers. By 2016, I can testify that those collectors are out there. If you have the material for sale and you can reach them, they will come. Be prepared to hold onto the material for years or until you apply stiff discounts.

OPG is still the closest source for reliable pricing on Golden Age books. They've had more than four and a half decades to get it right. The prices fluctuate from *OPG*, often down more often than up, as buyers know to push for discounts. Those old comics were produced in huge numbers that can't be replicated by today's publishers. They are from a time and comic book realm that can't be duplicated.

The end of the ten-centers felt like an era's end. Many buyers marked the transition point to twelve cents with some complaint. I've read the accounts from letters and talked to guys who remember how some comic book fans were shaken with disappointment when the price increase broke tradition. (Michelle Nolan commiserates with the others of that period. She remembers being just short of 14 when the price change hit. She still feels the youthful shock of the two-cent price increase!)

The publishers showed some concern. But the momentum of change brought on by exciting, new characters and eager new readers, quickly publishers' fears dissipated with the continued growth of a strong, youthful customer base ... and the arrival of the Age of Marvel.

Marvel prototypes. Marvel cast backwards as well as inwards for ideas at the dawn of their Silver Age. Stan, Jack and the others at Marvel wrote vignettes in their pre-hero titles, imagining characters and names like Groot, Dr. Droom and Fin Fang Foom. Somewhere amid all these stories were the seeds for Marvel's Silver Age heroes.

Some of the characters from back then seem to foreshadow the later heroes. Legend first had it that the Marvel origins for each hero were the concept of Stan Lee (but Jack Kirby and Steve Ditko, too) to compete with DC Comics. Stan and the others obviously looked for inspiration within their own library of comics. *OPG* lists what they call prototype issues identifying one-time characters from the pre-hero titles like *Tales of Suspense, Strange Tales, Journey Into Mystery,* and *Tales to Astonish.* The earliest issues of the *OPG* didn't identify prototypes, but at some point that data was entered.

Here are a couple of examples of what I'm leading to:

OPG touts *TOS* #16 (1961) as an Iron Man prototype, alluding that the character Metallo (also a DC villain!) was either an inspiration for Iron Man, perhaps one of many, or a direct link to Iron Man by design. This issue was published two years before Iron Man's arrival.

A character in *Journey Into Mystery* #73 (1961) appears in a 7-page story titled "The Spider Strikes." A scientist is exposed to radiation and sports the newly-acquired ability to shoot webs in issue #69 of *Strange Tales* (1959).

Marvel staffers needed source material, and all of their anthology stories were ripe for the plucking. For *OPG* and collectors, identifying all the prototypes must have taken some imagination to get from point A to point B. For instance, Issue #9 of *TOS* also lists an Iron Man prototype. I address this in another chapter, but the story from this issue, "The Return of the Living Robot," is about robots. *OPG* and others stretched the Iron Man connection, but perhaps they were able to glean information from Stan, Jack or the others stating that was the case. If that's not the case, then *OPG* provided an out by tagging the listing in *OPG* as "prototype-ish."

Uncle Ben and Aunt May, Ant-Man, Thor, Spider-Man, along with villains like Dr. Doom, the Stone Men, Toad Men and Magneto, all have prototype doppelgangers in earlier issues of the titles destined to house the real Iron Man, Thor, Professor X and Dr. Strange.

Collectibility varies. *OPG* differentiates the prototypes by assigning them slightly higher values than the "commons" around them. Fans are less likely to pay more for a copy because it features a prototype. They will invest if it's a high-grade prototype!

Significantly, the end of the ten-cent cover price neatly occurs when Marvel's prototype characters begin to manifest as the superheroes we all recognize. The Forensic Comicologist like things that wrap up neatly (cops too!).

14

Silver and Bronze Ages

Marvel Rules in the Age of Fandom

This is an easy chapter to write. I'm not going to reveal much that collectors don't already know. In the comic book world, it's a foregone conclusion that Marvel Comics runs the table for collecting popularity. Their titles and their characters are on most collectors' lips and wish lists. The leader of the pack of publishers is Marvel in the back-issue market; as a comic book store owner, I see sales and requests for back issues daily. DC holds a respectable second place, and the few remaining companies after DC can be lumped together with a small minority of followers.

I covered Marvel's origins and era changes briefly in previous chapters. The subject of Marvel Comics in the Silver Age warrants an entire book, and that's been done by others. What has not been comprehensively addressed is the collecting of Marvel Comics, at least not in any books I've read. The collector could use a little more background on the forces that drive comic book collecting or hamper it, especially in the vibrant Silver Age era. Both Silver and Bronze Age comics are hot. That's been true since the 1970s, when I lived through the transition from Silver to Bronze.

I found my collecting initiation for comics by the mid–1960s, at about the age of eight. Comic collecting for me was more random and spontaneous until that age. There weren't many places that sold comics in my part of town, even if I could get a ride from my father. My mother never even contemplated touring me around town just to buy funny books. The step-off point for collecting was one of those damned two-part stories in *Justice League of America*. Somehow I'd ended up with issue #21, which climaxed into a cliffhanger requiring issue #22. That took forever to find, even after pleading with Dad to get me to a more comprehensive magazine retailer miles from home.

> Michelle Nolan remembers finding *JLA* #22 at a bus stop in Redding, California, on her way to visit her grandparents. As happens with many of us collectors, her memory remains sharper around that moment than for many events since. She goes on to recall the temperature was 105 degrees, so getting off the bus couldn't have been pleasant. The copy she looked at had a 15-cent sticker affixed over the printed 12-cent cover price, something bus depots did back then.

The kids in my neighborhood were many, but comic book readers were fewer in number than one would expect from the heart of the baby-boomer generation (at least in my part of San Diego). I traded comics with just a couple of other kids also hamstrung by a lack of retailing in our ZIP code. What confounds some sports fans in our city today was true when I was a kid. There was and is just too much to do in this town other than reading comics and going to Chargers games. I lived north of a major east-west freeway system. South of Interstate 8 in older parts of San Diego, comic collectors could find retailers for new and used comics. North of the 8, the places to buy from were few in number. Places that I did find sold only new comics, and their ordering was haphazard and inconsistent. Garage sales were my best bet, and you know how that goes: catch as catch can!

Years passed when I felt seemingly on my own, searching out new comics and settling on just the old ones if I could find them. It wasn't until high school that I found ready-made locations to buy old and new comics. That timeline included San Diego's first comic book conventions and my employment at an honest-to-God comic book store. The absorption of those experiences granted me knowledge of what to collect beyond my own personal interests.

First of all, people like me were collecting whole runs of titles to fill in the boxes on homemade checklists. The key books in any run were not often recognized beyond their numerical order in a series (issue one was more expensive than issue two, issue two more than three, and so on). The age of Silver "first appearances" ended by 1970-ish. The Bronze Age was born simultaneously. We who lived comics were now caught up with the past and generating an era that future collectors, yet to be born, would envy.

We were continually buying new comics off the stands. Marvel and DC were inventing new characters for a market they perceived would thrive with new heroes and villains. Every other issue of something from DC and Marvel had a first appearance then. Those new costumed entries seemed to be no big deal to me until I saw what other, wiser collectors were doing.

Working at Richard Alf's Comic Kingdom back in the day allowed me to watch comic book fans and their developing rabid demand for Marvels as they got hotter than DCs. The hero-inception issues, the first appearances of the Silver Age Marvel heroes, were hot commodities even back then, and the books were only ten years old. The requests for *Amazing Fantasy* #15 and *Incredible Hulk* #1 (1962) always seemed to surpass the stock on hand. During that time I waded through tons of back issues at San Diego Comic-Con and swarms of smaller shows all across California. The concept of "wall books" was invented for comic conventions. Each show housed plenty of wall books, the best-of-the-best Silver Age keys, but there were a lot of fighters competing for those books. And they were affordable compared to what mid-level buyers could afford.

There's a point here I'd like to lean on a bit: the subject of "keys." As described in an earlier chapter, keys are significant issues of comics that contain important, valuable first appearances. Keys pertain to the first book in a run if that run is popular among collectors and dealers, and have greater value than the issues that surround it numerically. Those books we refer to as "common" or "filler" issues (filling a run). Central figures or plots, artistry or writing moments can be keys. First appearances do crop up all over the place in the Silver Age, allowing some non–number-one issues placement at or near the top rungs of key collectibility.

Here's an example: *Amazing Spider-Man* starts with issue #1, which is a key book. *Amazing Fantasy* #15 is Spidey's first appearance, but it is segregated by being the only issue to bear the title *Amazing Fantasy* (previously, it was one of Marvel's many horror/monster/

suspense anthology titles named *Amazing Adult Fantasy*). The *Amazing Spider-Man #1* retains secondary collectibility compared to *Amazing Fantasy* (*AF*) #15. By 2016, *AF* #15s were super-hot: *Action Comics* #1–style hot commodities, unaffordable for many. *Amazing Spider-Man* #1 is considered a consolation prize for die-hard key buyers hopped up on buying their dream book.

Amazing Spider-Man (or *ASM*) provides exciting benchmarks in the comic collecting hobby. The title is filled with desirable keys, while the character was Marvel's most popular superhero in the Silver Age. *ASM* had renowned first appearances in virtually every other issue after #1. Some issues introduced second-tier characters who didn't quite make it to key status. Other issues featured return appearances by newly popularized villains or heroes and can be considered keys or "semi-keys" of lesser importance. *ASM* has the distinction of producing key books throughout the Silver Age and well into the Bronze Age. These are important, expensive keys that continue to increase in value while retaining high visibility and market desire.

> *Amazing Spider-Man* presented a lot of important characters on both sides of the law, as well as love interests. Comic books thrive on new characters, but few have generated as many key appearances as *ASM*. Even before Marvel's movies in the new millennium amplified the popularity of their comic book characters, Spider-Man's rogues and allies were fan favorites. Marvel's other titles populated the entire Marvel Universe with comparable personnel, but few resonated as strongly as Spidey's people.

When you look at the roster of key issues populating the early issues of *ASM*, most are considered firsts and semi-keys, with an almost unbroken line beginning with #1 all the way up to #23. These issues are all part of the 38 issues greatly sought for Steve Ditko–drawn and co-plotted Silver Age stories that collectors are constantly saving for. When I compare *ASM* to the next popular issue of its time, *Fantastic Four*, the lineage of keys is somewhat less. The *Fantastic Four* is a great title (it says so at the top of each Silver Age issue!) but the villains, outside of Dr. Doom (and the wildly collectible issue #4, featuring the resurrection in comics of the princely Sub-Mariner), don't translate into the present with the same fierce collectability we find with Spider-Man's world. *Amazing Spider-Man* carries the heaviest roster of keys and collectible issues from the Silver and Bronze Age Marvel Universe.

Times and tastes change continually. *Fantastic Four* used to be Marvel's top dog in reference to a modest number of key issues. It was touted as Marvel's flagship title and was the earliest in Marvel's Silver Age superhero line. Jack Kirby's innovative and well-crafted plots and breakdowns featured some of Stan Lee's best dialogue. A gradual detachment from the *Fantastic Four* by comic readers, and the fallout from several criticized movies, relaxed the grip of some of *Fantastic Four*'s later keys. Marvel even drifted the team of core characters away from each other, canceling their title and leaving their fates to question.

The Marvel Universe was born in 1961 with *Fantastic Four* #1. *Spider-Man, Iron Man, The Hulk, Thor, Dr. Strange, Captain America, Ant-Man, Daredevil, The X-Men* and *Sgt. Fury* exploded with popularity, both as reads and as collectibles. DC Comics was seemingly less exciting at the same time, grinding out stories for children with insipid, predictable plots and wooden characters. (DC's war comics were an exception for kids of my generation. Still, they had a monthly, formulaic quality to the plots and action.) Marvel wrote stories with fallible characters. Those characters had distinct personalities and shared the same hang-ups as their readers. Older kids, college age students and hip adults enjoyed Marvel Comics. Their attentiveness helped mold Marvel's Universe into a mythical place that was part fiction and part real. People bought Marvels because they wanted to see what the fuss was all about and because Marvels were good, really fresh material. Marvel's success in paper translated to success on paper as their circulation figures increased.

Marvel enjoyed annual sales increases, inducing Martin Goodman to push distributor Independent Distribution into contract talks. Goodman wanted more favorable printing terms and the ability to produce more titles, since Marvel's characters were still confined to just a handful of books. Goodman won the right to publish his comic book characters in greater quantities of titles, guaranteeing Marvel the certainty that they could dominate the comic book world.

Goodman needed expansion. He wanted to sell Marvel by the end of the decade, and a larger publishing empire unencumbered by DC's restrictions would inflate his company's value on the open market. Marvel would remain on the ascent until near the end of the decade and a change of leadership. Those 1960s Marvels would forever remain the best of what happened at Marvel. That magic decade, the 1960s, influences collector habits today. The end of the 1960s also foretold a change in eras for comics.

I was born in 1955, considered the middle years of the Baby Boomer period (1946–1964). My generation watched television transition from black-and-white to color. More stations were available to television set owners as the clunky antennas made way for cable boxes. San Diegans could now get more than four or five English-speaking networks (and one Mexican station). Gas was remarkably cheap for just a little longer, but that also changed with the comic book eras. By the end of the 1960s San Diego and Los Angeles were smothering under heavy brown layers of smog. Smog was a normal part of Southern California living and routinely colored the skies sickly shades of grays and browns, especially during the hotter months. Unleaded gas was just around the corner.

As a kid in San Diego, I remember "smog alerts" during the latter part of summer and early fall. The air quality would degrade to the point where my throat felt scratchy and irritated when I was outdoors. Everybody felt it; outdoor activity was restricted by parental suggestion in the hot summer months, so kids like me stayed inside and read comics. Without the distraction of the outdoors, my friends and I would sit around a house somewhere in the neighborhood and read whatever comics were at hand. We shared the reads and laughed at the stupid stuff Jimmy Olsen and Lois Lane did. We bonded with that facet of our youth in the era of Silver Age comics.

Batman debuted on television in 1966. We read *Batman* comics and thought the TV show was much cooler. We didn't yet see the silliness that would mark the show and likely kill it, yet would save *Batman* comic books from cancellation. The TV show turned into a movie with theatrical release. I can't tell you how big that was with *Batman*'s main TV villains teamed up against the Dynamic Duo!

Marvel developed a severely budgeted cartoon series that brought all their Silver Age characters to the small screen. I could never find those TV shows on local television stations (they were only accessible to some if their TVs could pull in Los Angeles stations). So DC was the company of choice for kids my age influenced by television. I've since seen some of the cartoons, but the animation wasn't nearly as good as Tex Avery, Disney or Warner Brothers cartoons. Marvel was out there, but their characters were unfamiliar if you started reading in the late 1950s. DC reigned in the superhero market at the beginning of the 1960s.

Marvel gathered steam with guys like me because it dramatized aspects of our lives as we reached our late teen years. The flat perspectives of DC's heroes were easily supplanted by Spider-Man's angst and constant setbacks as he tried so hard to improve his lot in life. His comic book presence lured a lot of later readers (me included), and many of us sought out copies of his earlier adventures. By the end of the 1960s, Spider-Man was the favorite target of all kinds of collectors, so naturally the copies of his early back issues were in high demand at even the most unlikely back-issue locations (and at prices that seemed to push the envelope).

Used-book stores, mostly in the downtown area, obtained comic book back issues from whatever sources were available. Those stores tended to tighten access to the older issues with their own systems of specialized pricing. Ken Krueger's newsstand in Ocean Beach (a community of San Diego) displayed back-issues and treated them as valuable collectibles. Ken was one of the founders of the San Diego Comic-Con, and his input and commitment to comics helped elevate their collectibility. Ken and the others formed a group of proponents heavily influenced by their relationship to comic books. They were a mixture of pre–World War II kids and baby boomers slightly older than me who saw wealth in the buying and selling of all kinds of comics.

They also truly loved comic books. It was easy enough in those days to end up at some collector's house and get caught up in various discussions about the "whys" and "wherefores" of our realm. There were no "speculators" among us in that time of brimming energy for all things comic book.

Lanning's Bookstore, an old-school used-book store, was located downtown around 9th or 10th and Broadway. In the early 1970s, as my quests for back issues grew more expansive (and I got a driver's license!), I explored locations further from home. Lanning's was on my list, but I started there a little too late. The owner, an older woman, had her regulars, and they routinely picked through her selection of old comics. There was a certain irony to shopping for comics at Lanning's, for she had different reasons to possess old comic books. To my dismay, she used them to line the bottom of the parrot cage next to her register! I'd walk in the door and see that damn bird pooping all over barely recognizable Golden Age comics that old lady Lanning had dismembered to cover the floor of the cage. Tragic!

Comic Grinder posted an interview of San Diego Comic-Con board member and veteran Jackie Estrada in 2012. Jackie was also a fan of Lanning's. I know Jackie and liked what she shared with interviewer Henry Chamberlin:

> My high school sweetheart was Davy Estrada. We went to San Diego State together. We got into comics. And we'd go, every week, to downtown San Diego, to Lanning's Bookstore. Mrs. Lanning's Bookstore, with the cobwebs hanging from the ceiling and all the old magazines, and a shopping cart with a bin of coverless comics in it! They would have *Walt Disney's Comics & Stories, Little Lulu*, things like that.

That was Lanning's.

Early San Diego Comic-Con builder Ken Krueger's bookstore in one of San Diego's beach communities respected comic books and put great effort into displaying and selling them. Ken was a true futurist and a really good guy, mentoring an entire generation of future fans.

This group's position in the scheme of things guaranteed a future for more than collecting just comics. Their reach extended to comic strips, original art, pulps and science fiction, Big Little Books, vintage toys, satire magazines, *Playboy* magazine, other adult crossovers, fantasy, old movies and more. All

Right and below: This copy of *Detective Comics* #31 presents one of the most sought-after, iconic Batman covers of all time. Neal Adams's adaptation for *Batman* #227 raised the bar for collectible 1970s comics. Neal played with the theme one more time with New 52 *Detective Comics* #49. *Detective Comics* #31 (1939) © DC Comics. Used with permission, *Batman* #227 (1970) © DC Comics. Used with permission and New 52 *Detective Comics* #49 (2016) (© DC Comics. Used with permission).

this generated an escalation in popularity with the first San Diego Comic-Con, at least in the world of my hometown. Now suddenly a convention brought together the immediate fans and those who were curious. The people on the fringe who didn't really know the core collectors became the core collectors. Some began operating within the convention, while others began writing the rules. Comics became cool again like they'd been in the 1940s, but to two generations together instead of two separated by an era.

Guests from the comic book companies showed up at our convention, as they would back in New York and other shows that popped up nationwide. These men and women trumpeted their characters' successes and their own, becoming heroes of sorts themselves. Marvel took a front seat in the show, with Stan Lee firmly portraying the face of Marvel. He echoed the consideration that Marvel's comics were the best and the most exciting. DC and the much smaller companies brought guests to shows, but none of them had a committed leader who was a recognizable showman.

Neal Adams, Jim Steranko, Jack Kirby and others were magnetic comic celebrities who personalized the comic books they were a part of. The world recognized them as singular talents, not necessarily attached to any one company. Even Marvel stalwart Kirby had separated from Marvel by the early 1970s, representing himself first, and his comics second.

Adams and Steranko began their comic book work in the Silver Age. So many of DC and Marvel's artists working in the sixties began their careers in the preceding decades that it was unusual to identify new talent. Fabulous mainstays like Gil Kane, Don Heck, John Romita, Irv Novick, Joe Kubert, Russ Heath, Murphy Anderson, and of course Jack Kirby were already established artists for either company. By the time the end of the Silver Age was near, some of these men were ready to hand the reins of the daily grind off to others. Some were ready to retire; some continued to work. Not only were these artists endearing to readers, they were also prolific. They produced nonstop entertainment for their companies in the late 1950s and throughout the 1960s, steadfastly working into the 1970s.

Some of the artists would continue to draw for comics even as fans began to sway towards a newer generation of talent. I watched the stars of four-color, the artists, surface at early comic conventions one after another. I could see that those men and women were fans like me, but then, not like me. They were the heart and soul of our hobby. Their names lit up the pages of Silver Age Marvel Comics thanks to Stan Lee and Marvel's position on their talent. But the conventions took them to stratospheric status. Suddenly, Neal Adams (The Pencil!), Jack "The King" Kirby, and the others were accessible (Steve Ditko was and forever remained inaccessible). That was the key to the fan growth spurt that I saw in the beginning of the 1970s. All those dudes were there to meet fans, hand off samples of their talent, and promote projects that wouldn't be advertised in the comics. Some of the artists weren't financially comfortable, so the fan movement gave them a vehicle to sell some of their work. Most of the artists didn't own their work; those pages were still in the hands of their publishers. But they could do sketches, re-creations and the like.

I often wonder what my beloved hobby would have been like if Steve Ditko had attended shows. His mystique was encouraged more for not being around than for his talent, and he was super-talented in comic books. I know the bios say he teaches art in the Northeast. I've read about brief encounters with super-fans he responded to. Occasionally, Ditko surfaces with published work, often distributed through Diamond

Distributors. Otherwise, he's a "No comment—I let my work speak for me" kind of guy. Another "what if?"

I think the most amazing aspect of artists and conventions was the effort behind various cons to seek out and locate people. There are super-fans who work with the conventions to seek out artists and writers who have long since retired from the scene. There are also comic book guys who bring other lost talents back to the forefront.

By bringing their talent out from behind their easels, we made the artists become superstars. For the fans, creators began to reach Hollywood status. Some creators were known but rarely seen; others came to conventions out of obscurity or out of curiosity to see what the fuss was all about. All were welcomed by fans in numbers the writers and artists could only have wondered about. I saw and talked to quite a few artists while I gathered autographs or sought out sketches. My friends and I could even run into them in the hallways and at restaurants or even at parties. For some of them the experiences must have been jarring, like the shock of being approached by a stream of strangers when you're a celebrity. Their arrival at conventions built a celebrity status that I liken to rock stars.

I was at San Diego-Con in 1998 when I met an older gentleman shopping for particular Zane Grey comics from Dell Publishing. He searched for them because he had painted many of the covers and was at the con to walk down Memory Lane. I asked him if he was with anyone or perhaps had contact with the convention staff. He said no. He and his wife were there on their own, just sight-seeing. I was pretty excited. I felt like I had just discovered a treasure, but I didn't know what to do with him. I asked him to tell me a little about his career with Dell, so he humored me a bit with his tale:

He started working for Dell in their paperback book division doing covers for their westerns. His editor kept him working but couldn't generate enough work to pay him a decent salary. The editor made a suggestion: he asked if he'd be willing to paint comic book covers. The artist (and I'm ashamed to say I've forgotten his name) agreed and continued painting for Dell for a living.

What was interesting was the way Dell's offices were laid out. The artist told me that he worked in an office building in New York, riding the elevator each day to work. He entered the offices and walked down a long, quiet hallway lined with closed office doors. He entered his office to paint the art for paperback book covers.

When his editor brought him on board to do the comic book cover versions, he simply crossed the hall to another nondescript door and went to work at another easel. He said he had a few friends, but very few Dell employees were singled out for their work. They were there to paint and draw with little fanfare. That was the way things were done in the 1960s.

By late 1998, the artist was amazed at the world that had grown up around him. We took a little stroll around the dealers' room and talked. He underscored his history at Dell. He remembered it fondly, but said it wasn't for him. In the long run he wanted to work in commercial art where the money was, and he felt comics were no place to make a living.

I felt the contrary, but he was the veteran, so I could only listen. I did find a convention representative who had connections to guest administration, so I turned the artist over to the handler in the hope that the artist could find a seat in my world.

I remember when Shelly Moldoff was just beginning to make the rounds at shows in California. I first saw him at Wonder Con in the 1990s in Oakland seated at a table one aisle over, selling pages of art and taking commissions. Shelly worked on *Batman* beginning in 1953, drawing Batman during the "silly" phase. He drew until 1967, never getting any published credit for ghosting Bob Kane. But his star rose with the fans at the conventions. He found a path that allowed him to claim his place in the limelight and make a little extra cash.

I met another Golden Age great at a small convention in Arizona. This show was a two-day affair, but it had big aspirations. Arizona, especially the Phoenix area, has always had comic book back-issue stores of merit and people who could fill a convention with the kind of exhibitors who could draw in back-issue fans. One fan I couldn't have predicted was old Golden Age great Mart Nodell. Mart was in his eighties when I met him. He was at this Arizona show having breakfast before the beginning of the first day. He was with his wife, Carrie, and they were conversing over what to expect. This was Mart's first West Coast comic con and only the second since coming out of a 35-year retirement.

Mart was invited to the show after another entrepreneur had seen him publicly. That guy allowed Mart to announce to the world that he was the original creator of Green Lantern in 1940. Actually, Mart designed the art and costume for Green Lantern, but none of us were going to argue with him. Like other artists, he retired from comics to get into commercial art. He saw no financial future doing comic books in the 1940s.

In each case, comic conventions were instrumental in bringing these veterans to light. Whether it was a first chance to meet *Daredevil/Dracula* artist Gene Colan during one of his many appearances or another legend like Mart Nodell or Shelly Moldoff for the first time, conventions and the back-issue fans who admire them made it all happen, and still do.

For a man my age, no reminisce is more golden than seeing and meeting Jack "The King" Kirby at almost every San Diego Comic-Con in the 1970s. Being there back then seems magical to me now. The younger fans express bewilderment when I tell them I was able to hang out with an icon. The closest they can get to that image is paying $100-plus to get Stan Lee to autograph a comic book at a show or convention. That is, if they are lucky enough to get to see him.

These celebrated artists created outstanding work and highly identifiable art styles: Gil Kane and his distinct, muscular portrayal of human calves and turned-up noses, hooked me on *Green Lantern*. Joe Kubert drew exciting, gripping illustrations in DC's war titles; John Romita on *Amazing Spider-Man*; Murphy Anderson's work on *Hawkman*; John Buscema on *Avengers* (and later *Conan the Barbarian*, starting in 1970). Heath and his photographic framing graced the DC war comics; Curt Swan was by far the best Superman artist for me, especially when inked by Anderson. The distinct variety in styles gave even the youngest readers the ability to tell each artist from the others.

Men like Curt Swan, Gene Colan, Wayne Boring, Don Heck, Carmine Infantino and others would be forever tied to the character projects they were assigned to draw: Colan on *Daredevil*; Infantino on a streamlined Flash from the onset of the Silver Age. Infantino also played a role in keeping *Batman* alive when circulation looked bleak in the early 1960s. Don Heck, George Tuska and even Wally Wood (for a short time) piloted Daredevil and Iron Man through their titles. Wayne Boring's barrel-chested Superman didn't fly through the air; he powered through it!

The two companies maintained their stables of art talent and rarely let them slip to the competition. Exceptions did occur, of course. Ditko returned to Charlton, where he could be paid to do what he wanted, free of the more confining structure he felt at Marvel. Mike Esposito of DC's Andru-and-Esposito art team-ups in the 1960s used a pseudonym at Marvel, and guys like Neal Adams worked where they wanted to. Neal Adams, like Jim Steranko, was a pure product of the second half of the 1960s Silver Age. Neal had worked briefly for Archie Comics before taking on the role of "dynamic, new cover artist" at DC. Neal's dramatic illustrative and fluid pencils anchored him at DC and changed everything about collecting comics. His art was exciting; his covers featured cliffhanging drama that seemed more vibrant than other cover art at DC.

At Marvel, Stan Lee hired a talent off the street named Jim Steranko. Jim wore classy clothes to the office and promised Marvel he could deliver eye-catching pencils. His first assignment took the second-tier character Nick Fury from *Strange Tales* and walloped the readers with his cinematic flair for using imagery to tell the story. Together, Adams and Steranko engaged comic book readers with unique art styles that were their way of showing off capabilities uncommon for Marvel and DC. Marvel liked its "house style," even encouraging newcomers Barry Smith and Rich Buckler to present Kirby-like pencils. Adams and Steranko stirred up comic fans because their art took comics to a new level. Suddenly comic book art looked adult in context and seemed aimed at taking comics more seriously.

Both men shined brightly but left mainstream comics all too early, leaving a library of must-have comic books for collectors. Even today, both men are sought after for autographs, sketches and interviews. The fascination for collectors of those late Silver Age/early Bronze Age issues from both artists continues today. Adams's seminal art on Denny O'Neill's scripted *Green Lantern/Green Arrow* series is a list-topper for comic book aficionados. Steranko's *Nick Fury* (not forgetting his short run on *Captain America* and the stunning cover for *Incredible Hulk Special* #1) was his tour-de-force for artistic storytelling. His pop art and stunning cover art sells copies of *Nick Fury* long past its absence on the stands.

My mind boggles at what could have been with an Adams/Steranko art team-up back in the day!

Bob Kane and the legendary editor Julius Schwartz were forever recognized movers and shakers. But it was the hot artists like Steranko and Adams who mesmerized crowds big and small at shows. Stan Lee could stand at a podium, sit on a panel or sign autographs in a dealers' room and grab the most attention. He made the Silver Age his own and convinced us all to "Make Mine Marvel!"

Sadly, many of these admired icons were from a different time and are favored by an increasingly older comic book fan base. I attended a San Diego Comic-Con in the early 2000s and walked the room for a while, catching a break from my exhibitors' booth. I walked amongst the tables in Artist Alley and saw an older artist with no line at his table. I didn't recognize Jim Mooney seated at a booth, but I certainly remember his 1960s work for DC. Jim had sketches for sale, including a Batman sketch, for reasonable prices. Jim was another 1960s DC icon and should have had a few people hanging around as fans do at these shows.

I like Jim's work and bought the Batman sketch, having him sign it to me. There was never a line at his booth. His situation was shared by others at that show and subsequent shows I attended. The Old Guard was celebrated, but perhaps not enough.

Stan Lee was forever a dominant man in our hobby and the comic book industry. He controlled the output of a company seemingly on his own. His name was emblazoned across Marvel's titles. He had his own editorial "Soap Box" in each Marvel issue. Stan positioned himself as the face and soul behind the Marvel Movement. He appeared to rise above the rest of the talent at Marvel (or any other company) and to speak his own brand of philosophy. He spent so much time speaking and working on outside projects that others were needed to complete chores that once were all his.

This was a point in time where Marvel reached a zenith. It was near the end of the 1960s and America was embroiled in cultural and radical change. Marvel preferred to stay on the sidelines and only marginally addressed the realities of the world as I saw it. Marvel was much more preoccupied with growth within the company. Martin Goodman, the publisher at Marvel, sensed a chance for his company to challenge DC and their distribution control over Marvel's title output. Marvel was making money and wanted to double-down on their titles.

Marvel entered a new realm where success came with high costs. Creative, innovative personnel at Marvel began to leave. Two shapers in particular, Steve Ditko and Jack Kirby, had had enough, and took their ideas and energy elsewhere. Stan was busy as well, but not necessarily writing or dialoguing comics. He found replacements in Archie Goodwin, Roy Thomas and others, and by 1968 comic book buyers like me saw definite changes.

Suddenly, Marvel comic books were printed on better paper with glossier covers and none of those dreadful mis-cuts prevalent in their comics since the 1950s. Gone too were the names that we knew signified a story or art style. Ditko's replacement, John Romita, had a completely different pencil. His version was a thicker Peter Parker with slightly less detail. Marvel's changes included fewer but larger panels per page, so fewer stories could be concluded in one comic. Now readers like me were learning about the costly necessity of buying sequential issues to complete one story. And those stories were not cheap. By 1969 the new management wanted to squeeze more money out of Marvel, so cover prices went up from twelve cents to fifteen. If you were a Marvel completist, and many of us Boomers were, you could no longer be certain you could afford all of Marvel's superhero line. Three cents wasn't that much, but my allowance by the end of junior high school was about five dollars a week. I took a job as a paperboy to make my comic book ends meet!

Marvel still avoided our reality in their storytelling. They did opt to string together a few controversial subjects, mostly memorable in *Amazing Spider-Man*. *ASM* issues #96 through #98 dealt with the subject of illicit drug use through Harry Osborn, Spidey's best friend and the son of the Green Goblin. Marvel's three-issue story arc was not looked upon favorably by the Comics Code Authority, so their approval stamp was held back. Stan made the decision to print without the stamp on the title's covers. The content of the story was definitely anti-drug, but the CCA lacked the flexibility to modify its censorship on that issue. Stan's decision to run the story forced change within the Code. It also created a set of three more key issues for later collectors.

Consequently, within a short time DC allowed Denny O'Neill and Neal Adams to pursue the subject of narcotics in their successful *Green Lantern/Green Arrow* series—*GL/GA* #85 and #86 in 1971. The crushing discovery that Green Arrow's own ward and junior partner in crime fighting was experimenting with heroin earned the praise of civic leaders and parents alike. The New York mayor at the time, John Lindsay, wrote a letter congratulating

DC on its brave steps to bring public awareness to the drug epidemic through comics. The letter was published in *GL/GA* #86.

The Forensic Comicologist liked the sudden cultural awareness and boldness of the story so much he used it as the subject matter for a college project.

For educational purposes, this is a good point in the chapter to refer to the era change for comic books. The social changes in America were now being reflected, albeit carefully, in comic books. Racism, war, political corruption, corporate greed and more brought us Silver Agers into the upheaval that was the transition from the 1960s into the 1970s. Marvel and DC allowed their comics to reflect more mature themes. Readers who stuck with the Silver Age from its inception were now old enough to want more relevance in their comics. The characters we laughed about at DC, like Jimmy Olsen and Lois Lane, suddenly made gains in social and societal awareness. Heroes such as Superman, flawless in their design and performance, were reduced in power to make them vulnerable, closer to the human condition.

DC provided readers with a Batman who operated with predictable readiness for years. His capers usually involved Robin (often in peril). The 1960s TV show kept the characters afloat at a time when their publication future was at risk. The TV show reaffirmed their monetary value, but the stories were still told in DC time, not real time. The need to be more astute in relationship to America's reality entered the world of Batman. With the input of plots from writers like O'Neill, Frank Robbins and others, Batman's character took on more meaning. Batman worked solo without Robin and collided with society's social ills. Even Vietnam found its way into a Bat story, something usually kept at a distance in the comic book world.

The uplifted plot content and meaningful adult art meant that teens and young adults in 1970 were no longer protected from the problems in the real world. Readers my age, if curious enough, could bridge the gap between a serious Batman story and the news on television. Our young consciences were being elevated through comics. The comics that embodied those changes became collectible. Adams's menacing portrayal of Batman in three different titles (*Detective Comics*, *Batman* and *Brave and the Bold*) created comics considered highly collectible today.

The end of the Silver Age was poignant not just for style points but for sales points too. DC's dominance with higher circulation figures surrendered to Marvel with the end of the 1960s. For a brief time Marvel's sales zenith was well above what DC could produce. Marvel's new owner eventually separated from its contract with DC altogether and bought its own distribution network. Marvel generated new characters with the dawn if the 1970s. Characters such as Iron Fist, Wolverine, Shang-Chi, Blade and Luke Cage sprang up from new talent working at Marvel. These heroes were well accepted by readers at a time when the general thought was that superheroes were unsustainable.

Marvel's post–Kirby character inventions were generally less marketable outside of their comic book appearances. All the movie money was generated from the Kirby-era heroes and villains. Marvel and NetFlix introduced a string of Marvel's "street" heroes on NetFlix's subscription network. The early success of *Daredevil*, *Jessica Jones* and *Luke Cage* indicated strong viewer appeal for these characters and more. I loved the shows, 13 episodes of thoughtful, entrancing storytelling for each show. The characters were well-cast and the subdued New York street vibe added realism to their tales.

Marvel's other television entry was *Agents of SHIELD* on ABC. I watched the show through all of its seasons, enjoying it for the most part. Marvel reacquired the movie and TV rights to another post–Kirby character, Ghost Rider, and added him to the cast. The show, for me, languished in the second couple of seasons. I really wanted Marvel to provide first-tier heroes and villains. What I got was less satisfying with their versions of the Inhumans. With Ghost Rider introduced in season 4, that all changed. I welcomed the appearance of a costumed Marvel stand-out; he made the season much more palatable.

I shopped at a supermarket near my house, Alpha-Beta Market. The store was adequate in size for its time and had been in operation at that location since 1964. By 1970 other chains had opened in larger shopping centers and were attracting more and more locals. None of those stores sold comics, and the Alpha-Beta Market chain must have taken notice. Comics that were once ignored and then prominently displayed were racked by happenstance placement in the store's magazine area. No thought was given to the ordering, so there was no sense to the arrangement of the comics that the store ordered from the local magazine distributor. Finally, just after Jack Kirby's *Kamandi* #1 for DC hit the stands (1972), Alpha-Beta stopped carrying comic books altogether. Those spots on the magazine racks were replaced by adult-friendly monthlies or gossip rags for the titillated masses.

DC invented new characters within and outside the superhero realm. Their success rate for new villains and heroes created after 1968 was met with reader ambivalence. Kirby's Fourth World characters started out strong, the ideas behind the stories coming from Kirby's powerful imagination. The three titles appeared almost simultaneously: *New Gods, Forever People* and *Mister Miracle*. They had great Fourth World titles, Jack Kirby art and new characters in the DC universe. But sales lapsed after a year or so and quickly ended those short-lived additions to DC Comics' line-up. Evidently, the DC fans were grounded in DC mainstays, and the Marvel guys preferred Marvel. Or else we'd have to believe that Kirby's Fourth World was just not interesting enough to grab and hold readers.

At the beginning of the 1970s, DC's sales figures were dropping while Marvel's innovations were raising sales numbers. DC worked vigorously to match Marvel, but ran afoul of less successful circulation numbers once their cover prices ballooned up to twenty-five cents in 1975–1976. Choices in new titles were clear attempts to mimic Marvel's four-color rendition of Robert E. Howard's *Conan the Barbarian*, horror/monster titles, and other non-hero Marvel start-ups. DC's *Sword and Sorcery, Claw the Unconquered, Kong the Untamed* and Steve Ditko's *Stalker* failed soon after arrival. DC's long-running horror/mystery/science fiction titles were ripe for mimicry by Marvel. Marvel had a stable of old reprints that dovetailed nicely into their own fantasy titles. With the Code relaxing its rules, Marvel was able to reprint some of their old work while allowing a few new stories to be printed.

Eventually the changes in reader tastes steered many of them away from comics and led to a plunge in sales numbers for both companies. There are several reasons for the decline. Among them were other, more desired forms of entertainment, increased comic book cover prices, and my personal take: the comics were just not as good as they were at the end of the Silver Age.

Here's a breakdown strongly based upon my impressions and history broken down by genre (and this section pertains to collectibility today):

> The superhero market lived with steadily decreasing numbers for paid circulation around DC and Marvel's core caped characters. An example taken from Comichron.com gathered stats that placed *Amazing Spider-Man* at the top of Marvel's circulation chart in 1968. *ASM* sold 373,303 copies on average that year. By 1974 that figure had dropped to 288,232 and by 1978 had slipped to 258,156. DC's *Superman* was still a powerhouse seller back then, trumping even *Batman*. *Superman* sold 636,000 copies on average versus *Batman* at position #2 with 533,450. By 1979 they were at 223,000+ and 166,640, respectively.

Both companies had started out the decade with strong, popular titles. Adams's influence on certain Marvel and DC comic characters led those titles to circulation increases. The Batman family titles probably benefited more than other by Adams's participation at DC. The same can be said about Marvel's *Avengers* during Adams's run (the Kree/Skrull war story arc).

Neal Adams' place in comic book lore is noteworthy on many fronts. Neal did two store signings with us at Southern California Comics. At one of those signings Neal was asked why he ended up doing art for a brief period on *X-Men*. Neal was energetic when he explained that Stan Lee hired him to work for Marvel because Lee saw Adams' impact on DC sales. Lee wanted the same. So Neal worked briefly on several titles. When Lee asked him what other titles he would choose to draw, Adams asked, "What's your weakest selling title?" Stan replied that it was *X-Men* (which would go to reprints in 1970 and be cancelled in 1975 in that format). Neal said, "Give it to me," and so for a short period Adams' art stunned readers of that title.

The Superman family of titles was written to a somewhat more mature level just ten years after readers were growing tired of Lois Lane's attempt to wheedle love out of Superman. Superman gained resistance to Kryptonite in *Superman* #233 (1971) and found his alter ego changing jobs. Jimmy Olsen fell under the influence of Jack Kirby's pencils while Lois Lane developed a social awareness. Green Lantern and Green Arrow found social causes worth fighting for. That maturation would not be turned back for either character.

The Flash and *Wonder Woman* survived the transition from era to era, both having had their starts in the Golden Age. Each title went for the long haul before cancellation and rebooting in the mid–1980s. A note about these two titles: 2015–2016 saw a marked increase in Flash popularity, probably due to the TV show. Back-issue sales picked up domestically and abroad. At the 2016 Comic-Con International, we sold a large portion of our Silver and Bronze Age *Flash*es to American dealers for resale, and a French dealer for the same purpose.

Wonder Woman was hot before the then-unreleased movie *Batman v Superman: Dawn of Justice*. Her stint in that movie and subsequent casting for upcoming films (including her own solo project) propelled sales of *Wonder Woman* beyond our capacity to stock the title.

What took place at the dawn of the Bronze Age was the distressing revelation that both DC and Marvel were losing their readership. Despite socially aware stories, new characters and new art talent by 1969, the number-one selling title in the 1970s was *Archie Comics*.

Traditional veteran writers and artists were being replaced by new people, with styles often less recognizable. Whole genres were taken over by people I never heard of. One changing group of DC's output was its war comics. DC had held onto that important market for two decades by the beginning of the Bronze Age. DC's Big Five titles all got started in the 1950s with strong reader following. *Our Army At War* featuring Sgt. Rock, *Our Fighting Forces, Star Spangled War Stories, All-American Men of War,* and the widely read *GI Combat* with the Haunted Tank succeeded through the 1960s. Of the five, *All-American Men of War* folded in 1966, before the Bronze Age. The other four either capitalized on their flagship characters or experimented with new ones: The Losers, Enemy Ace and the Unknown Soldier celebrated various levels of success.

DC's infusion of a sociological mentality, reaching out to fans with occasionally topical results, changed the structure of its core heroes. Batman, Superman, Green Lantern, Aquaman, the JLA, and others were drawn into "real time" to answer real-world concerns. Out of all these changes, DC generated few key issues outside of Neal Adams's touch. *GL/GA, Batman, Detective Comics,* and a couple of *Brave and the Bold*s are still the DCs most in demand because of his work. *Atom, Hawkman* and *Aquaman* had been good reads with consistent stories, but they were still canceled. *Strange Adventures,* featuring Adams's surprise breakout hero Deadman, couldn't survive on its own, and saw his storyline wrapped into *Aquaman* before both were terminated.

Stepping away from the costume set, DC and Marvel almost simultaneously generated two similar creature heroes: Swamp Thing and Man-Thing. Either character fits the superhero category, while both can easily slip into the monster/horror column.

Both swamp creatures are carried over into occasional storylines, although Swamp Thing has had greater success in the modern era with his own titles. (Both first appearances were in anthology titles: Swamp Thing in *House of Secrets* #92 and Man-Thing in *Savage Tales* #1.) Both characters have been springboards for other first appearances of collectibility (Constantine in *Swamp Thing* #37 and Howard the Duck in *Fear* #19, when Man-Thing owned that title). Strangely, *House of Secrets* #92 is a much more desired collector's item than *Savage Tales* #1. Perhaps it's because *Savage Tales* was a magazine format, not necessarily convenient to collect. Or the fact that it was Conan's first outing at Marvel as an illustrated character, not sought out much for the Man-Thing appearance.

While I address *House of Secrets*, I should mention that DC hit a new wellspring of interest with the new material in all their horror/mystery titles. *House of Mystery, Unexpected* and *Weird Mystery* showcased new art talent for DC while Marvel was producing horror titles with reprints from the 1950s. Bernie Wrightson, Mike Kaluta and Jeff Jones entered the arena of hot artistry while older artists of particular fame saw print again. I loved seeing icons like Alex Toth, Wally Wood and Joe Orlando join a new breed of imported artistry from the Philippines. Alfredo Alcala and countrymen Nestor Redondo, Ernie Chan, Tony DeZuniga and more became go-to guys for DC. Just a handful of DC's horror/mystery comics are prized, but it is most definitely due to the art.

The Filipino artists were led to the United States by Alfredo Alcala, Nestor Redondo and others. Alcala was already famous in his home country as an outstanding illustrator. He and a few others had a studio in the Philippines where they trained new talent for work there and abroad. By the 1970s, Alcala and the others were working for virtually every comic book publisher in America. They became the as-yet unfamiliar names working at DC.

The Filipinos were quick, hard workers, which stunned editors at Marvel and DC. Joe Orlando, an executive at DC (and former EC artist) hired Alcala to do the art on their war and horror/mystery titles. Alfredo and many of the others worked fast, churning out more pages than comic book editors were prepared for, cementing their jobs in America.

I was always impressed with their style. Many of the Filipino artists drew with great detail, more so than some of the artists on DC and Marvel's top-tier titles. Eventually I saw some of their work transit over to Batman and other superheroes.

At a San Diego convention in the early 2000s, my business partner Gino stopped at a dealer's booth to leaf through a stack of low-priced original art. The pages were all published works from 1980s DC titles, mostly war and horror. To Gino's amazement, the art was cheap, only four dollars a page, and it was all Filipino artists. Gino and I bought the whole stack and made a good deal of coin selling them off at our store.

The art was beautiful and so detailed for titles that were soon to be canceled by DC. The guys from the Philippines were underutilized by DC, and probably Marvel. They could have kept on working on all the titles across the board for as long as they wanted work.

Conan has seen better days as well. When he first appeared in 1970, all of us were bowled over by the art style and the fantastic action. Conan ruled in both *Conan the Barbarian* and *Savage Sword of Conan*, the latter in a black-and-white magazine format (and supposedly a much more mature storyline). In San Diego, a military town, Conan reigned supreme with marines and sailors. Some stories were adapted from Conan novels, while the vast majority usually pitted Conan against monsters and wizards made up by Roy Thomas and others. Maybe it was the repetitive stories or the decline in the military population locally, but Conan virtually dropped off the map after the 1980s in San Diego.

The Silver Age and Bronze Age superhero selection for collectibility is exhausting. New key back issues materialize as often as announcements are made regarding a character's TV or movie debut. DC bred the beginnings of the Silver Age with superheroes only a few months and years before Marvel's similar point of creation. What DC did not do was retain dominance in sales over Marvel by the dawn of the next era. Marvel's superhero characters shattered DC's numbers (even though both companies lost circulation until things turned around in the later 1980s). Marvel kept *Amazing Spider-Man* as its number one best-seller with *Fantastic Four* taking second place. *Thor* retained its post–Kirby mythos, but failed to produce meaningful keys after #168 and #169 (Galactus' appearances). As the series continued, Marvel extended the Asgard mythology while putting Thor through his god-sized battles and family machinations.

One exception to *Thor*'s lack of identifiable keys well into the 1980s was issue #337. Walt Simonson took on the writing and art chores for *Thor* with this issue. Simonson brought his easily identifiable pencils and fresh writing to the comic. Simonson's first desire was to create a new character: Beta Ray Bill. Bill was initially a monster in appearance but would quickly become a hero and ally of Thor. Readers responded to the new hammer-wielder and Bill enjoyed newborn popularity.

I've seen plenty of copies of #337 for sale over the years; it was a heavily speculated comic book in its day. I've seen multitudes of copies out there rendering that issue relatively common. Yet GPA lists finished prices for copies in 9.4 and greater at over $100. Create a Marvel key and they will come.

The Forensic Comicologist can barely keep up with the consistent rise and fall of Marvel key issues.

15

Bronze Age

Marvel, Large and in Charge

Near the end of the Silver Age in 1970, Marvel's new ownership allotted more title options. *Tales of Suspense* split into *Iron Man* and *Captain America*. *Tales to Astonish* gave Hulk and Sub-Mariner their own self-titled monthly comics. Marvel experimented with second-tier heroes by providing the Silver Surfer with his own 18-issue series. The Surfer was a spin-off from the *Fantastic Four* and was written with a certain social relevance by Stan Lee, reminiscent of O'Neill and Adams of *Green Lantern/Green Arrow* (published about two years prior). Stan's writing was at its best, and it was said that after that run ended, Stan would never let anyone else write for the character but him. *Silver Surfer* was always a favorite, not only of mine, but my father. He felt Stan's stories were written "up" to his level.

Marvel knew that to thrive they needed to create new titles. Nothing as strong as the early Silver Age characters had come out of the "House of Ideas" since Kirby left. Heroes like Silver Surfer, Ka-Zar, the Invaders and the Inhumans were granted space in either their own titles or half space in ongoing anthologies like *Amazing Adventures* and *Astonishing Tales*. The Inhumans did a set in *Amazing Adventures* with Neal Adams art before landing their own self-titled 32-page comic. Neither the Inhumans nor the Invaders were new to the Marvel universe. *Fantastic Four* had been the staging point for the Inhumans (now gaining new life as their characters saw TV screen time while movie rumors abounded). Meanwhile, the *Invaders* told new tales of the *All-Winners Squad* of the 1940s.

What Marvel needed was to jettison the thinking of the past and allow its current crop of writing talent the freedom to invent new bankable heroes. For you key collector types, this period of Marvel creativity yielded important issues galore. Besides the aforementioned *Inhumans* and *Invaders* #1s, we have the following: *Special Marvel Edition* (previously a reprint tile) giving us *Shang Chi, Master of King Fu* with issue #15. *Iron Fist* started out first in *Marvel Premiere* (a typical try-out title much like DC's *Showcase*) before beginning again with issue #1. Of course, we see the rise of Conan beginning with a brief run in the *Savage Tales* magazine. His Barry Smith-endowed artwork propelled Conan to instant four-color stardom. Sabretooth found his way onto the path of fame with *Iron Fist* #14. His opposite, Wolverine, spun off out of *Incredible Hulk* #181 and became the darling of the 1970s. Wolverine eventually ended up as a teammate of the re-imagined X-Men in *Giant-Size X-Men* #1. The *Giant-Size* titles from Marvel encompassed a short period of production in the mid–1970s. They contained a mixture of new and reprinted material, depending on the chosen title.

Marvel's cavalcade of key appearances from the Bronze Age continued with Luke Cage. He began in *Luke Cage—Hero for Hire* as a prison experiment, giving him near-invulnerable skin and accompanying strength. Luke's invention followed the popularity of the style of black cinema that produced the likes of John Shaft in the *Shaft* movies of the 1970s. Cage became an urban legend who provided a hero for the denizens of New York's darkest streets. Issue #1 is a hot collectible commodity. (Marvel reduced the cover art for its titles at the time *Hero for Hire* came out. The cover art was boxed into a frame, presumably to stand out against competition on the sales racks. The result for *Hero for Hire* #1 was a heavy black border that shows every crease and dimple. That makes it difficult to find super high-grade copies today.)

Luke Cage was not Marvel's first black character. That honor goes to Black Panther, first featured in *Fantastic Four* #52 right after the Silver Surfer/Galactus trilogy. But Cage was Marvel's stab at introducing an inner-city street hero to comics. Cage was the reluctant warrior who adopted a now-familiar "with great power comes great responsibility" mentality. Luke's lifestyle was tinged with the daily survival of a man struggling to get by on the mean streets of New York with no job, no formal training or education, and no future prospects.

By issue #17 Luke became Power Man with a title change. He eventually formed a dynamic duo with Iron Fist in issue #48. Cage couldn't sustain his own title without an assist after "blaxploitation" films ran their course.

Some 1970s characters had gumption but no longevity. *The Cat* and *Red Wolf* tried to make a go of it along with *Shanna The She-Devil*. There's minimal collectible success flowing from those three titles. Same is true for the venerable Spider-Family. *Amazing Spider-Man* set standards for key collectibles with a handful of Bronze Age must-haves. *Marvel Spotlight* brought us Spider-Woman. She got her own self-named title, but that item is dubious for investment success at this date.

Speaking of Spider-Woman, those of us who grew up on DC comic books were exposed to their characters' derivations early on with the initial creation of Superboy. That was in 1944 and was successful enough to ultimately launch Supergirl and even stories of Superman when he was a baby. Of course Krypto the Superdog (1955) stretched the joy of baby boomer kids for all things Super. DC made this Superman Family a thing and brought the philosophy of "more is better" into the world of Batman. And so it went, with super-extended families and/or sidekicks for DC well into the 1960s.

Marvel, on the other hand, kept their hero lineage simple: one power, one person. Looking back at Marvel's replication of genres copied from other companies in the 1950s, its reluctance to cram similar characters into their universe was refreshing. That's why Spider-Woman was such an anomaly. It felt like Marvel was surrendering to cruder plot devices, a suspicion that was confirmed for me when the world saw *Savage She-Hulk* for the first time. Unlike DC's unrepentant exploitation of the Superman theme decades before, Marvel cast the She-Hulk and Spider-Woman characters in an effort to "do it" before another company could invent and license the names. Maybe so, but neither character has been commercially successful in the volatile back-issue market.

Perhaps one of the more contrived Marvel characters is Moon Knight. He seems an amalgam of Batman, Dracula, and at least a dozen other characters with similar powers, problems and backgrounds. His claim to originality is that he has multiple personalities, or does he?

Moon Knight arrived in a two-part adventure in *Werewolf By Night* #32 and #33. Issue #32 is an overwhelmingly lucrative key book. *Moon Knight* titles came and went, starting over at issue #1 numerous times. *Marvel Spotlight* gave Moon Knight a two-issue solo tryout before he earned his own title. There is some fanfare for those two issues (#28 and #29), but really none for any of his subsequent appearances.

Speaking of *Werewolf By Night,* by 1970 the Comics Code Authority had relaxed its standards. Now, monsters were free to wreak havoc in comics again after 15 years of suppression.

The Monster of Frankenstein, Tomb of Dracula, and the aforementioned *Werewolf By Night* were three new titles in the early 1970s. Each title generated a #1 issue that retains some value today. They contained quality art and stories by past luminaries like Gene Colan, Marv Wolfman, Mike Ploog and Gerry Conway. The Man-Thing started in a title called *Fear* (1970–1975), following his debut in *Savage Tales,* before transitioning to his own *Man-Thing* title. In turn, *Fear* (with Man-Thing) showcased one of the most creative swipes at the comic book industry in general with Howard the Duck. Howard was a talking duck from another planet with a wry sense of humor and a driving need to get away from humans and return home. Steve Gerber's *Howard the Duck* (1976) got his own title and enjoyed a three-year stint. Howard was born from a mystical nexus of realities, which is a good point to refer to Doctor Strange.

The good doctor shared page space in *Strange Tales* for years before splitting the title. He retained sole position in the book with issue #169 (a Marvel key). He resurfaced later in his own title, *Doctor Strange* (1974). Issue one of that series continues to increase in value with the doctor released as a movie in 2016. His page partner in *Strange Tales,* Nick Fury, got his own short-lived title. *Nick Fury* issues #1–#7 are highly prized for the Jim Steranko cover art.

Another helping of Bronze Age originality from *Strange Tales* became Dr. Strange's replacement in that title. Brother Voodoo failed to gain recognition, but the invention of Lee and Kirby's Warlock (formerly Him) took over for Brother. Warlock was spacey in concept and wondrous in art, with Jim Starlin calling the shots. His stories took him into Marvel's space-based universe and pitched him against a whole new host of off-planet drama. That development in outer space was accompanied by Captain Marvel, started in a former reprint title called *Marvel Super Heroes* (1967). He gained *Captain Marvel* stature at the beginning of the Bronze Age and has stayed afloat ever since. For a brief period in the title's run Starlin's cosmic plots and elaborate art style made *CM* famous with unique and odd existential plots. The Starlin run on *CM* is highly collectible today, especially the emergence of Thanos the universal threat. *Marvel Super Heroes #13 was* Captain Marvel's second spin in comics (not to be confused with two other, earlier permutations of that name). That issue is all the rage now because it featured the first appearance of Carol Danvers, who would transcend her ordinary life by becoming Ms. Marvel and gaining a short-lived self-titled series. In turn, Danvers has morphed into the newest version of Captain Marvel. That role has been cast for an upcoming Marvel movie, so issue #13 is red hot to collect!

All of the above inventions—plus Nova, Defenders, the original Guardians of the Galaxy and more—illustrate a period at post–Kirby Marvel. New talent was challenged to come up with new characters. The writers had different values, different points of view, and different goals for the comic characters they brought to publication.

The dawning of Marvel's Bronze Age displayed prowess at inventiveness, but also reduced panel counts per page and increased cover prices. Marvel was subjecting its readership to new heroes, but many of them did not succeed in that era. What comic buyers had to deal with was an atmosphere where post–Kirby, post–Adams, and more importantly, post–Stan Lee guidance left us with fewer panels per page with higher cover costs. An inevitable loss of buyers was imminent.

> An excerpt from the *Great American Novel* shares, "[I]n October 1971 Marvel used a sneaky trick: they raised their page count and price. DC heard in advance and did the same. But DC had to buy their paper a year in advance so was locked into the higher page count. The next month Marvel dropped their pages and prices again, while DC had to keep their prices high. For the whole year Marvel grabbed market share, and kept a lot of it even after DC went back to normal."

Marvel's circulation increase and decline followed the path of most post–Kirby story involvement. The dips in distribution figures also corresponded to cover price increases, which happened more frequently in the inflation-plagued 1970s than the previous four decades combined. The new characters that Marvel crafted after 1968 retain levels of collectibility, but their importance collectively did little to keep Marvel's sales numbers at their highest peak. Their Bronze Age titles (roughly 1970–1980) showed diversity in subject matter compared to DC's determination to work within the superhero bracket. The general trend was that DC's sales dropped as readers chose Marvel over DC.

DC flourished as the more desirable of the two companies when they re-engaged the comic book market in the late 1950s. Their progressive new versions of old heroes were well-timed with the new-age block of readers. DC's star rose with the TV element and adult growth of its characters. The *Batman* TV show evidently came along at the right time. *Batman* the comic book was considered for cancellation by DC, an unthinkable action by the time Greenway Productions introduced the first season of *Batman* on network TV in 1966. The phenomenally popular second time on screen for *Batman* (forget the lackluster 1940s serials) not only helped keep *Batman* afloat but guided DC to rethink how the character had been manhandled for so long. They retooled *Batman* and *Detective Comics* to reflect a better-developed character and re-involved him in crime-solving instead of monkeying around with aliens. Shelly Moldoff, Carmine Infantino and others were now tasked with returning Batman to crime-fighter status with the art and stories.

The earliest Batman titles of the 1970s were perhaps the best of any era for Batman. Neal Adams's art was installed on many covers and into a handful of interiors in all three Bat titles from that period (with the exception of *World's Finest*, although Adams did handle art chores in a couple of issues). They are without a doubt the hottest collectible comic book grouping of the Bronze Age. No other titles from the 1970s come close in such a wide swath of issues on everyone's bucket list. Neal Adams's work almost singlehandedly helps these issues retain their top-tier status on the resale market against all of DC's other Bronze comics.

There are several Bat keys from the Adams run:

Batman Issue #227, the classic Gothic cover Adams did in tribute to *Detective Comics* #31 (1939).
Batman Issue #232, the first appearance of Ra's al Guhl.

Batman Issue #234, the first appearance of Harvey Dent as Two-Face since the Golden Age.
Detective Comics #400, the first appearance of Man-Bat.

These are high-water marks for DC, Batman, Adams and back-issue dealers, if they can find them. No other titles like the Bat titles have generated Bronze Age keys for DC. The remaining DC titles and post–Adams Bat titles remain lackluster for memorable new characters or stories, at least as far as Bronze Age collectors are concerned.

Marvel's *Amazing Spider-Man* and *X-Men* titles still retain the greatest concentration of Bronze Age keys collectively. *X-Men* and *Amazing Spider-Man* are indicative of the differences between DC and Marvel. DC kept on with steady stories that yielded virtually no bankable new heroes (except maybe Firestorm), while *Amazing Spider-Man* brought us Punisher, the death of Gwen Stacey, and the inception of the clone saga. *X-Men* made use of Wolverine, brought us Storm, Colossus, and Nightcrawler, and closed out the 1970s with Kitty Pryde and Alpha Flight.

X-Men featured Dave Cockrum's first art for Marvel, redefining the look of characters who had all but disappeared months before. He and Len Wein brought new life to the old team in the summer of 1975 with *Giant-Size X-Men* #1. The new team members were a success, allowing them to transition into *X-Men*, taking up with issue #94 after the original series had ceased publication in June of 1975. Cockrum's art was instantly recognized by many of us, feeling it was better than anything else at Marvel. He had a different style that seemed more real-life. I saw a different dynamic in Dave's work that I hadn't enjoyed since Neal Adams had stood the industry on its head just a few years before.

Reading through Cockrum's on-line history, I was surprised to learn that he invented Nightcrawler long before working at Marvel. The character was novel for his appearance, and Cockrum was able to insert him into the brand-new X-Men ensemble cast.

John Byrne replaced Cockrum as artist with issue #108, generating sort of a semi-key for those who target those things. John brought co-plotting and writing skills to *X-Men* along with his pencils. Byrne was born in England but immigrated to Canada with his family when he was a child. Maybe it was a fondness for his new Canadian identity that eventually led him to agitate for Wolverine's permanency within the ranks of the X-Men. That allegiance allowed Wolverine to stand out as a popular X-Man, making him the comic book sensation he is today.

Overall, DC's 1970s line-up allowed some its characters to mature, but they still lacked the daily, human flaws that defined Marvel heroes. DC attempted to expand its universe mythos, but the stories felt inadequate to me. I much preferred Marvel's goings-on, and apparently I wasn't alone, as reflected decades later by the volume of late 1970s Marvel back-issue sales compared to DC sales. Even then, neither company was set to create a magnum opus for the ages. The other readers of the day must have agreed when you look at the sales dip that made 1980 a low-water mark for both DC and Marvel. I felt that the end of the 1970s demonstrated that comics had all but expended their creativity, at least at the story level.

I'll beat this dead horse just a little more when I identify two low points for Marvel's seeming lack of inventiveness. Just imagine what I thought when I saw Dazzler (1981) or Rocket Racer (1977) for the first time. These were two disco-influenced characters that foretold Marvel's attempt to relate to a young, hip crowd, leaving legacy readers like me disappointed.

I was disappointed to see and feel the growing absences of the Golden Age pencilers as they faded away from comics. Guys like Irv Novick, Herb Trimpe, Joe Kubert, and of course Jack "The King" Kirby were seen less and less. Great artists like Dick Giordano, John Romita, John Buscema (and brother Sal) were being supplemented by a force of talented artists from overseas, Alfredo Alcala and the studio artists in the Philippines, plus new talents from Spain (José Luis García and Gonzalo Mayo). Curt Swan and Murphy Anderson no longer tackled Superman, while Carmine Infantino began to edit comics instead of drawing them. Neal Adams was long gone from Batman. Jim Aparo, mentored somewhat by Adams, had his own sleek style for The Bat. Jim did take up art chores on *Aquaman* before it was canceled and turned to *Adventure Comics* on an anthology feature.

Aparo's art has always been suitably elegant. He held the art reins on the long-lasting Batman title *Brave and the Bold* for ten years. That's a pretty serviceable heritage for any artist in our hobby, but Aparo's work there generated no key books of significance. DC kept the title as a bimonthly, allowing it a role in placing Batman in at least one story with every character in the DC Universe. I think I blew it off when Batman teamed with Kamandi, Jack Kirby's young survivor from an alternate future.

For me, comic book stories felt replicated and uninspiring. They were just reads. No revelations developed of any historic note. The characters were cookie-cutter, as though the industry was just fulfilling itself by meeting deadlines. Even the collectibility of Bronze Age comics felt forced. Everything seemed the same. I read few sustainable stories that I can reflect upon now that were written in the later Bronze Age. There are exceptions; *Uncanny X-Men* will always stand above the other titles. It was such a breath of fresh air. *X-Men* had gone from feeling like a second-tier title in the second half of the 1960s to a brief domain for Neal Adams so he could give it new life. He was not there long enough to make a lasting difference, and before long it sunk into reprint mode. That was the only time I'd seen any Marvel title end its existence with reprinted stories of its inception.

Uncanny X-Men, the easily recognized version of the re-created X-Men, thrived through two sets of artist/writer combos. Len Wein/Dave Cockrum and Chris Claremont/John Byrne mastered the mutant drama with a mixture of old and new characters. Bringing Wolverine into the fold was genius. As far as I'm concerned, *X-Men* retooled to become the flagship read over *FF* and *Amazing Spider-Man* (the Clone Saga barely sustains). If only those titles had produced the memorable storylines that *X-Men* did, maybe their resale success in the present would be greater.

The remaining comic book publishers of old, Gold Key, Charlton and Archie, were still there, but their output seemed targeted for a younger audience. New publishers and independent types like Warp Graphics, Steve Ditko's *MR. A*, and the visionary Jack Katz held true to core audiences with shared imaginations who wanted to work without editorial restrictions in four-color print.

I titled this chapter "Marvel Rules!" without qualifying that statement. So here it is: after decades of selling comics, I find it fairly easy to identify and explain trends. There are Golden Age trends, Silver Age trends, and more trends right up to the present. The trend that this chapter refers to is how popular Marvel comics are in the back-issue market. This chapter is meant to convey a sense of what was happening in comic books for roughly two decades. Whatever any of the publishers were doing, their efforts weren't enough to topple Marvel in the charts. With all the time that has passed, nothing has changed that fact.

Marvel Comics' long list of titles is generally the most asked for at my store. We run the shop seven days a week, responding to phone calls, in-store shoppers, e-mails, personal messages through Facebook, or chat sites and even handwritten letters. Any request to buy something eventually passes over my desk. I see what everyone is asking for, and for the most part it's Marvel. Some Marvel titles have increased in demand and popularity, like *Daredevil*, *Amazing Spider-Man* and *Hero for Hire*. These are all tied into cinematic releases, but *ASM* is also a legacy title. The Silver Age issues were in high demand in the Bronze Age with the earliest issues commanding more money than some of the other Marvels.

Unfortunately for collectors and dealers alike, other Marvels have not fared so well. We can use the *Fantastic Four* as an example. Even before the first *FF* movies appeared, the *FF* as a comic book title, once self-styled as "The World's Greatest Comic Magazine," was losing readers as we saw customers dropping the title. The back issues were not faring any better. I used to be able to sell anything below issue #30 fairly often, but that's not the case anymore, at least not if I don't severely discount them. The unevenly received movies didn't help. I figure the only segment within that austere title that has current demand at competitive prices is the Silver Surfer/Galactus trilogy, issues #48–#50 (1966). Even with the first issue from 1961, the super-team that started the Marvel Revolution has seen times with stronger demand.

Putting all that aside, Marvel Comics commands the market because that's what my customers tell me with their cash, credit cards or PayPal.

The era of the Galactus/Silver Surfer trilogy is considered a seminal Jack Kirby and Stan Lee triumph. Jack's art and imagination and Stan's verbose dialogue drilled the popularity of those comics into at least two generations of fans. For Marvel fans, this is just one of several Marvel stories that still resonate and produced keys. There is a small selection of story arcs, famous covers or special art that signify milestones in Marvel Mania times. I've listed a few that come quickly to memory.

The list includes Gwen Stacey's death in *ASM* #121–122 (1973), plus the *Avengers* Kree/Skrull war with Neal Adams's involvement (*Avengers* #89–#97, 1971–1972), which was written by Roy Thomas and drawn effectively by John and Sal Buscema. *Tales of Suspense* produced a story in which Cap battled Nazi Sleeper robots through three issues in 1965–1966 (#72–#74). In *Amazing Spider-Man* #31–#33 (1965), Peter must save his aunt against all odds seemingly stacked against him (including a building!). *Captain America* struck again with Steranko pencils and covers. He handles issues #110, #111 and #113 (1969), bringing a hip modernization to the title, much like his take on *Nick Fury*. Steranko surfaces again on my list with *Nick Fury* #1–#7 (1968) and his pop-art style and Dali covers. His covers alone could sell the least likely titles.

Jim Starlin's art on *Captain Marvel* was another extraordinary example of talent that was captured by Marvel Comics. In 1973 he joined Mike Friedrich on issue #25 and began a story arc *OPG* lists as the "1st Thanos Saga." This is yet another Bronze Age event for Marvel that houses key issues, the sequence finishing up by #34.

There are probably other Marvel "tour-de-force" issues that will come to mind right after this book is published. I was 61 by the end of 2016, so don't jump all over me with "What abouts…!"

Within the framework of prominent issues, little if anything produced by Marvel after the early 1970s is as pronounced as the list above. Outside of some firsts, the remaining

Bronze Age period lacks resonance for Marvel. The malaise that seemed to surround comics as the new decade approached was disheartening, enough to make Howard the Duck cry. Price increases and my own maturation distracted me from buying many newsstand comics. I preferred buying old comics, collecting and reading them. It says something when I can attest that EC Comics from 25 years in the past provided me with more entertainment than most of what was being produced by 1980.

I know I wasn't alone. Comic books' true legacy was and is what they stimulated in a new generation of creators. Those creators and others produced the future popularity of comics in the next decade, the Copper Age.

I still worked at a comic book store when speculation fever broke out thanks to direct market distribution. One of the benefactors of this inception was Atlas/Seaboard Comics in 1975, the year I started working at a comic book store. Published out of New York by Marvel's former owner, Martin Goodman, the upstart company attempted to become the third party in a two-party race for comic book fandom (Marvel and DC representing the other two parties). My friends and I bought the comics, as did lots of others, but I just could not generate interest in them. The line brought guys like Howard Chaykin, Steve Ditko, Neal Adams and more back into the daylight with characters they wanted to do and with better perks and pay. Fans who thought this was a seminal moment for future comic investment bought quantities of many of the titles. I did not see it that way.

There was a new capacity to buy as many comics from direct distribution as any of us wanted. This dovetailed with the frequency of comic conventions to sell them for speculative profit. The titles for the most part were not that entertaining. I watched buyers hoard Atlas/Seaboard comics while guys like me felt Marvel's new stuff was the way to go. *Howard the Duck* and *Doctor Strange* seemed more lucrative to me. We got on board with DC when they printed Mike Kaluta's wonderfully rendered *Shadow* (1973) or CC Beck's return to the Golden Age version of Captain Marvel aka *Shazam* (1973).

In 1974 Atlas/Seaboard saw what we saw: that the time was ripe to introduce new comic books into a world where stores existed that only sold comic books. Unfortunately for them, *Planet of the Vampires, Iron Jaw* and the like painted their limitations within the titles. Others such as *Police Action, Brute,* and *Cougar* were not likely to latch onto an audience. Chaykin's *The Scorpion* plus *Grim Ghost* and the horror titles stood a chance, but none of them made it past their fourth issue before the company folded. As it turned out, Atlas/Seaboard was a company doomed, or maybe ahead of its time. Successful start-ups that could hold their own against Marvel and DC would have to wait for another decade.

The Forensic Comicologist wanted the Atlas/Seaboard titles to be good, but they weren't. Maybe if the publications had gone on longer, the company would have retooled them to work. Those comics didn't even have the chance to ease past their growing pains. Chaykin's *The Scorpion* was a standout among the other Atlas/Seaboard titles. With its demise, Chaykin simply moved it over to Marvel and changed the character's name to Dominic Fortune. Fortune was showcased in *Marvel Premiere* #56 (1980), but his Depression-era pulp character was not a stable way to build a platform. I give props to Chaykin for revisiting pulp-type characters right up to the present.

16

Generation Termination
(or, Changing of the Guard)

Many changes occurred for me in 1980. I was hired by the police department after years of construction work and other odd jobs. I was rootless in my ambitions. I preferred and found more joy in hands-on work and comic book dealing than pursuing more college in the fields of anthropology and paleontology. Girls and play outranked grades and career.

Comic book collecting was well into the second generation of fandom. The first gen was and will always remain the guys who started out as kids in the Golden Age and remained fans of collecting well into the Bronze Age. These were the men and women who wanted and sought out Big Little Books, pulps, funny animal/humor comics, westerns, Disneys and teen comics. Men wanted their childhood favorites like superheroes and science fiction. Women wanted Katy Keene, Archie and romance comics. Both sides wanted television and movie-themed Dell and Gold Key comics. Gilberton allowed production of *Classics Illustrated* to meet an insatiable demand well into the 1980s. Their stories were considered safe for children. If the stories were good enough for school reading assignments, then they were safe enough for comics.

Katy Keene's self-titled comic book ran from 1949 to 1961. Although it was never a title designed for my interest, my shop has encountered many grown women who loved the character as kids. Katy's comics featured clothing designs submitted by the readership. If the editors chose particular designs, they were drawn into the comics. Those drawings were printed so that they could be cut out by readers to dress up their own dolls. Occasionally, we have inquiries for particular issues. Some of those readers are around, searching for their published submissions, so they can relive their pasts with pride and amusement.

But folks were aging and their values were not necessarily the values of their kids and grandkids. A simple way to compare the changes is to look at the obvious differences in childhood entertainment, like cartoons and live television. I grew up with my dad's favorites: *Buck Rogers*, *John Wayne* westerns, and *Alley Oop*. These characters appeared in comics, the movies, and BLBs, and eventually turned up on television as Saturday afternoon entertainment. As kids we all got a kick out of the corny special effects or nonstop action. The black-and-white *Flash Gordon* and *Buck Rogers* serials of the 1930s cracked me and my friends up. The cheesy sparkler exhausts on their rocket ships and tin man robots played against our more sophisticated 1960s sensibilities! And why did Buster Crabbe play both heroic roles? Was it that hard to find actors to be action film stars?

Our cartoons were pretty cool compared to my dad's. Sure, he had the Fleischer roto-scoped *Superman*, along with *Bugs Bunny* shorts and Disney full-length features. We had Roadrunner and Coyote, *Space Ghost*, *Fireball XL5*, all the Warner Brothers cartoons from three different decades, and more. Even the 1930s *Popeye* animation was cycled through afternoon cartoons well into the 1960s.

By contrast, the kids who were of television age by the early 1980s found sustenance in shows and comics featuring *GI Joe*, *Transformers*, *Smurfs*, *He-Man*, *Robotech* and other Japanese influences. Those cartoons were by design generally less violent, less sadistic, less gun-oriented than cartoons from the past. The cartoons of my day amped kids out; that morning and weekend fix of animated violence numbed some of us to the real thing. The 1980s cartoons seemed made to mellow kids out. That is a fundamental example of a cultural change. My father's generation slowly disappeared from my culture, to be replaced by another generation.

We all know America went through social changes by the 1980s, with more children living in single-parent households. Don't try to fact-check me on this; just accept it. Some kids either had one parent who worked, or two parents both working, creating the term "latchkey kids." These were the kids who returned home from school with no mother or father there to greet them. They entertained themselves, got schoolwork done, found after-school programs, or got into trouble. The social changes wrought by this family evolution included kids who raised themselves without the same influences. The influences from the world around them helped produce a generation who craved edginess to their entertainment. They weren't getting it from TV in the afternoons, so they looked elsewhere. Comic books were one choice, and that choice was met with the arrival of Chris Claremont and Frank Miller and the 1982 release of their *Wolverine Limited Series* (1982). For the first time we experienced a solo story for Wolverine and witnessed the primal fury of the character. Young readers ate that stuff up! I know because of the hundreds of copies I've purchased over the years for resale from that generation. Compared to other stories coming out of Marvel, I found this Wolverine story arc to be enlightening. The same can be said of Miller's chores as the writer for thirty some-odd issues of *Daredevil* (1979), altering the dramatic weight of Matt Murdock to that of a tragic hero.

Frank Miller enters the comic-book favorite pantheon with these two titles. The afore-mentioned Miller titles are considered collectible, common but highly prized by those who remember their first exposure to them in the early 1980s. Miller started *Daredevil* with issue #158 and a high-grade copy can sell for hundreds.

Miller's groundbreaking achievement entered the arena of comic book competition with his *Batman—The Dark Knight Returns* (1986), four-issue, prestige format, graphic novels. The limited series grew famous for its dark, edgy portrayal of an older, bitter Batman coping with the unwanted interference of others. That story is considered a turning point in the change in the direction fans wanted comic books to go by the mid–1980s. Not all fans, but a number high enough to bring feedback that the publishers noticed.

Dark Knight was followed by Alan Moore's ferocious entry into an original, stand-alone story with unique characters. *Watchmen* (1986) understood what fans were looking for, even if they did not. Again, the fate of comic publishing was hastened in a new, volatile direction by a sage with something angry to say. Incidentally, *Watchmen* comics were collectible but held negligible value until the announcement of the movie. Prices swelled right up until the theatrical release. The movie's content drew mixed reviews and emotions, but a hiccup in the predicted success removed the anointment of value from the back issues. That value reduction has never regained ground.

I read these stories and was a little unsettled by the dark quality of the heroes. Fans were talking and showed an inclination to see what other dark machinations the creative comic book community imagined.

I review all this to illustrate the social change in our country. Broken homes and broken lives were reflected with more accuracy by the changing attitudes in comics. Readers wanted the gritty reality more in tune with their perception of real life. The price paid for this was a disconnection between my parents' comic books and our own. The twenty-somethings were engrossed in the angry and macabre that also drew some of their influences from the underground comics (comix!) of ten years before. The younger kids were entertained by the cartoons less harmful to their psyches.

As a kid I loved the science fiction/monster movies of the 1950s. They were run incessantly on Saturday afternoons on San Diego television. When the 1980s rolled around, "slasher" movies were "in." Younger audiences loved the "over the top" violence. Slasher films were their brand of horror, designed to give them the blood-curdling thrills that my films could not. They were also looking for entertainment that was for them and not for their parents.

So they were ripe for their own thing when *Teenage Mutant Ninja Turtles* arrived in 1984.

TMNT has become a worldwide phenomenon, spawning comics, merchandise, cartoons and live-action movies. The Turtles are even perfectly situated to appeal to subsequent generations of small children forever. They will always be rejuvenated in the light of well-intended *TMNT* stories.

To accentuate the importance of *TMNT* as a comic book series, the first printing of #1 sold for an easy five figures in the marketplace of 2016. Even the second printing can sell for big bucks, topping out in the low hundreds in 9.8! Clearly *TMNT* #1 is an investment-grade book.

By the early 1980s there was a clear societal movement to collect all things vintage, especially with the movie *American Graffiti* (1973), the TV show *Happy Days* (1974–1984), and a resurgence in popularity for old movies for those who waxed nostalgic. A new generation of viewers all spoke of the affection for times, people, places and events that preceded them. Slipped into all that reverence were the things from the past that could make money.

Traditionally, comic books made few collectors a lot of money, changing hands in more of an "in-house" collecting world. Those of us who grew up alongside the First Gen comic book fans in the 1960s made a little money selling comics, mostly through local newspaper ads or comic conventions in the 1970s. Some had made a go of it offering mail-order catalogs through trade publications and comic books. But in the materialistic 1980s, many people were catching a whiff of the hyped success stories surrounding comic book dealing.

Things were propelled along by the people publishing comic books. The label "Collector's Item" was unabashedly used in regards to comic books as soon as they were published (it would take the beginning of the next decade to see "Collector's Item" emblazoned across new comic books as they hit the stands, as if they actually would be prized investments). People bought into this malarkey and bought multiple copies for their future retirement plans. Newbies sought out comics wherever they could find them to cash in on potential resale bonanzas. Comics that were less than ten years old suddenly got sucked up and churned out as collectible and profitable. The 1980s and the 1990s were breeding a culture with an aptitude for collecting (and selling!).

I don't remember the stories behind half the collections I acquired in the 1970s. Acknowledging that, I somehow ended up with a run of *Famous Monsters of Filmland* (1958) beginning with the first issue. I grew up a fan in the 1960s, but really did not have a concept of Forrest J Ackerman's historical significance to Sci-Fi Americana until my early attendance at Comic-Con. I'd seen him at shows as either a guest or a celebrated attendee (my future business partner Gino got to take a private tour of his house, the Ackermansion, later in life).

Anyway, I was seated at my booth at the 1976 San Diego Comic-Con against one of the exhibit hall walls with my displays and boxes in place when an older couple approached me. Now stop me if you've heard this before, but I recognized Forry and his wife now standing in front of me. Forry said "Hi" and looked at the *FMOF* #1 showcased on my wall display and asked to see it. I held it out to him and he took it to look it over. He asked if I had more, so I placed a box containing the rest of the copies on my display table. The issues were in numerical order. He let his fingers walk across the tops of the magazines, commenting to his wife (and I'll never forget this) that all the years he ran the magazine he never owned a complete run of this title. His wife smiled, indulging her husband and suggested that he buy these. He had a sort of, "Sure, why not?" look on his face. He waxed nostalgic and decided to buy them to fill a hole in his memories. He cut me a check, thanked me and moved on.

I'll never know if Forry was serious about wanting the mags or if he was helping a young exhibitor make a little cash doing what he loved. I will always remember it as a gracious gesture.

As a longtime comic book back issue retailer, I look back over the decades with certain favoritism. I cherish the Golden Age and Silver Age comics. The Golden Age was the Golden Age while the Silver Age is my legacy period, my "Golden Age" to look back upon when I'm much older. The Bronze Age stuff is what it is, a reference point to a new direction for comics. The 1980s "Copper Age" reflects a new timeline for a new set of fans. Those fans have different values and different likes that will someday trigger a certain feeling of fondness when they look back to their childhood. Naturally, my aged peers and I do not feel the same nostalgia for something like *Transformers*, not like the guy who was a kid when he saw a *Transformers* (1984) comic book the first time it hit the stands. The 1980s generation eats up the comic books that highlight their childhoods. These new generation collectors and their speculator nemesis now value *Transformers* to the tune of several hundred dollars for high-grade copies of #1. They may not have the same affection for a high-grade issue #1 of *Howard the Duck* from a decade earlier, but many hold other Marvel Silver Age keys in reverence, like *Iron Man* #1 (1968). They're willing to shell out hundreds of dollars for nice copies for a popular character that exists in their current timeline; with *Howard*, not so much. What they do hold dear is the influx of passion for characters who were invented or written for them in the 1980s. *Omega Men* (1982) introduced Lobo in issue #3. *The New Teen Titans* (1980) featured Deathstroke's first outing. *Tales of the Teen Titans* #44 (1984) saw the creation of Nightwing, the matured version of the Dick Grayson/ Robin character of old. DC's mini-series *Legends* (1986) returned a failed Silver Age super-group to comics called the *Suicide Squad*, and it became a movie in 2016.

The fans are probably still strip mining bargain bins nationwide for cheap 1980s books that might hold yet another invaluable first appearance. I see pickers and collectors scouring our boxes constantly for 1980s first appearances, since they are affordable and plentiful. Some Johnny-come-latelys are still trying to slyly shoehorn their way in, naively believing none of this activity had been dominant before they came a-calling. All walks of life have been exploiting and collecting comics, but some are still just crawling.

I used to denigrate the 1980s comics as fodder for bargain bins and wastes of space for investment. Not anymore. The current masters of comic book collecting see the 1980s as their Golden Age and I respect them for that. They are perhaps a vanguard for more fervent 1980s collecting to come. Plus, material is easy and cheap to come by, and I can make money selling it inexpensively.

Clearly, the bulk of the 1980s material isn't worth more than the original cover price. The prized books so far sell for hundreds, not thousands, with a few exceptions (*TMNT* #1) as addressed earlier. A few issues were quickly propped up in value by movies and seemed to go to four digits in value.

Incredible Hulk #271 (1982) is one example. The movie *Guardians of the Galaxy* (2014) generated collector interest in a host of lesser-tier Marvel characters. One of those, Rocket Raccoon, made his first appearance in this issue. At the time of the movie release, the book shot up into the $500+ range; even more for graded, signed copies. That issue seemed about to explode beyond $1,000, and then the weeks after the movie's release cooled the book down.

Strangely, Rocket Raccoon had appeared elsewhere earlier, but that knowledge didn't seem to be common. It seems that a different version of Rocket appeared in the 1970s in one of Marvel's magazines: *Marvel Preview* (1976). Rocket was a back-up story to the featured character, Satanna (Satan's hot daughter) in issue #7. Now eighteen months after that wildly successful and fun *Guardians* movie, all value indications for *Incredible Hulk* #271 trend down. Perhaps the movie sequel will push the value back up.

DC Comics has some 1980s strengths. I'm often handed copies of this or that series for potential resale because of some character that's movie-bound. A prime example that's a hot riser is #49 of *DC Comics Presents* (1982). Superman and Shazam try to get a handle on Captain Marvel's nemesis/evil doppelganger(?), Black Adam. Both Black Adam and Captain Marvel (the DC version) are getting their movies together as this is written. Incidentally, Captain Marvel has been locked up in copyright by Marvel for some time. DC titles their version Shazam to remove any chance of litigation or licensing infringement.

Unfortunately, DC, like Marvel, has some false starts. *The Flash* TV show was expected to promote some 1980s villains, provoking speculators to hunt down those particular issues for resale. Nothing like that has yet resonated at our store. The *Gotham* TV show excited collector/speculator fans, as well. *Gotham* revealed a slew of villainous first appearances, some from the latter days of Batman comic books. One character who menaced Gotham was a bad guy called Firebug, first identified in 1979 in *Batman* #318. That issue was being touted as a collector's item even though almost nothing introduced on the show has yet to produce a collectible comic book. My lesson is to teach caution when assuming some random character's appearance on the screen, big or small, is going to generate anticipated earnings.

The Marvel magazines produced briefly in the 1970s were all black-and-white productions (with one Spider-Man exception). They were Marvel's attempts at copying Warren Magazines' success with their horror and sci-fi titles *Creepy, Eerie and Vampirella*. The magazine format excused publishers from the restraints and censorship of the Comics Code Authority. We readers considered the stories to be more mature. Marvel went so far as to print their first issue of *Savage Tales* (with Conan) wearing a "Mature Readers" label. *Savage Tales* was an anthology magazine. Eventually *Savage Sword of Conan* was produced for Conan's growing readership, while *Savage Tales* and the rest of the Marvel line of magazines faded out of production.

Incidentally, the popularity of the movie brought younger customers looking at comic book stores to find more *Guardians of the Galaxy*. Since many are not readers, the comics tended not to satisfy. Apparently there's a large difference between the thrill of the movie and the thrill of the read.

Other customers equated the success of the movie with success in buying keys and reselling them. These people jumped on board, often spending foolishly and then waiting as long as a nanosecond to try to resell for a profit. I see a few of those guys still around trying to get serious, but most folded up their tents and moved onto some other get-rich-quick scheme.

I was out of the collecting aspect of the hobby for a few years in the second half of the 1980s. I read new comics, even shopped for them with my teenage son at local stores. I wanted to be entertained and it entertained him. I found it to be a great bonding tool for a father and his boy. The stores were plentiful back then and clearly there were already too many comic book stores out there for customers to support. Outside of stores, comics were prevalent at swap meets, just like they were when I was a kid in the 1960s.

The drive to find comics at swap meets, flea markets and garage sales remains active. The current crop of comic book people is largely made up of those born in the 1980s and 1990s, but they're merciless when it comes to hunting down comics. These folks bridge the gap that otherwise permeates an American culture filled with non-comic book people. This book is actually written for those comic book people. There are a lot of hasty decisions being made that could create problems this book hopes to prevent.

I count myself lucky that my son, now grown and a police officer as well, loves comics. But even he has little affection for the old comics, the comics I treasure. His Golden Age is the 1980s and he's content to own and reread that stuff, mostly Batman comics.

The San Diego Comic-Con attracted a couple of thousand people in the mid–1970s and looked to house five times that many once the show moved to San Diego's existing convention center. The best years of the show, for me, were at the old El Cortez Hotel built in the early 1920s. The hotel and convention staff's tolerance for the zany crowd could only go so far. By 1980 the show had to move in order to expand. It ended up at the city's convention center, blocks away from the El Cortez. The convention center was large enough to hold an expanded exhibitor hall, but it lost the amenity of a connected hotel and restaurant.

Back in that time, if you were in town for the show and wanted a convenient place to stay, you ended up walking blocks or spending more than maybe you could afford. The featured hotel for the con was the also old Hotel San Diego on Broadway when that part of downtown San Diego had not yet been gentrified. There were a lot fewer people in costume back then, and they sure felt uncomfortable walking streets occupied by massage parlors, prostitutes, street people, gangsters, homeless, beggars and the like, all under the constant, watchful eyes of passing patrol officers. Certainly no place to haul your expensive back issue purchases through!

It was freaky seeing the young con attendees in outlandish costumes strolling in singles, pairs and groups to find restaurants, reach hotels, and show off their attire. I knew these same streets for years as anything but a playground for costumed comic book people. Clearly my generation has competition from Gen X and Z, the Millennials and Comic Con: The Next Generation!

Keith Ahlstrom is a long-time customer at our store. He's also a San Diego Comic-Con veteran with memories reaching back to the El Cortez Hotel days. Here's Keith in his own words:

"I don't remember the year, it might have been 1975 or 1976, but it was just like Eisner's Comic-Con booklet cover with the Spirit sitting by the pool (1975). Except in my case there was Stan Lee on one side and Jack Kirby on the other, each with his own crown puffing away on a cigar.

"The funny thing back then is even though smoking was not allowed inside, it seemed everyone I met had a cigar except Steranko. I was a performing magician when I was younger and so was Steranko. I remember one year spending hours talking about magic with him. The first time I met him I only had a *Fantastic Four* #88 on me and I remember I was out of cash (always happens at the con). I told him that and he signed it. To this day I still have it.

"Will Eisner was incredibly nice when I met him. I wish I could say the same about Bob Kane. Both Sheldon Moldoff and Jerry Robinson were great and shared lots of time and art. Every year I got something from Mr. Moldoff. I remember asking him to draw Harley Quinn for me and he said it was the first time he had drawn the modern version (he put her on a lot of pictures after that).

"Industrial Light and Magic was there and talked about some copies of *Star Wars* going out with footage of Luke and Biggs that was later removed. The version shown at the premier in San Diego sponsored by B-100 (local radio) had the footage at the Valley Circle Theater. They also said that George Lucas would never let it come out on video since he hated the size of TV screens. Also they talked about it being in 13 parts just like a serial from the 1930–40s."

That con, though, was emblematic of the universal changes in collecting behavior and comic cons in general. More back-issue people were sold space at the con. More guests were appearing. More original art, science fiction, movie posters and movie memorabilia popped up. Video game floor machines got a small corner, so those vendors could entice players for the first time at that show. T-shirt salespeople got to spread out and sell more rock and roll shirts (cheap bootleg knock-offs, as near as I could tell, before any agency thought to crack down on that stuff at our Con).

The 1980s comic conventions still operated in a Wild West environment, with few rules to curtail behavior. No one running the show was overly concerned about the dealers' room. Tables were paid for and sellers set up. That was about it. You paid more for a wall space and those were preferable for most exhibitors. We placed our boxes on the tables and went to the floor for extra display space. If you wanted to fill your booth to capacity, that was no problem. You just sat in a chair in the aisle. Dealers and deals spun around the room while the fear of theft was as yet nowhere near the epidemic level it is now. Not everyone had mastered wall displays, so many of us used our table tops to show off the good stuff. We simply covered it up with heavy, transparent plastic sheets to stop potential pilfering.

The 1980s will be forever indelibly marked as the transition point where I knew back-issue sales were here to stay. At the end of the 1970s many of us wondered how much longer this could go on. By the end of the 1980s the prices to get into the show seemed expensive, yet everybody went. In fact, the end of the 1980s pushed Comic-Con beyond the convention center's ability to contain it, much as had happened ten years before. Both the con and the hobby were growing way past my expectations of collecting a generation ago.

The second generation of fandom, post–Baby Boomers, was muscling in on the Old Guard's turf. Anime? Video games? What else is next?

Comic-Con booked itself into the new San Diego Convention Center in 1991 on the bay. Even though this building was new and magnificent by San Diego standards, it was clearly too small. San Diego had trouble booking large-scale conventions that required the square footage of a Los Angeles or San Francisco-sized arena. The San Diego Comic-Con was growing faster than anticipated and within a few years of occupation had begun to outgrow its surroundings.

The 1996 Republican National Convention (RNC) occupied the convention center for a week that summer. There was growing criticism about the small size of the building, so the pressure was on to expand it.

A multimillion-dollar expansion alleviated some of the claustrophobia, but that was only temporary. Once the San Diego Comic-Con renamed itself Comic-Con International, it was clear to me that the convention committee intended to go bigger, maybe "out-of-town" bigger.

As of 2016, San Diegans were still collectively waiting for the con and the city to find a solution to keep the show in town. Pessimistically, the con spokespeople clearly wanted to stay, but felt no option to move if the city did not expand the convention site. LA was tempting San Diego's greatest show to leave town permanently. The city struggled to find the money post-2008 mortgage collapse and city officials' budget bungling. But we loyal locals could not fathom losing Comic-Con.

The San Diego Chargers needed a new stadium; the then current one needed to be gutted or torn down. The city had attempted to meld the needs of the Chargers with the needs of the convention center. Several plans had been introduced, putting together a package deal inclusive of a new stadium and convention center expansion. Much of the tone of the rhetoric was the citywide debate over putting the Chargers into a new stadium built with a convention center expansion. The rub was the source of all the money to build this megaplex. Then the Chargers left for Los Angeles and the stadium problem solved itself. The big question remains: what happens to San Diego's own Comic-Con International?

One unfortunate side-effect of the maturing of the hobby is the knowledge lost. The skills we all used to make smart purchases are not necessarily being implemented by new fans. By the 1990s the souls who set the smartest aspects of collecting in motion were not influencing collectors as they once were. The *Overstreet Price Guide* formed guidelines to grades that were not necessarily considerations for new collectors. Even into the new decades, collectors are content to let someone else do the grading for them.

With the proliferation of third-party grading, there seems to be a complete lack of interest by way too many guys raised as kids in the 1980s and 1990s to learn how to grade. The era when they would collectively discuss grades has been replaced by an unfettered interest in paying whatever the price-gun cost is, minus the inevitable results of a request for a discount.

The weekly subscription publication *Comic Buyer's Guide* (1971–2013) was popular for news, editorials and ads for many years. Guest writers and knowledgeable columnists shared stories about the hobby and working within it. The Internet more than likely is responsible for putting it into the print periodical graveyard where other newspapers and magazines are now entombed.

Those writers and columnists are spread out all over the Net lecturing, teaching, sharing and commenting on the state of the industry and the hobby. But sometimes at my store or at conventions it seems collectors are not paying attention. We used to argue grading back in the day and discuss which dealers were cheating us. That concern was one point of the driving force that created Certified Guaranty Corporation (CGC) under the umbrella company Certified Collectibles Group (CCG). CGC sold the idea of providing a service for comic book people to protect them from getting cheated, and make a profit doing it. Nowadays the average collector leans too heavily on third-party grading for his own comfort. They've got to get back to basics so they can have a greater understanding of why grades are the way they are. Too many don't ask questions.

The 1980s/1990s kids are set perfectly to exploit the comics they grew up with. The Millennials have inherited the mantle of chief collectors. They encourage each other to haunt back-issue opportunities for gems that will be graded for profit on eBay. The 1980s books are easy to come by, cheap, and potential winners if the movies or TV pick up on a particular 1980s title. One other distinction exists for the Millennials: they care as much about toy collecting as they do for comics. Some do both, while others collect toys and have no comic book interest. Non-sports trading cards are part of the Millennials' target collectibles. They're shared with older fans, so the card companies target everyone. The 1990s saw the surge in all kinds of trading card subjects from comic characters to movie and television shows, from porn to popular artists—even cards based upon history.

In the hands of the 1980s kids, all these collectibles mean something to them they may have trouble sharing with their elders. The modern comics, the toys, the cards are all quantities the Millennials can call their own.

One thought I want to share is a fact repeated often at my store. We receive calls and see walk-ins daily offering to sell us comic book collections. This frequent occurrence can be quite lucrative for both the owner and for us. Generally, the older the comics (older than the 1980s), the better the chances of both sides being happy with the prices. But when the owner is not appreciative of the purchase price we might offer, they tend to feel a little miffed. It can be a tad unpleasant as the owner looks for an alternative price or responds in a surly fashion.

One of the more common responses to getting what they consider bad news is the now classic statement: "Well, I'll just pass them onto my kids." I don't chide the owner, but I warn them that after years of buying and selling comics, I see it's rare that the next generation wants the comics. That's especially true if the subsequent generation is a teen or pre-teen. Two dynamics are at work here:

1. The kids are not interested in comic books, new or old. The root reason for today's younger kids is a complete detachment from the idea of reading comic books. They like the movies, they like the toys and games, but actually reading them does not entice. So our "Generation Termination" observation realistically removes "passing comic books onto the kids" as a serious option.

2. My generation didn't necessarily appreciate or find interest in the hobbies and entertainment of my parents. Teens tend to dislike the

The author wants you! To collect comics smartly, ca. 2016.

things their parents like; it's a part of youth. Comic books are definitely from another generation, so if you are a parent with comic books and you want to sell them, be prepared to sell. Your kids would rather have the money than the comics!

I have one funny El Cortez Comic Con story that I love telling over and over again. It involves the annual masquerade ball held each year. As I remember, there was always a masquerade ball on the Saturday evening of the Con.

In the 1970s the ball was held in the large banquet room above the exhibitors' room across the street from the hotel. The banquet room was large enough to seat about 300 people, and each year that room was packed with fans eager to see cool, handmade costumes.

The event was hosted by a popular rock station DJ named Gabriel Wisdom. He stood at a podium with a microphone that you could barely hear at the back of the room. On this particular night, Wisdom wore a scaled-back Thor costume complete with Viking helmet and hammer. The hammer was mesmerizing because it was plated with mirrors and picked up all the lighting like a disco ball. He swung that thing around throughout the show, dazzling everybody.

Anyway, the show started and costumes marched onto the stage one-by-one. Each model got a couple of minutes to walk across the stage, turn so we could see 360 degrees of the outfit, and then maybe say a few words for the audience. That night we had the usual assemblage of *Star Trek* uniforms, fairies, and a pretty complex Iron Man outfit that kept dropping off pieces of armor on the stage. All-in-all, these shows were more funny than serious and a good laugh-fest for me and my friends. So we were pretty stirred up when Cheech Wizard walked on stage.

For those of you not familiar, Cheech Wizard was the fantasy creation of Vaughn Bodé, an avant-garde artist and cartoonist born from the 1960s counter culture movement. Cheech was the embodiment of the hippie culture, wandering around in peace looking for women, parties and a good time. He was garbed in tan leggings and an oversized wizard's soft conical hat that covered his head down to his hips.

Our Cheech Wizard wore the exact same outfit with the creator's own mimicked hat design. He wore the tan leggings, but from my seat in the middle of the audience they appeared to be thin, opaque pantyhose.

So I assumed it was a he as the model spun around in pirouette fashion clearly enjoying the moments under the bright lights. I mean really bright lights sparkling off the mirrored hammer twirling in the host's hands. Wisdom was not sure what to make of Cheech. Not being familiar with the character, he had the model walk closer to the edge of the stage where the lights were brighter and then—Oops! *He* wasn't wearing any undergarment beneath the pantyhose! Wisdom noticed at the same time as the people in the seats, and let out a howl as the audience exploded into laughter.

Now I'm not being insensitive because Cheech seemed to relish the added attention. In fact, ushers had to coax "him" off the stage while the audience continued to fall all over itself with laughter. I know I never laughed so hard in my life, but hey: that's Comic-Con!

The Forensic Comicologist knows those types of surprises won't happen again at a convention with rules and censorship strongly enforced. That kind of innocent behavior at con will usually guarantee an escort with security out the door.

17

Third-Party Grading

Tired of getting ripped off? I know I grew weary of the pitfalls of comic book collecting ages ago. What pitfalls, you ask? Well, I'll tell you…

I'm old enough to remember comic book grading in its infancy. Terms like "Good," "Fine," and "Mint" were effectively used to cover the complete gamut of condition permutations. Since the Internet had not yet been invented, national comic book dealers produced catalogues, which were offered through ads in comic books, fanzines, or newspaper classifieds. Buying comics through catalogs could be risky pending each dealer's interpretation of grading (accuracy was not always a consideration). One legendary East Coast dealer is remarkable for stretching grades with such statements as: "Tape is not a defect!" I believed him—for a short time. Comics were cheap by today's standards. Collecting comics was more about filling runs than quick turnarounds to make fast bucks.

Buying was blindly done through the mail. Thus, buyers had no picture to work from. The grand surprise was what came through the mail. A five-dollar mint copy of *Daredevil* #1 (1964) could manifest as a low-grade good, or even coverless. Arguments through the mail ensued. If you were lucky, maybe a phone number was included. In those days, phone numbers rarely changed, and just about everybody was in the phone book.

Early national mail order dealers such as Robert Bell and Howard Rogofsky set trends with their tireless catalogue production and world-class, back-issue acquisition skills. I still see their old classifieds in late Silver Age comic books. Those guys depended on collectors like me being in some agreement with the condition of the comics they sold.

Comic conventions arrived in the mid–1960s, a little later on the West Coast. In 1970, the *OPG* was born and was sold at shows and stores. The early editions tried to establish uniform grading standards, with terminology reminiscent of those used by the coin collecting culture. Words like Good, Fine, or Mint took on sister categories: "Fair," "Very Good," "Very Fine," and others. Brief qualifiers described the requirements to fit into any category. These descriptions were basic at first, then took on more detail as grading was refined. Soon smaller incremental grades attempted to fill in gaps in terminology. Half grades were developed and then included in *Overstreet*'s grading tiers. Terms like Very Fine (VF) were sometimes followed by Very Fine/Near Mint (VF/NM). Very Fine Plus was added to the mix, splitting VF and VF/NM. The fine gradients of identifying defects in comics dictated that a VF+ was necessary when VF was not enough and VF/NM was too much.

The *Overstreet Price Guide* introduced grading in a uniform, column fashion. Three columns, Good, Fine, and Mint, headed the tiered prices for titles and issue numbers. This was not the first attempt at pricing standardization. Two men, Michael Cohen and Tom

Horsky, co-wrote an earlier price guide in 1965 titled *The Argosy Comic Book Price Guide*. It was an innovative one-shot specific to a legendary Hollywood outlet, Argosy Book Store. For both books, the intent was the same: to standardize comic book back issue pricing by utilizing grading tiers to do the job. The *Argosy* was a minor effort, however, not comparable to the scope of the *Overstreet Price Guide*.

Overstreet Price Guide's ambitious start copyrighted a grading tier system for collectors. They could see values in different grades, using formatted books resembling price guides for coin collecting. *Overstreet Price Guide* designed a guide to account for any comic based upon damage, defects and natural wear and tear from repeated handling. Robert Overstreet and original comic fan Jerry Bails tasked themselves with the invention of a comprehensive reference book that timed itself perfectly with the baby boomers' infatuation with reading and collecting comic books.

The condition of back issues was less a problem than simply finding them. Resale for many secondary collectors was not yet a defining factor with comic books. I looked around my neighborhood at garage sales on Saturdays. In the 1960s there weren't a lot of people competing at the garage sale level and comics were really cheap. Condition was not yet a specific choice. Most collectors were kids looking for comics to read. Barber shops and doctors' and dentists' offices were great places to find old comics. Back then, owners thought comics pacified kids in waiting rooms. I remember every place my parents had to take me for an appointment had comics on small tables. They were almost always *Archie* family comics or *Richie Rich* comics (many different titles). The comics were often roughly handled and nobody ever seemed to mind if customers took them home. If you wanted them, they were yours for the taking!

Overstreet Price Guide helped change that. It amplified comic book collecting relevance and established the back-issue market as an entity with its own culture, separate from the publication and sale of new, monthly comics.

I purchased my first copy of the *Overstreet Price Guide* at the 1973 or 1974 San Diego Comic-Con. That was my earliest exposure to *Overstreet Price Guide*. I read it and educated myself on the significance of the various grading standards. Early *Guides* printed bare-bones descriptions for the still-narrow gauge of grading standards. I made comprehensive notes in margins and gaps of every page where the *Overstreet Price Guide*'s information was lacking. I found arguing grading points with dealers and other fans could be more educational and competed with *Overstreet Price Guide* for comprehensive information. Vice versa, I was selling at cons by 1976 and nothing put grading comics in perspective more than being challenged by potential buyers. At least *Overstreet Price Guide* and its contributors took the time to create initial standards the public willingly accepted.

I was at the first San Diego Comic-Con when it moved to its next location, Golden Hall in the San Diego Community Concourse/Convention Center. This occurred after the El Cortez Hotel had separated from Comic-Con.

The room designated for exhibition was roughly twice the size of the hall back at the El Cortez. It was also the first comic convention location with docks to unload vehicles. Gone were the days where we had to find uptown street parking and then walk hundreds of yards to get our comics into the building. Now, it was a stop at the back of the dealers' room, with a dock master to keep everything orderly.

I had a table and sold back issues in a room filled with people doing the same. Set-up was on Wednesday and the show ran for an exhausting five days through Sunday. The move to the new venue caused the fire marshal to allow more people to queue up to get into the dealers' room. More people meant new people, so our displays attracted more and varied opportunities to sell. I saw lots of new faces and a greater variety of buyers.

In the late morning on Saturday of one early show at the new venue, a kid of about 12 stood at my table looking down at *Avengers* #1 (1963). I had my best comics on the table with thick, clear plastic covering them to prevent theft. Most back-issue dealers are inherently wary of unaccompanied children, especially when it comes to expensive comics. That plastic was a great deterrent.

The kid asked for the price and grade on my *Avengers* #1. His request was a surprise because kids don't know that grades matter, but I indulged him and told him it was a Fine priced at $150. The kid was unfazed and he asked to see the book. Part of me wanted to tell him to scram, but being the budding pro I was becoming, I took the book out from under cover and opened it for him. He debated the grade with me by counting the spine creases that broke color. The little scamp actually argued the accuracy of the grade, forcing me to take a stand. An obvious thought was "Why bother?" but being the consummate professional, I exercised patience and let him burn himself out, figuring he couldn't possibly afford it anyway. I resigned myself to a no-sale result and put the book back under plastic as the kid said he'd think about it.

Minutes passed and I saw the kid return to face me across the table. He said "Hi" and pulled out a $100 bill and a $50 bill, asking to buy the *Avengers* #1. I was stunned! That was good money for one comic back then, and I had now dealt with what would be the youngest big spender I'd ever encountered. There was no parent around whom I could see and the boy didn't appear to be in direct contact with one. I didn't know how valid this sale was going to be, but business was business. The deal was done and he was happy.

I got schooled. Serious collectors come in all shapes, sizes and ages.

In the 1970s it seemed everybody carried an *Overstreet Price Guide* at conventions. Nothing was ever printed in the *Overstreet Price Guide* that indicated prices dropped. *Overstreet* tended to allow comic book prices to either rise or display no change. Within the past decade, *OPG* has shown a willingness to reduce prices.

Overstreet Price Guide continues to print sales figures for key comics based upon tracked sales. Advisor input is welcome with *OPG* soliciting sales figure opinions in the fall of each year. After CGC's debut, documented sales of key comics included third-party encased books. By 2016, sales figures in *Overstreet Price Guide* are either in synch with documented third-party graded copies or are an alternative to what happens in the marketplace. Potential buyers can tab into online statistics sites like GPAnalysis, to see if their desires are affordable at any given moment. *OPG* can only adjust annually.

Just about everybody wants to see the prices rise if the copies are in their possession. Comic collectors and dealers love to see upward movement in the prices. The validation for their ownership comes from a perpetual increase in the value of their comics. Back in the day, my peers and I couldn't wait to get the new *OPG* to see what price increases were posted.

I had a copy of Avon Publishing's *Mask of Fu Manchu* #1 (1952), picked up at the monthly Rose Bowl swap meet in Pasadena in the mid–1970s from acquaintance Loren Marks. It was about an eight-dollar purchase at about VG but it was cool, all–Wally Wood art. Back then, there was a strong demand for Wood's work. Each year I would zip to the *Overstreet Price Guide* listing and see a minor price bump. That was very encouraging and mirrored what every other comic book back-issue person was doing. Dealers were quickly re-pricing their books. Collectors were salivating over their comics. All we ever saw was upward movement. In fact, the worst-case scenario for any comic book listing in *Overstreet Price Guide* was that a price stayed put.

That would all be altered by the arrival of *Wizard Magazine* (1991). For the uninitiated, *Wizard* was a slick comic book fan magazine devoted to the newest, hottest publications in comics. *Wizard* also had a price guide. Their version utilized one column per page of NM prices but with instructions on how to calculate reduced prices for lesser grades. I perused several issues of *Wizard* for this chapter to discover the origins for their NM prices, but your guess is as good as mine.

One significant option *Wizard* offered was the willingness to devalue books. They had a snappy, pastel-colored coding system built into their charts that identified price trends for each book. Pink indicated that prices went up, blue indicated prices went down, green meant "this one's new," and yellow announced that a book "was hot."

A lot of their "facts" seemed speculative and self-serving, designed to grab attention to sell more *Wizard Magazine*s. The design did get a lot of attention. I witnessed *Wizard* fans buy the magazine each month for the price guide first and the articles second. The constant price fluctuations spurred on speculators who couldn't care less about the articles.

Wizard related to modern comics better than vintage issues. Any attempt by a contemporary to talk prices to me or the others using *Wizard* for prices was met with scorn. *Wizard* was cognizant of the images that sold *Wizard*: anything with Wolverine. Wolverine graced the *Wizard* covers more often than Pamela Anderson appeared on *Playboy* magazine, but it could have been close!

The *Overstreet Price Guide* emerged as the Bible for collectors and dealers alike. No deal at a booth was struck without at least one party consulting the *OPG*. Grades were not defined as tightly in early fandom, but *OPG* gradually put more effort into it, eventually publishing companion grading guides.

OPG's pricing structure illustrated how better copies of desirable titles could increase in value on a regular basis. That frequency was measured by *OPG* on an annual basis. Only much later did *OPG* attempt to circulate a regular monthly update, with minimal success. *OPG*'s *Fan* was *Overstreet*'s attempt in the 1990s to compete with *Wizard*. *OPG*'s *Fan* (1995) ended publishing in 1997, having replaced another *Overstreet* publication called *Overstreet's Comic Book Monthly*. Ultimately, grading tightened up and savvy buyers were wary of price-gunned copies (nothing more than a grocery store price sticker) without accompanying grades or obvious, sloppy grading.

Slowly but surely, grading matured from stylized interpretation to formulaic, objective terms. The grades in between grades were filled in so "Good" and "Fine" were split by "Very Good's" cousins "Good Plus," "Good-Very Good," "Very Good Minus," "Very Good Plus," "Very Good-Fine," and then "Fine Minus." Interpretative grading was replaced by finite categories where the grade of any book could be compartmentalized. These segmented levels forced every book into near-strict grades, theoretically removing the argument about a grade.

At the other end of the spectrum, this attention to grading detail effectively changed the way high-grade copies were evaluated. The overly optimistic "Mint" category was elevated to a near-impossible grade to achieve. Instead, the grade "Near Mint" was chopped into the new levels of separation. "Near Mint" or "NM" was book-ended to include "Very Fine-Near Mint," "Near Mint Minus," "Near Mint," "Near Mint Plus" and back to "Mint," or "Gem Mint."

In 1992, Marvel published their pamphlet on collecting comics. Running eight pages and the size of a comic book, this instructional item was meant to give newbies a brief guide on how to collect.

Unfortunately, Marvel's *Reader's Digest* version of the more comprehensive *OPG* was laughable, especially by today's standards. I don't know if anyone took this publication seriously, but check out the grading guide the writer put in a yellow box on page seven:

Condition

Before you can price it, you have to determine the condition of a comic.

Poor: Badly damaged, missing chunks or pages.

Good: Complete, well-read with some small tears or creases, a good deal of wear and tear.

Fine: Average wear with a tight and shiny cover, very small tear or crease on edges, no writing on comic.

Very Fine: Slight wear just beginning around staples or along spine. Flat, clean and shiny.

Near Mint: Only one or two tiny defects -- almost perfect.

Mint: Perfect, no defects.

When you are determining condition, you have to consider the cover *and* inside pages.

Marvel's one and only attempt to explain comic book grading; from the 1990s.

This thin shot at education is cute for its brevity and light-heartedness, although I fear the writer and publisher actually felt this was a genuine tool for collectors. I had never seen one of these until 2016. Sadly, this scant information on "Condition" is all a lot of collectors now know.

There were no encapsulated, third-party graded comics back before the dawn of the 21st century. There were clubs or associations that were held in esteem by others, offering their own grading services. The finished product was not sealed, but came with certification or guarantee. One group, the AACC (American Association of Comic-book Collectors) was a national, incorporated organization/fan club that set up booths at conventions and offered grading opportunities for fans. The service came with a charge. By then, plenty of entrepreneurs charged others to grade comics; some people were confident enough to charge for their expertise. Unfortunately, none were experts carrying validated certificates of approval backed by any organization that protected all parties involved. No one had acceptable public authority to lock particular comic books into any grade for all time. There were and are great graders with solid reputations, but they still have to defend a grade, if the copy comes without necessary inalienable documentation. No container existed to seal in a graded book to prevent tampering. No grader was accredited on one coast whose work would be accepted by a collector on the opposite coast.

It was thought by many of my peers and others that West Coast dealers graded stricter than East Coast dealers. That theorem has been bounced back and forth for years. Good luck getting a win in an open forum on that subject!

There are ethical comic book graders, but until the late 1990s there was little to prevent a grader from being unscrupulous. Graders had the opportunity to manipulate grades to their benefit or for the benefit of a customer. Conversely, the recipient of an accurately graded book could easily replace that book with a lower-graded copy, fooling many. The keys to foiling corruption are grader accountability and a proper container.

Comic books and their fans generally conducted business through print or in person prior to the Internet. I don't remember ever calling a dealer to work a deal unless it was a local guy. eBay's arrival in the late 1990s changed all that by connecting sellers and buyers in real time and on a grand scale. eBay allowed both parties to cut out the middleman and communicate instantly through e-mail (eventually supervised almost entirely by attentive eBay watchers). Web sites blossomed and transactions took place at all hours of the day. The infatuation with business at computer speed added volume to comic book shoppers. The United States Postal Service even seemed to be making money from increased interstate shipping.

Inevitably, a rise in scams, corruption, or plain old incorrect grading drove people crazy. Nobody could trust the Internet for business involving old comic books, especially on eBay. It was a free-fire zone for bad or incompetent sellers, who took easy advantage of buyers both gullible and savvy.

Contention over deals frustrated enough of the right people. Concerns for the need to produce a society with safe, consistent, inarguable grading practices were voiced nation-wide. Chat sites aired grievances while victims harangued eBay to correct wrongs. Getting ripped off online became commonplace: misgraded books and subsequent complaints were reaching a crescendo. How would we trust anyone?

During my years as a police officer I investigated many traffic accidents. The most hor-rific accidents often involved motorcycles. The frequency of motorcycle accidents led me and my peers to conclude that there are two kinds of motorcycle riders: those who have crashed and those who are going to crash. It seemed that literally no rider could be safe forever. Similarly, my feelings about eBay are based on countless examples of fraud and deception. Conveniently, the motorcycle analogy fits dealings on eBay. My theory changes to two kinds of eBay shoppers: those who have been ripped off and those who are going to get ripped off. 'Nuff said!

Enter CGC.

Originally founded and headquartered in 2000 in New Jersey, Comics Guaranty LLC (CGC) moved to Sarasota, Florida (its present-day location). CGC is actually an independent business within the auspices of an umbrella organization, the Certified Collectibles Group. CGC officially kicked off operations in 2000, the first company to offer a third-party grading alternative to the "open range" our hobby had.

CGC's inception brought a new grading format into common use. The ten-point tier system was introduced to streamline comic book grading. The ten-point system was recognized by *OPG* in 1999 as the heir to an older 100-point system and any other system. The old "poor-fair-good" assignments were matched up with a numbering system that would eliminate some of the grade foolishness that had existed up to the new millennium.

Some examples of corrupted usage of the old grading system included the additions of pluses and minuses to enhance grades. A VG+ in the hands of ne'er-do-wells might increase to VG++ or the more improbable VG+++. Comic book guys with no concept of correct terminology were known to exaggerate the grading chart with indefensible grades like VG-VF, Excellent, or NM-/VF. The ludicrous derailment of the grading terms often advertised grades that exposed the grader's lack of expertise, or an unwillingness to comply with terms that many of us understood and were comfortable with. The ten-point grading system was designed to remove amateur attempts to fudge on the grading with the old style. Dealers thought the ten-point system was lighthearted, banter-suited grading with extra plusses. If I asked a dealer why there were so many plusses, he would respond, "Well, it's a really strong VG+." Hey, I was a cop. I'm used to taking the fun out of everything!

CGC is a business, grading comic books, magazines, photographs and documents for profit. Other grading services have long encapsulated collectibles such as coins, cards and documents. But in the comic book world, there have only been small-market graders uninvolved in permanent encapsulation. Also, their lack of universal exposure kept demand lower. Once graded, the independent graders offered no way to lock in the grade of a comic. The book was not sealed in any way to prevent tampering or copy-switching. What was needed was a sealed container, much like the containers used in the coin and trading card hobbies.

"Encapsulation" of comic books for decades meant relegation to paper or plastic bags. Custom-made comic book bags became widely available in the early 1970s. Plastics of this nature were manufactured from common oil by-products, leftover chemicals derived through the transformation of raw oil into refined gasoline. The bags of the day were composites of chemicals solidified into polyethylene (polypropylene bags came along at some point).

Mr. Ubiquitous posted a page on the Internet site ComicVine.com. Titled *Comic Book Care*, it provided definitions explaining the differences between polyethylene and polypropylene (edited for content):

> Polyethylene is inert, translucent and creates a lower static charge than polypropylene, and those are the three main characteristics which make it a superior archival or storage material. An inert substance, according to chemists, is not readily reactive with other elements, in that it cannot produce other chemical compounds. In other words, molds, mildews, and discolorations will not occur with an inert substance, so there's no way a polyethylene sleeve can damage your collectible, nor can damage readily occur to it. Polypropylene is also inert, but that's where the similarities end.
>
> The translucent nature of Polyethylene prohibits a greater amount of light than the transparent Polypropylene. Light can be particularly harmful to collectibles, especially magazines, comics, books, photographs, artwork or any kind of cover or jacket that has color and/or photos or illustrations. By inhibiting the overall amount of harmful light that affects your collectible, the risk of fading is minimized.

The eternal battle between the forces of light and darkness wage war in comic book collecting in our lifetimes. Mr. U continues:

The lower static charge produced by Polyethylene as opposed to the higher charge emitted by Polypropylene means that Polyethylene will attract much less dirt, dust and other foreign, organic elements. And it is those elements which produce damage to collectibles.

Polyethylene is more flexible than Polypropylene. By contrast, Polypropylene is stiff and hard, while Polyethylene is soft and pliable. The relatively rough surface of Polypropylene has the potential to produce scratches to the surfaces of collectibles while the potential for scratching by Polyethylene sleeves is minimal.

I checked our store inventory and noted that we carry comic book bags from four different manufacturers. Three are polypropylene and one is Mylar D.

Now this poly-information may make your head hurt and cause you to go "Huh?" Really, I get these questions. The answers may be much tougher than answering, "Where does the sun go?" Comic collectors can be picky, finicky and somewhat fussy. They want their comics just right, their bags and boards just right, and their boxes just right. Placing this information in my book will make my life a lot easier for future comic book supply questions. Maybe you readers will gain enough information to do my job for me.

Poly bags are chemically inert, meaning that they do not react chemically with other substances, such as comic book paper. Unfortunately, both polypropylene and polyethylene are considered "short-term care" solutions. Both types do age, generally displaying a foggy or discolored quality that is not suitable for long-term storage of documents or comics. The better bags to use are Mylar: formed from a film-like version of polyester that is much stronger and more durable than the less expensive comic book poly-bags. Mylar is considered a step up from the softer, more flexible poly-bags, but the cost is considerably more.

With all these permutations of bags, there was still no permanently sealable container for comic books. Hard shells had been invented, such as Chris Pedrin's screw-down "Fortress." Unfortunately, the Fortress is a two-way container that allows access, and thus, the ability to tamper.

CGC finally invented a strong container with several components and a "lock-down" outer shell. The inner workings consist of micro-chamber filter paper squeezed between the covers and the front and back pages. This paper blocks ink transfer between the cover and adjacent page. It also absorbs pollutants trapped within the comic book and container. The comic itself is heat-sealed within an inert, plastic envelope made of Barex, which is similar to Mylar for longevity and conservation elements.

A CGC container is most noted for its outer shell. The hard plastic container literally is the face of CGC. Each graded comic from their company houses an information card mounted across the top. The company's name headlines the pertinent details about the book and its contents. Each container has sealed, corner locking snaps that close together when the two halves of the outer Perspex shells are pressed together. It's this "one-way" mechanism that protects the integrity of each graded book. As long as the locks are unbroken, the vitality of the grade remains unchanged. If the locks are broken, the grade of the contained book becomes suspect. The locks guarantee security by their very presence.

Remember, cracking open the slabs is a crime! (Not really.)

When CGC first began production, the sealed info card was printed with a different font. This font for the numerical grade was small and difficult to read if viewed as a picture over the Internet. A subsequent redesign enlarged the font and repositioned the grade for easier identification. This was especially helpful when perusing eBay. The pictures sellers posted on eBay were often tilted and skewed. The remarkable indifference by many posters towards clear, large and high-resolution pictures was and is still common. The first-generation CGC labels presented the numerical grades and serial numbers in small font that was almost impossible to read if the photo was not dead-on. The second-generation container was adequate and addressed the Internet photo-hosting dilemma with larger font.

By 2016, CGC had evolved into its third container design. I prefer the new design with its sturdier nature and design changes that allow containers to be easily manipulated out of comic book boxes. There were initial problems with the inner well somehow damaging the comic book contents. The edges of the comic book, notably the top edge, showed signs of a wavy alteration brought on by an unknown transformation process. CGC attempted to correct the problem by returning to the original Barex-formula inner well. By August 2016, I continued to read online complaints from unhappy CGC customers. The complaints introduced two new terms to my world: "Newton Rings" and "creep engine."

Newton Rings refer to the oily sheen visible in CGC containers that gives off a prismatic effect (or rings). It's an optical effect created between two layers of plastic and light. These rings were first discovered by Isaac Newton, which is why they are called Newton Rings. The use of the term in our hobby derives from the effect given off by the container when the Mylar inner well that surrounds the book and the hard plastic holder come into contact.

Creep engine is a term best defined by an article in comicsheatingup.net (June 17, 2016): it occurs "where the comics inside bunch up together causing waviness. This is a result of force on the outside causing the book inside to move."

The best analogy I can provide for creep engine is my own experience with flooring. I used to work for a small contractor. I was trained in light construction and commercial remodeling of homes and businesses. One of my skills was laying down parquet and laminate flooring. To do flooring properly, there needs to be an expansion space along at least one side near a wall. Wood expands and contracts for the duration of its existence. Wooden floors do the same. They have a tendency to buckle if there's no expansion pocket allowing the floor to "breathe."

Apparently, CGC's containers need breathing space due to the pressures on either edge of the contained comic book. Comic books expand and contract to some degree; after all, they are born from wood pulp. Such pressures will cause a comic book to bow or wrinkle in the container.

I purchased a *Star Wars* #1 (1977) from a buddy in early July of 2016. The grade was 9.8 and the copy was flat. Three weeks later the top of the copy was wavy. It did appear that the book had begun to compress against the right and left sides of the container, causing it to buckle in the center just like a wooden floor. I returned the copy.

CGC's grading standards were once shrouded in mystery. The company has not published their standards to date. CGC has publicly stated, however, that its standards differ from *OPG*. Third-party grading by conscientious graders often lined up with *OPG*'s standards. Almost every correct grader I ever met adhered to the baseline set by *OPG*. CGC's grading seems tightly woven into the fabric of the grading comprehension most of us have learned through *OPG*. Any differences are generally subtle in either a positive or negative light.

The grading standards within our hobby do change. There are standards published by retailers that may not match *OPG*, CGC/CBCS, or each other. Sometimes there's an outcry for change that originates from concerns and complaints that the "old" way of doing things needs to evolve. One case of a change I agree with involved the severity of grading a nice-looking comic book that was missing a coupon. Or perhaps it was missing a non-story panel in an otherwise better-looking copy than a Fine.

For years *OPG* posted that defect in a grade no better than 1.0 (Fair). If you were the owner of a popular book that had great cover appearance but was missing a coupon, you would have grieved over that 1.0 grade.

One of the benchmark issues that caused *OPG* to re-examine its policy involves *Incredible Hulk* #181 (1975). Marvel ran a contest crossing into 1975 involving stamps that could be cut from the pages of Marvel comic books. The "Value Stamps" were collected into books buyers mailed away for. Marvel Value Stamps ran through every issue of Marvel comic books for about a year, including *Incredible Hulk* #181. Many stamps were cut out. Many buyers have been burned over the years by not checking to see if the stamp was present in their copies of #181. Many more felt the sting when they sent their copies off to CGC for grading and got them back graded at a lowly 1.0. Debates about the caustic grade devaluation led to theories that nice copies missing the stamp would decline to somewhere between a 2.0 and 3.0. Those were nice thoughts, but *OPG* refused to climb into the debate and stood pat at 1.0.

After years of debate about devaluing a really popular book over missing a lowly coupon-style part of a non-story page, *OPG* made an announcement. They decided to upgrade the quality of a nice copy missing the Marvel Value Stamp to 1.5. The grade 1.0 would apply if the copy was hammered to begin with, but consideration had to be given to the unpopular possibility that better-looking copies would sink all the way down to the bottom. Some collectors lobbied for higher, but *OPG* settled on 1.5 and there it stands.

The grading companies allow some leeway with the direction they may wish to go with this missing coupon issue. CGC has presented higher grade copies missing coupons with "Qualified" grades.

I took the following statement off CGC's Web site:

> A Qualified label is used by CGC for certified books that have a significant defect that needs specific description, or to note an unauthenticated signature (one which was not witnessed by CGC). For example, a comic book with a missing coupon that otherwise grades 6.0 will receive a Qualified grade, avoiding a considerably lower grade. CGC would give this book a Qualified grade of 6.0 and a Label Text notation "Coupon missing from page 10, does not affect story."

OPG does not address "Qualified" and CBCS avoids the Qualified label, as well.

No dealer is truly crying about the missing Marvel Value Stamp tragedy too much because sellers can still charge whatever they want. For example, in 2016 we sold an apparent 5.0 copy of #181 missing the stamp for $400. The 2016 *OPG* calculated their value of the book at about $90.

The buyers want what they want!

CGC Signature Series Label

Even without detailed descriptions of CGC's grading standards, comparisons with *OPG* and other third-party systems indicate most agree with each other.

Our store has submitted hundreds of comics to CGC (and CBCS), almost since their inception. In a roundabout way, we determined that our grading, following the well-known

OPG instructions, more often closely resembles the CGC/CBCS product than not. We make mistakes and CGC makes mistakes. Our tendency is to pre-grade a book before submission. If the book comes back matching, or close to matching our grade, we call that a success. We estimate that 75–80 percent of our submissions match our pre-grade. The other 10–15 percent of the submissions return within half a grade on either side of ours. That's close enough in low and mid-grades but not good enough in high grades. The remaining percentages indicate that CGC/CBCS and I did not agree. Maybe I missed something during pre-grade or CGC/CBCS made a mistake. CGC/CBCS freely acknowledges their potential for grader errors. They have a system in place to take second looks at those possible slip-ups.

Neither company will guarantee a grade before examining a book. To quote CGC's Web site: "The assigned grade represents our opinion, as grading is subjective." Your viewpoint may not be shared by CGC. Submitters without true grading talent tend to regard their comics with great optimism. Their books look all minty-fresh and worthy of third-party scrutiny. I've encountered plenty of people who sent in "high-grade" copies only to get label shock in the return mail. Their 9.4s turned into 6.0s or worse for inexplicable reasons (to them, at least).

For untested consumers, it's wise to understand that trying to reason why a grade came back lower than expected cannot be done by staring angrily through two layers of plastic. All grading companies offer the grader's notes for each comic book. The notes identify defects that affect grading. Submitters should go with those notes rather than speculate that CGC/CBCS are "too harsh/don't know what they're doing/wow, I think they got it wrong," etc. Those kinds of concerns can be worked out ahead of time if submitters find others beforehand who are talented enough to corroborate a suspected grade.

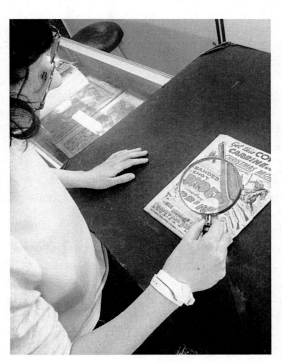

Examine them closely for defects and restoration. A little effort goes a long way toward preventing buyer's remorse later.

We all understand the process of evaluating a comic book. Page color, structure, defects, staple positioning, and paper flatness all play a part. Some defects are obvious; others, not so much. Aside from issues with restoration, simple paper impressions, indentations, and other subtle flaws may require visual aids to uncover. Reading glasses and magnifying glasses will confirm defects not readily seen without the right ambient or direct lighting.

The bottom line is this: collectors submitting comics for grading should have either a working knowledge of grading or an assist from someone who is trained. Third-party grading submissions can be pretty steep from tier to tier. It's important that a submitter do a little math before sending anything in.

Let's go over some examples:

A typical submission to CGC depends on the age and/or value of the comic book; easy enough to complete if a correct value is already attached. Getting to that point is the trick. Once again, I'm showing concern for the significance of correctly graded comics.

For example, I had a recent customer show me a submission that had just returned in the mail. It was a copy of *Incredible Hulk* #181, the mondo-desirable 1970s icon with Wolverine's first appearance. The grade was a 6.0 with moderate spine creasing. The owner was disappointed. He had purchased the copy raw on eBay, which had advertised it with a grade of "Very Fine." *OPG* priced the book in "Fine" at $300. The owner paid around $600 for the copy. *OPG* has the "Very Fine" grade priced at $750 (GPA much higher), a significant markup from $600 if the grade was accurate. According to CGC, it was not, so buyer beware.

Shipping is an expensive addition. CGC maintains a chart on the back of their submission for pre-calculating shipping costs (for USPS registered only). Fed Ex costs are also quoted, but I prefer using the post office. The submitter's *Incredible Hulk* #181 was tagged at $750 when submitted, so we will go with that value for shipping. Shipping for that price range was $31 (in 2016). That's just for one book, which includes insurance and a tracking number. The price ramps up with an increased quantity of books, even if their prices remain within the same tier.

Let's look at this *Incredible Hulk* #181 from the GPA angle. The submitter was not aware of the GPAnalysis site. If he had only known, a decision not to take a chance on the eBay offering would have been reinforced. The market value put an 8.0 copy at over $1,300 at that time! But the book came back at a 6.0. He paid for a VF but received a market-value Fine; he got no break against retail. After matching purchase price and CGC costs against *OPG* and GPA, we see that he might have been better off buying a graded copy. He spent extra money to get a copy graded that he might have purchased already slabbed for the same price.

I can quote countless episodes of similarly disappointing optimism. If the *Incredible Hulk* buyer had received a properly graded raw copy of the book from the eBay seller, then his post CGC 8.0 grade would have rewarded his $600 eBay purchase, even after adding third-party grading fees. Those fees, by the way, could have reached another $129 with the two-way shipping included. The seller graded inaccurately, often an issue on eBay, and the buyer believed the seller. Undoubtedly, the buyer can live with the 6.0 (Fine). His copy, like so many *Incredible Hulk* #181s, will increase in value. Demand for that book is ultra-strong. On the other hand, the buyer better train to be more wary, and the seller should get a clue.

CGC is not the only third-party grading company. CBCS, operated by well-known collecting figures in the hobby, is the most recent domestic competition for third-party comic book grading. CBCS is located in the same region as CGC and offers plans and services tweaked slightly in subtle differences from CGC. Both companies run comparable services at similar prices. The prices will always be considered fair by some, exorbitant by others.

Florida is an ideal state to own a business. There's no state income tax and the sales tax is a fair 6 percent. A lot of third-party grading fans pray that CGC or CBCS (or both) will either relocate to a state closer to their cities, or open a satellite branch within easier, physical reach. California, my state, is unlikely to receive such a facility. It's expensive for residents, and some say we are taxed to death. Nevada, like Florida, has no state income tax. However, neither company publicly claims they're interested in moving.

CBCS operates with a different set of grading tiers with competitive submission prices (competitive to CGC). Both companies offer signature guarantees. These guarantees, or Signature Series tiers, are all the rage. Plenty of signers exhibit or are guests at comic cons. With a CGC or CBCS witness in tow, fans get their favorite comic signed, present or not. Both companies will accept the properly witnessed signature and attach the appropriate verified signature label. The most popular signatures (with Stan Lee's handwriting at the top of the list) can garner extra market value.

Here's an example: I'll use copies of *Amazing Spider-Man* #129 to show pricing contrast. 9.6 is a nice, common, high-grade copy. There are plenty of archived sales of that issue in that grade on various Internet sites. For simplicity I'll use GPA.

The most recent sale of an *Amazing Spider-Man* #129 in CGC 9.6 sold in December 2015 for $2,475. A copy in the same grade signed by Stan Lee sold in October 2011 for $4,750. A couple of more recent sales included other signatures with Lee. Those copies broke $3,000.

Of course, the differences in value must accommodate the costs involved with getting those signatures. CBCS adds one sweetener to their verification process—they will authenticate "non-witnessed" signatures. For an additional fee, they will run a signed comic book through a signature authentication service. That works for all of us who got comics signed back in the day by heavyweights like Lee plus Jack Kirby, Siegel and Shuster, Bob Kane and others who have departed.

If I didn't say so before, we can all benefit from real tight, third-party grading. The world of shady dealings does not ignore grading comics. Too many comic books have been tampered with for decades. They bear clear or faint marks of restoration, which are value-killers in our world for most comics. Restoration can be tricky to detect, so we rely on the grading companies to sniff it out. Ideally, we don't want the shock of finding out our *Amazing Spider-Man* #129 has been tampered with in order to enhance its appearance. The grading companies won't alert you to that dilemma without payment up front. A talented (usually well-experienced) comic book dealer or collector can spot restoration. Ask one for guidance and an examination of your books prior to submission; many of us are happy to oblige. Just remember, no one is obligated to provide a screening service without compensation.

In June 2014 one soul sold a restored *Amazing Spider-Man* #129 in 9.4 (Near Mint) for $513. This sale was recorded on GPA, so the seller is generally unknown. An unrestored copy was worth $2,189 and rising at the beginning of 2017. I cannot emphasize enough the importance of understanding grading in our hobby. The financial consequences at stake can be too high for the risk.

Both companies retain the grader's notes for each comic book they handle. The notes can help dispel an owner's doubts about the grade of a submitted book. People who submit to grading are often dismissive of the subtleties of grading. Faint creases, fingernail impressions or other tiny instances of damage to a comic book go unnoticed by novices. If any collector wants to learn how to grade well, he can just drop a ton of money on bad choices and send them off for grading!

Third-party grading excels in restoration detection. Comic book restoration takes

Both photographs: Comic book restoration comes in many flavors, but it's not uncommon to see completely rebuilt Golden Age comics come to market. The *Batman #1* has extensive amateur restoration: color touch, pieces added, tear seals, reinforced, reglossed, 10th and 23rd pages married. That's quite a bit of work to bring it to market at around $27,000 in 2017. The *Detective Comics #2* is complete, but with most of the pages loose, with some attached with heavy taping, and ink added to the cover, which is trimmed. The book is scarce in any grade; this copy retailed for $4000 in 2017. The stigma of restoration is less intimidating with the oldest, rarest Golden Age. *Batman #1* (1940) © DC Comics. Used with permission and *Detective Comics #2* (1937) (© DC Comics. Used with permission).

many forms: trimming, color-touch, tear-seals, and so on. Restoration can be any level of amateur hands-on work up to nearly undetectable pro-level work. Let somebody else waste money on eBay buying a suspicious book and then sending it in for grading. You should make the smarter choice after the comic enters the market again. CBCS and CGC are noteworthy for employing people well-studied in restoration detection. This is the plus that most consumers have no exposure to. Again, look locally for help in this matter before you commit to a potential money disaster!

GPAnalysis allows members to link to specific comics whose sale(s) have been documented on their site. By clicking on any of the columns of grade, a pop-up window will display the various recorded copies in that grade. The records generally cover the most recent three-year period. The certificate number for each book graded links the viewer to more information, but not the grader's notes. The exception is for restored copies. Whatever restoration notes appear on the container label will be grafted onto the GPA link.

One aspect of restoration that can be trickier to detect than others is trimming. Older comics with uneven or torn edges look a lot better when they are cleaned up a bit. Marvel comics in its infancy (circa 1958–1966) suffered from a manufacturing malformation we call "Marvel chipping." The edges of some newly printed copies were torn, jagged or missing chips of paper. The reasons were dull knives when the paper was cut on the assembly line. The machines would have to be stopped every few dozen or more cuts to sharpen the knives. The paper in line right after the stoppage suffered the worst of the dull cuts. These were just comic books to the workers, so nobody got too excited about replacing them with fresh copies. They got bundled up with the rest for distribution.

Copies from that time tend to have covers that overhang the contents, which add to the misery for later collectors. Amateur hack jobs were employed probably in the '60s the moment someone was dissatisfied with his purchase. Out came the scissors or the paper cutter. When the collecting world evolved into a way to make money, some entrepreneurs sat down and reasoned that a well-trimmed copy would look better and sell for more.

"Marvel chipping" entered the pantheon of terminology ages ago. What confuses many is how to grade the books. Some see Marvel chipping as a serious defect to be graded as any other similar defect. Others view it as less than an issue because the comic book was made that way. My experience has taught me that the grading companies adhere to the former, not the latter. Marvel chipping = bad.

Years later we are all stupefied by how many trimmed copies are out there and how little value is attached to them. The grading companies have identified an untold number of copies. Dealers like me have identified them at our store, intercepting them before an unsuspecting owner sent them off for grading.

There are several other third-party grading companies operating on three continents as of 2017. Professional Grading Experts, or PGX, does business out of Eugene, Oregon. Their website boasts: "We grade smarter … we grade faster." Comic book fans who submit to PGX like the fast turnaround time and cheaper submission prices. Compared to CGC/CBCS, PGX appears to be a bargain for third-party submissions. PGX has been around for a few years but has yet to claim the universal acceptance that CGC enjoys (with CBCS coming on strong).

A former Australian comic book store owner, Grant Adey, opened a third-party grading company in his country. Like CGC, CBCS and PGX, HALO offers a locking, hard plastic container that seals in each graded comic book. HALO is supported by the theory that they can operate as a regional version of CGC. For them, the shipping costs alone from the U.S. to Australia are prohibitive. It's just too expensive to mail CGC containers by weight alone, never mind the price attached to shipping expensive valuables across the globe. HALO localizes third-party grading to that region, assuming enough customers exist there to make the business profitable. Grant is currently training a U.S. associate to spread his company to our continent.

A fifth company, The Vault, specializes in more modern comics, Copper Age and above.

Recently, a national comic book retailer, Midwest Comic Books, opted to offer their own graded comics. Their system promotes itself this way:

Midwest Comic Grading (MCG) came into existence as the grading unit of Midwest Comic Books (MCB). However, we also desired to offer comic book lovers, collectors, buyers and sellers **lower cost**

options to just hard shell grading. I feel the companies that offer only that form of encapsulation do a good job but many people own newer, higher-grade comics that may want to get them graded, but don't want to pay the higher price to have them placed inside an acrylic holder. Ever since grading became a profession, many wished that they could get professional grading done here in the Midwest and not have to ship their books across the country. Therefore, MCG is acting both as a grading unit for MCB and trying to fill a void in both affordability and availability in the world of comic book grading. All professional graders, whether grading coins, currency, or comics are charged with placing your items under a microscope to determine their condition and therefore value.

Their container is described as a "rigid non-hard shell grading" shell.

Controversy arises when the consumer realizes that MCG will grade their own books. The descriptions of their container choices indicate that some form of irreversible seal is applied to prevent tampering. I see a perceived conflict of interest and have seen Facebook comments reflecting my same concerns. This type of conflict has already cost other graders their reputations and presumably business. We are taught that the "third" in third-party grading symbolizes agenda-free credibility. A company that stacks the deck in their favor without outside accountability is considerably close to the business equivalent of an oligarchy. It's benign as long as the buyers appreciate that MCG's grades may not reflect general standards for grading.

In February 2017, CBCS introduced a similar service matching MCG. Here's the introductory announcement quoted from CBCS's web site:

> CBCS is proud to offer a new grading service, Raw Grade. This service is an inexpensive and fast method of providing customers with independent third-party grade for comic books, magazines or treasury edition books.
>
> This new service is designed for customers who are looking for a fast and reliable grade that will help these collectors sell books without incurring the full cost associated with traditional grading and encapsulating. This service is directed at those collectors who feel that their return on investment does not warrant traditional grading, those who are seeking to sell their collections quickly and those who choose not to invest in traditional grading.
>
> Books graded using the Raw Grade service are evaluated, graded and placed in a Mylar bag with a backing board. The grade is displayed on a sticker that is adhered to the front of the Mylar bag. The bag is also sealed with a tamper-evident sticker to provide security.
>
> The Raw Grade service does not include a restoration check; it is strictly an evaluation of the book's condition at the time of grading.
>
> The Raw Grade service is not meant to provide long-term protection for comics. Customers wanting to have their books graded and protected should utilize our traditional grading service....

The motivation for this additional service can be as simple as a new, somewhat acceptable revenue stream. CBCS got around one nagging omission in the world of comic book grading: treasury-sized grading. No company has designed an encapsulating, hard-shell container for treasury-sized periodicals, but at my store we get inquiries about any third-party grading company that could comply. CBCS will use their hybrid style to grade treasuries, a process in demand.

It is not my business with this book to discuss the open dialogues on the various chat sites. I will say that an initial firestorm of denigration opened up on certain chat sites about this new CBCS plan. I read similar arguments against it using the same comments I posted just a page back. This modified grading system and its harsh critics remind me of the same harsh critics that attacked CGC when it was new. The naysayers were abundant, but not so much now.

Time can be harsh on small businesses. Third-party grading companies are no exception. CGC and CBCS work hard to solicit business, setting up submission sites at various comic book conventions to supplement office submissions. That extra work buffers their safety nets to help ensure profit.

All the grading services related to comic books spring from a concept that only dates back to the dawn of the new millennium. It's still the "wild country" out there, so be prepared to expect changes.

As discussed earlier, a singular advantage to third-party grading is to attach an inarguable grade and quality to submitted comic books. The grade cannot change once the comic is sealed in its container. But there are plenty of instances in which the containers have been tampered with. One common scenario is to gingerly pop the corner locks, doing as little damage as possible. Then, offenders will split open the inner plastic well to unseal the comic book using a sharp blade to minimize damage. This act maintains the ruse that the inner envelope hasn't been tampered with. Typically, the copy is replaced with a lesser-graded copy of the same issue, matching the title and issue number to the label affixed at the top.

Advanced design changes are attempting to foil the bad guys and spoil their tampering efforts. Concerned container owners can inspect the outer case for cracks, chips, or broken locks, which could be evidence of tampering. Glue and even tape have confounded container owners with fake resealing attempts. Always inspect a container before taking possession of a third-party graded comic book. This caution applies when buying a graded comic on eBay, or any other website or auction. Not being able to inspect a book before taking possession is a risk, and crooked eBay sellers take advantage of the opportunity. Tampering is easy to get away with if a consumer is unaware it happens.

Tampered products that end up being delivered through the mail can provide a challenge for the buyer. An experienced thief will make it difficult to get justice. A seller who is caught selling tampered containers may not have been aware, either. Use common sense when buying third-party graded books from a distance. Inspect them closely when buying in person.

In summary, remember one thing: grading can be a contentious vocation. It's a beautiful day when a buyer and a seller can agree on a particular comic book. The grade of a book is as important as are the comic book title and issue.

There are old-school purists dismissive of third-party grading. Turning a three-dimensional comic book into a two-dimensional wall hanging is abhorrent to them. Who's to argue? Their only possible quandary with this choice is what happens next. Popular opinion on eBay demonstrates that sales of particular comic books are enhanced by third-party grading. Raw copies often sell for less if at all. Collectors who sit on groups of particular vintage comics need to seriously consider the ramifications of leaving them raw. Today's buyers want the fear of restoration reliably removed. The savviest dealer can't reassure all buyers that a book is unrestored, especially over the Internet. Neither can every buyer rely on every seller's grades. Grades matter. Restoration is a massive concern. Even grading companies can miss it during a grading examination.

Understanding restoration can certainly enhance the skill-sets of comic book collectors. There's plenty of information on the Internet addressing restoration (Or, you can wait for *Forensic Comicologist* Volume 2, already good to go!).

A forensic comicologist must be prepared to admit mistakes and move on. At my store we sell a lot of raw copies of back issues that we graded prior to sticker pricing them. The sticker will often show a hand-written grade from one of my staff members. Most of the time buyers agree with our grades. People who have purchased books we graded often submit them for professional grading to either CGC or CBCS. Out of those submissions we run about eighty percent accurate with another fifteen percent coming in at about a half a grade within range of ours.

Sometimes we don't get close enough and are at odds with the third-party grader. As a business we have all kinds of store policies, but we don't have a policy to cover grading conflicts. As it happens, we had a conflict like that with a regular customer, Alex. I don't remember what the book was, maybe an issue of *Iron Fist*, or something like that. We had it graded a 9.0 and Alex bought it for that grade.

Alex sends everything he ever buys into CGC, so he sent this 9.0 in. It came back months later a disappointing 7.5, which is a considerable monetary decrease from a 9.0. He was not happy. I felt a little flushed as well because it's embarrassing to get the grade wrong. The book wasn't very expensive and certainly not worth the effort to debate the grader's notes, so I offered to cover Alex's expenses and buy the book back from him. He opted to be very gracious about the mistake. He knew he had now officially spent more money on the book than it was worth with CGC's grade. Alex opted to keep the book and declined my attempts at compensation.

My submission history with CGC goes back to 2002. In all that time I've never received a grade higher than 9.8. I've submitted hundreds of my own books, both vintage and modern. Still, no 9.9s or 10.0s. The same is true with CBCS. Both companies are stingy with those top grades.

On the other hand, our store submits for customers as well. We've submitted hundreds of books for others within a 14-year time frame. Again, 9.9s and 10.0s elude us. That is, until 2014 when one of our walk-ins brought a small stack to send into CGC. One of the books was a copy of *X-Men: Omega* published in 1995, touted as the final battle for the Age of Apocalypse. This was a book that was manufactured with a shiny Mylar cover along with its sister one-shots, *X-Men: Prime* and *X-Men: Alpha*.

Our customer got it back a 10.0. That was his first submission and he got a 10.0! I know 9.9 and 10.0 grades are rare, but sometimes fishing for 10.0s is like playing the slots in Las Vegas. I stand at the dollar slots for hours, mindlessly inserting coins or playing credits while sipping free cocktails. After decades of repeated entertainment, the best hit I have to show is a $400 win. On at least one occasion the seat next to me remains empty. At some point I'll assume the machine I'm playing is cursed so I scoot over to the empty seat and begin coin insertion. As soon as the vacated seat is spotted another gambler takes it. He inserts five coins to play the maximum bet and … he wins the jackpot! Really?

Such is my history with CGC 10.0; CBCS too, for that matter.

Meanwhile, I had a customer come into our shop to work a trade. He was interested in off-loading a stack of third-party graded books. That stack included PGX books, modern comics from the past two to three years. He acquired the graded books from the collector who had submitted them. The non–PGX copies were graded at 9.6s and 9.8s. The PGX copies were almost all 9.9s and 10.0s. How the heck did that happen? Most of those super high-grade copies were from DC's eye-grabbing phase, but that doesn't mean that style of comic book will be granted 10.0 status automatically. Certainly not a whole group submitted in one volley.

CGC's census doesn't even list any graded 10.0s for *Justice League* (2011) issue #23.4, yet PGX handed it out as part of a group of other 10.0s from one submission.

In my Las Vegas analogy, if I gambled on the Strip at the PGX Casino, I would not have changed seats.

18

Pricing

When I think of pricing comic book back issues, I think of the old ways: convention prices. For years I've attended comic conventions where the dealer prices seemed higher than average. Back in the day, we collectors called that "con-pricing" (as in convention pricing, not convict pricing). We had the *Overstreet Price Guide* to set prices and we darn well followed them. But at conventions you saw a different pricing structure in play. The prices were often bumped a little, especially by out-of-town dealers.

Their rationale was fine: they were trying to use higher prices to offset travel and hotel costs. And nobody was really trying to hide this knowledge. Most dealers explained to prospective customers that "convention pricing was perfectly normal and acceptable." If you didn't want to pay their prices, there were still plenty of others to buy from. Locals and small-time players could easily get a booth or table at most cons.

Those new faces and small-time dealers were the most desired back-issue retailers in the room. Dealers tended to swarm them at set-up on Day One and clean out their back issues before anyone else got to them. Normal back-issue collectors wanted to find them because their prices were either fair or low (another reason dealers preyed upon them). The newbies didn't travel a show circuit to learn the fine art of overpricing; they had comics they wanted to sell without the nuances of skilled back-issue sellers. We consistently attended the local San Diego Con and were able to rebuild our back-issue inventories off the new players.

All sides knew a new guy selling at the con might have copies of comics in high demand or copies that had not been seen before. Nowadays that's next to impossible. No new blood finds its way into our San Diego convention to sell comic book back-issues. The badges for random attendees are made from the rare earth metal unobtainium, and so nobody carrying a briefcase full of comics can get in. No new dealer can get in to sell because there are rarely any new spots available for exhibitors. On the almost unheard-of occasion when a new dealer gets a chance at a spot, he or she is overwhelmed by the high cost of exhibiting.

I know a lot of local comic book guys. Quite a few of them do some back-issue dealing on the side using Facebook, swap meets and Craigslist to conduct business. Their options for grander arenas have increased recently with the steady proliferation of conventions within driving distance of their homes or shops. Admission prices at those shows don't frighten off attendees, so if a seller is lucky enough to get a spot at a good con, he is likely to make money, but not Comic-Con International. The costs are way too high for most of those guys. At $6,300 (2017 price) for our two end caps, it's even a little scary for me when I write the check each year!

Let me get back to pricing. I wasn't there as an adult in the very beginning of the formalized movement to establish recognized prices for back issues. My history includes knowledge that beginning in the earliest days of comic books, there were retailers for "used" comics. Magazine stands, bookstores and businesses where kids congregated often had older copies up for grabs.

By the mid–1960s, fanzines and letters columns in new comic books had begun to connect buyers and sellers from all over the country who wanted to talk comics and shop comics. The same fanzines and comics posted ads for retailers selling back issues. By 1964 fandom was connecting and collecting in earnest. The money was still small change when you consider that a typical back-issue ad offered comic books from less than ten years before. The prices could reach lofty heights up to about 40 cents a copy, except in rare cases with mostly first issues. Neal Adams was just getting started revolutionizing the Batman family with his mature and dramatic art style. His art was in demand and his back issues were perilously high at seventy-five cents! The comic book store I worked for in 1975 stretched the Adams back-issue prices up to two dollars a copy. Outrageous!

Reviewing Marvel's *All About Collecting Comic Books* (1992) pamphlet, I quote this almost hysterical claim: "Comics are today's *hot* collectibles, up there with baseball cards, coins and stamps. Single comics have sold for thousands of dollars. Even the one you bought last year for $3.50 is already worth more than four times its original price." I beg to differ.

Jack Kirby was at his peak providing rising publisher Marvel Comics with an art and story backbone that would never be repeated. For twelve cents I could get *Batman*'s 200th issue. For fifteen cents each I could get *Fantastic Four*'s 100th issue and *Amazing Spider-Man*'s 100th issue brand new. The back issues for those titles were rising as well, up to a quarter a copy for the fan favorites. Nearly 50 years later, those same twelve- and fifteen-cent cover priced books are going for hundreds and hundreds of dollars.

The middle of the 1960s and beyond saw regular fan publications like *Rocket's Blast Comic Collector* filled with catalogs and classified ads buying and selling comic books. It was at this point the *OPG* transitioned from Bob Overstreet's collective years of gathering painstaking statistics to a full-fledged book, recognized by most of us as the Bible of comic book knowledge and back issue pricing. Its inception in 1970 heralded a new environment for collecting and provided primitive rules in the form of grading.

In 1971, teenager Alan Light created his own comic book fan newspaper, offering a subscription service through the mail. The newsprint publication eventually contained articles, classified ads, reviews and photos. He titled it *The Buyer's Guide for Comic Fandom*. San Diego comic collecting brothers Steve and Bill Schanes sold comics from home. On my one visit to their beach area home, they handed me a copy of the *Buyer's Guide*. I'd never seen or read anything about it. Like everything else comic books in San Diego in 1973, there was a great disconnection between comic book fans. The rising popularity of the local comic book convention was changing all that. The *Buyer's Guide* added the national element to collecting. I read it and then subscribed, bringing a more worldly view to my tastes. Suddenly, I could be a back-issue player. I could run small ads selling comics or I could buy from anyone posting ads. There had been nothing locally as accessible to the rest of the country, providing a wealth of old comics for sale. (I never saw a copy of *Rocket's Blast* in town until 1975.)

In the early days of *Overstreet's Price Guide*, the writers would preface copies with the following statement:

> Comic book values listed in this reference work were recorded from convention sales, dealers' lists, adzines, and by special contact with dealers and collectors from coast to coast. Prices paid for rare comics vary considerably from one locale to another. We have attempted to list a realistic average between the lowest and highest range observed. The reader should keep in mind that the prices listed only reflect the market just prior to publication. Any new trends that have developed since the preparation of this book would not be shown.

OPG goes on to explain, "The values listed are reports, not estimates. Each new edition of the *Guide* is actually an average report of sales that occurred during the year." All prices were subject to change with each new *Overstreet Price Guide*.

Back then we couldn't wait for the new *OPG* to see how much our collections had improved in value. Its annual arrival meant many collectors were going to get an uptick in the values of their comic books.

OPG's delivery date usually occurred in the spring, not long before San Diego Comic-Con's summer show. We bought our copies from local comic book stores. If you were a convention back-issue dealer at the dawn of Comic-Con, you brought your copy home to re-price your comics for the show every year. I'm talking boxes of comics per dealer. No dealer wanted to be caught short on a chance to make another ten percent on a comic that was $6 last year and $6.50 now.

The alternative was to choose to be lazy and not do the work. Lazy is as lazy does, but it also improves the dealer's chances of outselling an opponent. If two dealers sat side-by-side at Con and one was clearly reworking the books with a copy of *OPG* held open while the other did nothing and his prices were last year's prices, well … so much the better for some buyers!

By 1970, the world of comic books had changed. New comics were fifteen cents, the first San Diego convention arrived (Golden State Con), and the first *OPG* saw print. All this happened as I reached high school and began my focused investment in all things comic book.

I met many others looking to buy old comic books. Two friends and fellow students from high school, Roland Pritchard and Ken Marr, were as far into comic books as I was. Comic book hunters who preceded me were well into the search. I'd run into some of these guys at swap meets and garage sales, and through classified ads in the local newspapers. Residents in my own neighborhood routinely held garage sales. Those neighbors easily fed my growing appetite for comic books because their kids didn't seem to care about comics as much as I did. Strangely, I tended to find more *Mad Magazines* and DC Comics than Marvels and the others.

Some of the San Diego guys I met were already established back-issue dealers, mostly through local ads. One or two were advertising in comic book classified ads or fanzines' ad sections. Two such comic book devotees were future friends and mentors of mine: Ski Mark Ford and Greg Pharis.

Ski was a local beach guy who was physically and mentally more mature than many of us recent high school graduates by 1973–1975. Ski was connected to other dealers all over the U.S. and was the only "player" I knew in the hobby. He was adept at moving back issues, having been mentored by comic book collecting pioneer Ken Krueger, recognized as one of the founders of Comic-Con and an early super-fan. Ken ran a newsstand in the beach area. I met him in the early 1970s before he sold off the stand and moved on.

Ken was one of Ski's business influences, setting groundwork for Ski's knowledge of pricing. In turn, Ski helped nudge me into becoming a savvy comic book retailer. Among other aspects of the business, Ski introduced me to the *OPG* and encouraged me to read it from cover to cover. I found the listings in the book to be profoundly inspiring. With the added extra bits of knowledge and history within each title, I tasked myself with the challenge of making a hobby into a living. I applied the practical, pricing knowledge to my own back-issue pricing workload.

My other instructor was Greg Pharis. We met when he was running newspaper ads selling and buying comics from his home. I first met him in 1969, answering one of his ads selling comics. We eventually worked together and became friends. We are still friends almost 50 years later. Greg was my boss at Richard Alf's Comic Kingdom in the mid–1970s. He taught me more about the comic book marketplace than the guy we worked for, and Richard had his name on the sign!

Greg was a dutiful dealer, honest with ethics and everything. He worked without an agenda and conducted business as he saw fit, adhering to a code of conduct that he thought was slowly disappearing from our culture, the kind of values he felt were more respected a generation before. Greg craved the simplicity and genuine honesty he felt existed when comic books were young. He treasured the comic books of a bygone era for their strict portrayal of the difference between good and evil; there was little of the blurred lines that appeal to comic book fans today. Greg did have a way with pricing and selling comics. He understood grading, more so than a lot of his future customers. He developed a following of customer and fans who felt Greg was so fair with his pricing that he had to be losing money on sales!

Greg used the *OPG* because he believed it was the best source for pricing. He was often outraged by the pricing antics of others and was especially put off by "those East Coast dealers," as we called them. Neither he nor I could ever reconcile the differences between the East Coast dealers and us. Greg knew many of the comic book guys in San Diego and felt that they were markedly fairer in the way they did business. Since I was a few years younger than Greg, I would hear the complaints, but still had to catch up on the experience. That experience came with selling and buying at San Diego Comic-Con.

Plenty of East Coast dealers showed at the con even in the early days. I encountered many, did business with some, and learned a lot about the groundwork of retailing. I also bought into the belief that the East Coast dealers, at least some of the ones who sold at con, did do business differently from us. Their inventories and prices reflected qualities that figuratively "broadcast" a feeling of dominance over the local yokels.

Not all of us were as naïve about retailing comic books as the East Coast guys thought. Older men like Tom French and Ken Krueger, both instrumental to San Diego Comic-Con's early existence, held their own, while young bucks like Ski would give East Coasters a hard time. Ski was a bear of a man who literally bullied fair prices and discounts out of those guys.

Both Ski and Greg understood that back issues were fun, profitable and had a future.

None of us could predict how far that future would extend or how expensive it would get. No one ever said that comic books would last into the following century. We all thought back issues were "on the clock" because "those crazy prices" were unsustainable.

Pricing Today

What I wouldn't give for yesterday's comic book pricing! It was all so simple: convention dealers with wonky grading and *OPG* were leading us all into the future. But the future is today, and pricing techniques have changed. So there's a lot of confusion, misunderstanding and downright subterfuge in that aspect of our hobby.

To begin, a lot of collectors misunderstand what it means to buy and sell comic books for a living, especially at the convention and store levels. There is a mass assumption about what dealers pay to acquire collections from collectors who were out of the hobby for years while sitting on boxes of comics they gathered decades before. Too often they believe that the modern comics they purchased in the recent past increased in value. When the truth is provided from someone at my level in the business world of comics, the reaction is often shock and disbelief. There is often an expectation that their comics generally have appreciated in value from the cover price. Some collectors of more recent comics view the vintage of their comics as significant enough to earn them more money than they paid. That's often true enough if the comics were purchased off the stands before the 1980s. A collection that was purchased after that period, even at "collector's prices," is often not the bonanza one is looking for now.

I've dealt with many collectors selling their comics. I've also purchased from many fellow dealers that I'm acquainted with and ones I've only met once. Everybody has his own purchasing style and purchase pricing. Many have learned, from overpaying, how to trim the fat, while others don't have enough liquidity to keep up with other dealers. They don't get to select collections to buy; they have to hunt them down and hope the owner entertains their offer. With all the "meat-eater" dealers out there, a bargain buyer has to step up with his best offer before the owner looks for someone better known and more noteworthy as a pro spender. This is where I come in.

I started off small-time with little money to burn. I learned how to find and buy collections in the 1970s. By the beginning of the new millennium, I saw how much stuff was out there in the seemingly inexhaustible supplies of comic collections. There's another one for sale around each corner every day.

My rise to successful dealer was not meteoric. It was slow and plodding, with hiccups and bad deals at every step. I learned a lot and spent a lot collectively. At the age of 60, I figure I had developed enough pricing knowledge to teach others. Any forensic comicologist worth his or her salt had to pay a lot of dues over a great period to gain trust. There ain't no school for what we do!

All dealers have a tendency to eye competition with a cautious approach. We don't know if the other guy is "worthy" of being in the room with us. By worthy I mean reliable, honest, experienced and independent. Too many rookies see the hobby through rose-colored glasses, ready to make a killing without much forethought.

There is a phrase that runs through my thoughts when I look at comics to buy for collecting and resale: "I will debate the grade, but not the price." The dealer can charge whatever he wants. The grade can be inconsistent between two people, or downright wrong.

A second line—"stick with the grade, argue the price"—pertains to discounting a comic book. If the grade is solid, then figure out if the seller will bend the price. Although most of us want full price, there is a clear understanding that discounts are commonly requested. No one is out of line for asking. Only the most stubborn retailer will resist a discount request. I'll probably hear some complaint about this statement, but it is fact; we just don't like advertising it.

I've seen dealers come up the ranks as slowly as I did and then operate on an even keel with the others. I've also seen dealers flop around with poor attitudes and poor sales performance. Those folks will lie to themselves to stay in the game. I give you a few examples:

I've watched swap meet guys pay a couple of hundred dollars to set up for a weekend day, maybe two days. Their inventories are modest without being salted with a proper number of popular books to make a splash. If they read the swap meet crowd right, they will end up selling a couple of hot items and a small number of inexpensive bulk comics. In all likelihood, they spend an active, pleasant day before driving off with barely any profit. I know; I've been there. I found swap meets to be places to learn the craft, but I've never boasted about a day of strong sales. The buyers see swap meets as places to get deals, so some will be put off by collector's prices. Others are there to grind an exhibitor down so they can feel good about themselves or buy comics for their own resale purposes.

Swap meets, like garage sales and the like, are ground-level job experience and provide a small modicum of comic book sales experience. It's tough to feel optimistic when it seems few buyers like your fair prices and the weather threatens to drop buckets on you or burn you to death.

The key to the pricing learning curve is repetition. A large volume of repetitive sales will do the trick. Prospective comic book dealers will learn in time what prices the market will really tolerate. The social media will link people together one-on-one and provide not only a market to do business but a forum to judge that business. There are plenty of opinions, a lot of wisdom and experience and room for a new player to be greeted warmly before getting started. With settings like the closed groups on Facebook, anyone can feel at ease because the members want to know who you are and what you have. A lot of them participate without an agenda and will give fair opinions about pricing. The nature of a closed group limits the opportunities to buy and sell to that group, so the members still must reach outside for more tangible prices.

That brings me to the next example: comic book stores. A proper comic book store that stocks back issues is less common than 10 years gone by. The store that does stock a worthwhile number of back issues will lay claim to a vast amount of pricing experience. The sheer number of sales sets trends in pricing, giving the talented owner the ability to price accurately and consistently. If the owner gets no feedback, he or she is probably not making many sales.

That sales repetition will tell the owner if *OPG* is working, if discounting from *OPG* is working, or if another system is the key. We use *OPG* and discount books that have been hanging around too long. *OPG* is less favored for high-grade books, keys and third-party graded books. The book's pricing is not "evergreen" enough to keep up with fluctuating pricing changes that affect more desirable grades and keys.

The buyer needs to understand that sellers make choices and so do the buyers, often by not buying. Not by arguing and assertion through attitude or demand. I've been confronted by too many men and women who prefer to tell me what I'm going to do rather than ask if I'm willing to discount. I have no idea if they think their sales pitch is a buying tool, but I know who the "tool" is. Me being the shy, retiring flower that I am, I have always stymied the demanders. At the store and convention level I know of few experienced sellers even willing to entertain the demanders.

The stores have to have the patience of Job with some of their inventories. Comics rapidly build up in back-issue boxes and can't all be "in your face" in glass cases and mounted on the walls. In display boxes they tend to disappear from the owner's awareness. If that's the case, they may lie around for years. At some point the wisest storeowners will consider making sales decisions. We do. We cycle out the oldest stuff after a few years in inventory and either sell them on eBay or reduce them for the store. Either works. If not, there's always a comic convention (Michelle Nolan is adamant that Heroes World Con in Charlotte, North Carolina, is the world's best con!).

Comic conventions: I love them, but I could eventually live without them. There has been and still is a tremendous amount of prep work for me before a show. It would take a chapter just to itemize and explain all the things I have to do to stay on my toes and make the shows work on my terms. This, of course, involves pricing. I use *OPG*. I use GPAnalysis. I use eBay. I use my own store sales figures. I use other dealers. I use experience and common sense.

There are other sources: chat boards where thoughts about pricing are debated endlessly. Round-filing: where the dealer doesn't want to work too hard and just price-guns everything to nice, round numbers that make sense to that dealer. We use the price gun where it makes sense to us and to our customers. I'm not going to grade an obvious low-end copy of *Fantastic Four* #94, about a $12 book, when I can price it $5 and guarantee a quicker sale. I know that the $12 *OPG* price is awkward to justify, but $5 takes no effort to justify.

I suppose one could try to learn the pricing game by copying other dealers. I've never done it, but I have seen lame attempts by others to go that way. One individual used to take advantage of our friendship by calling me for prices. I'd get calls frequently asking how much he should price this book and that. I was happy to help, at first. Then it became annoying. I asked him to consider the lessons he'd already learned, having sold comics for years, but he was more interested in cutting corners without expending effort. He's out of the comic book business now.

Networking: this is the alternative to copying others. Facebook groups network when a particular comic or collection of comic books surfaces within a group and the "hive mind" discusses a fair price. I like the democracy of the decision, but I learned a long time ago that people can be talked into doing just about anything. We acquire a strange variety of collectibles throughout each year. Sometimes the con is the only place they stand a chance of selling. To get to the price point, we are willing to ask help from others. For the sake of simplicity, we take the good will of another and his or her advice and run with it on small-dollar items. On big-ticket items we have to have corroboration. One source outside of proven sales is not enough.

> In late 2016 there was a flurry of activity on Facebook and certain chat sites aimed at one particular comic book dealer. That dealer was caught "shilling" his auctions on eBay. The shill on eBay, a seller, uses additional eBay bidder usernames to artificially increase bids on auctions. Sometimes, others are employed using alternate bidder names to do the same job. It violates eBay rules and is patently unfair to bidders. Like a firestorm, this seller was spread out across social networking and treated as a crook. His e-mail profile was hammered with such severity that eBay banned him from their site.
>
> Shoddy dealers who work so blatantly to cut corners selling comic books on the Internet are favorite targets of Internet subscribers and trolls alike. Nobody can stay hidden and no cheater can stay under the radar. After reading the posts about this seller, I got the impression that comic fans are out there waiting for these events. Once they finish savaging that current villain, they're onto the next.
>
> The seller in this case was also set up in several other venues selling comics. Time will tell if he suffers irreparable damage from his actions.

Then we have the guy who prices comic books from "God knows where." These guys, both dealers and stores, baffle and frustrate me. I've seen them countless times at their booths or their shops with handwritten Post-Its or uniform price stickers that have no basis in proven stats that I can find. I see dealers who appear to price through the front of the comic book bag and then hang in there with the price even when a potential buyer looks inside and sees the back cover is damaged. It's clear the seller worked fast with no regard to get the most money from an unsuspecting customer who won't ask questions. I also see stores everywhere I go that can only tell me "That's market value" for a comic that I would try to sell correctly for half the amount. I would prefer to do business with a store or dealer who simply said, "That's what I want to sell it for."

I've said it before and I'll repeat it here: if the seller doesn't post a grade on the price sticker, be wary. The dealer who does post the grade has made a written commitment to that grade. He or she can be challenged by a customer. At least the customer has a starting point that makes sense and can always argue the written grade. No posted grade = mystery grading = debatable pricing. That can be a dealer's kiss of death if it gets around the room that he or she is just pricing for the sake of gouging.

At comic conventions, buyers look for dealers they can trust. That can be an uphill battle if it's based on pricing. Sticking with my rule of thumb and shopping for posted grades on raw comics aligns these shoppers with dealers who feel the same way they do. The dealers don't want to argue with you, they want to sell to you. If you make consistent purchases from the dealers who price according to a system you trust, then you can begin to trust those dealers.

The Forensic Comicologist makes a living pricing comic books. He relies on his sources to price accurately. If he feels that his sources are off, he adjusts accordingly. If he buys comics, most often for resale, he will use the "grade on the sticker" identifier to choose whom he will buy from. The FC has cut loose a lot of dealers from his "buy list" over the years, dealers with grades (or lack thereof) or prices that didn't jive. They failed to generate a climate of trust or consistent accuracy.

More About Pricing

I've adroitly handled as much about pricing comics for sale and attaching values as I think anyone reading this chapter can stand. So how about we take the conversation a different direction?

We engage people lugging their comic book collections into our shop as a daily occurrence. We "advertise" religiously that we buy comic books. We don't pay for a lot of advertisements, per se: we just put it out there publicly and we've been the place to go for countless numbers of comic collections. People bring their comics to us for any number of reasons, but word has been repeated that we pay a fair price. We don't pay extravagantly, but we have a large resource pool for cash to afford just about any collection. That purchase force sends more collections our way than almost any other local dealer. The bottom line is I have a vast amount of experience to draw from. Therefore I claim shot-caller status when it comes to purchasing comic book collections.

I mentioned that people sell for several reasons; they also want what they want for several reasons. They can be distrustful of dealers and unsure of themselves. They think they're sitting on gold mines and want the appropriate reward. Some collection owners are under the misconception that their comics are worth more than reality dictates, but they don't know our reality as comic book dealers.

I prefer the collection owners to be at ease during the deal. If they're tense, they tend not to listen to me as they try desperately to absorb the news about my price, good or bad. Numbers can confound people, especially percentages. For my purposes it's best if the collection owner is allowed to ask questions to relieve any inner turmoil at his own speed. This all adds up in varying ways to handle different people with different collections within several common scenarios.

Let me break down how I pay for comics with a couple of those scenarios:

Scenario 1: A Modern Age Collection Walks into My Store

This scenario plays out every day at Southern California Comics. We either get a call ahead of time or someone shows up with a collection of comic books spanning the 1980s to the present. The collection is housed in a combination of ten short and long comic book boxes the owner has stored, or hauled across the country for years. They were inherited from a relative or purchased by the owner who read each one. He or she is done with them and feels now's the time to sell, what with all the comic book movies.

We help the owner carry the boxes into the shop from the parking lot and begin the inspection process. In the beginning we treated these comic books with singular value. Each comic book had a particular price much like *OPG* taught us. I'd pay upwards of a quarter to fifty cents for a comic from the 1980s or 1990s that I would attempt to sell for three or four dollars. This was how we sold common comic books back in the old days, so

I went with what I knew. But I was selling in the 1990s and modern comics didn't carry the same weight as they did twenty years before. eBay helped to negate *OPG* values.

Before eBay, back-issue retailers had a sort of stranglehold on the retail market. If you wanted something as a collector, you chose a dealer's catalogue, infant Web sites, the few conventions that existed, or local hubs. After eBay, collectors could quickly connect with buyers and sellers. Suddenly, middlemen not attuned to the new way of doing business found themselves being left behind. Worse, if they failed to understand what eBay was all about, they couldn't modify their business models; comic books they routinely sold for certain prices could be had cheaper on eBay.

Dealers who were set in their ways with *Overstreet Price Guide* prices were being knocked back on their pins by a decreasing customer base who found identical copies on eBay. Now, people could finish a new comic book read and sell it on eBay for anything they could get; they didn't have to fuss with dealers, storage and comic book stores. Some eBay sellers sold comics at prices that gave the impression they didn't care what they got; they just wanted to be on eBay. *OPG* prices appeared to be high to a new generation of collectors who didn't read the book. They felt comfortable with whatever prices they saw on eBay. Those prices were often cheaper than *OPG*, especially with more recent comics. The truth was, they were right.

As my inventory built up, I brought it to the con to sell on as much square table footage as I could afford. This is before I teamed with others and expanded from convention sales to our store. We quickly learned that the public would not embrace *OPG* pricing on common 1980s and 1990s books. (This business plan attracted a few people, but not a lot.) My competitors were split between doing the same thing and just selling them for bulk prices. My future business partner was already adapted to con pricing and realized that modern books would move faster and yield proper profit at nice round figures, such as $1.00 per comic (or the greater incentive of 12 for $10).

I changed to the same philosophy and saw more sales potential immediately. Many buyers just want to read the comics, not invest in them, so a dollar seems fair or even generous. We opened the store with our famous dollar bins and have ridden the success of that decision for years.

Of course, we couldn't succeed buying single issues at twenty-five or fifty cents on the dollar. So we lowered our purchase pricing for those dollar book collections. We sank to a dime a copy. While that seemed cheap and insulting, it didn't stop collections from entering our domain. People have heard of worse, with urban legends of stores buying comic book collections by the pound!

Buying comic books by the pound!

At this point we were still getting the public to respond to our store. Comic-Con was our big money-maker, but the costs and restrictions to operate there were enormous and growing too fast each year. Suddenly, selling dollar books at conventions was no longer financially feasible unless we did something to lower costs. The Con won't offer help, so we had to lower the costs of what we paid for bargain books: we dropped our price to a nickel a comic. Outrageous! But it worked then and continues to work now. We tend to go to great lengths to explain to sellers what the true monetary value of a Modern Age collection consists of, using the hundreds of boxes of similar comic books in our store as examples. More often than not, a nickel a book is accepted by the owner.

Some owners claim they just want to "get rid of" their comics. We give them the nickel-a-book get-rid-of price and they choke in disbelief. "Get rid of" is their euphemism for "Pay me some money and I'd like it now." They may walk and look for another buyer, but pickings are slim. There are not a lot of stores buying common back issues in bulk. Often as not, the trail leads right back to us.

In Scenario 1 we purchased the collection of ten boxes, broke it all down, and sent most of the contents to the dollar bins.

SCENARIO 2: A MODERN AGE COLLECTION WITH SOME KEY BOOKS AND BETTER 1980s TO 1990s COMICS

With this better collection, I separate out the common, bargain books and then isolate the comics I deem to have better value. From those, I split off the comics that would normally sell for more than a dollar at our store. Commonly, we would target comics that get rounded down to the $3–$5 range. Those might get the seller twenty-five cents a copy or better. Often as not, though, we already have depth in our inventory with those issues, so we may show less interest if we can't get them cheaper than a quarter.

Finally we are left with the "cream of the crop": the comics that will sell for better numbers and are often the key books in a collection. Key means first appearances, first issues or "flavor of the month" titles or issues due to some movie or some such, like an *Incredible Hulk* #271, the first Rocket Raccoon appearance in monthly comics. It's truly a comic that would have been ignored two years prior to the *Guardians of the Galaxy* movie release.

Those better comics defend a better purchase price from dealers like me. We explain their significance to the owner even if it is unnecessary. Collection owners want to feel respected and know they can trust the dealer they're working with. Disclosing important tidbits of information that gains these owners an insight into their collection's value builds that trust. They already feel slammed by the nickel-a-book news, so enlightening them with the better news helps to seal the deal.

I have to assign values to the best stuff. That means my staff and I have to grade those to give them proper values. There is a sticky situation involving attaching values. *OPG* is only good to a point, and then pricing comics is beyond that reference. Other sources get us closer to achievable prices. Internet pricing, our own inventory, and other price references exist for us to draw upon. However, we don't have the luxury of holding the owner at bay for hours while we go through the comics one-by-one. Mostly, my experience gives me confidence to speed through the best books and attach purchase prices based upon similar, repetitive buys. The rest of the collection is counted off into stacks to get bulk prices.

The best books deserve to be purchased at prices fair to both parties. I'm comfortable with paying an average 50 percent of retail for really "good" books, especially if those key books are older and scarcer. I'm willing to pay more if the books are absolute gems, such as a comic grading in the 9s against the 10-point scale. That would work with just about any 1960s comic book key.

In this scenario I've offered a nickel a comic for the largest portion of a Modern Age collection. I paid more for a few books likely to sell for more at my store, titles like *Wonder Woman, Harley Quinn, Deadpool, Batman* and *Amazing Spider-Man.* I paid the best for high-grade key copies such as *New Mutants* #98, *Amazing Spider-Man* #300 and *Batman Adventures* #12. If the buyer will take a check, he can cash it immediately. If the buyer wants cash, I can get that quickly at the bank. There's no third option for buying comics at our store. PayPal could be a consideration if someone wanted the money wired to his bank account.

Some customers who sell to us have no bank accounts. They only want cash. The Forensic Comicologist has to go into interrogation mode to confirm the collection is legit. The lack of a bank account, PayPal account or even a credit card is enough to spur suspicion. The Forensic Comicologist will place phone calls to other stores and check with one or two Craigslist guys to see if this collection stinks.

However, if the collection is fine, the owner takes a check, and my staff is now actively processing the comics, the best books will be graded by more than one person at the store. This style of committee grading locks in what we feel is a tight grade.

SCENARIO 3: A VINTAGE COLLECTION WALKS INTO THE STORE

Let's define "vintage" as comics predating the mid–1970s. I see late 1970s comic books and their later counterparts way too often. They are not as "on the radar" as you might think, considering their age. There exists a general lack of significance among late 1970s comics and few key issues were written. The exceptions are the growing influence of movies on first appearances in comics, no matter how insignificant. Otherwise, much of the production from that time period is relegated to bargain status.

Let's play this scenario out with a much cheerier outcome for the collection owner looking to sell. Let's imagine the collection consists of one thousand comics from the 1970s. That's a good reference point because it encompasses a lot of keys and a lot of bargain-commons. A thousand comics, if bagged and boarded, occupy about four comic book long-boxes.

I see near-complete runs of *Amazing Spider-Man, Avengers, Fantastic Four* and other Marvel titles. There are no DCs, nor any other publisher. That's not unusual. Marvel dominated back then, and the remaining companies mostly consisted of Archie Comics, Gold Key, Harvey and Charlton; these are not companies that I see often in quantity in the back-issue market when I'm buying collections.

Archie comics from the Silver Age are considered "kid-safe." The violence is cartoonish and the stories are generally accepted by parents. Archie comics were produced with a myriad of titles with characters from Archie's life. Those comics sold widely to children and show the marks of time, especially when they are offered for resale. I've rarely seen an Archie title that didn't look well-loved and well-read. They are perennial dollar comics at our store.

The *ASM*s are heartening because some of the most potent 1970s keys belong in that run. A lot of *ASM* "commons" have value greater than $50–$100 in high grade. The issues below #150 tend to carry the greatest value and desirability. After #150 and well into the later 1970s, well … not so much. They really need to hit CGC/CBCS 9.6 and higher to make a market impression.

In our scenario, the *ASM*s are the wealth of the collection. The other Marvel titles are certainly better sellers than at just a buck apiece. After running through the collection, I end up with a box of better comics, a larger box of commons that could go either way, and a small box of keys. The keys consist of legendary collectible icons like the *ASM* #121, #122 and phenomenal #129. Issues #121 and #122 portray the famous "Death of Gwen Stacy" story arc. These are rare examples of a two-part key set; the #121 is slightly more desired than the #122. The #129 is the first appearance of Punisher and one of the most increasingly valuable collectibles in our hobby. The *Fantastic Four*s and the rest of the comics have keys in fewer than 1 in 50 issues. So let's concentrate on those Spideys.

Remember, this is an exercise in pricing. I'm looking over those three key *ASM* issues and a couple of others for quality, so I know what I will do to move them later. The copies are nice. I estimate the three will grade out to 9.0–9.2 status. The below stats reflect GPA/CGC prices:

(2016) #121 9.0 and 9.2 are stalled at about $600.
(2016) #122 9.0 and 9.2 $350 and $500, respectively.
(2016) #129 9.0 and 9.2 around $1,300 in each grade, but on the rise because of the NetFlix Daredevil series and a stunning legacy of popularity.

The owner may or may not know their value, but I tell him regardless. Honesty trumps subterfuge. I pitch half price for my buy-in on the keys. I'm willing to go to 60 percent if I have to; this means my retail will have to go up to counter the higher purchase price. The owner is cool with 50 percent; now what about the remainder?

Well, there's the dilemma. I have stock depth in those other *ASM*s, so I don't really want them at a percentage of retail. If I did, I'd pay less than a third, even in high grade. So maybe I pay $3 on a comic that *OPG* calls $25 and I'm lucky if I get a fast $15. This accounts for about 100 of the issues of *Amazing Spider-Man* in the collection.

I dig out the keys from the other Marvel titles in the collection and assign values for the purchase. Then I count the majority of the rest as commons and assign one lot price at somewhere less than a dollar a book. There's little dickering in this deal because my explanations were so concise I left little for the owner to speculate about.

Even though I base my selling prices on inventory, GPA, *OPG* and other sources, let's be honest: the keys are what almost anyone wants to see and talk about. I will use GPA where applicable, but those grades are well within CGC's purview. I want to establish prices that exist in writing somewhere. I don't want to have to defend prices because others will find them too expensive. So if I don't like the GPA prices and *OPG* has them covered, and higher, I may go that way.

The fact is that to run a business, I regard all overhead as a hurdle. Pricing is the greatest hurdle. If I don't have a proper markup I'm wasting my time and will not succeed. If I pay too little and charge too much, I'm going to get gutted for being on the wrong side of business. Once again, I'm wasting my time and I will not last in business.

One major upside to a collection of such magnitude, especially a collection with the

ASM keys in high grade, is that the markup on the keys to full retail can offset a lack of sales for the commons. If I paid, let's say, $3,000 for the collection of one thousand comics, the *ASM* keys may book retail at that price. Then the rest of the books are gravy (profit).

SCENARIO 4: WHEN THE COLLECTION IS TOO OLD AND TOO COOL, SO I'M GOING TO HAVE TO PAY WELL

All dealers dream of the big find, the comic collection sent from heaven, a collection with all the manna a buyer could want! I've purchased a few of those collections, mostly Gold and Silver Age with nice copies of key books liberally sprinkled within. These are the collections that most of us only hear about. These are the kinds of extraordinary opportunities that make the national news and end up in the hands of the wealthiest, best connected retailers.

They get them because they advertise so well they are given brand-name status as high-rolling buyers and sellers. They can also back up their reps with heavy wallets and firm promises that they can spend whatever it takes. Or the collections end up in the hands of the big auction houses, floating the comics past a large array of shoppers. Those collections are not purchased outright by the auction companies so they have no money up front, unless a stipend was paid to the owner ahead of the auction's close.

My store seeks out collections of all sizes. We endeavor to cover the purchase with one, up-front payment so we can own it outright and immediately. My business must have a lot of liquidity to firm up our promises to collection owners that we can afford any cost. When a really cool collection surfaces, we can beat out some of our closest competitors.

I have yet to meet collection owners who contacted me to sell, yet who didn't have an idea of the value of their comics. It doesn't take long for the Internet to educate them of the potential value of their comics (perceptions right or wrong). Their search brings them to me for reasons I've discussed earlier. The "trust factor" and readiness to spend big bucks appeal to sellers. The ability to have the deal worked in person is also a strong draw.

The collection is brought to my store so I can begin the examination process with the help of staff and computers, along with a few tools to identify restoration. In this case the collection consists of about 400 comic books from the mid–1930s into the early 1940s. It's an original owner collection passed down to a son now middle-aged. There are not many traditional, key books, but anything from the 1930s is significant; they all become genuine collectibles just from scarcity and age alone.

There are early *Superman* issues, early *More Fun Comics*, *Famous Funnies* and a group of various Centaur titles highly prized by Golden Age collectors; really scarce stuff. The owner's father passed years ago; he wants the best price he can get. He's from Los Angeles, so he passed by a lot of my competitors to get to me. He expects to get paid well or he'll consider walking.

I normally want a collection of this magnitude at a generous half retail. Some of the copies are low grade, a few coverless or missing pages or panels. I feel like they're somewhat of a burden to speculate on, so I concoct prices based on what I will have to do to eventually move them. My numbers jive with his thoughts. He knows those copies are much less valuable.

Half price is considered a universally fair amount. The majority of the 1940s comics outside of the aforementioned *Superman*s are funny-animal issues, some slow to move. I shrug when I explain their sluggish sales to the owner. I'm reluctant to pay more than one-third of retail. Even that's a lot, but they are lesser-known and I like really old comics. He senses my squeamishness and settles on a third of *OPG*, or less, depending on condition for those copies.

Once they're purchased, I dig a little deeper into the Centaur titles to figure out if there's a ceiling beyond *OPG* for me to work with. I contact a Centaur-collecting friend and he helps me work out serious prices for those comics. The *Superman* comics begin with issue #3. That's "super" low numbering, but those issues are still relatively available, so no one is fighting hard to find them. I pay half price and price them at full-price according to *OPG*. The least important comics will get priced by *OPG*. In all likelihood, many of those will be discounted anywhere from 10 percent to 50 percent in less than three years.

SCENARIO 5: BUYING KEY COMICS FROM MY PEERS

Dealers thrive on the exclusivity of key book sales. Acquiring those books can be tough. Collectors are so intrigued by key comics that it seems to be all anyone is looking for. There's such a demand among collectors for *New Mutants* #98 and *Incredible Hulk* #181 that it feels like nobody wants much else. Back-issue dealers need those books for show to keep the right collectors interested, even if their sales mean little profit. Often that means guys like me have to make a "trip to the well."

The Well. The place connected comic book dealers go to resupply their key books, otherwise known as "the other dealers." Convention dealers historically meet and greet, sell to and buy from each other in the earliest hours of any comic book show before and during the arrival of the attendees. The dealers work all the time to acquire the books that will sell well for the best money, often taking offers up front from other dealers in case they fear a poor show. Or because that's their comfort level, or they like doing that sort of business with those particular dealers.

Whatever the reason, I'm one of them. Before Southern California Comics hit its stride, the only way the store could get meaty collectibles was to buy from convention dealers. That was at a time when it was just as crucial to our survival to take the offers for some of our books from fellow retailers.

The pricing is up to the dealer selling. One dealer, often as not, does not need to discount and sell his best books to another dealer as badly as the first dealer needs those books for resale in a different environment. Perhaps a small dealer does relish the chance at "fat" money from a larger dealer looking to restock his baseline of key comics. Maybe two dealers are on equal footing, but one needs a momentary infusion of cash. Dealer "A" brought a new collection to a convention for the very first time. Dealer "B" scours the show early to look for comics for his depleted inventory and sees dealer A's collection before the other dealers. B scours A's booth and asks if they can work a deal. A wants the money and B wants the comics, so they dicker over percentages and off they go.

Dealer to dealer, a 20 percent discount seems to be the traditional discount. The better books may only get 10 percent while the best books are yours for the taking—at full price. At one show, I provided a discount of 30 percent to a dealer. He had selected a lot of commons I had room on and 30 percent worked for both of us. At other shows among other dealers at other times, discounts could be steeper. On rare occasions, one dealer might make an offer the other can't refuse and the entire booth changes hands. That was a much more common affair at the San Diego Con/Comic-Con International when anybody could get a booth. Lots of strangers to our exhibition hall found space and were quickly enveloped by the tribe.

This is all well-known and accepted behavior. Perhaps the seller is being nice to an acquaintance or friend. Perhaps one dealer has made a commitment to spend enough money to make it worthwhile for dealers. It could also be to complete a promise or for the dissolution of debt. Whatever the reason, we've all learned to compensate by "jacking up the prices" on the books we just purchased from Dealer A to gain a small percentage bump above sticker, providing an additional price advantage.

There are reluctant dealers who won't work with others. There are those who require much coaxing, but other dealers seem ready to give up the farm. There are examples of dealers at Comic-Con International and elsewhere who start a show with a rock in their stomach, nervous they will have a bad show. Their concern is palpable to approaching dealers. They want to dispel worry, so they might be quick to jump at the offers early on from approaching dealers. Some of the biggest dealers nationally seek relationships with those guys. Then, each year when they see them at a show like San Diego, they get preferential choice of the keys before anyone else, and at better discounts.

The approaching dealer now may own a wealth of both dealer-supplied keys and maybe commons. He or she can resell them immediately or bring them home to an audience who doesn't have con exposure. Having newly refreshed glass cases filled with all those lovely key books in a store that was virtually empty just a week before brings in a lot of business. Those newly displayed, un-sleeved aces draw a lot of attention and help the store maintain its relevance.

Ultimately, any approaching dealer will boast that the thrill of the hunt makes all the above scenarios worth the effort. Making a living off dealing back issues is tough but fun. You have to know a lot to get it done right. Smart pricing, and knowing when to cave in a little, helps propel business forward. You make allies of your peers and your customers. Keep the BS to a minimum and you will earn respect.

I wouldn't trade my status or experiences as a back-issue comic dealer for anything. It has been a long, entertaining ride. My time as a forensic comicologist has helped me breed allies and business partners. I've had huge gains and significant losses. I've earned trust from some and seen others part ways. We can't all be friends, but we can all respect, if grudgingly, those dealers, collectors, buyers, sellers and traders who adhere to a code of conduct that would make any forensic comicologist proud.

Bibliography

Adler, J. April 2017. "The Greytone Process." *The Lantern.* Retrieved from: http://www.wtv-zone.com/silverager/greytone.shtml.

Anthony, H. June 17, 2016. CGC new case debate explained [web-log comment]. *Comics Heating Up.* Retrieved from: comicsheatingup.net/2016/06/17/cgc-new-case-debate-explained/.

Barlass, T. 2013. "Unofficial Spider-Man Home Page." *Spider-Fan.* Retrieved from: www.spiderfan.org/fax/comics.html.

Benton, M. 1989. *The Comic Book in America.* Dallas: Taylor.

_____. 1993. *The Illustrated History of Crime Comics.* Dallas: Taylor.

Blackbeard, B., and Bill Williams. 1977. *The Smithsonian Collection of Newspaper Comics.* Washington, D.C.: Smithsonian Institution Press.

Bretall, B. 2015. *Comic Spectrum.* Retrieved from: www.comicspectrum.com.

Canote, T. May 16, 2010. "Harvey Comics Dark Secret" [web log comment]. Retrieved from: www.mercurie.blogspot.com/2010/05/harvey-comics-dark-secret.html.

Chukueke, N. July 2016. "What Is Comic Preservation?" *Welcome to Comic Preservation.* Retrieved from: www.comicpreservation.com.

Conroy, T. October 3, 2011. "The Need for a Re-Evaluation of the Use of Alum in Book Conservation and the Book Arts." *The Book and Paper Group Annual* 8. Retrieved from: www.cool.conservation-us.org/coolaic/sg/bpg/annual/v08/bp08-02.html.

Coville, J. 2016. "See You in the Funny Pages." *The History of Comic Books.* Retrieved from: www.thecomicbooks.com/old/Platinum.html.

Creep Engine. June 24, 2016. *Comic Book Forum Boards* [web forum comments]. Retrieved from: www.the-comic-book-forum.boards.net/board/42.

Daniels, L. 1995. *DC Comics: Sixty Years of the World's Favorite Comic Book Heroes.* New York: Bullfinch Press/Little, Brown.

Dark Side of the Sun. June 3, 2014. "Comic Book Grading." *Comic Vine.* Retrieved from: www.comicvine.gamespot.com/comic-book-grading/4015-44517/.

Drew. April 2017. "Halo Certification Comic Book Grading & Encapsulation." *Urban Fiction.* Retrieved from: www.urbanfiction.bigcartel.com/product/halo-certification-comic-grading.

Feirtag, K. 2016. "1998 Hall of Fame Inductee: Frank Frazetta." Museum of Illustration. Retrieved from: www.societyillustrators.org/frank-frazetta.

Forro, L. 2017. *Comic Book Memories II.* Retrieved from: pristine.webspaceforme.net/Facebook/comicbookmemories2/gerber/gerber.html.

Frost, A. 2016. *An Informal History of the Comic Book Industry.* Retrieved from: www.scriptgraphics.weebly.com/comicbook-history.html.

Gagliano, R. April 2017. "Why Polyethylene Rather than Polypropylene?" *Downtown Magazine.* Retrieved from: www.dtmagazine.com/polyvspoly.html.

Gerber, E. 1989. *The Gerber Photo-Journal Guide to Comic Books*, vols. 1–2. Minden, NV: Gerber.

Goulart, R. 1986. *Ron Goulart's Great History of Comic Books.* Chicago: Contemporary Books.

_____. 1990. *The Encyclopedia of Comics.* New York: Facts on File.

_____. 2000. *Comic Book Culture.* Portland, OR: Collectors Press.

Goza, D. 2017. "An Informal History of the Comic Book Industry" [web log entry]. *Script Graphics Comics and Stories.* Retrieved from: www.scriptgraphics.weebly.com/comicbook-history.html.

Gunnison, J., J. Locke, and D. Ellis. 2000. *The Adventure House Guide to Pulps.* Silver Spring, MD: Adventure House.

Haines, L. 1998. *The Business of Comics.* New York: Watson-Guptill.

Hake, T. July 25, 2013. *Argosy Comic Book Price Guide.* Hake's Americana and Collectibles. Retrieved from: www.hakes.com/Auction/ItemDetail/83889/THE-ARGOSY-COMIC-BOOK-PRICE-GUIDE-WITH-MAILER-AND-BUYING-LISTS.

Haspel, M. February 19, 2015. CGC comics guarantee. *CGC Comics.* Retrieved from: www.cgccomics.com/grading/cgc-comics-guarantee.asp.

Horn, M. 1999. *The World Encyclopedia of Comics.* Philadelphia: Chelsea House.

Jones, G. 2004. *Men of Tomorrow: Geeks, Gangsters, and the Birth of the Comic Book.* New York: Basic Books.

Kirby, J., and J. Simon. 2009. *The Best of Simon and Kirby.* London: Titan.

Kistler, A. October 23, 2005. "Alan Kistler's Profile on the Martian Manhunter" [web log comment]. *Monitor Duty.* Retrieved from: www.monitorduty.com/?p=1087.

Konda, K. February 24, 2014. "The Origin of 'With Great Power Comes Great Responsibility' & 7 Other Surprising Parts of Spider-Man's Comic Book History." *We Minored in Film.* Retrieved from: www.weminoredinfilm.com/2014/04/22/the-origin-of-with-great-power-comes-great-responsibility-7-other-surprising-parts-of-spider-mans-comic-book-history/.

Lesser, R. 1997. *Pulp Art*. New York: Gramercy Books.

Lowery, L. 2012. "The Beginning." *Big Little Books*. Retrieved from: www.biglittlebooks.com/historyofBLBs.html.

Malloy, A. 1993. *Comic Book Artists*. Pennsylvania: Wallace-Homestead.

Marshall, J. October 6, 2014. "How and Why Comic Books Are Drawn at 10 by 15 Inches: Individual Preference Becomes Industry Standard." *Art of the Comic Book*. Retrieved from: www.artofthecomicbook.com/history/art-reduction.htm.

Mautner, C. January 2, 2011. "Fantagraphics to Publish the Complete Carl Barks." *Comic Book Resources*. Retrieved from: www.cbr.com/exclusive-fantagraphics-to-publish-the-complete-carl-barks/.

McKracken, Z. 2014. "Marvel and DC Sales Figures." *Great American Novel*. Retrieved from: www.zak-site.com/Great-American-Novel/comicsales.html.

Miller, J. 1969-present. "Comic Book Sales by Month." *Comichron*. Retrieved from: www.comichron.com/monthlycomicssales.html.

Mr. Ubiquitous. September 2009. FYI: "Polyethylene Vs. Polypropylene" [web log comment]. *Comic Book Care*. Retrieved from: comicvine.gamespot.com/comic-book-care/4015–44586/forums/fyi-polyethylene-vs-polypropylene-5914/.

Moldoff, K., and S. Moldoff. January 2011. Sheldon Moldoff. *Sheldon Moldoff*. Retrieved from: www.sheldon-moldoff.com/home-page/welcome-to-sheldon-moldoff-com/.

Nelson, M. 2011. *Comic Book Pedigrees*. Retrieved from: www.comicpedigrees.com/about-us.php.

Newton's Rings. April 2017. *City Collegiate*. Retrieved from: http://www.citycollegiate.com/newtonsrings.htm.

Nolan, M. 2009. "Gerber 8, 9, and 10 Ratings, Part One." *CGC Enewsletter*. Retrieved from: www.cgccomics.com/news/enews/2009/May/article6.asp.

Overstreet, R. 2010. *Official Overstreet Comic Book Companion*, 11th ed. New York: Random House.

Overstreet, R., and A. Blumberg. 2006. *Official Overstreet Comic Book Grading Guide*, 3rd ed. New York: Random House.

Perez, J. May 16, 2016. "6 Bizarre Stan Lee Prototypes of Famous Marvel Characters" [web log comment]. Retrieved from: www.dorkly.com/post/77943/stan-lees-weird-prototype-versions-of-6-famous-marvel-characters.

PGX Comics. April 2017. Grading services. Retrieved from: www.pgxcomics.com.

Rozanski, C. 2016. CGC comics part one. *Mile High Comics Database*. Retrieved from: www.milehighcomics.com/tales/cbg02.html.

Schuddeboom, B. July 14, 2016. Comiclopedia: Alex Raymond. *Lambiek Comiclopedia*. Retrieved from: www.lambiek.net/artists/r/raymond.htm.

Scott's classic comic corner: Measuring scarcity [web log comment]. *Comic Book Resources*. Retrieved from: www.goodcomics.comicbookresources.com/2009/05/20/scotts-classic-comics-corner-measuring scarcity/.

Shooter, J. 2011. "Comic Book Distribution." Retrieved from: www.jimshooter.com/2011/11/comic-book-distribution.html/.

Siefert, M. October 30, 2011. 1962: "DC Explains Its First Ever Price Increase from 10 Cents to 12 Cents." *Bleeding Cool*. Retrieved from: www.bleedingcool.com/2011/10/30/1962-dc-explains-its-first-ever-price-increase-from-10-cents-to-12-cents/.

"So What Are Bronze-Age Marvel Price Variants?" April 24, 2010. Retrieved from: www.bronzeagemarvelvariants.blogspot.com/2010/04/so-what-are-bronze-age-marvel-price.html.

Solomon, C. 1994. *The History of Animation: Enchanted Drawings*. Avenal, NJ: Wings Books.

Spurgeon, T. August 2008. *Jack Kamen, 1920–2008*. Retrieved from: www.comicsreporter.com/index.php/jack_kame_1920_2008/.

Steve ID. November 1, 2013. "Charlton Comics Publishing History." *ComicVine*. Retrieved from: www.comicvine.gamespot.com/charlton/4010–125/.

Steinhoff, R.J. December 19, 2011. "The CGC Census and Market Values." *The Comic Book Daily*. Retrieved from: www.comicbookdaily.com/collecting-community/by-the-numbers/the-cgc-census-and-market-values/.

Sundin, S. November 21, 2011. *Make It Do: Scrap Drives in World War II*. [Web Log] Retrieved from: www.sarahsundin.com/make-it-do-scrap-drives-in-world-war-ii-2/.

Surdham, D. March 24, 2015. "Comic Books and Censorship in the 1940s." *OUPblog*. Retrieved from: blog.oup.com/2015/03/comic-books-censorship-history/.

Thompson, D., and D. Lupoff. 1998. *The Comic Book Book*. Carlstadt, NJ: Krause.

Weist, J. 2004. *100 Greatest Comic Books*. Atlanta, GA: Whitman.

Writer Tim. April 2017. Alfredo Alcala. *Wizard's Keep*. Retrieved from: www.wizards-keep.com/index.asp?Page=alfredo-alcala—62810916.

Yardley, W. January 30, 2014. "Gary Arlington, a Force in Underground Comic Books, Is Dead at 75." *The New York Times*. Retrieved from: www.nytimes.com/2014/01/31/books/gary-arlington-a-force-in-comic-books-is-dead-at-75.html?

Index